THE SCOTTISH WEB DIRECTORY

THE SCOTTISH WEB DIRECTORY

OVER 10,000 HOUSEHOLD NAMES & OFFICIAL WEBSITES

Compiled by Roderick Millar, Robbie McLaren,
Ian Mclean and Alice Millar

•

Clive and Bettina Zietman

In association with Scottish Enterprise

Publisher's note

Every possible effort has been made to ensure that the information contained in this book is accurate at the time of going to press, and the publishers and authors cannot accept responsibility for any errors or omissions, however caused. No responsibility for loss or damage occasioned to any person acting, or refraining from action, as a result of the material in this publication can be accepted by the editor, the publisher or any of the authors.

This directory aims to provide easy access to the web sites of Scottish 'household' names on the internet. It does not claim to be comprehensive. Neither Scottish Enterprise nor Kogan Page in any way endorse or recommend any of the web sites listed.

First published in 2003 by Kogan Page Limited

120 Pentonville Road
London N1 9JN

22883 Quicksilver Drive
Sterling VA 20166-2012
USA

Kogan Page website: www.kogan-page.co.uk

Scottish Enterprise website: www.scottish-enterprise.com

This first Scottish edition is based on and includes material from The Incredibly Indispensable Web Directory compiled by Clive and Bettina Zietman, and also published by Kogan Page.

The inclusion of websites listed in this directory does not imply that they have been endorsed or recommended by Kogan Page Ltd or Scottish Enterprise

---

British Library Cataloguing-in-Publication Data

A CIP record for this book is available from the British Library

ISBN 0 7494 3816 9

Typeset by Bibliocraft Ltd, Dundee
Printed and bound in Great Britain by Cambrian Printers Ltd., Aberystwyth

arts & entertainment

business

children

education, training & research

environment

food & drink

government

healthcare

help!

hobbies & leisure

information sources

living

museums, libraries & information

personal finance

places

science & nature

shopping

sport

technology

travel

Scotland: the best place to do e-business

Charlie Watt, Senior Director, E Business, Scottish Enterprise

eBusiness is changing the way companies interact and communicate with each other and their customers and it is set to play an increasing part in Scotland's future prosperity.

Scotland is fast emerging as a leading player in the European marketplace for electronic business solutions, applications and research. It is arguably one of the most advanced of all the major European nations in terms of ICT uptake and usage.

The people, skill supply, the cross fertilisation of ideas and talents, and the ability to interact and form partnerships with other businesses all help to encourage some of the world's largest and most successful companies to Scotland as the place to do eBusiness.

Added to this, we also have a world-class research and development community, active in both the academic and commercial sectors, coupled with the ability to deliver a steady stream of innovative products and processes that can be profitably marketed in Europe and around the world.

Scotland currently has 13 universities, nine specialist higher education institutions, 46 further education colleges conducting world-class research and development.

Hundreds of companies have reaped the rewards of doing eBusiness in Scotland and this number is growing rapidly. Last year 35 per cent of Scottish companies had a web presence, compared with 39 per cent in 2002. In 2001 only 14 percent of Scottish businesses had introduced a facility allowing customers to order online. This year that figure has grown to 20 per cent.

In fact, seven percent of the annual turnover of all Scottish companies currently comes from website activity, whether online transactions or enquiries that result in sales. This translates into £2.6 billion of business sales activity in Scotland being generated each year from the Internet.

Although we can not afford to be complacent, it is heartening to see that Scotland is making steady progress. The latest DTI International Benchmark survey, which was released in early December, shows Scotland coming second only to London in a study of 10 UK regions in the use of eBusiness and third behind USA and Germany against a league of top technologically aware countries.

However we want to do more to raise awareness of the benefits of eBusiness. It helps companies reach more customers, improve their contact with suppliers and clients, reduce their cost base and boost their bottom line. It is not about technology for it's own sake; it's about helping companies develop a competitive edge in an ever expanding global market place.

And Scottish Enterprise is playing a key role in driving forward the eBusiness revolution. We are committed to developing an integrated approach to eBusiness; educating companies about its advantages in order to stimulate demand and helping the supply sector provide the type of services and products companies need.

This year, our target is to help 1425 more companies market and transact online and we have a number of initiatives in place that will help us achieve this target. In fact we are likely to substantially exceed this target.

Project ATLAS was launched in February 2002 to help build a world class telecoms infrastructure for all Scottish businesses.

The multi-million pound project will increase the choice of telecoms suppliers for companies in business parks around the country, driving down broadband prices and increasing availability. It will also increase the number of businesses using broadband, giving telecoms companies in Scotland access to many more customers.

The national government initiative, UK Online for Business, is another major project that is designed to help UK firms exploit the business benefits of information and communication technologies (ICTs).

Part of a nationwide partnership between the government, industry, the voluntary sector, trades unions and consumer groups, UK Online for Business provides companies with advice, free publications and an e-commerce pack detailing the best way to grow their eBusiness.

Scottish Enterprise is also heavily involved in managing the DTI fund for innovative use of broadband which aims to raise awareness of the business benefits of broadband. It features eight projects including broadband demonstration centres, technology evaluation pilots and broadband trials as well as a website which explains in simple terms what broadband is about.

We are also behind the popular Winners at the Web (W@W) Awards, which reward Scotland's most dynamic and innovative e-businesses. The annual competition carries prizes totalling £100,000. See www.scottish-enterprise.com for further information.

These initiatives are all geared towards turning Scotland into a European centre of excellence for e-commerce. The clear objectives

must now be to ensure that Scotland continues to be at the forefront of the developments in the digital economy and is regarded as the most technologically aware and advanced country in Europe.
For more information, visit
www.scottish-enterprise.com/ebusiness

Preface

Welcome to the first edition of the Scottish Web Directory. This book is for all internet users who are either based in Scotland or have in an interest in things Scottish. The sites listed are in noway Scots-parochial, the wider world is well represented, but where a local Scottish source is relevant and appropriate it is given priority.

the internet problem

The internet is an extraordinary resource, but it has certain practical problems. Firstly it is labyrinthine. It almost certainly contains information on any subject that you care to imagine, however, tracking down a particular nugget of information can be time-consuming and complicated. Search engines can be an excellent guide to this labyrinth, but like the Minotaur in the legend they can be dangerous creatures, providing you with thousands of 'related' sites to your query that are, in fact, irrelevant and take you in the wrong direction. Often the problem is too much information rather than too little.
The second problem in finding your ideal site is that although its content may be of high quality, little may have been spent on marketing it. Since the fizz went out of the internet bubble there has been a noticeable shift of emphasis from product sales sites to product information sites. The latter are much cheaper to set up and, in contrast to sites that 'trade', virtually costless to run. This is reflected in the promotion of these sites as they are not revenue earners, they are allocated limited marketing funds and so can become difficult to locate. Search engines typically list those sites that promote themselves best. In addition, many search engines are designed to list sites by their popularity, which is measured by the number of people that visit them. If a site is well publicised then it will be visited frequently and a virtuous circle of promotion starts regardless of the quality of the site. Most organisations these days have acquired straight-forward website addresses, that state clearly and simply who they are, but there is still a significant minority of excellent sites that hide their lights under bushels. These sites rarely appear in simple web searches.

our solution

This guide is designed to avoid these problems and to provide an incredibly indispensable guide. We have done the searching for you!

With the initial concept that, for our readers, a Scotland sourced site will be better received than one from, say, Australia, we have catalogued our sites with this 'Scotland-centric' approach in mind. For example, in the Food & Drink section, the whisky and beer listings receive more recognition than the wines and other spirits. Similarly in the Sports section Football and Rugby take priority over Baseball or Cricket, and we highlight Scottish sports such as Shinty and Curling whereas others guides might miss them out altogether.

We have also focused our chosen sites, where possible, on the official organisations and associations for different areas of interest. As the internet is constantly developing, a directory such as this cannot expect to list all the current 'movers and shakers' in every discipline. By directing you to the relevant official sites you will be able to find regularly updated information and further links. That said, we have listed as many individual companies, charities and other services as time and quality permits.

It is the case that certain sections of the directory are less website rich than others. In Food & Drink, for example, many restaurants, regardless of their quality, do not have websites of their own although some are featured through the well-known restaurant guides and we direct you to these. Other sections are far more fruitful and in these we have carefully chosen sites that give the greatest breadth and quality of information. Finally, it is obvious that some sections clearly have little Scottish based information to offer. This is frequently because the relevant organisation has a UK wide remit, in which case we list that; or there is no Scottish representation in the category, such as for car manufacturers, where we then give the international listing as the topic is of general interest.

developing the directory

The directory must develop with the internet. While we have used our collective 'Scottish' judgement on which sites to include and which to omit, it is inevitable that we have overlooked some areas and left out some sites we ought to have included. We very much hope that readers will inform us about any sites they think ought to be in the book that currently are not. Please send any suggestions to info@kogan-page.co.uk.

Finally my thanks go to all who helped do the careful and time-consuming research for this book, particularly Robbie McLaren, Ian McLean, Elaine Ofori, Emma Clayton and Alice Millar.

Roderick Millar
October 2002

- actors & actresses
- art
- ballet
- clubs
- comedy
- events
- film
- funding, organisations & regulation
- literature
- magazines & websites
- music
- promotors & directors
- radio
- stadia & concert halls
- television
- theatre
- tickets

actors & actresses

Adam Sandler
www.adamsandler.com

Alan Cumming (Fan Club)
www.angelfire.com/wa/AlanCumming

Alicia Silverstone
www.alicia-silverstone.net

Alyssa Milano
www.alyssa.com

Anna Friel
www.netshopuk.co.uk/annafriel

Anthony Hopkins
www.nasser.net/hopkins

Antonio Banderas
www.antoniobanderasfans.com

Arnold Schwarzenegger
www.schwarzenegger.com

Audrey Hepburn
www.audreyhepburn.com

Ava Gardner
www.avagardner.org

Ben Affleck
www.affleck.com

Bob Hope
www.bobhope.com

Brad Pitt
www.bradpitt.com

Brian Cox
www.coxian.com

Bruce Lee
www.brucelee.org.uk

Burl Ives
www.burlives.com

Cameron Diaz
www.cameron-diaz.com

Carrie Fisher
www.carriefisher.com

Cary Grant
www.carygrant.co.uk

Cheryl Ladd
www.cherylladd.com

Christian Bale
www.christianbale.org

Christopher Lambert
www.christopherlambert.org

Claire Danes
www.claire-danes.com

Clint Eastwood
www.clinteastwood.net

Courteney Cox
www.courteneycox.net

Craig Charles
www.craigcharles.co.uk

Daniel Day-Lewis
www.danielday.org

David Boreanaz
www.celebrityblvd.com/davidboreanaz

David Schwimmer
www.davidschwimmer.net

Don Johnson
www.donjohnson.com

Doris Day
www.dorisday.com

Dougray Scott
www.dougrayscottinfocus.com

Errol Flynn
www.errolflynn.net

Ewan McGregor
www.ewanspotting.com

Gail Porter
www.gail-porter-world.co.uk

George Clooney
www.georgeclooney.org

Gillian Anderson
http://gaws.ao.net

Gwyneth Paltrow
www.gwyneth.cjb.net

Harold Lloyd
www.haroldlloyd.com

Harrison Ford
www.harrison-ford.net

Helena Bonham-Carter
www.helena-bonham-carter.com

Ian McKellen
www.mckellen.com

Ingrid Pitt
www.pittofhorror.com

Jack Ryder
www.jackryder.cjb.net

Jim Carrey
www.jimcarreyonline.com

Jimmy Stewart
www.jimmy.org

John Hannah
www.johnhannah.net

Jonny Lee Miller (Fan Site)
www.jonnyleemiller.co.uk

Joseph Smith
www.joesmith.com

Josh Hartnett
www.joshhartnett.com

Kate Winslet
www.kate-winslet.org

Keanu Reeves
www.keanunet.com

Kelly Brook
www.kellybrookonline.com

Ken Stott (Fan Club)
http://kenstott.8m.com

Kevin McKidd (Fan Site)
http://kevin.mckidd.port5.com

Kevin Spacey
www.spacey.com

Kristen Johnston
www.kristenjohnston.net

Laura Fraser
www.laurafraser.bravepages.com

Leonard Nimoy
www.nimoy.com

Leonardo di Caprio
www.leonardodicaprio.com

Martin Lawrence
www.martin-lawrence.com

Matt Damon
www.mattdamon.com

Meg Ryan
www.megryan.net

Mel Gibson
www.melgibson.com

Melanie Griffith (Fan Club)
www.antoniobanderasfans.com/melanie_griffith

Melissa Joan Hart
www.melissa-joan-hart.com

Morgan Freeman
www.morganfreeman.com

Nicolas Cage
www.cage-cave.avalon.hr

Nicole Kidman (Fan Club)
www.nicolekidman.org

Pamela Anderson Lee
www.pamelaandersonlee.com

Paul Nicholls
www.paul-nicholls.com

Robert Carlyle
http://robertcarlylesite.tripod.com/uncobraw

Robson Green
www.robsongreen.com

Roy Rogers
www.royrogers.com

Sandra Bullock
www.sandra.com

Sean Connery
www.seanconnery.com

Sheree J Wilson
www.shereejwilson.com

Stephen Collins
www.stephencollins.com

Thomas Dolby
www.thomas-dolby.com

Timothy Dalton
www.timothydalton.com

Tom Cruise (Fan Club)
www.tomcruise.fans.net

Tony Curtis
www.tonycurtis.com

Tony Hancock (Fan Club)
www.staff.ncl.ac.uk/nigel.collier/index2.html

Tori Spelling
www.tori-spelling.com

Val Kilmer
http://vkn.com

Wes Craven
www.wescraven.com

Will Smith
www.willsmith.net

William Shatner
www.williamshatner.com

Winona Ryder
www.winonaryder.org

art

Associations & Institutes

Arts Council
www.artscouncil.org.uk

Association of Art Historians
www.gold.ac.uk/aah

Association of Illustrators
www.aoi.co.uk

British Arts Festivals Association
www.artsfestivals.co.uk

British Council Scotland
www.britcoun.org/scotland

Institute of Contemporary Arts
www.ica.org.uk

National Acrylic Painters Association
www.artarena.force9.co.uk/napa

National Art Library
www.nal.vam.ac.uk

National Portraiture Association
www.natportrait.com

RSA
www.rsa.org.uk

Galleries & Exhibitions

Aberdeen Art Gallery
www.aagm.co.uk

Aberdeen Maritime Museum
www.aagm.co.uk

An Lanntair
www.lanntair.com

An Tobar
www.antobar.co.uk

An Tuireann
www.AnTuireann.org.uk

Andrew Carnegie Birthplace Museum
www.carnegiemuseum.co.uk

Andrew Logan Museum of Sculpture
www.andrewlogan.com

Arbroath Museum
www.angus.gov.uk/history.htm

Banchory Museum
www.aberdeenshire.gov.uk/banchory.htm

Burrell Collection
www.clyde-valley.com/glasgow/burrell.htm

Centre for Contemporary Arts
www.cca-glasgow.com

City Art Centre, Edinburgh
www.cac.org.uk

Courtauld Institute
www.courtauld.ac.uk

Crawford Arts Centre
www.crawfordarts.free-online.co.uk

Culzean Caslte
www.nts.org.uk/culzean.html

Dalmeny House, South Queensferry
www.dalmeny.co.uk

Dean Gallery
www.natgalscot.ac.uk

Duff House Country Gallery, Banff
www.duffhouse.com

Dumfries & Galloway Arts Association
www.dgaa.net

Dundee Contemporary Arts
www.dca.org.uk

Eden Court
www.eden-court.co.uk

Edinburgh City Art Centre
www.edinburgh.gov.uk/city_art_centre/web/cac

Falconer Museum, Moray
www.moray.gov.uk/museums

Fruitmarket Gallery
www.fruitmarket.co.uk

Glamis Castle
www.great-houses-scotland.co.uk/glamis

Glasgow Gallery of Modern Art
www.clyde-valley.com/glasgow/modart.htm

Glasgow School of Art
www.gsa.ac.uk

Harbour Arts Centre
www.harbourarts.co.uk

Hopetoun House
www.hopetounhouse.com

Hunterian Art Gallery
www.gla.ac.uk/museum

Hunterian Art Gallery, Glasgow
www.gla.ac.uk/museum/artgall

Huntly House Museum
www.cac.org.uk

Inverleith House, Edinburgh
www.rbge.org.uk/inverleith-house

Lyth Arts Centre
www.caithness.org

Marischal Museum, Aberdeen
www.abdn.ac.uk/~ant010

McLean Museum & Art Gallery, Greenock
www.inverclyde.gov.uk/museum/index.htm

McLellan Galleries
www.glasgowguide.co.uk/gpages/glasgow-mclgall1z.html

Museum of Childhood
www.edinburgh.gov.uk/CEC/Recreation/Leisure/Data/Museum_Of_Childhood/Museum_Of_Childhood.html

National Art Library
www.nal.vam.ac.uk

National Gallery
www.nationalgallery.org.uk

National Gallery of Scotland
www.natgalscot.ac.uk

National Museum of Photography, Film & Television
www.nmpft.org.uk

National Portrait Gallery
www.npg.org.uk

Paisley Museum & Art Galleries
www.renfrewshire.gov.uk

Peoples Palace Museum
www.glasgow.gov.uk/html/about/palace/palace.htm

Peter Anson Gallery, Buckie
www.moray.gov.uk/anson/ansonpag.htm

Photographers' Gallery
www.photonet.org.uk

Pier Arts Centre
www.pierartscentre.com

Pollok House
http://clyde-valley.com/glasgow/pollock.htm?12345

Proiseact nan Ealan – Gaelic Arts Agency
www.gaelic-arts.com

Robert Burns Centre, Dumfries
www.galloway.co.uk

Royal Academy
www.royalacademy.org.uk

Scottish Gallery, Edinburgh
www.scottish-gallery.co.uk

Scottish National Gallery of Modern Art
www.nationalgalleries.org

Scottish National Portrait Gallery
www.nationalgalleries.org

Serpentine Gallery
www.serpentinegallery.org

Shambellie House Museum of Costume, Dumfries
www.information-britain.co.uk/showPlace.cfm?Place_ID=1334

Shetland Arts Trust
www.shetland-music.com

St Mungo Museum
www.clyde-valley.com/glasgow/mungomus.htm

Taigh Chearsabhagh
www.taigh-chearsabhagh.org

Talbot Rice Gallery
www.trg.ed.ec.uk

Tate Gallery
www.tate.org.uk

The Lemon Tree
www.lemontree.org

Tramway
www.tramway.org

Wallace Collection
www.the-wallace-collection.org.uk

ballet

American Ballet Theatre
www.abt.org

Australian Ballet
www.australianballet.com.au

Birmingham Royal Ballet
www.brb.org.uk

Bolshoi Ballet
www.bolshoi.ru

Continental Ballet
www.continentalballet.com

Copenhagen International Ballet
www.koelpin.com

Frankfurt Ballet
www.frankfurt-ballett.de

Hamburg Ballet
www.hamburgballett.de

Hong Kong Ballet
www.hkballet.com

Kirov Ballet
www.kirovballet.com

Moscow Flying Ballet
www.flying-ballet.com

National Ballet of Canada
www.nationalballet.ca

New York City Ballet
www.nycballet.com

Northern Ballet Theatre
www.nbt.co.uk

Rambert Dance Company
www.rambert.co.uk

Royal Ballet
www.royalballet.org

Royal Ballet School
www.royal-ballet-school.org

Sadler's Wells
www.sadlers-wells.com

Scottish Ballet
www.scottishballet.co.uk

clubs

Scotlands Clubbers Guide
www.s1play.com/clubs

Scotlands Night Clubs Rated
www.ukclubs.tv/clubratings/mapscotland2.asp

UK Clubs
www.ukclubs.tv

comedy

Abbott & Costello (Fan Club)
www.city-net.com/abbottandcostellofc

Attila the Stockbroker
www.attilathestockbroker.com

BBC Comedy Zone
www.comedyzone.beeb.com

Ben Elton
www.ben-elton.com

Chewin The Fat
www.chewinthefat.co.uk

Comedy Store
www.thecomedystore.co.uk

Comic Relief
www.comicrelief.org.uk

Dame Edna
www.dame-edna.com

Danny La Rue
www.dannylarue.com

Dilbert
www.unitedmedia.com/comics/dilbert

Eddie Izzard
www.izzard.com

Fascinating Aida
www.fascinating-aida.co.uk

French & Saunders
www.frenchandsaunders.com

George Formby
www.georgeformby.co.uk

Graham Norton
www.grahamnorton.co.uk

Jongleurs
www.jongleurs.com

Laurel & Hardy
www.laurel-and-hardy.com

Lee & Herring
www.leeandherring.com

Listings of Scottish Comedy Gigs
www.homeandaway.com/
Scotland_comedy.htm

Monty Python Online
www.pythonline.com

Morecambe & Wise
www.morecambeandwise.co.uk

Naked Video
http://tv.cream.org/arkn.htm

Penn & Teller
www.sincity.com

Rab C Nesbitt (Fan Site)
www.argyll.demon.co.uk/Rab.html

Reeves & Mortimer
www.come.to/vicandbob

Rowan Atkinson
www.hsn.dk/rowan

Scottish Comedy
www.scottishcomedy.com

events

Aldeburgh Productions
www.aldeburgh.co.uk

Arts Worldwide
www.artsworldwide.org.uk

Association of Scottish Games & Festivals
www.asgf.org

BAFTA Awards
www.bafta.org

Berlin International Film Festival
www.berlinale.de

Blues & Roots Music Festival
www.bluesfest.com.au

Booker Prize
www.bookerprize.co.uk

Brit Awards
www.brits.co.uk

British Arts Festivals Association
www.artsfestivals.co.uk

British Federation of Festivals for Music, Dance & Speech
www.festivals.demon.co.uk

Cannes Film Festival
www.festival-cannes.fr

Crufts Dog Show
www.crufts.org.uk

Dance Umbrella
www.danceumbrella.co.uk

Edinburgh Festival
www.edinburghfestivals.co.uk

Edinburgh Fringe Festival
www.edfringe.com

European Festivals Association
www.euro-festival.net

Fleadh Festival
www.fleadhfestival.com

Gig on the Green
www.gigonthegreen.com

Glasgow International Jazz Festival
www.jazzfest.co.uk

Glastonbury Festival
www.glastonbury-festival.co.uk

Ideal Home Show
www.idealhomeshow.co.uk

International Festival of Chocolate
www.chocfest.com

International Workshop Festival
www.workshopfestival.co.uk

Just For Laughs – International Comedy Festival (Montreal)
www.hahaha.com

Laurence Olivier Awards
http://pilgirl.tripod.com/olivier.html

Listings of Scottish Events
www.rampantscotland.com

Moscow State Circus
www.moscowstatecircus.co.uk

Motor Show
www.motorshow.co.uk

Music Festivals UK
www.aloud.com/festival.shtml

Music Festivals Worldwide
www.festivals.com

Oscars
www.oscar.com

Raindance Film Showcase
www.raindance.co.uk

Royal Highland Games
www.braemargathering.org

Scottish Festivals & Celebrations
www.scottishradiance.com

Sundance Film Festival
www.sundance.org

T in the Park
www.tinthepark.com

Tony Awards
www.tonys.org

Toronto International Film Festival
www.bell.ca/toronto/filmfest

Whitbread Book Awards
www.whitbreadbookawards.co.uk

film

Cinemas

ABC
www.abccinemas.co.uk

Apollo
www.apollocinemas.co.uk

Caledonian
www.caledoniancinemas.co.uk

Carlton Cinema
www.stirling.co.uk/arts/cinema.htm

Cinemark
www.cinemark.com

Cineworld
www.cineworld.co.uk

Circle
www.circlecinemas.co.uk

Circuit Cinema
www.circuit-cinema.co.uk

Dominion Cinema
www.dominioncinemas.net

Empire
www.empireonline.co.uk

Filmhouse
www.filmhousecinema.com

Imax
www.imax.com

Odeon
www.odeon.co.uk

Pathe
www.pathe.co.uk

Picture House
www.picturehouse-cinemas.co.uk

Reeltime
www.reeltime-cinemas.co.uk

Screen
www.screencinemas.co.uk

Showcase
www.showcasecinemas.co.uk

UCI
www.uci-cinemas.co.uk

Virgin
www.virgin.net/cinema

Warner
www.warnervillage.co.uk

West Coast
www.westcoastcinemas.co.uk

Films

About a boy
www.about-a-boy.com

Alien Resurrection
www.alien-resurrection.co.uk

American Beauty
www.americanbeauty-thefilm.com

American Psycho
www.americanpsycho.com

Anastasia
www.anya.com

Angela's Ashes
www.angelasashes.com

As Good As It Gets
www.spe.sony.com/movies/asgoodasitgets

Austin Powers
www.austinpowers.com

Back to the Future
www.bttf.com

Batman & Robin
www.batman-robin.com

Bicentennial Man
www.ravecentral.com/bicentman.html

Billy Elliot
www.billyelliot.net

Black Hawk Down
www.spe.sony.com/movies/blackhawkdown

Blair Witch Project
www.blairwitch.co.uk

Boogie Nights
www.boogie-nights.com

Bourne Identity
www.thebourneidentity.com

Braveheart
www.paramount.com/braveheart

Carry On
www.carryonline.com

Celebrity
www.miramax.com/celebrity

Chicken Run
www.chickenrun.co.uk

Dancer in the Dark
http://dancerinthedark.co.uk

East is East
www.eastiseast.co.uk

Elizabeth
www.elizabeth-themovie.com

End of Days
www.end-of-days.com

End of the Affair
www.spe.sony.com/movies/endoftheaffair

Entrapment
www.foxmovies.com/entrapment

Eyes Wide Shut
www.eyeswideshut.com

Godzilla
www.godzilla.com

Goldmember
www.austinpowers.com

Gone in 60 Seconds
www.gonein60seconds.com

Grease
www.greasemovie.com

Hannibal
www.mgm.com/hannibal

Harry Potter
www.harrypotter.com

Hideous Kinky
www.kwfc.com/filmography/hideouskinky.shtml

High Fidelity
www.studio.go.com/movies/highfidelity

Highlander
www.highlander-official.com

Hilary & Jackie
www.virtualurth.com/movies/hilaryandjackie.html

Honest
www.honestthemovie.com

Incredible Hulk
www.incrediblehulk.com

Independence Day
www.id4.com

Jackie Brown
www.jackiebrown.co.uk

James Bond
www.jamesbond.com

Jerry Maguire
www.jerrymaguire.com

Julien Donkey-boy
www.juliendonkeyboy.com

Lock, Stock & Two Smoking Barrels
www.lockstock2barrels.com

Lord of the Rings
www.lordoftherings.net

Lost in Space
www.dangerwillrobinson.com

Matrix Reloaded
www.whatisthematrix.com

Men In Black
www.meninblack.com

Men in Black 2
www.meninblack.com

Midsummer Night's Dream
www.fox.co.uk/midsummer

Minority Report
www.minorityreport.com

Mission Impossible
www.missionimpossible.com

Mission Impossible 2
www.missionimpossible.com

My Dog Skip
http://mydogskip.warnerbros.com

Nightmare on Elm Street
www.elmstreet.co.uk

Notting Hill
www.notting-hill.com

Oscar Wilde
www.oscarwilde.com

Prince of Egypt
www.prince-of-egypt.com

Psycho
www.universalstudios.com/home/psycho

Reign of Fire
http://bventertainment.go.com/movies/reignoffire

Rocky Horror Picture Show
www.rockyhorror.com

Rugrats Movie
www.rugratsmovie.com

Rules of Engagement
www.rulesmovie.com

Runaway Bride
www.runawaybride.com

Saving Private Ryan
www.rzm.com/pvt.ryan

Scooby Doo
www.scoobydoo.com

Scream 3
www.scream3.com

Shakespeare in Love
www.miramax.com/shakespeareinlove

Sleepy Hollow
www.sleepyhollowthemovie.co.uk

Snatch
www.snatch-the-movie.com

South Park The Movie
www.southparkmovie.com

Spiderman
www.spiderman.sonypictures.com

Star Wars
www.starwars.com

Star Wars Episode 2
www.starwars.com/episode2

Stuart Little
www.stuartlittle.com

Sum of All Fears
www.sumofallfearsmovie.com

Tarzan (Disney's)
www.tarzan.co.uk

The Avengers
www.the-avengers.com

The Beach
www.virgin.net/thebeach

The Bone Collector
www.thebonecollector.com

The Governess
www.spe.sony.com/classics/governess

The King & I
www.thekingandi.com

The Mummy
www.themummy.com

The Out-of-Towners
www.outoftowners.com

The Patriot
www.thepatriot.com

The Perfect Storm
www.perfectstorm.net

The Phantom Menace
www.starwars.com/episode-i

The Postman
www.thepostman.com

The Road to Eldorado
www.roadtoeldorado.com

The Saint
www.thesaint.com

The Talented Mr. Ripley
www.talentedmrripley.com

The Thomas Crown Affair
www.mgm.com/thethomascrownaffair

The World is Not Enough
www.jamesbond.com/bond19

There's Something About Mary
www.aboutmary.com

Thin Red Line
www.thethinredline.co.uk

Time Code
www.timecode2000.com

Titanic
www.titanicmovie.com

Tomorrow Never Dies
www.tomorrowneverdies.com

Toy Story 2
http://disney.go.com/worldsofdisney/toystory2

Trainspotting
www.miramax.com/trainspotting

Tumbleweeds
www.tumbleweeds-movie.com

Turbo: A Power Rangers Movie
www.powerrangersturbo.com

Viva Rock Vegas
www.vivarockvegas.com

Waterworld: Quest for the Mariner
www.mca.com/unicity/waterworld

Wild Wild West
www.wildwildwest.net

Wizard of Oz
www.thewizardofoz.com

You've Got Mail
www.youvegotmail.com

Production Companies & Studios

20th Century Fox UK
www.fox.co.uk

Bollywood
www.bollywood.org.uk

Buena Vista International
www.bvimovies.com

Castle Rock
www.castle-rock.com

Columbia Tristar
www.spe.sony.com/movies

Dimension Films
www.dimensionfilms.com

Disney
www.disney.com/disneypictures

Ealing – NTFS
www.ealingstudios.co.uk

Edinburgh Film Studios
www.edinburghfilmstudios.co.uk

Elstree
www.elstreefilmstudios.co.uk

FilmFour
www.filmfour.com

Fine Line Features
www.flf.com

Ginger Productions
www.goginger.com

HDS
www.hds-studios.com

Hollywood
www.hollywood.com

Leavesden
www.leavesdenstudios.com

Lucas Film
www.lucasfilm.com

MCA Universal
www.mca.com

MGM
www.mgm.com

Miramax
www.miramax.com

New Line
www.newline.com

October Films
www.octoberfilms.com

Orion
www.orionpictures.com

Paramount
www.paramount.com/motionpicture

Pathé
www.pathé.co.uk

Picture Palace Productions
www.picturepalace.com

Polygram Video
www.polygramvideo.co.uk

SMG
www.smg.plc.uk

Steven Spielberg Dreamworks
www.spielberg-dreamworks.com

Teddington
www.teddington.co.uk

Three Mills Island
www.threemills.com

United International Pictures
www.uip.com

Universal
www.universalstudios.com

Universal Pictures
www.universalpictures.com

Walt Disney
www.disney.go.com/studiooperations

Wark Clements
www.warkclements.com

Warner Brothers
www.movies.warnerbros.com

West Freugh
www.backlot.co.uk/westfreugh

funding, organisations & regulation

Academy of Motion Picture Arts & Sciences
www.orcars.orgAmerican Film Foundation
www.americanfilmfoundation.com

American Film Institute
www.afionline.org

Antonine Films
www.antoninefilms.co.uk

Association of British Theatre Technicians
www.abtt.org.uk

Association of Motion Picture Sound
www.amps.net

Association of Mouth & Foot Painting Artists Worldwide
www.amfpa.com

Association of Professional Theatre for Children & Young People
www.designer.co.uk

BAFTA
www.bafta.org

BBC
www.bbc.co.uk

British Academy of Dramatic Combat
www.badc.co.uk

British Board of Film Classification
www.bbfc.co.uk

British Copyright Council
www.britishcopyright.org.uk

British Film Commission
www.britfilmcom.co.uk

British Film Institute
www.bfi.org.uk

British Films Catalogue
www.britfilms.com

British Music Information Centre
www.bmic.co.uk

British Phonographic Industry
www.bpi.co.uk

British Screen Finance
www.britishscreen.co.uk

British Society of Master Glass Painters
www.bsmgp.org.uk

British Universities Film & Video Council
www.bufvc.ac.uk

British Video Association
www.bva.org.uk

Broadcasting Standards Commission
www.bsc.org.uk

Cartoonists' Guild
www.pipemedia.net/cartoons

Cinema Organ Society
www.cinema-organs.org.uk

Cinema Theatre Association
www.cinema-theatre.org.uk

Community Development Foundation
www.cdf.org.uk

Community Fund Scotland
www.community-fund.org.uk

Community Media Association
www.commedia.org.uk

Copyright Licensing Agency
www.cla.co.uk

Crafts Council
www.craftscouncil.org.uk

Department for Culture, Media & Sport
www.culture.gov.uk

Digital Arts Development Agency
www.da2.org.uk

Directors' Guild of Great Britain
www.dggb.co.uk

Directors' Guild of Great Britain
www.dggb.co.uk

Edinburgh Film Focus
www.edinfilm.com

Emmys (Academy of Television Arts & Sciences)
www.emmys.org

Equity British Actors' Union
www.equity.org.uk

Film & Video Umbrella
www.fvumbrella.com/explorernew.html

Film in Edinburgh
www.edinburghguide.com/aande/film

Films made in South West Scotland
www.dumgal.gov.uk/services/depts/comres/screencommission/films.htm

Fine Art Trade Guild
www.fineart.co.uk

First Take Films
www.firsttakefilms.com

Foundation for Art & Creative Technology
www.fact.co.uk

Freeform Arts Trust
www.freeform.org.uk

Glasgow Film Fund
www.filmcentre.co.uk/faqs_fund.htm

Glasgow Film Office
www.glasgowfilm.org.uk

Glasgow Film Theatre
www.gft.org.uk

Guild of Film Production Accountants & Financial Administrators
www.gfpa.org.uk

Guild of Television Cameramen
www.gtc.org.uk

Heritage Lottery Fund
www.hlf.org.uk

Incorporated Society of Musicians
www.ism.org

Independent Television Commission
www.itc.co.uk

Independent Theatre Council
www.itc-arts.org

International Arts Bureau
www.international-arts.org

International Thespian Society
www.etassoc.org

Magic Circle
www.themagiccircle.co.uk

Media Trust
www.mediatrust.org

Millennium Commission
www.millennium.gov.uk

Moving Image Society
www.bksts.com

Museums & Galleries Commission
www.museums.gov.uk

Music Industries Association
www.mia.org.uk

National Campaign for the Arts
www.artscampaign.org.uk

National Council for Voluntary Organisations
www.ncvo-vol.org.uk

National Endowment for Science, Technology & the Arts (NESTA)
www.nesta.org.uk

National Foundation for Youth Music
www.youthmusic.org.uk

National Foundation for Youth Music
www.youthmusic.org.uk

National Lottery Charities Board
www.nlcb.org.uk

New Opportunties Fund
www.nof.org.uk

New Producers' Alliance
www.npa.org.uk

Performing Rights Society
www.prs.co.uk

Phonographic Performance Limited
www.ppluk.com

Piano Tuners' Association
www.pianotuner.org.uk

Producers' Alliance for Cinema & Television
www.pact.co.uk

Production Managers' Association
www.pma.org.uk

Scottish Arts Council
www.sac.org.uk

Scottish Highlands & Islands Film Commission
www.scotfilm.org

Scottish Screen
www.scottishscreen.com

Production Managers' Association
www.pma.org.uk

Royal Television Society
www.rts.org.uk

Society of Television Lighting Directors
www.stld.org.uk

Sonic Arts Network
www.sonicartsnetwork.org

Soros Documentary Fund
www.soros.org/sdf

South West Scotland Screen Commission
www.sw-scotland-screen.com

The Film Council
www.filmcouncil.org

Writers' Guild of Great Britain
www.writers.org.uk/guild

literature

Allan Ramsay
www.ebs.hw.ac.uk/EDC/edinburghers/alan-ramsay-elder.html

Ambit Magazine
www.ambit.co.uk

Anne Frank
www.annefrank.com

Arthur C Clarke
www.acclarke.co.uk

Arvon Foundation
www.arvonfoundation.org

Association of Scottish Literary Studies
www2.arts.gla.ac.uk/ScotLit/ASLS

Book Trust
www.booktrust.org.uk

Catherine McCormack
http://members.tripod.com/~SurferGirl415/cmcormack.html

Christopher Brookmyre
www.brookmyre.co.uk

Douglas Adams
www.douglasadams.com

Fay Weldon
www.tile.net/weldon

Helen Keller
www.hki.org/helen.html

Hugh McDiarmid
www.yfinnie.demon.co.uk/contents4thistle1.html

Iain Banks
http://lucid.cba.uiuc.edu/~rkeogh/banks

Ian Fleming
www.ianfleming.org

Ian Hamilton Finlay
www.ubu.com

Ian Rankin
www.ianrankin.net

J K Rowling
www.jkrowling.com

John Grisham
www.jgrisham.com

John Steinbeck
www.steinbeck.org

JRR Tolkien
www.tolkien.co.uk

Ken Follett
www.ken-follett.com

Lewis Carroll
www.lewiscarroll.org/carroll

Lord Byron
www.lordbyron.ds4a.com

Margaret Drabble
www.tile.net/drabble

Poetry Book Society
www.poetrybooks.co.uk

Poetry Review
www.poetrysoc.com

Robert Burns
www.robertburns.org

Robert Louis Stevenson
www.unibg.it/rls/rls.htm

Rudyard Kipling
www.kipling.org.uk

Scottish Authors – Slainte
www.slainte.org.uk

Scottish Poetry Library
www.spl.org.uk

Shakespeare Birthplace Trust
www.shakespeare.org.uk

Sir Arthur Conan Doyle
www.sherlockholmesonline.org

Sir Thomas Urquhart
www.users.globalnet.co.uk/~crumey/thomas_urquhart.html

Sir Walter Scott
www.kirjasto.sci.fi/wscott.htm

Stephen King
www.stephenking.com

magazines & websites

Amateur Stage
www.uktw.co.uk/amstage

Art Guide
www.artguide.org.uk

Art Libraries of UK & Ireland
http://arlis.nal.vam.ac.uk

Art Review
www.art-review.co.uk

Arts Business
www.arts-business.co.uk

BBC Music
www.bbcworldwide.com/musicmagazine

BBC Music Magazine
www.bbcmusicmagazine.beeb.com

Cable Guide
www.cableguide.co.uk

Casting Weekly
www.ndirect.co.uk/~castingw

Circa
www.recirca.com

Dotmusic
www.dotmusic.com

G-Wizz
www.g-wizz.net

Galleries Magazine
www.artefact.co.uk

Gramophone Magazine
www.gramophone.co.uk

Hitchhikers Guide to the Galaxy
www.h2g2.com

International Directory of Art Libraries
http://iberia.vassar.edu/ifla-idal

International Movie Database
www.imdb.com

List
www.listmag.com

Live Art Magazine
http://art.ntu.ac.uk/livemag

Media Week
www.mediaweek.co.uk

MP3
www.mp3.com

Musician
www.musician.com

Musician's Guide
www.musiciansguide.com

Musicscotland
www.musicscotland.com

New Musical Express (NME)
www.nme.com

Opening Line
www.openingline.co.uk

Popcorn
www.popcorn.co.uk

Q
www.qonline.co.uk

Radio Times
www.radiotimes.co.uk

Rolling Stone
www.rollingstone.com

Route Online
www.route-online.com

Satellite World
www.satelliteworld.demon.co.uk

SceneOne
www.sceneone.co.uk

Screen International
www.screendaily.com

Spotlight Casting Directory
www.spotlightcd.com

Teletext
www.teletext.co.uk

The Raft
www.c3.vmg.co.uk

The Stage
www.thestage.co.uk

Theatre
www.uktw.co.uk/theatremag

Time
www.time.com

Time Out
www.timeout.com

Tune Web
www.darsie.net/tuneweb

TV Times
www.tvtimes.co.uk

Ultimate Band List
www.ubl.com

Variety
www.variety.com

Warner ESP (Music Catalogue)
www.warneresp.co.uk

World Wide Arts Resources
www.world-arts-resources.com

music

Akai
www.akai.com

Bagpipe Web Directory
www.bobdunsire.com/bagpipeweb

BBC Scottish Symphony Orchestra
www.bbc.co.uk/scotland/musicscotland/bbcsso

Boosey & Hawkes
www.boosey.com

Chappell
www.uk-piano.org/chappell

Classical Piano
www.classicalpiano.com

College of Piping
www.college-of-piping.co.uk

Fender
www.fender.com

Guitar Tabs Universe
www.guitartabs.cc

Harmony Central
www.harmony-central.com

Highland Music Trust
www.heallan.com

HMV
www.hmv.com

Irish Traditional Music Archive
www.itma.ie

Kemble Pianos
www.uk-piano.org/kemble

Marshall Amplification
www.marshallamps.com

National Youth Choir of Scotland
www.nycos.co.uk

National Youth Orchestra of Scotland
www.nyos.co.uk

Piping Centre
www.thepipingcentre.co.uk

Premier Percussion
www.premier-percussion.com

Scottish Chamber Orchestra
www.sco.org.uk

Scottish Fiddle Orchestra
www.sfo.org.uk

Scottish Folk Directory
www.scottishfolkdirectory.com

Scottish Independent Music Scene
www.harenet.demon.co.uk/sims

Scottish Music Information Centre
www.smic.org.uk

Steinway
www.steinway.com

The Gig Guide
www.gigguide.co.uk

Yamaha
www.yamaha.co.uk

Artists

911
http://c3.vmg.co.uk/911

A-ha
www.a-ha.net

A1
www.a1-online.com

Abba
www.abbasite.com

AC/DC
www.elektra.com/retro/acdc

Adam Ant
www.adam-ant.net

Aerosmith
www.aerosmith.com

Alanis Morisette
www.alanismorisette.com

Alice Cooper
www.alicecoopershow.com

All Saints
www.theallsaints.com

America
www.venturahighway.com

Animals
www.animals.mcmail.com

Anne Murray
www.annemurray.com

Another Level
www.anotherlevel.co.uk

Aqua
www.aqua.dk

Atomic Kitten
www.atomickitten.co.uk

Atomic Rooster
http://atomicrooster.com

Aztec Camera
www.killermontstreet.com

B*Witched
www.b-witched.com

B-52's
www.theb52s.com

Backstreet Boys
www.backstreetboys.com

Bananarama
www.bananaramaweb.com

Barbra Streisand
www.barbra-streisand.com

Barclay James Harvest
www.bjharvest.co.uk

Barry Manilow
www.manilow.com

Bay City Rollers
www.lesmckeown.com

BB King
www.bbking.com

Be-Bop Deluxe
http://billnelson.com

Beach Boys
www.beach-boys.com

Beastie Boys
www.beastieboys.com

Beatles
www.beatles.com

Beautiful South
www.beautifulsouth.co.uk

Beck
www.beck.com

Bee Gees
www.beegees.net

Bellamy Brothers
www.bellamybros.com

Belle & Sebastian
www.belleandsebastian.co.uk

Big Brother & the Holding Company
www.bbhc.com/BigBrother.htm

Big Country
www.bigcountry.co.uk

Billie Piper
www.billie.co.uk

Billy Idol
www.billyidol.com

Billy Joel
www.billyjoel.com

Bjork
www.bjork.co.uk/bjork

Bjorn Again
www.bjornagain.com

Black Sabbath
www.black-sabbath.com

Blondie
www.blondie.net

Blur
www.blur.co.uk

Bob Dylan
www.bobdylan.com

Bob Marley
www.bobmarley.com

Bob Seger
www.segerbob.com

Bon Jovi
www.bonjovi.com

Boy George
www.boy.george.net

Boyzone
www.boyzone.co.uk

Brandy
www.foreverbrandy.com

Britney Spears
www.britneyspears.co.uk

Bruce Springsteen
www.brucespringsteen.net

Buzzcocks
www.buzzcocks.com

Capercaillie
www.capercaillie.co.uk

Cardigans
www.cardigans.net

Cat Stevens
www.catstevens.co.uk

Catatonia
www.catatonia.com

Celine Dion
www.celineonline.com

Charlie Parker
www.charlieparker.com

Chemical Brothers
www.algonet.se/~inftryck/chemical

Cher
www.cher.com

Chicago
www.chicagotheband.com

Chris De Burgh
www.cdeb.com

Chris Isaak
www.repriserec.com/chrisisaak

Christina Aguilera
www.christina-aguilera.com

Clash
www.westwaytotheworld.com

Cleopatra
www.cleopatramusic.com

Cliff Richard
www.cliffrichard.org

Cocteau Twins
www.cocteautwins.com

Coldplay
www.coldplay.com

The Corries
www.corries.com

Corrs
www.corrs.com

Cosby, Stills, Nash & Young
www.csny.net

Craig David
www.craigdavid.co.uk

Cranberries
www.the-cranberries.net

Crash Test Dummies
www.crashtestdummies.com

Croft No Five
www.croftnofive.com

Culture Club
www.cultureclub.net

Cure
www.thecure.com

Dannii Minogue
www.dannii.com

Darius Danesh
www.darius-danesh.org.uk

David Bowie
www.davidbowie.com

David Cassidy
www.davidcassidy.com

David Essex
www.davidessex.com

David Knopfler
www.knopfler.com

Deacon Blue
www.rickyross.com

Dean Friedman
www.deanfriedman.com

Deep Purple
www.deep-purple.com

Del Amitri
www.delamitri.com

Depeche Mode
www.depechemode.com

Des'ree
www.desree.co.uk

Destiny's Child
www.destinyschild.com

Diana Ross
www.dianaross.com

Divine Comedy
www.thedivinecomedy.com

Dixie Chicks
www.dixiechicks.com

Dolly Parton
www.dolly.net

Donny & Marie Osmond
www.donnyandmarie.com

Doobie Brothers
www.doobiebros.com

Doors
www.thedoors.com

Duran Duran
www.duranduran.com

Dwight Yoakam
www.wbr.com/nashville/dwightyoakam

Elton John
www.eltonjohn.com

Elvis Costello
www.elvis-costello.com

Elvis Presley
www.elvis-presley.com

Emerson Lake & Palmer
www.emersonlakepalmer.com

Eminem
www.eminem.com

Emma Bunton
www.emma-lee-bunton.com

Enigma
http://enigma.kaizo.org

Enya
www.repriserec.com/enya

Eric Clapton
www.repriserec.com/ericclapton

Everything But The Girl
www.ebtg.com

Fairport Convention
www.fairportconvention.co.uk

Faith Hill
www.faithhill.com

Fatboy Slim
www.normancook.cjb.net

Frank Sinatra
www.sinatra.com

Fugees
www.fugees.net

Future Pilot AKA
www.futurepilotaka.com

Gabrielle
www.gabrielle.co.uk

Garbage
www.garbage.com

Gary Barlow
www.garybarlow.mcmail.com

Genesis
www.genesis-web.com

Geneva
www.nuderecords.com/htm_geneva

George Benson
www.georgebenson.com

George Harrison
www.allthingsmustpass.com

George Michael
www.aegean.net

Geri Halliwell
www.gerihalliwell.co.uk

Gerry Marsden & the Pacemakers
www.gerrymarsden.com

Glen Campbell
www.glencampbellshow.com

Glen Miller Orchestra
www.glennmillerorchestra.com

Glitter Band
www.glitterband.fsnet.co.uk

Gloria Estefan
www.gloriafan.com

Golden Earring
www.golden-earring.nl

Grateful Dead
www.dead.net

Greg Lake
www.greglake.com

Guns N' Roses
www.geffen.com/gunsnroses

Hall & Oates
www.hallandoates.org.uk

Hanson
www.hansonline.com

Harry Connick Jr
www.hconnickjr.com

Hawkwind
www.hawkwind.com

Heaven 17
www.heaven17.com

Hollies
www.hollies.co.uk

Honeyz
www.honeyzstyle.2ya.com

Hootie & the Blowfish
www.hootie.com

Howard Jones
www.howardjones.com

Hue & Cry
www.lindawho.com

Ian Dury
www.iandury.co.uk

Iron Maiden
www.ironmaiden.co.uk

Isaac Hayes
www.isaachayes.com

Isley Brothers
http://sonymusic.com/artists/theisleybrothers

Jamiroquai
www.jamiroquai.co.uk

Janet Jackson
www.friendsofjanet.com

Jean Michel Jarre
www.jeanmicheljarre.com

Jeff Beck
www.epicrecords.com/jeffbeck

Jennifer Lopez
www.jenniferlopez.com

Jethro Tull
www.j-tull.com

Jewel
www.jeweljk.com

Jim Diamond
www.jimdiamond.com

Jimi Hendrix
www.jimi-hendrix.com

JJ 72
www.jj72.com

Jo Dee Messina
www.jodeemessina.com

Joan Armatrading
www.joanarmatrading.com

Joan Baez
www.baez.woz.org

Joe Brown
www.joebrown.co.uk

Joe Cocker
www.joediffie.com

Joe Jackson
www.joejackson.com

Johnny Cash
www.johnnycash.com

Jon Bon Jovi
www.jonbonjovi.com

Joni Mitchell
www.jonimitchell.com

Joy Division
www.worldinmotion.net/joydivision.htm

Judy Tzuke
www.tzuke.com

Julian Cope
www.juliancope.com

Julian Lennon
www.julianlennon.com

Julie Felix
www.herebedragons.co.uk

Julio Inglesias
www.julioiglesias.net

Kajagoogoo
www.kajagoogoo.com

Kavana
www.c3.vmg.co.uk/kavana

KC & the Sunshine Band
www.heykcsb.com

Kd lang
www.kdlang.com

Kenny Rogers
www.kennyrogers.net

Kinks
http://kinks.it.rit.edu/okfc

Kiss
www.kissonline.com

Korn
www.korn.com

Kula Shaker
www.kulashaker.co.uk

Kylie Minogue
www.kylie.com

LeAnn Rimes
www.rimestimes.com

Led Zeppelin
www.led-zeppelin.com

Lenny Kravitz
www.virginrecords.com/kravitz

Leonard Bernstein
www.leonardbernstein.com

Leonard Cohen
www.leonardcohen.com

Level 42
www.level42.com

Levellers
www.levellers.co.uk

Lighthouse Family
www.lighthousefamily.com

Lightning Seeds
www.lightningseeds.com

Limahl
www.limahl.co.uk

Limp Bizkit
www.limpbizkit.com

Lou Reed
www.loureed.org

Lulu
www.lulu.co.uk

Luther Vandross
www.epicrecords.com/luthervandross

Lynyrd Skynyrd
www.lynyrdskynyrd.com

Macy Gray
www.macygray.com

Madness
www.madness.co.uk

Madonna
www.wbr.com/madonna

Mandy Moore
www.mandymoore.com

Manic Street Preachers
www.manics.co.uk

Mansun
www.mansun.co.uk

Marc Almond
www.marcalmond.co.uk

Mariah Carey
www.mcarey.com

Marillion
www.marillion.com

Marilyn Manson
www.marilynmanson.net

Mark Knopfler
www.mark-knopfler-news.co.uk

Martine McCutcheon
www.martinemccutcheon.com

Mary Chapin Carpenter
www.marychapincarpenter.com

Mary J Blige
www.mjblige.com

Massive Attack
www.massiveattack.co.uk

Mavericks
www.themavericks.com

Meat Loaf
www.meatloaf-oifc.com

Melanie C
www.northern-star.co.uk

Metallica
www.metclub.com

Michael Bolton
www.michaelbolton.com

Michael Jackson
www.mjnet.com

Michael Nyman
www.michaelnyman.com

Mike Oldfield
www.mikeoldfield.org

Miles Davis
www.miles-davis.com

Moody Blues
www.moodyblues.co.uk

Morrissey
www.morrissey.co.uk

Natalie Imbruglia
www.natalie-imbruglia.co.uk

Neil Diamond
www.neildiamondhomepage.com

Neneh Cherry
www.nenehweb.com

Nitty Gritty Dirt Band
www.nittygritty.com

Norman Greenbaum
www.spiritinthesky.com

Oasis
www.oasisinet.com

Ocean Colour Scene
www.oceancolourscene.com

Olivia Newton John
www.onlyolivia.com/onj.html

Osmonds
www.osmond.com

Ozzy Osbourne
www.ozzy.com

Pastels
www.cogsci.ed.ac.uk/~jonathan/pastels.html

Patsy Cline
www.patsy.nu

Paul Young
www.paul-young.com

Paula Abdul
www.undermyspell.com

Pet Shop Boys
www.petshopboys.co.uk

Peter Andre
www.amws.com.au/a/andre-peter

Peter Gabriel
www.petergabriel.com

Peter Tork
www.petertork.com

PJ Harvey
www.pjh.org

Placebo
www.placebo.co.uk

Placido Domingo
www.placido-domingo.com

Pogues
www.pogues.com

Portishead
www.portishead.co.uk

Primal Scream
www.primalscream.org

Prince
www.npgmusicclub.com

Proclaimers
www.proclaimers.co.uk

Prodigy
www.theprodigy.co.uk

Public Enemy
www.public-enemy.com

Puff Daddy
www.puffdaddy.com

Pulp
www.rise.co.uk/pulp

Queen
www.queen-fip.com

Quincy Jones
www.wbr.com/quincyjones

Radiohead
www.radiohead.co.uk

Ralph Vaughan Williams
www.cs.qub.ac.uk/~J.Collis/RVW.html

Ramones
www.officialramones.com

Ray Charles
www.raycharles.com

REM
www.wbr.com/rem

Ricky Martin
www.rickymartin.com

Ringo Starr
www.ringotour.com

Robbie Williams
www.robbiewilliams.co.uk

Rod Stewart
www.wbr.com/rodstewart

Roger Daltrey
www.rogerdaltrey.net

Roger Waters
www.roger-waters.com

Roger Whittaker
www.rogerwhittaker.com

Rolf Harris
www.rolfharris.com

Rolling Stones
www.the-rolling-stones.com

Ronan Keating
www.ronankeating.net

Roy Orbison
www.orbison.com

Roy Wood
www.roywood.com

Runrig
www.runrig.co.uk

S Club 7
www.sclub7.co.uk

Sarah McLachlan
www.sarahmclachlan.com

Seal
www.wbr.com/seal

Searchers
www.the-searchers.co.uk

Shakin Stevens
www.shaky.net

Shania Twain
www.shania-twain.com

Sheena Easton
www.sheenaeaston.com

Sheryl Crow
www.sherylcrow.com

Shola Ama
www.shola-ama.com

Simon & Garfunkel
http://legacyrecordings.com/simonandgarfunkel

Sinead O'Connor
www.sinead-oconnor.com

Six Mile Bridge
www.loosegoose.com/6mb

Sixpence None the Richer
www.sixpence-ntr.com

Smashing Pumpkins
www.smashing-pumpkins.net

Smokey Robinson & the Miracles (Fan Club)
www.edgenet.net/smokey_miracles

Sparks
www.sparksofficialwebsite.com

Spice Girls
www.spicegirlsforever.co.uk

Spinal Tap
www.spinaltap.com

Squeeze
www.squeezefan.com

Status Quo
www.statusquo.co.uk

Steps
www.stepsofficial.com

Stereophonics
www.stereophonics.co.uk

Stevie Nicks
www.nicksfix.com

Stiltskin
www.stiltskin.org.uk

Sting
www.stingchronicity.co.uk

Suede
www.suede.co.uk

Supergrass
www.supergrass.com

Supertramp
www.supertramp.com

Suzanne Vega
www.vega.net

Tammy Wynette
www.tammywynette.com

Tears for Fears
www.sonymusic.com/artists/TearsForFears

Tennage Fan Club
www.teenagefanclub.com

Texas
www.texas.uk.com

Tina Turner
www.tina-turner.com

Tom Jones
www.tomjones.com

Tom Petty
www.tompetty.com

Toni Braxton
www.tonibraxton.net

Tony Bennett
www.tonybennett.net

Tori Amos
www.tori.com

Travis
www.travisonline.com

Tricky
www.trickyonline.com

Trisha Yearwood
www.mca-nashville.com/trishayearwood

Turtles
www.theturtles.com

U2
www.u2.com

UB 40
www.ub40-dep.com

Ultra
www.eastwest.co.uk/ultra

Ultravox
www.ultravox.org.uk

Van Halen
www.van-halen.com

Vanessa Mae
www.vanessa-mae.org

Vengaboys
www.vengaboys.com

Verve
www.the-raft.com/theverve

Village People
www.villagepeople-official.com

Westlife
www.westlife.co.uk

Wet Wet Wet
www.wetwetwet.co.uk

Whitney Houston
www.whitney-houston.co.uk

Will Smith
www.willsmith.net

Willie Nelson
www.willienelson.com

Wishbone Ash
www.wishboneash.com

Wyclef
www.wyclef.com

Composers

Chopin
www.chopin.org

Henry Purcell
www.bl.uk/exhibitions/purcell

Stephen Sondheim
www.sondheim.com

Opera

La Scala
http://lascala.milano.it

Royal Opera House
www.royaloperahouse.org

Royal Scottish National Orchestra
www.rsno.org.uk

Scottish Opera
www.scottishopera.org.uk

Orchestras – Scottish

BBC Scottish Symphony Orchestra.
www.bbc.co.uk/bbcsso

BT Scottish Ensemble
www.btscottishensemble.co.uk

OrchestraNet
www.orchestranet.co.uk

Royal Scottish National
www.rsno.org.uk

Scottish Chamber Orchestra
www.sco.org.uk

Orchestras

Adelaide Symphony Orchestra
www.aso.com.au

Ambache
www.ambache.co.uk

Association of British Orchestras
www.abo.org.uk

BBC Philharmonic Orchestra
www.bbc.co.uk/orchestras/philharmonic

BBC Symphony
www.bbc.co.uk/orchestras/so

Berlin Philharmonic
www.berlin-philharmonic.com

Boston Symphony
www.bso.org

Chicago Symphony
www.chicagosymphony.org

Israel Philharmonic
www.ipo.co.il

Los Angeles
www.la.phil.org

National Association of Youth Orchestras
www.nayo.org.uk

New York Philharmonic
www.nyphilharmon.org

New Zealand Symphony Orchestra
www.nzso.co.nz

Philharmonia
www.philharmonia.co.uk

Royal Philharmonic
www.rpo.co.uk

Seattle Symphony
www.seattlesymp

Toronto Symphony
www.orchestra.on.ca

Vienna Philharmonic
www.vienna.at/philharmoniker/vph

Vienna Symphony
www.weiner-symphoniker.at

Record Companies

21st Century Music
www.21stcentury.co.uk

A&M
www.amrecords.com

Arista
www.aristarec.com

Atlantic
www.atlantic-records.com

Beggars Banquet
www.beggars.com

Chandos
www.chandos-records.com

Columbia
www.columbiarecords.com

Creation
www.creation.co.uk

Decca
www.decca.com

ECM
www.ecmrecords.com

EMI Chrysalis
www.emichrysalis.co.uk

Epic
www.epicrecords.com

Geffen
www.geffen.com

Grapevine
www.grapevine-label.co.uk

HMV
www.hmv.co.uk

Hyperion
www.hyperion-records.co.uk

Island
www.island.co.uk

Legacy Recordings
www.legacyrecordings.com

MCA
www.mcarecords.com

Mercury
www.mercuryrecords.com

Ministry of Sound
www.ministryofsound.co.uk

Naxos & Marco Polo
www.hnh.com

Nimbus
www.nimbus.ltd.uk

Parlophone
www.parlophone.co.uk

Polydor
www.polydor.co.uk

Polygram
www.polygram.com

QED Productions
www.qed-productions.com

Sony
www.sonymusic.co.uk

Sony Classical
www.sonyclassical.com

Telstar
www.telstar.co.uk

Tower
www.towerrecords.co.uk

Universal Music Group
www.umusic.com

Virgin
www.virginrecords.co.uk

Warner Brothers
www.wbr.com

Studios

Abbey Road Studios
www.abbeyroad.co.uk

RAK Recording Studios
www.rakstudios.co.uk

promotors & directors

Directors' Guild of Great Britain
www.dggb.co.uk

Raymond Gubbay
www.raymond-gubbay.co.uk

Robert Stigwood Organisation
www.rsogroup.com

Stephen Berkoff
www.east-productions.demon.co.uk

radio

UK

Atlantic
www.atlantic252.com

BBC Asian Network
www.bbc.co.uk/england/asiannetwork

BBC Radio 1
www.bbc.co.uk/radio1

BBC Radio 2
www.bbc.co.uk/radio2

BBC Radio 3
www.bbc.co.uk/radio3

BBC Radio 4
www.bbc.co.uk/radio4

BBC Radio 5
www.bbc.co.uk/radio5

BBC Radio Scotland
www.bbc.co.uk/scotland/radioscotland

BBC World Service
www.bbc.co.uk/worldservice

Borders FM
www.radioborders.co.uk

Central FM
www.centralfm.co.uk

Classic FM
www.classicfm.co.uk

Discovery FM
www.discoveryfm.net

Forth FM (Edinburgh)
www.radioforth.co.uk

Fresh Air FM
www.freshairfm.co.uk

Heartland FM
www.heartlandfm.co.uk

Highlander Radio
www.scottishradio.net

Isles FM
www.islesfm.co.uk

Kingdom FM
www.kingdomfm.co.uk

Lochbroom FM
www.lochbroomfm.co.uk

Moray Firth Radio
www.mfr.co.uk/indexone.html

Nevis Radio
www.nevisradio.co.uk

New Atlantic 252
www.atlantic252.co.uk

Northsound
www.northsound1.co.uk

Northsound AM
www.northsound2.co.uk

Oban FM
www.oban-org.co.uk/obanfm/obanfm.htm

Q96
www.geocities.com/Hollywood/Hills/9419

Radio Clyde AM
http://clyde2.com

Radio Clyde FM
http://clyde1.com

Radio Nan Gaidheal
www.bbc.co.uk/scotland/alba

Radio North Angus
www.radionorthangus.org.uk

Radio Tay AM
www.tayam.co.uk

Radio Tay FM
www.tayfm.co.uk

Real Radio
www.realradiofm.com

Score Digital
www.scoredigital.co.uk

ScotRadio
www.live365.com/stations/240319

Scottish Internet Radio
www.scottish.internetradio.co.uk

Scottish Radio Holdings
www.srh.org.uk

SIBC
www.sibc.co.uk

Talk Radio
www.talk-radio.co.uk

Talk Sport
www.talksport.net

Virgin Radio
www.virginradio.com

Voice of America
www.voa.gov

Westsound FM
www.west-sound.co.uk/westsound/westfm

stadia & concert halls

Aberdeen Exhibition & Conference Centre
www.aecc.co.uk

Aberdeen Music Hall
www.ifb.net/webit/musichal.htm

Barrowlands
www.glasgow-barrowland.com

Birmingham NEC
www.nec.co.uk

Celtic Park
www.celticfc.net

Corn Exchange
www.ece.uk.com

Edinburgh International Conference Centre
www.eicc.co.uk

Hampden Park
www.hampdenpark.co.uk

Ibrox
www.ibrox-stadium.com

McDiarmid Park
www.stjohnstonefc.co.uk

Murrayfield Stadium
www.sru.org.uk

National Indoor Arena
www.nia-birmingham.co.uk

Pittodrie
www.afc.co.uk

Royal Opera House
www.royaloperahouse.org

SECC
www.secc.co.uk

television

Channels

ABC
www.abc-tv.net

Anglia
www.angliatv.co.uk

BBC
www.bbc.co.uk

BBC News
www.news.bbc.co.uk

Border TV
www.border-tv.com

Bravo
www.bravo.co.uk

Carlton
www.carltontv.co.uk

Carlton Select
www.carltonselect.com

Central
www.centraltv.co.uk

Challenge TV
www.challengetv.co.uk

Channel 4
www.channel4.co.uk

Channel 5
www.channel5.co.uk

Channel Television
www.channeltv.co.uk

CNN
www.cnn.com

Digital Gaelic Television
www.teleg.co.uk

Discovery
www.discovery.com

Disney Channel
www.disneychannel.co.uk

E4
www.e4.com

Euro TV
www.eurotv.com

Film Four
www.filmfour.com

Golf Channel
www.thegolfchannel.com

Grampian
www.grampiantv.co.uk

Granada
www.granada.tv.co.uk

Granada Plus
www.gplus.co.uk

Granada Sky
www.gsb.co.uk

HTV
www.htv.co.uk

ITV
www.itv.co.uk

Living
www.livingtv.co.uk

LWT
www.lwt.co.uk

Meridian
www.meridiantv.co.uk

MTV
www.mtv.co.uk

NBC
www.nbc.com

ONDigital
www.ondigital.co.uk

Sci-Fi Channel
www.scifi.com

Scottish Television
www.stv.co.uk

Scottish TV
www.scottishtv.co.uk

Sky
www.sky.co.uk

Web TV
www.webtv.com

Critics

Victor Lewis-Smith
www.lewis-smith.com

Personalities

Edith Bowman
http://european.mtve.com/shows/vjbiog_edith.shtml

Nicky Campbell
www.bbc.co.uk/fivelive/campbell

Billy Connolly
www.billyconnolly.com

Tam Cowan
www.dailyrecord.co.uk/columnists/tamcowan

Dougie Donnelly
www.bbc.co.uk/pressoffice/biographies/biogs/sport/dougiedonnelly.shtml

Hazel Irvine
http://news.bbc.co.uk/sport1/hi/tv_and_radio/football_focus/1480508.stm

Lorraine Kelly
http://gm.tv/index.cfm?articleid=442

Ally McCoist
www.aquestionpfally.com

Carol Smillie
www.bbc.co.uk/homes/programmes/presenters/carol.shtml

Production Companies

Aardman Animations
www.aardman.com

Addictive Television
www.addictive.com

Ginger Media Group
www.ginger.com

Hat Trick Productions
www.hat-trick.co.uk

Mentorn
www.mentorn.co.uk

Mersey Television Company
www.merseytv.com

Programmes

Alan Partridge
www.alan-partridge.co.uk

Babylon 5
http://babylon5.warnerbros.com

Baywatch
www.baywatchtv.com

BBC Comedy Zone
www.comedyzone.beeb.com

BBC Schools
www.bbc.co.uk/education/schools

Beechgrove Garden
www.beechgrove.co.uk

Beverly Hills 90210
www.helicon7.com/90210

Bewitched
www.bewitched.net

Big Brother
www.channel4.com/bigbrother

Blind Date
www.blinddate.co.uk

Brookside
www.brookie.com

Buffy the Vampire Slayer
www.buffyslayer.com

Bugs
www.bugs.co.uk

Cagney & Lacey
http://w3.one.net/~voyager/candl.html

Castaway 2000
www.bbc.co.uk/theheatison

Challenge Anneka
www.mentorn.co.uk/challenge

Changing Rooms
www.bbc.co.uk/changingrooms

Channel 4 Schools
www.schools.channel4.com

Charlie's Angels
www.charliesangels.com

Chewin the Fat
www.chewinthefat.co.uk

Cold Feet
www.coldfeetonline.co.uk

Coronation Street
www.coronationstreet.co.uk

Dawson's Creek
www.dawsons-creek.com

Dempsey & Makepeace
www.dempseyandmakepeace.de

Dr Quinn Medicine Woman
www.drquinn.com

Due South
www.duesouth.com

Eastenders
www.bbc.co.uk/eastenders

Emmerdale
www.emmerdale.co.uk

ER
www.ertv.com

Frasier
www.frasier.mcmail.com

Friends
www.friends.warnerbros.com

Gardeners' World
www.gardenersworld.beeb.com

Gladiators
www.lwt.co.uk/gladiators

GMTV
www.gmtv.co.uk

Have I Got News For You
www.haveigotnewsforyou.com

Hawaii Five-O
www.mjq.net/fiveo

High Road
www.highroad.co.uk

Hill Street Blues
www.net-hlp.com/hsb

Holby City
www.bbc.co.uk/holbycity

Holiday
www.takeoff.beeb.com

Hollyoaks
www.hollyoaks.com

Home & Away
www.homeandaway.seven.com.au

Horizon
www.bbc.co.uk/horizon

Jerry Springer Show
www.universalstudios.com/tv/jerryspringer

Kavanagh QC
www.kavanaghqc.co.uk

Knight Rider
www.knight-rider.com

League of Gentlemen
www.roystonvasey.co.uk

London Tonight
www.londontonight.co.uk

Lost in Space
www.lostinspacetv.com

Men Behaving Badly
www.menbehavingbadly.com

Monarch of the Glen
www.bbc.co.uk/monarch

Monty Python
www.montypython.net

Mr Bean
www.mrbean.co.uk

Neighbours
www.neighbours.com

North Tonight
www.northtonight.grampiantv.com

Northern Exposure
www.netspace.org/~moose/moose.html

NYPD Blue
www.nypdblue.com

Oprah Winfrey
www.oprahshow.com

Peak Practice
www.peakpractice.co.uk

Planet of the Apes
www.foxhome.com/planetoftheapes

Railway Children
http://therailwaychildren.carlton.com

Red Dwarf
www.reddwarf.co.uk

Scotland Today
www.scotlandtoday.scottishtv.co.uk

Scotsport
www.scotsport.co.uk

Scottish Passport
www.scottishpassport.co.uk

Seinfeld
www.seinfeld.com

South Park
www.southpark.co.uk

Space 1999
www.space1999.net

Star Trek
www.startrek.com

Stars In Their Eyes
www.starsintheireyes.co.uk

Starsky & Hutch
www.spe.sony.com/tv/shows/sgn/sh

Taggart
www.scottishtv.co.uk/drama

Talk TV
www.talktv.co.uk

TFI Friday
www.tfifriday.com

The Bill
www.thebill.com

The Fast Show
www.bbc.co.uk/comedy/fastshow

The Home Show
www.home-show.co.uk

The Point
www.thepointonline.co.uk

The Prisoner
www.the-prisoner-6.freeserve.co.uk

The Saint
www.saint.org

The Sweeney
www.thesweeney.com

They Think It's All Over
www.talkback.co.uk/theythink

Today's the Day
www.mentorn.co.uk/tdd

Tomorrow's World
www.bbc.co.uk/tw

Tomorrow's World Plus
www.twplus.beeb.com

Top Gear
www.topgear.beeb.com

Top of the Pops
www.totp.beeb.com

Who Wants to be a Millionaire?
www.phone-a-friend.com

Wish You Were Here?
www.wishyouwerehere.com

World at War
www.theworldatwar.com

World in Action
www.world-in-action.co.uk

X-Files
www.thex-files.com

theatre

Companies

784 Theatre
www.784theatre.com

Bench Tours
www.benchtours.com

Birds of Paradise Theatre
www.birdsofparadisetheatre.co.uk

Boiler House
www.boilerhouse.org.uk

Dance Base
www.dancebase.co.uk

Macrobert
www.macrobert.org

NTC Touring Theatre Company
www.ntc-touringtheatre.co.uk

QuicksilverTheatre Company
www.quicksilvertheatre.org

Rocket Theatre Company
www.rockettheatre.co.uk

Scottish Youth Theatre
www.scottishyouththeatre.org

Soho Theatre Company
www.sohotheatre.com

Suspect Culture
www.suspectculture.com

TAG Theatre Co
www.tag-theatre.co.uk

Tara Arts
www.tara-arts.com

Theatre Babel
www.theatrebabel.co.uk

Theatre Cryptic
www.cryptic.org.uk

Tram Direct Theatre Co
www.tramdir.dircon.co.uk

Visible Fictions Theatre Co
www.visiblefictions.co.uk

Wee Stories Theatre Co
www.weestoriestheatre.org

Productions

Art
www.dewynters.com/art

Beautiful Game
www.beautifulgamemusical.com

Buddy Holly Story
www.mpcgroup.co.uk/buddy

Carousel
www.shubert.com/carousel.html

Cats
www.reallyuseful.com/cats

Chicago
www.chicagothemusical.com

Doctor Dolittle
www.doctordolittle.co.uk

Evita
www.thenewevita.com

Fosse the Musical
www.fosse.uk.com

Grease
www.grease-tour.com

Houdini The Musical
www.houdinithemusical.com

Jekyll & Hyde
www.jekyll-hyde.com

Les Miserables
www.lesmis.com

Lord of the Dance
www.lordofthedance.com

Mamma Mia!
www.mamma-mia.com

Miss Saigon
www.miss-saigon.com

My Fair Lady
www.tcfhe.com/myfairlady

Notre Dame de Paris
www.albemarle-london.com/notredame.html

Phantom of the Opera
www.thephantomoftheopera.com

Riverdance
www.riverdance.com

Rocky Horror Picture Show
www.rockyhorror.com

Saturday Night Fever
www.nightfever.co.uk

Spend, Spend, Spend
www.spendspendspend.net

Tap Dogs
www.tapdogs.com

The King & I
www.kingandi.co.uk

Theatres

Aberdeen Music Hall
www.aberdeencity.gov.uk/acc/WhatsOn/PerformanceVenues/venue_mh.asp

The Arches
www.thearches.co.uk

Byre Theatre
www.byretheatre.com

Carnegie Hall
www.carnegiehall.co.uk

Church Hill Theatre
www.edinburgh.gov.uk/CEC/Recreation/Leisure/Data/Church_Hill_Theatre/Church_Hill_Theatre.html

Citizens Theatre, Glasgow
www.citz.co.uk

Dundee Rep Theatre
www.dundeereptheatre.co.uk

Eden Court Theatre, Inverness
www.edencourt.uk.com

Federation of Scottish Theatre
www.scottishtheatre.org

Festival Theatre, Edinburgh
www.eft.co.uk

His Majesty's Theatre, Aberdeen
www.aberdeencity.gov.uk/acc/WhatsOn/PerformanceVenues/Default.asp

Pavilion Theatre, Glasgow
www.paviliontheatre.co.uk

Perth Theatre
www.perth.org.uk/perth/theatre

Pitlochry Festival Theatre
www.pitlochry.org.uk

Playhouse, Edinburgh
www.gold.co.uk/playhouse.html

Royal Exchange Theatre Company
www.royalexchange.co.uk

Royal Lyceum Theatre, Edinburgh
www.infoser.com/infotheatre/lyceum

Royal National Theatre
www.nt-online.org.uk

Theatre Royal, Glasgow
www.theatreroyalglasgow.com

Tramway Theatre
www.tramway.org

Traverse Theatre, Edinburgh
www.traverse.co.uk

Tron Theatre, Glasgow
www.tron.co.uk

Usher Hall
www.usherhall.co.uk

tickets

Albemarle of London
www.albemarle-london.com

BBC Ticket Unit
www.bbc.co.uk/tickets

First Call
www.first-call.co.uk

Global Tickets
www.globaltickets.com

Group Line
www.groupline.com

Hot Tickets Direct
www.hotticketsdirect.com

Lastminute.com
www.lastminute.com

Red T
www.redt.co.uk

Ripping Records
www.rippingrecords.com

SECC Tickets
www.secctickets.com

Society of Ticket Agents & Retailers
www.s-t-a-r.org.uk

SRU
www.sru.org.uk

Theatre Tokens
www.theatretokens.com

Ticket Line
http://events.edinburgh.gov.uk

Ticket Select
www.stoll-moss.com

Ticketmaster
www.scotland.ticketmaster.co.uk

Tickets Direct
www.tickets-direct.co.uk

Tickets Online
www.tickets-online.co.uk

Tickets Scotland
www.tickets-scotland.com

Ticketselect
www.stoll-moss.com

Ticketweb
www.ticketweb.co.uk

Wayahead
www.wayahead.com

West End Theatre Bookings
www.uktickets.co.uk

What's On Stage
www.whatsonstage.com

- advertising agencies
- agriculture
- architecture
- automotive
- aviation
- chambers of commerce & local enterprise companies
- chemicals
- computer training
- couriers
- electrical & technological
- energy
- engineering
- finance
- food, beverages & tobacco
- insurance
- leisure
- livery companies & guilds
- magazines & websites
- manufacturing
- marketing
- materials & construction
- media
- metals & mining
- modelling agencies
- office supplies & services
- paper & packaging
- pharmaceutical
- printing & publishing
- private investigators
- professional bodies & associations
- professions
- real estate
- recruitment
- retail
- services
- shipping & shipbuilding
- standards
- stock & commodity exchanges & financial listings
- telecommunications
- trade unions & associations
- transport
- US corporations
- utilities

advertising agencies

1576 (Edinburgh)
www.1576.co.uk

Abbott Mead Vickers
www.amvbbdo.co.uk

Addison Wesley Longman
www.awl.com

Advertising Age
www.adage.com

Barkers Scotland
www.barkersscotland.co.uk

Bartle Bogle Hegarty
www.bbh.co.uk

Bates Dorland
www.bates-dorland.co.uk

Beer Davies
www.beerdavies.co.uk

BMP DDB
www.bmp.co.uk

Charles Barker
www.cbarker.co.uk

CHJS
www.chjs.co.uk

Coltas Ltd (Glasgow)
www.coltas.co.uk

Davidson Advertising (Glasgow)
www.davidsonadvertising.co.uk

Dewynters
www.dewynters.com

DMBB
www.dmbb.com

Dryden Brown
www.dryden.co.uk

Duckworth Finn Grub Waters
www.dfgw.co.uk

Edmonds Advertising (Edinburgh)
www.edmonds.co.uk

Faulds Advertising (Edinburgh)
www.faulds.co.uk

FCB
www.fcb.com

Ginger Marketing (Glasgow)
www.gingermarketing.co.uk

Grey
www.grey.co.uk

Gupta Partnership (Edinburgh)
www.guptapartnership.com

HHCL
www.hhcl.com

Indigo Bridge Ltd (Kirkcaldy)
www.indigobridge.com

J Walter Thompson
www.jwtworld.com

Joslin Shaw
www.joshaw.co.uk

Lawrence Creative (Glasgow)
www.lawrencecreative.com

Leo Burnett
www.leoburnett.com

Lowe Howard Spink
www.lowehoward-spink.co.uk

McCann Erickson
www.mccann.com

Mearns & Gill Advertising (Aberdeen)
www.mearns-gill.com

Osprey Scotland (Edinburgh)
www.ospreydesign.co.uk

Paling Walters Targis
www.palingwalters.com

Poulter
www.poulter.co.uk

RDW
www.rdw-advertising.co.uk

Saatchi & Saatchi
www.saatchi-saatchi.com

Scotti Internet Marketing (Stirling)
www.scotti-internet-marketing.co.uk

The Leith Agency (Edinburgh)
www.leith.co.uk

Wam-McCann Erickson (Edinburgh)
www.mccann-online.co.uk

Young & Rubicam
www.yandr.com

Professional Bodies

Advertising Association
www.adassoc.org.uk

Advertising Standards Authority
www.asa.org.uk

Committee of Advertising Practice
www.cap.org.uk

European Advertising Standards Alliance
www.easa-alliance.org

Institute of Practitioners in Advertising
www.ipa.co.uk

Internet Advertising Bureau UK
www.iabuk.net

agriculture

Agricultural Equipment Association
www.aea.uk.com

Agriknowledge
www.agriknowledge.co.uk/Arable/
arableindex.htm

Countrywide Farmers
www.countrywidefarmers.co.uk

DEFRA
www.defra.gov.uk

Farm Animal Welfare Council
www.fawc.org.uk

Farm Direct
www.farm-direct.co.uk

Farm Retail Association
www.farmshopping.com

Farm Talking
www.farmtalking.com

Farmers Weekly Interactive
www.fwi.co.uk

Farming UK Directory
www.farminguk.co.uk

Food Future
www.foodfuture.org.uk

National Association of Farmers Markets
www.farmersmarkets.net

National Farmers Union
www.nfu.org.uk

National Farmers Union of Scotland
www.nfus.org.uk

Rare Breeds Survival Trust
www.rbst.demon.co.uk

Royal Agricultural College
www.royagcol.ac.uk

Rural Heart
www.ruralheart.com

Scottish Agricultural College
www.sac.ac.uk

Scottish Association of Farmers Markets
www.scottishfarmersmarkets.co.uk

Scottish Executive Dept of Environment & Rural Affairs
www.scotland.gov.uk/who/dept_rural.asp

Scottish Research Information System
www.scottishresearch.com

Small Farms Association
www.small-farms-association.co.uk

Society of Ploughmen
www.ploughmen.co.uk

Tenant Farmers Association
http://ntfm670.facility.pipex.com/tfa

Tractors Direct
www.tractorsdirect.org.uk

Young Farmers Clubs
www.nfyfc.org.uk

Animal Health

Institute for Animal Health
www.iah.bbsrc.ac.uk

Arable

Arable Research Centres
www.arable.co.uk

Arable Research Institute Association
www.aria.org.uk

Association of Independent Crop Consultants
www.aicc.org.uk

British Beet Research Organisation
www.bbro.co.uk

British Potato Council
www.potato.org.uk

Institute of Arable Crop Research
www.iacr.bbsrc.ac.uk/iacr/tiacrhome.html

International Grains Council
www.igc.org.uk/index.htm

Cattle

Aberdeen Angus Cattle Society
www.aberdeen-angus.com

Ayrshire Cattle Society
www.ayrshires.org

British Belgian Blue Cattle Society
www.belgianblue.co.uk

British Cattle Veterinary Association
www.bcva.org.uk

British Charolais
www.charolais.co.uk

British Limousin Cattle Society
www.limousin.co.uk

British Piedmontese Cattle Society
www.tumpline.co.uk/piemontese

British Simmenthal Cattle Society
www.britishsimmental.co.uk

British White Cattle Society
www.britishwhitecattle.co.uk

Dexter Cattle Society
www.dextercattlesociety.co.uk

National Beef Association
www.nationalbeefassociation.co.uk

Premium Cattle Health Scheme
www.cattlehealth.co.uk

The Highland Cattle Society
www.highlandcattlesociety.com

Welsh Black Cattle Society
www.welshblackcattlesociety.org

White Park Cattle Society
www.whitepark.org.uk

World Guernsey Cattle Federation
www.worldguernseys.org

Dairy

British Sheep Dairying Association
www.sheepdairying.com

Dairy Crest
www.dairycrest.co.uk

Express Dairies
www.expressdairies.co.uk

Food Standards Agency Scotland
www.food.gov.uk/scotland

Graham's Dairies
www.grahams-dairies.co.uk

Milk Development Council
www.mdc.org.uk

Mitchell's
www.mitchells-scotland.com

Organic Dairy Farming
www.iger.bbsrc.ac.uk/igerweb/ruminant/rn-orgdairy.html

Robert Wiseman Dairies
www.wiseman-dairies.co.uk

Royal Association of British Dairy Farmers
www.rabdf.co.uk

Deer

British Deer Farmers Association
www.bdfa.co.uk

Deer Commission for Scotland
www.dcs.gov.uk

Fish Farming

C+H Aquaculture
www.chaqua.com

IntraFish
www.intrafish.com

Forestry

BJ Unwin Consultancy
www.bjunwin.co.uk

British Christmas Tree Growers Association
www.bctga.co.uk

CKD Finlayson Hughes
www.forestry-scotland.co.uk

Forestry & Timber Association
www.forestryandtimber.org

Forestry Commission
www.forestry.gov.uk

Royal Scottish Forestry Society
www.rsfs.org

Small Woods Association
www.smallwoods.org.uk

Timber Trade Federation
www.ttf.co.uk

Tree Council
www.treecouncil.org.uk

Organic

Dumfries & Galloway Organic Network
www.dg-organic.net

Organic Farmers & Growers
www.organicfarmers.uk.com

Organic Food Federation
www.orgfoodfed.com

Register of Organic Food Standards
www.defra.gov.uk/farm/organic

Scottish Green Party
www.scottishgreens.org.uk

Scottish Organic Directory
www.organicdirectory.ndo.co.uk

Scottish Organic Producers Association
www.sopa.org.uk

Soil Association
www.soilassociation.org

Pigs

Gloucester Old Spots
www.stockmaster.co.uk/oursite/gospbc

Pig Resources Page
www.cullen.org.uk/pig

Rural Development

Countryside Agency
www.countryside.gov.uk/index.htm

Countryside Alliance
www.countryside-alliance.org/policy/Development.html

Crofters Commission
www.crofterscommission.org.uk

InfoRurale
www.inforurale.org.uk/inforurale

Rural Development Network
www.ruralnet.org.uk

Scottish Executive Rural Devlopment Committee
www.scottish.parliament.uk/official_report/cttee/rural.htm

Sustainable Rural Resources
www.rural-resources.co.uk

Sheepdogs

International Sheepdog Society
www.isds.org.uk

World Sheepdog Championships
www.sheepdogchampionships.co.uk

architecture

Edinburgh Contemporary Architecture
www.edinburgharchitecture.co.uk

Edinburgh University School of Art & Architecture
www.caad.ed.ac.uk

The Lighthouse
www.thelighthouse.co.uk

Scottish Architecture
www.scottisharchitecture.com

Scottish Executive: Architecture
www.scotland.gov.uk/whatwedo.asp?topic=architecture

The Cockburn Association
www.cockburnassociation.org.uk

automotive

Consortium for Automotive Recycling
www.caregroup.org.uk

Dennis
www.dennis-group.co.uk

Henlys
www.henlys.com

Inchcape
www.inchcape.com

Kwik-Fit
www.kwik-fit.com

Lex Service
www.lex.co.uk

Motor Vehicle Repairers' Association
www.mvra.com

Retail Motor Industry Federation
www.rmif.co.uk

Scottish Motor Trade Association
www.smta.co.uk

Car Hire

1car1
www.1car1.com

A G Lees (Galashiels)
www.aglees-cars.com

Alamo
www.alamo.com

Alldrive 4x4
www.scottish-towns.co.uk/perthshire/auchterarder/alldrive/index.html

AMK Self Drive
www.amkselfdrive.co.uk

Avis
www.avis.com

Clarkson Glasgow
www.carhirescotland.com

Disables Car Hire Companies
www.mobility-unit.dft.gov.uk/mavis/fact19.htm

Easycar
www.easycar.com

EuropCar
www.europcar.com

Guy Salmon
www.guysalmon.co.uk

Hertz
www.hertz.com

Kenning
www.e-sixt.co.uk

Motorhome Rentals
http://freespace.virgin.net/montana.motorhomes

Portree Coachworks
www.portreecoachworks.co.uk

Manufacturers

Society of Motor Manufacturers
www.smmt.co.uk

Manufacturers – Cars

Alfa Romeo
www.alfaromeo.co.uk

Audi
www.audi.co.uk

Bentley
www.rolls-royceandbentley.co.uk/bentley/index.htm

BMW
www.bmw.co.uk

Caterham
www.caterham.co.uk

Chrysler
www.chrysler.com

Citroen
www.citroen.co.uk

Daewoo
www.daewoo-cars.co.uk

Daihatsu
www.daihatsu.com

Ferrari
www.ferrari.it

Fiat
www.fiat.co.uk

Honda
www.honda.co.uk

Hyundai
www.hyundai-car.co.uk

Jaguar
www.jaguar.com/uk

Kia
www.kia.co.uk

Lada
www.lada.co.uk

Lamborghini
www.lamborghini.co.uk

Lexus
www.lexus.co.uk

Lotus
www.lotuscars.co.uk

Marlin
www.marlincars.co.uk

Maserati
www.maserati.it

Mazda
www.mazda.co.uk

Mercedes
www.mercedesbenz.co.uk

Mitsubishi
www.mitsubishi-cars.co.uk

Morgan
www.morgan-motor.co.uk

Nissan
www.nissan.co.uk

Peugeot
www.peugeot.co.uk

Porsche
www.porsche.co.uk

Proton
www.proton.co.uk

Renault
www.renault.co.uk

Rover
www.rover.co.uk

Saab
www.saab.co.uk

Seat
www.seat.co.uk

Skoda
www.skoda.co.uk

Subaru
www.subaru.co.uk

Suzuki
www.suzuki.co.uk

Toyota
www.toyota.co.uk

TVR
www.tvr.co.uk

Vauxhall
http://buypower.vauxhall.co.uk/index.jhtml

Volkswagen
www.volkswagen.co.uk

Volvo
www.volvocars.volvo.co.uk

Manufacturers – Commercial

Ford
www.ford.co.uk

Iveco
www.iveco.com

LDV
www.ldv.co.uk

Sales & Service

Barnetts
www.barnettsmg.com

G&R Grandison
www.grgrandison.co.uk

Scottish Motor Auction Group
www.smag.co.uk

Taggarts
www.taggarts.co.uk

aviation

Aviation Industry Group
www.ai-group.co.uk

Aviation Today
www.aviationtoday.com

chambers of commerce & local enterprise companies

General

Bedfordshire
www.beds.chamber.co.uk/main/main6.htm

Birmingham
www.bci.org.uk

Bradford
www.bradford-cbr-of-trade.freeserve.co.uk

British
www.britishchambers.org.uk

British Chambers of Commerce
www.chamberonline.co.uk

Cambridge
www.cambridgechamber.co.uk

Central & West Lancashire
www.lancschamber.co.uk

Central Scotland
www.central-chamber.co.uk

Dorset
www.wdi.co.uk/dcci

East of England
www.go-eastern.gov.uk

Exeter
www.exeter-chamber-of-commerce.co.uk

Guernsey
www.industry.guernsey.net

Liverpool
www.liverpoolchamber.org.uk

Manchester
www.mcci.co.uk

North Derbyshire
www.derbyshire.org

Northern Ireland
www.nicci.co.uk

Oxford
www.oxlink.co.uk/coc

Plymouth
www.plymouth-chamber.co.uk

Rotherham
www.rccte.org.uk

Shropshire
www.shropshire-chamber.co.uk

Somerset
www.somerset.businesslink.co.uk

Southern Derbyshire
www.tec.co.uk/map/sderby.html

Suffolk
www.suffolkchamber.co.uk

Thames Valley
www.thamesvalleychamber.co.uk

Wolverhampton
www.wton-chamber.co.uk

York & North Yorkshire
www.yorkchamber.co.uk

Foreign

American
www.uschamber.org

Association of European Chambers of Commerce (Euro Chambres)
www.eurochambre.be

Austrian
www.wk.or.at

Dutch
www.nbcc.demon.co.uk

International Chambers of Commerce
www.iccwbo.org

Singaporean
www.britcham.org.sg/asp/general.asp?MenuItemId=65

Scotland

Aberdeen
www.aberdeenchamber.co.uk

Aberdeen & Grampian Chamber of Commerce
www.agcc.co.uk

Argyll & the Islands Enterprise
www.aie.co.uk

Cairngorms Chamber of Commerce
www.aviemore.co.uk

Caithness & Sutherland Enterprise
www.case-lec.co.uk

Central Scotland Chamber of Commerce
www.central-chamber.co.uk

Clydesdale Chamber of Commerce
www.clydesdalechambers.org.uk

Dumfries & Galloway Chamber of Commerce
www.actionexport.co.uk/assistance/coc_assistance.html

Dundee & Tayside Chamber of Commerce
www.dundeechamber.co.uk

Edinburgh Chamber of Commerce
www.ecce.org

Fife Chamber of Commerce & Enterprise
www.fifechamber.co.uk

Glasgow Chamber of Commerce
www.glasgowchamber.org

Inverness & Nairn Enterprise
www.ine.co.uk

Inverness Chamber of Commerce
http://inverness-chamber.co.uk

Lochaber Enterprise
www.hie.co.uk/lochaber

Moray Badenoch & Strathspey Enterprise
www.hie.co.uk/mbse

Mull & Iona Chamber of Commerce
www.mull.zynet.co.uk/mullindx.html

Orkney Enterprise
www.hie.co.uk/orkney

Perthshire Chamber of Commerce
www.perth.org.uk

Ross & Cromarty Enterprise
www.hie.co.uk/race

Scottish Chambers of Commerce
www.scottishchambers.org.uk

Scottish Enterprise

www.scottish-enterprise.com

Scottish Enterprise – Ayrshire
www.scottish-enterprise.com/about/lecs/ayr

Scottish Enterprise – Borders
www.scottish-enterprise.com/about/lecs/borders

Scottish Enterprise – Dumfries & Galloway
www.scottish-enterprise.com/about/lecs/dumfries

Scottish Enterprise – Dunbartonshire
www.scottish-enterprise.com/about/lecs/dunbart

Scottish Enterprise – Edinburgh & Lothian
www.scottish-enterprise.com/about/lecs/edin

Scottish Enterprise – Fife
www.scottish-enterprise.com/about/lecs/fife

Scottish Enterprise – Forth Valley
www.scottish-enterprise.com/about/lecs/forth

Scottish Enterprise – Glasgow
www.scottish-enterprise.com/about/lecs/glasgow

Scottish Enterprise – Grampian
www.scottish-enterprise.com/about/lecs/grampian

Scottish Enterprise – Lanarkshire
www.scottish-enterprise.com/about/lecs/lanark

Scottish Enterprise – Renfrewshire
www.scottish-enterprise.com/about/lecs/renfrew

Scottish Enterprise – Tayside
www.scottish-enterprise.com/about/lecs/tayside

Shetland Enterprise
www.hie.co.uk/shetland

Skye & Lochalsh Enterprise
www.hie.co.uk/sale

Western Isles – Local Economic Forum
www.wilef.co.uk/membership.asp

Western Isles Enterprise
www.hie.co.uk/welcome.asp.LocID-hienetlecwie.htm

chemicals

AGA Group
www.aga.com

Alcan Chemicals
www.chemicals.alcan.com/contact/europe/euro_indx.htm

Association of British Pharmaceutical Industries
www.abpi.org.uk

BOC
www.boc.com

BP Chemicals
www.bpchemicals.com

British Aerosol Manufacturers Association
www.bama.co.uk

British AgroChemicals Association
www.baa.org.uk

British Association for Chemical Specialities
www.aecportico.co.uk/Directory/BACS.shtm

British Biotech
www.britbio.co.uk

British Pest Control Association
www.bpca.org.uk

British Society of Perfumers
www.bsp.org.uk

Burmah Castrol
www.burmah-castrol.com

Celltech Chiroscience
www.celltech.co.uk

Chemdex (Chemistry search portal)
www.chemdex.org

Chemical Industry Association
www.sourcerer.co.uk/html/english/cia.htm

Chemicals Technology
www.chemicals-technology.com

Dynamic Chemicals
www.dynamic-chemicals.co.uk

Ferguson Menzies
www.fergusonmenzies.co.uk

Fertilizer Manufacturers Association
www.fma.org.uk

Imperial Chemical Industries
www.ici.com

Laporte
www.inspec.co.uk

Nobel Enterprises
www.nobel-enterprises.com

Picon
www.picon.com

Royal Society of Chemistry
www.rsc.org

Scottish Society for Contamination Control
www.s2c2.co.uk

Soap & Detergent Industry Association
www.sdia.org.uk

Solvents Industry Association
www.sia-uk.org.uk

Specialised Organic Chemical Sector Association
www.socsa.org.uk

Tan Chemicals
www.taninternational.com/Company.html

The Sourcerer (Chemical Industry portal)
www.sourcerer.co.uk

computer training

Airhouse Studios (Borders)
www.airhousestudios.co.uk

Clip ICT
www.clipict.co.uk

Deafblind Scotland
www.deafblindscotland.org.uk

Direct Scotland
www.directscotland.co.uk

EuroScot
www.euroscot.net/computertraining

EWTC (Edinburgh)
www.ewtc.co.uk

Freeskills
www.freeskills.com

Glenholm (Borders)
www.glenholm.dircon.co.uk

iTrain Scotland (Edinburgh)
www.itrainscotland.co.uk

Netconx (Glasgow)
www.netconx.co.uk/netcon

Quality Training (Stirling)
www.quality-training.co.uk

Sunrise Systems (Edinburgh & Angus)
www.sunsys.com/training.htm

couriers

Acorn Express
www.acornexpress-uk.com

Amtrak
www.amtrak.co.uk

Arrow Express
www.arrow-express.co.uk

Arrow Gold Star
www.arrowexpress.com

Business Post
www.business-post.com

Caledonian Couriers (Glasgow)
www.caledoniancouriers.co.uk

Central Couriers
www.centralcouriersltd.co.uk

City Couriers
www.citycouriers.co.uk

City Link
www.city-link.co.uk

Crossflight
www.crossflight.co.uk

DHL
www.dhl.co.uk

Eagle Couriers (Edinburgh & Glasgow)
www.eagle-couriers.co.uk

Ecosse World Express
www.ecosseworldexpress.co.uk

Federal Express
www.fedex.com

Five Ways Express
www.5ways.mcmail.com

Go Delivery Services
www.google.godelivery.co.uk

ICC
www.icc-couriers.co.uk

International Association of Air Travel Couriers
www.aircourier.co.uk

Jeeves Couriers (Aberdeen & North East)
www.jeeves-couriers.fsnet.co.uk

Lynx
www.lynx.co.uk

MBE (Aberdeen)
www.mbe.uk.com

Mercury
www.mercurycourier.com

Moves
www.moves.co.uk

Parcel Force
www.parcelforce.co.uk

Pegasus Express
www.pegasusexp.co.uk

Post Office
www.consignia.com

Premier Despatch (Livingstone)
www.premier-apc.co.uk

Priority Couriers
www.prioritycouriers.co.uk

Pronto Despatch (Inverness & Aberdeen)
www.prontodespatch.co.uk

React Transport (Glenrothes)
www.react-transport.co.uk

Royal Mail
www.royalmail.com

Securicor Express Delivery
www.securicor.com/omegaexpress

Securicor-Omega
www.securicor.co.uk

Sprint
www.sprintexpress.co.uk

TNT
www.tnt.co.uk

UPS
www.ups.com

World Courier
www.worldcourier.com

Professional Bodies

National Courier Association
www.nca.couk.com

Road Haulage Association
www.rha.org.uk

electrical & technological

Cookson Group
www.cooksongroup.co.uk

Danka Business Systems
www.danka.com

Eidos
www.eidos.com

Invensys
www.invensys.com

Logica
www.logica.com

Lynx Group
www.lynx-group.co.uk

Misys
www.misys.co.uk

Parity Group
www.parity.co.uk

Psion
www.psion.com

QXL.com
www.qxl.com

Racal Electronics
www.racal.com

Sage
www.sage.com

Scoot.com
www.scoot.com

Sema Group
www.semagroup.com

Smiths Industries
www.smiths-industries.com

Directories

Applegate (electronics directory)
www.applegate.co.uk/elec

Electronic Scotland
www.electronics-scotland.com

Manufacturers

Aiwa
www.aiwa.co.uk

Bosch
www.bosch.co.uk

Braun
www.braun.com/global

Brother
www.brother.co.uk

Canon
www.canon.co.uk

Compaq
www.hp.com

Cookson Group
www.cooksongroup.co.uk

Dell
www.dell.co.uk

DeLonghi
www.delonghi.co.uk

Electrolux
www.electrolux.co.uk

General Electric
www.ge.com/uk

Glen Dimplex
www.glendimplex.com

Hewlett Packard
www.hp.com

Hotpoint
www.hotpoint.co.uk

Kenwood
www.kenwood.co.uk

Mitsubishi
www.mitsubishi.com

Moulinex
www.moulinex.com

NEC
www.nec.co.uk

Neff
www.neff.co.uk

Nokia
www.nokia.co.uk

Panasonic
www.panasonic.co.uk

Philips
www.philips.co.uk

Pioneer Electronics
www.pioneerelectronics.com

Psion
www.psion.com

Samsung Electronics
www.samsungelectronics.com

Siemens
www.siemens.co.uk

Smeg
www.smeguk.com

Toshiba
www.toshiba.co.uk

Whirlpool
www.whirlpool.co.uk

Professional Bodies

Institute of Electrical Engineers
www.iee.org

NIC EIC
www.niceic.org.uk

Services

C B Radio Sales
http://cb.radio.sales.8k.com

Campbell & McHardy (Elgin)
www.campbellandmchardy.co.uk

CE Services (Selkirk)
www.selkirk.bordernet.co.uk/ceservices

Dickson & Mahan (Stranraer)
www.sandmill.fsnet.co.uk/dandm.htm

Forth Electrical Services
www.fes-group.co.uk

GP Electric (Dumfries)
www.gp-electric.co.uk

Indigo AV (Stirling)
www.indigo-av.co.uk

Pat Fraser (Nairn)
www.patfraser.co.uk

Power Generation Services
www.powgen.fsnet.co.uk

Stirling Electrical Services
www.stirlingelectricalservices.co.uk

Who To Use
www.whotouse.co.uk/electricians.html

Web – sales

AudioVision
www.audiovisiononline.co.uk

Empire Direct
www.empiredirect.co.uk

Kelkoo
http://uk.kelkoo.com

Maplin
www.maplin.co.uk

Unbeatable.co.uk
www.unbeatable.co.uk

energy

AgipPetroli
www.agippetroli.it/uk/index.html

BP Amoco
www.bpamoco.com

British-Borneo Oil & Gas
www.british-borneo.co.uk

Burmah Castrol
www.burmah-castrol.com

Chevron
www.chevron.com

Conoco
www.conoco.com

Enterprise Oil
www.entoil.com

Exxon (Esso)
www.exxon.com

Gulf
www.gulfoil.com

Lasmo
www.lasmo.com

Mobil
www.mobil.co.uk

Premier Oil
www.premier-oil.com

Shell Transport & Trading Company
www.shell.com

Texaco
www.texaco.co.uk

Total
www.total.com

Xerox
www.xerox.com

Coal

RJB
www.rjb.co.uk

Scottish Coal
www.scottishcoal.co.uk

World Coal Institute
www.wci-coal.com

Electricity

Scottish & Southern
www.scottish-southern.co.uk

Scottish Power
www.scottishpower.plc.uk

Gas

Calor Gas Scotland
www.calorgasscotland.co.uk

Gleaner
www.gleaner.co.uk

Scottish Gas
www.gas.co.uk

Tech Auto
www.techauto-gas.co.uk

Hydro Electric

Scottish Hydro-Electric
www.hydro.co.uk

Nuclear

Scottish Nuclear
www.snl.co.uk

Oil

BP
www.bp.com

ExxonMobil
www.esso.com/eaff/essouk

Oil & Gas Directory
www1.slb.com/petr.dir

Shell
www.shell.com

TotalFinaElf
www.totalfinaelf.com/ho/en/index.htm

UK Offshore Operators Association
www.oilandgas.org.uk

UK Petroleum Industry Association
www.ukpia.com

Professional Bodies

Energy Industries Council
www.the-eic.com

Sustainable

British Biogen
www.britishbiogen.co.uk

British Hydro-Power Association
www.brit-hydro.cwc.net

British Photovoltaic Association
www.pv-uk.org.uk

British Wind Energy Association
www.bwea.com

Industrial & Power Association
www.ipa-scotland.org.uk

Scottish Energy Efficiency Office
www.energy-efficiency.org

Scottish Energy Environment Foundation
www.seef.org.uk

Scottish Renewables Forum
www.scottishrenewables.com

The Associate Parliamentary Renewable & Sustainable Energy Group
www.praseg.org.uk

Wavegen
www.wavegen.com

Western Isles Renewable Energy Partnership
www.w-isles.gov.uk/wiarep

engineering

ABB Ltd
www.abb.co.uk

AkerKvaerner
www.akerkvaerner.com

AMEC
www.amec.co.uk

Arup
www.arup.com

Babcock International
www.babcock.co.uk

Balfour Kilpatrick
www.balfourkilpatrick.com

Homer Burgess
www.homerburgess.com

Ingenco
www.ingenco.uk.net

KBR Engineering & Construction
www.halliburton.com

Mitsui Babcock
www.mitsuibabcock.com

Motherwell Bridge Construction
www.motherwellbridge.com

Newton Fabrications
www.newtonholdings.com

Orion Engineering
www.orioneng.co.uk

Palmers Engineering
www.palmers-group.com

Rolls Royce
www.rolls-royce.com

Scottish Engineering
www.scottishengineering.org.uk

Shipbuilders & Shiprepairers Association
www.ssa.org.uk

Thermal Engineering International
www.tei.co.uk

Weir Group
www.weir.co.uk

Wood Group
www.woodgroup.com

Professional Bodies

Construction Best Practice Programme
www.cbpp.org.uk/cbpp

Construction Confederation
www.thecc.org.uk

Engineering Construction Industry Association
www.ecia.co.uk

Engineering Council
www.engc.org.uk

Engineering Employers Federation
www.eef.org.uk

The Movement for Innovation
www.m4i.org.uk/m4i

finance

3i Group
www.3igroup.com

ABN Amro
www.abnamro.com

Advanced Currency Markets
www.ac-markets.com/EN/default.asp

American Stock Exchange
www.amex.com

Bank of America
www.bankofamerica.com

Banking Liaison Group
www.bankingliaison.co.uk

Barclaycard
www.barclaycard.co.uk

BNP Paribas
www.bnpparibas.com/en/home/default.asp

British Venture Capital Association
www.bvca.co.uk

Cazenove & Co
www.cazenove.co.uk

Chase Manhattan
www.chase.com

Close Brothers Group
www.cbcf.com

Coinco International
www.coinco.co.uk

Credit Lyonnais
www.creditlyonnais.fr

Credit Suisse
www.credit-suisse.com/en/home.html

Datastream
www.datastream.com

Deutsche Bank
http://group.deutsche-bank.de

Dow Jones
www.dowjones.com

Equitable Life
www.equitable.co.uk

Fidelity Investments
www.fidelity.co.uk

Financial Times
http://news.ft.com/home/uk

Franklin Templeton
www.templeton.ca

FTSE
www.ftse.com

Goldman Sachs
www.gs.com/uk/index.html

Hang Seng Bank
http://main.hangseng.com

ING Bank
www.ingbank.com

JP Morgan
www.jpmorgan.com

LINK Interchange Network
www.link.co.uk

M & G Group
www.mandg.co.uk

Merrill Lynch
www.ml.com

Mizuho Bank
www.mizuhocbk.co.jp/english/index.html

Morgan Stanley Dean Witter
www.morganstanley.com

Nomura
www.nomura.com

Perpetual
www.perpetual.co.uk

Provident Financial
www.providentfinancial.co.uk

Prudential
www.pru.co.uk

Rabobank
www.rabobank.nl

S&P Funds Service
www.funds-sp.com/win/en/Index.jsp

Salomon Smith Barney
www.salomonsmithbarney.com

Schroders
www.schroders.com

Scottish Amicable
www.scottishamicable.com

Societe Generale
www.socgen.com/en/index2.htm

Svenska Handelsbanken
www.handelsbanken.se

Travelex Foreign Exchange
www.fx4business.com

Wells Fargo Bank
www.wellsfargo.com

Banks & Building Societies

Abbey National
www.abbeynational.plc.uk

Agricultural Credit Bureau
www.lltps.co.uk/ACB

Alliance & Leicester
www.alliance-leicester.co.uk

Bank of England
www.bankofengland.co.uk

Bank of Scotland
www.bankofscotland.co.uk

Banks.com Directory
www.banks.com

Barclays Bank
www.barclays.co.uk

Capital One UK
www.capitalone.co.uk

Charterhouse Bank
www.charterhouse.co.uk/homebank

Citibank
www.citibank.com/uk

Clydesdale Bank
www.cbonline.co.uk

Co-operative bank
www.co-operativebank.co.uk

Committee of Scottish Clearing Banks
www.scotbanks.org.uk

Halifax
www.halifax.co.uk

Hamilton Direct Bank
www.hdb.co.uk

HSBC Bank
www.hsbc.co.uk

Legal & General
www.landg.com

Lloyds TSB
www.lloydstsb.com

National Savings & Investments
www.nsandi.com

National Westminster Bank
www.natwestgroup.com

NatWest
www.natwest.com

Noble Group
www.noblegp.com

Northern Rock
www.nrock.co.uk

Royal Bank of Scotland
www.royalbankscot.co.uk

Royal Bank of Scotland – Commercial Services
www.rbscs.co.uk

Royal Bank of Scotland – Financial Markets
www.rbsmarkets.com

Royal Bank of Scotland – International
www.rbsint.com

Royal Bank of Scotland- Corporate Banking & Financial Markets
www.rbs.co.uk

Scotia Capital
www.scotiacapital.com

Standard Bank London
www.sbl.co.uk

Standard Chartered Bank
www.standardchartered.com

Standard Life Bank
www.standardlifebank.com

Triodos Bank
www.triodos.co.uk

Consulting

Accenture
www.accenture.com

Arthur D Little
www.adl.com

BoozAllen Hamilton
www.bah.com

CAP Gemini Consulting
www.cgey.com

Deloitte & Touche
www.deloitte.co.uk

Ernst & Young
www.ey.com

KPMG
www.kpmg.co.uk

McKinsey & Co
www.mckinsey.com

PricewaterhouseCoopers
www.pwcglobal.com

Foreign

ABN AMRO, Netherlands
www.abnamro.nl

Agricultural Bank of China
www.abocn.com

Allied Bank, South Africa
www.allied.co.za

American National Bank
www.accessanb.com

American Savings Bank
www.asbhawaii.com

Arab Bank
www.arabbank.com

Asian Development Bank
www.adb.org

Australia & New Zealand Banking Group
www.anz.com

Banca Commerciale Italiana
www.bci.it

Banca d'Italia
www.bancaditalia.it

Banco Central Do Brasil
www.bcb.gov.br

Banco de España
www.bde.es

Banco de Portugal
www.bportugal.pt

Bangkok Bank, Thailand
www.bbl.co.th

Bank Austria
www.bankaustria.com

Bank of America
www.bankamerica.com

Bank of Baharian & Kuwait
http://bbkonline.com

Bank of Baroda
www.bankofbaroda.com

Bank of Canada
www.bank-banque-canada.ca

Bank of China
www.bank-of-china.com

Bank of Cyprus
www.bankofcyprus.com

Bank of Estonia
www.ee/epbe/en

Bank of Finland
www.bof.fi

Bank of Greece
www.bankofgreece.gr

Bank of Hawaii
www.boh.com

Bank of India
www.boiusa.com

Bank of Ireland
www.bankofireland.ie

Bank of Israel
www.bankisrael.gov.il

Bank of Japan
www.boj.or.jp/en

Bank of Kuwait & the Middle East
www.bkme.com

Bank of Latvia
www.bank.lv

Bank of Lebanon
www.bdl.gov.lb

Bank of Lithuania
www.lbank.lt

Bank of Mexico
www.banxico.org.mx

Bank of Montreal
www.bmo.com

Bank of Moscow
www.mmbank.ru

Bank of Mozambique
www.bancomoc.mz

Bank of New York
www.bankofny.com

Bank of Papua New Guinea
www.datec.com.pg

Bank of Portugal
www.bportugal.bt

Bank of Russia
www.cbr.ru

Bank of Slovenia
www.bsi.si

Bank of Thailand
www.bot.or.th

Bank of Tokyo
www.btm.co.jp

Bank of Wales
www.bankofwales.co.uk

Bank of Zambia
www.boz.zm

Bankers Trust, New York
www.bankerstrust.com

Bankgesellschaft Berlin
www.bankgesellschaft.de/en_index.html

Banque Centrale du Luxembourg
www.bcl.lu

Banque de France
www.banque-france.fr

Banque Nationale de Belgique
www.bnb.be

Banque Nationale de Paris
www.bnp.fr

Bermuda Monetary Authority
www.bma.bm

Bulgarian National Bank
www.bnb.bg

Canada Trust
www.canadatrust.com

Central Bank of Armenia
www.cba.am

Central Bank of Barbados
www.centralbank.org.bb

Central Bank of Bosnia
www.cbbh.gov.ba

Central Bank of Chile
www.bcentral.cl

Central Bank of China
www.cbc.gov.tw

Central Bank of Cyprus
www.centralbank.gov.cy

Central Bank of Iceland
www.sedlabanki.ias

Central Bank of India
www.centralbankofindia.co.in

Central Bank of Ireland
www.centralbank.ie

Central Bank of Jordan
www.cbj.gov.jo

Central Bank of Kenya
www.africaonline.co.ke/cbk

Central Bank of Malta
www.centralbankmalta.com

Central Bank of Swaziland
www.centralbank.sz

Central Bank of the Netherlands Antilles
http://centralbank.an

Central Bank of the Republic of Indonesia
www.bi.go.id

Central Bank of the Republic of Turkey
www.tcmb.gov.tr

Central Bank of the Russian Federation
www.cbr.ru

Central Bank of Trinidad & Tobago
www.central-bank.org.tt

Central Bank of Uruguay
www.bcu.gub.uy

Central Reserve Bank of El Salvador
www.bcr.gob.sv

Chase Manhattan
www.chase.com

Citibank
www.citibank.com

Commonwealth Bank of Australia
www.commbank.com.au

Credit Agricole, France
www.credit-agricole.fr

Creditanstalt
www.creditanstalt.co.at

Croatian National Bank
www.hnb.hr/eindex.htm

Czech National Bank
www.cnb.cz/en

Danmarks Nationalbank
www.nationalbanken.dk/uk

De Nederlandsche Bank
www.dnb.nl

Deutsche Bank
http://public.deutsche-bank.de

Deutsche Bundesbank
www.bundesbank.de

Dresdner Kleinwort Benson
www.dresdnerkb.com

Eastern Caribbean Bank
www.eccb-centralbank.org

European Central Bank
www.ecb.int

Federal Reserve Bank, San Francisco
www.frbsf.org

Federal Reserve System (USA)
www.federalreserve.gov

Fidelity Federal Savings Bank
www.fidfed.com

First Chicago
www.bankone.com

ForeningsSparbanken (Swedbank)
www.foreningssparbanken.se

Fuji Bank, Japan
www.fujibank.co.jp/eng

Grindlays Private Banking
www.pb.grindlays.com

Gulf International Bank
www.gibonline.com

ING Bank, Netherlands
www.ingbank.nl

Istituto di Credito Sammarinese
www.isc.sm

JP Morgan & Co
www.jpmorgan.com

Jordan National Bank
www.ahli.com

Muslim Commercial Bank, Pakistan
www.mcb.com.pk

National Australia Bank
www.national.com.au

National Bank of Bahrain
www.nbbonline.com

National Bank of Egypt
www.nbe.com.eg

National Bank of Moldova
www.bnm.org

National Bank of New Zealand
www.nbnz.co.nz

National Bank of the Republic of Macedonia
www.nbrm.gov.mk

National Commercial Bank, Saudi Arabia
www.alahli.com

Oesterreichische Nationalbank (Austria)
www.oenb.co.at/oenb

Ottoman Bank, Turkey
www.ottomanbank.com.tr/english

Philippine National Bank
www.philnabank.com

Punjab National Bank, India
www.pnbindia.com

Rabobank, Netherland
www.rabobank.nl

Reserve Bank of Australia
www.rba.gov.au

Reserve Bank of India
www.rbi.org.in

Reserve Bank of New Zealand
www.rbnz.govt.nz

Reykjavík Savings Bank, Iceland
www.spron.is

Rindal Sparebank, Norway
www.rindalsbanken.no

Scotiabank
www.scotiabank.com

Standard Chartered Bank
www.stanchart.com

State Bank of India
www.sbi.co.in

Sumitomo Bank
www.smbc.co.jp/global/index.html

Suomen Pankki (Finland)
www.bof.fi

Sveriges Riksbank (Sweden)
www.riksbank.se

Swiss National Bank
www.snb.ch

Top 100 Arab Banks
www.arab.net/arab-banks

Unibank, Denmark
www.unibank.dk

Union Bank of Switzerland
www.ubs.com

Wells Fargo
www.wellsfargo.com

World Bank
www.worldbank.org

Professional Bodies

Association of British Insurers
www.abi.org.uk

Association of Payment Clearing Services
www.apacs.org.uk

Association of Private Client Investment Managers & Stockbrokers
www.apcims.org

British Bankers' Association
www.bba.org.uk

British Insurers Brokers' Association
www.biba.org.uk

British Venture Capital Association
www.bvca.co.uk

Building Societies Association
www.bsa.org.uk

Chartered Institute of Public Finance And Accountancy
www.cipfa.org.uk

Council of Mortgage Lenders
www.cml.org.uk

Credit Card Research Group
www.ccrg.org.uk

Factors & Discounters Association
www.factors.org.uk

Financial Services Authority
www.fsa.gov.uk

Financial Watch
http://finance.wat.ch

Future & Options Association
www.foa.co.uk

HM Treasury
www.hm-treasury.gov.uk

International Risk Institute
www.riskinstitute.ch

International Underwriting Association
www.iua.co.uk

Investment Managers Association
www.investmentfunds.org.uk

National Association of Pension Funds
www.napf.co.uk

The World Bank
www.worldbank.org

World Savings Bank Group
www.savings-banks.com

UK

Arab Banking Corporation
www.arabbanking.com

Standard Chartered
www.stanchart.com

UBS
www.ubs.co.uk/privatebanking

Woolwich
www.woolwich.co.uk

food, beverages & tobacco

Bakeries

Alex Dalgetty (Bannocks & Black Buns)
www.galashiels.bordernet.co.uk/alexdalgetty

Ashers Bakery
www.ashers-bakery.co.uk

British Society of Baking
www.bsb.org.uk

Duncans of Deeside (Shortbread)
www.nettrak.co.uk/houseofcaledonia/duncans_of_deeside.htm

Eskside Bakery
www.esksidebakery.co.uk

Scottish Association of Master Bakers
www.samb.co.uk

William Sword Bakers
www.williamsword.co.uk

Breweries

Bass Brewers
www.bass-brewers.com

Belhaven Brewery
www.belhaven.co.uk

Caledonian Brewery
www.caledonian-brewery.co.uk

Diageo
www.diageo.com

Scottish & Newcastle
www.scottish-newcastle.com

Society of Independent Brewers
www.siba.co.uk

Confectionery

British Sugar
www.britishsugar.co.uk

Cadbury Schweppes
www.cadburyschweppes.com

Gaffney Confectionery
www.gaffneyconfectionery.co.uk

Golden Casket Group
www.millionssweets.co.uk

Great Glen Fine Foods
www.greatglenfinefoods.co.uk

Tate & Lyle
www.tate-lyle.co.uk

United Biscuits
www.unitedbiscuits.co.uk

Consulting

itsfood.com
www.itsfood.com

Dairy

Cheese.com
www.cheese.com

Dairy Crest
www.dairycrest.co.uk

Express Dairies
www.express-dairies.co.uk

Gourmet's Lair
www.gourmetslair.co.uk/scottish.shtml

McLelland & Co
www.mclelland.co.uk

Farmers Markets

Scottish Farmers Markets
www.scottishfarmersmarkets.co.uk

General Foods

Allied Domecq
www.allieddomecq.co.uk

Associated British Foods
www.abf.co.uk

Booker
www.booker-plc.com

Grampian Country Food Group
www.gcfg.com

Hazlewood Foods
www.hazlewoodfoods.com

Northern Foods
www.northern-foods.co.uk

Scotfruit
www.scotfruit.com

Unilever
www.unilever.com

Mineral Water

FSA Mineral Water List
www.foodstandards.gov.uk/foodindustry/42877

Natural Mineral Water Information Service
www.naturalmineralwater.org

Purely Scottish
www.purelyscottish.com

Water at Work
www.wateratwork.com

Water Coolers Scotland
www.watercoolersscotland.co.uk

Professional Bodies

Scottish Food & Drink
www.scottishfoodanddrink.com

Seafood

Aquascot
www.aquascot.uk.com

Fisher Foods Group
www.fisherfoodsgroup.com

International Fish Canners
www.intfishcan.com

JW Seafoods
www.summerislesfoods.com

Keltic Seafare
www.kelticseafare.com

Loch Duart
www.lochduart.com

Lossie Seafoods
www.lossie-seafoods.co.uk

Whitelink Seafoods
www.whitelink.com

Smokeries

Arbroath Fisheries
www.arbroath-smokie.co.uk

Tobacco

Davidoff
www.davidoff.com

Gallaher
www.gallaher-group.com

Imperial Tobacco
www.imperial-tobacco.com

Rizla
www.rizla.co.uk

Whisky

Allied Domecq
www.allieddomecqplc.com

Ballantines
www.ballantines.com

Dewar's Scotch Whisky
www.dewars.com

Douglas Laing & Co
www.douglaslaing.com/main.htm

Edrington Group
www.edringtongroup.com

Glenmorangie
www.glenmorangieplc.com

Gordon & Macphail
www.gordonandmacphail.com

Highland Distillers
www.grouse.com

Ian Mcleod & Co
www.ianmacleod.com

International Whisky Co Ltd
www.royalsilk.com

Inverhouse Distillery
www.inverhouse.com

Islay Whisky Society
www.islaywhiskysociety.com

Kyndal
www.kyndal.co.uk

Morrison Bowmore
www.morrisonbowmore.co.uk

North British Distillery Company
www.northbritish.co.uk

Pernod Ricard
www.pernod-ricard.com

Scotch Malt Whisky Society
www.smws.com

Scotch Whisky Association
www.scotch-whisky.org.uk

Scotch Whisky.com
www.scotchwhisky.com

United Distillers & Vintners
http://company.occ.com/undistill

Whisky Directory
www.scotlandonline.com/heritage/
heritage_whisky.cfm

insurance

Aegon UK
www.aegon.co.uk

AIG
www.aig.com

Allianz Cornhill Group
www.allianzcornhillinternational.co.uk

Allied Dunbar Assurance
www.allieddunbar.co.uk

AMP Pearl
www.amp-online.co.uk

Aon Group
www.aon.com

Association of Insurers & Risk Managers
www.airmic.com

Aviva Group
www.aviva.com

AXA
www.axa.co.uk

British Insurance & Investment Brokers' Association (BIIBA)
www.biiba.org.uk

BUPA
www.bupa.co.uk

CGU
www.cguplc.com

Co-operative Insurance Society
www.cis.co.uk

Cornhill
www.cornhill.co.uk

Eagle Star
www.eaglestardirect.co.uk

Endsleigh
www.endsleigh.co.uk

Hiscox
www.hiscox.com

Independent Insurance
www.independent-insurance.co.uk

Jardine Lloyd Thompson
www.jltgroup.com

Legal & General
www.legal-and-general.co.uk

Lloyd's of London
www.lloyds.com

London International Insurance & Reinsurance Market Association (LIRMA)
www.lirma.co.uk

Marsh McLennan Companies
www.mmc.com

Norwich Union
www.norwich-union.com

Old Mutual
www.oldmutual.com

Prudential
www.prudential.co.uk

Royal & Sun Alliance
www.royalsunalliance.co.uk

Scottish Amicable
www.scottishamicable.com

Scottish Provident
www.scotprov.co.uk

Standard Life Group
www.standardlife.com

Sun Life & Provincial Holdings
www.axa.co.uk

The Insurance Club
www.insuranceclub.co.uk

Unionamerica Holdings
www.unionamerica.com

Willis Corroon Group
www.williscorroon.com

Winterthur Life
www.winterthur-life.co.uk

Zurich Group
www.zurich.com

Professional Bodies

Association of British Insurers
www.abi.org.uk

British Insurers Brokers' Association
www.biba.org.uk

Chartered Institute of Loss Adjusters
www.cila.co.uk

General Insurance Standards Council
www.gisc.co.uk

Life Insurance Association
www.lia.co.uk

leisure

Airtours
www.airtours.com

Camelot Group
www.camelotplc.com

Compass Group
www.compass-group.com

Esporta
www.esporta.co.uk

First Choice Holidays
www.firstchoiceholidaysplc.com

Granada Group
www.granada.co.uk

Hilton Group
www.hiltongroup.com

J D Wetherspoon
www.jdwetherspoon.co.uk

Manchester United
www.manutd.com

PizzaExpress
www.pizzaexpress.co.uk

Rank
www.rank.com

Scottish & Newcastle
www.scottish-newcastle.com

Thistle Hotels
www.thistlehotels.com

Thomas Cook Group
www.thomascook.com

Thomson Travel Group
www.thomson-holidays.com

Whitbread
www.whitbread.co.uk

livery companies & guilds

Company of Water Conservators
www.waterconservators.org

Guild of Air Pilots & Air Navigators
www.gapan.org

Mercer's Company
www.mercers.co.uk

Worshipful Collection of Clock Makers
www.clockmakers.org

Worshipful Company of Bakers
www.bakers.co.uk

Worshipful Company of Barbers
www.barbers.org.uk

Worshipful Company of Carpenters
www.thecarpenterscompany.co.uk

Worshipful Company of Curriers
www.btinternet.com/~kestrels

Worshipful Company of Engineers
www.engineerscompany.org.uk

Worshipful Company of Fan Makers
www.fanmakers.co.uk

Worshipful Company of Farriers
www.wcf.org.uk

Worshipful Company of Framework Knitters
www.frameworkknitters.co.uk

Worshipful Company of Goldsmiths
www.thegoldsmiths.co.uk

Worshipful Company of Grocers
www.grocershall.co.uk

Worshipful Company of Information Technologists
www.wcit.org.uk

Worshipful Company of Ironmongers
www.ironhall.co.uk

Worshipful Company of Makers of Playing Cards
www.wopc.co.uk/cards/worshipful.html

Worshipful Company of Marketors
www.marketors.fsnet.co.uk

Worshipful Company of Professional Turners
www.rpturners.co.uk/aboutco.asp

Worshipful Company of Scientific Instrument Makers
www.wcsim.co.uk

Worshipful Company of Spectaclemakers
www.spectaclemakers.com

Worshipful Company of Stationers & Newspaper Makers
www.stationers.org

Worshipful Company of Upholders
www.upholders.co.uk

Worshipful Company of Wax Chandlers
www.waxchandlershall.co.uk

Worshipful Company of World Traders
www.world-traders.org

Worshipful Society of Apothecaries
www.apothecaries.org

magazines & websites

Accountancy
www.accountancymag.co.uk

Accountancy Age
www.accountancyage.co.uk

Banker
www.thebanker.com

BBC Business
http://news.bbc.co.uk/1/hi/business/default.stm

Better Business
www.better-business.co.uk

Bloomberg
www.bloomberg.co.uk

Business Daily
www.businessdaily.com

Business Week
www.businessweek.com

Business Wire
www.businesswire.com

Campaign
www.campaignlive.com

CFO Europe
www.cfoeurope.com

Commodities Now
www.commodities-now.com

Economist
www.economist.co.uk

Electric News
www.electricnews.net

Euromoney
www.euromoney.com

European Business Forum
www.europeanbusinessforum.com

Executive Magazine
www.executive-magazine.co.uk

Farmers Weekly
www.fwi.co.uk

Farmweek Journal
www.mortonnewspapers.com

Financial Times
http://news.ft.com/home/uk

Forbes
www.forbes.com

Fraser of Allander Institute: Scottish Economy
www.fraser.strath.ac.uk

Harvard Business Review
http://harvardbusinessonline.hbsp.harvard.edu

Insider
www.insider.co.uk

Investment Week
www.invweek.co.uk

iVenus
www.ivenus.com

Law Society Gazette
www.lawgazette.co.uk

Lexis-Nexis
http://news.ft.com/home/uk

Lloyd's List
www.lloydslist.com

London Evening Standard Business Day
www.thisislondon.com/dynamic/news/business.html

Marketing
www.marketing.haynet.com

Media Week
www.mediaweek.co.uk

News Now
www.newsnow.co.uk

Retail Week
www.retailing.co.uk

Reuters
www.reuters.co.uk

Reuters Money Network
www.moneynet.com

Royal Bank of Scotland: Economy Briefings
www.rbos.co.uk/economics

Scottish Business am
www.businessam.co.uk

Scottish Development International
www.scottishdevelopmentinternational.com

Scottish Enterprise
www.scottish-enterprise.com

Scottish Enterprise e-business
www.ecommerce-scotland.org

Scottish Financial Enterprise
www.financescotland.com

Six Mag
www.sixmag.com

Slashdot
www.slashdot.org

Sunday Herald
www.sundayherald.com

The Herald
www.theherald.co.uk

The Scotsman
www.thescotsman.co.uk

Yahoo Finance
http://biz.yahoo.com

Small Business

Bank of Scotland – Business startup
www.bankofscotland.co.uk/business/startup/index.html

Barclays Small Business
www.business.barclays.co.uk

Better Business
www.better-business.co.uk

Business Bureau
www.businessbureau.co.uk

Business Intelligence
www.business-intelligence.co.uk

Business Link
www.businesslink.org

Business Zone
www.businesszone.co.uk

Credit Cash
www.credit-to-cash.com

Dun & Bradstreet
www.dnb.com

Federation of Small Businesses
www.fsb.org.uk

Fit for the Future (CBI Best Practice site)
www.fitforthefuture.org.uk

Highlands & Island Enterprise
www.hie.co.uk

Home Business UK
www.homebusinessuk.co.uk

Is4profit
www.is4profit.com

National Business Angels Network
www.nationalbusangels.com/home

Royal Bank of Scotland – Startups
www.royalbankscot.co.uk/small_business/default.htm

Small Business Gateway (Scottish Enterprise)
www.sbgateway.com

Small Business Portal
www.smallbusinessportal.co.uk

Small Business Service
www.sbs.gov.uk

Start Business
www.startbusiness.co.uk

Startups
www.startups.co.uk

Strathclyde University Business Research
www.marketing.strath.ac.uk/dcd

Success4business (Lloyds TSB site)
www.success4business.com

manufacturing

AEA Technology
www.aeat.co.uk

Aggreko
www.aggreko.com

Ahlstrom
www.ahlstrom.com

Anti-Counterfeiting Group
www.a-cg.com

Arjo Wiggins Appleton
www.paperpoint.co.uk

Arran Aromatics
www.arran-aromatics.co.uk

Aulds the Bakers
www.aulds.co.uk

Avon Rubber
www.avonrubber.co.uk

Babcock BES
www.babcockbes.co.uk

BAE Systems
www.baesystems.com

Berisford
www.berisford.co.uk

Britax International
www.britax.com

Business Mentoring Scotland
www.businessmentoringscotland.org

CFM
www.cfm.co.uk

Coats Viyella
www.coats-viyella.com

Courtaulds
www.courtaulds.com

Design, Manufacture & Engineering Management
www.dmem.strath.ac.uk

Fife Fabrications
www.fifab.com

First Technology
www.firsttech.co.uk

FKI
www.fki.co.uk

Gaeltec
www.gaeltec.com

GKN
www.gknplc.com

Hoover
www.hoover.co.uk

ISI Solutions
www.isigroupplc.com

Laird
www.laird-plc.com

Linn Products
www.linn.co.uk

Lochcarron Weavers
www.lochcarron.com

Make It In Scotland (site for children)
www.makeitinscotland.co.uk

Morgan Crucible
www.morgancrucible.com

Morris Funriture
www.morrisfurniture.co.uk

NCR
www.ncr.com

Nikon Precision (Europe)
www.npeurope.com

Nylonic
www.nylonic.co.uk

Orkney Herring Company
www.orkneyherring.com

Ortak Jewellery
www.ortak.co.uk

Peter Scott Knitwear
www.peterscott.co.uk

Pilkington
www.pilkington.com

Presentation Products
www.giftpacks.co.uk

Reckitt Benckiser
www.reckitt.com

Regional Manufacturing Exhibitions
www.industry.co.uk

Replen
www.replen-esp.net

Rood Technology
www.roodtechnology.com

Rynex
www.rynex.co.uk

Scottish Development International
www.scottishdevelopmentinternational.com

Scottish Engineering
www.scottishengineering.org.uk

Scottish Manufacturing Show
www.scottishmanufacturing.co.uk

Scottish Quality Management Systems
www.sqms.co.uk

Taylor Group
www.tgdiecasting.co.uk

Technology Scotland
www.technologyscotland.org

Thales Optronics
www.optronics.co.uk

TI
www.tigroup.com

Tomkins
www.tomkins.co.uk

TT
www.ttgroup.com

Weatherford Completion Systems
www.weatherford.com

Weir
www.weir.co.uk

Xantak
www.tyresafe.com

York Electromagnetics
www.yorkemc.co.uk

marketing

7-26
www.7-26.co.uk

AC Nielsen
www.acnielsen.co.uk

Avian Communications
www.avian.co.uk

Barlow Doherty
www.barlowdoherty.com

be Cogent (Airdrie)
www.becogent.com

Beechwood Communications
www.beechwood-communications.co.uk

Border Marketing Company
www.bordermc.co.uk

Carnegie Worldwide
http://194.152.84.28/carnegieweb/sporthos_text.htm

The Crimson Edge
www.crimsonedge.co.uk

The Edinburgh Consultancy
www.edinburghconsultancy.com

ENDAT (Stirling)
www.endat.com

Ginger Marketing
www.gingermarketing.co.uk

Gold
www.gold.co.uk

Incognito Consultants
www.incognito-consultants.com

Indigo Bridge
www.indigobridge.com

Insync marketing
www.get-insync.com

KLP Euro RSCG
www.klpeurorscg.com

The Leith Agency
www.leith.co.uk

M2V Marketing
www.m2v.co.uk

Marketing Advantage DDB
www.maddb.com

Marketing & Creative Handbook
www.mch.co.uk/scotlandindex.html

Marketing Databasics
www.marketingdatabasics.com

Metis Marketing
www.metis.co.uk

Navigator Responsive Advertising
www.navigator-ra.co.uk

Only U Direct Marketing
www.only-u.co.uk

Pelorus Marketing Solutions (Dornoch)
www.pelorus.co.uk

Plan B (Ayr)
www.planbonline.co.uk

PRM
www.prm.co.uk

Replyline (Dunfermline)
www.replyline.co.uk

Skybridge Group
www.skybridgegroup.com

Stewart Miller Associates
www.smas.co.uk

Story UK
www.storyuk.com

Strategic Business Solutions
www.s-b-s.com

Professional Bodies

Chartered Institute of Marketing
www.cim.co.uk

Direct Marketing Association
www.dma.org.uk

PR Scotland – agencies listings
www.pr-scotland.com/agencies

materials & construction

AAF Industries
www.aaf.co.uk

Barratt Developments
www.ukpg.co.uk/barratt

Bellway
www.bellway.co.uk

Berkeley Group
www.berkeleygroup.com

BICC
www.bicc.com

Blue Circle
www.bluecircle.co.uk

Bovis Construction
www.bovis.com

Bryant Group
www.bryant.co.uk

Caradon
www.caradon.com

Costain
www.costain.com

George Wimpey
www.wimpey.co.uk

Hanson
www.hansonplc.com

John Laing
www.john-laing.com

Persimmon
www.persimmon.plc.uk

Readymix
www.readymix.com

Rockwool
www.rockwool.co.uk

Rugby Group
www.rugbygroup.co.uk

Shanks
www.shanks.co.uk

Tarmac
www.tarmac.co.uk

Taylor Woodrow
www.taywood.co.uk

Travis Perkins
www.travisperkins.co.uk

Vibroplant
www.vibroplant.com

media

British Sky Broadcasting
www.sky.co.uk

Capital Radio
www.capitalradio.plc.uk

Carat
www.carat.com

Carlton Communications
www.carltonplc.co.uk

Daily Mail & General Trust
www.dmgt.co.uk

Flextech
www.flextech.co.uk

Johnston Press
www.johnstonpress.co.uk

Newsquest
www.newsquest.co.uk

Reed Elsevier
www.reed-elsevier.com

Reuters
www.reuters.com

Scottish Media Group
www.scottishmedia.com

United News & Media
www.unm.com

Virgin
www.virgin.com

metals & mining

Alcoa
www.alcoasystems.co.uk

Anglo American
www.angloamerican.co.uk

AngloAmerican
www.angloamerican.co.uk

Association of British Mining Equipment Companies
www.abmec.org.uk

Bodycote International
www.bodycote.com

British Mining Database
www.ap.pwp.blueyonder.co.uk/bmd.htm

Caledonia Mining Corp
www.caledoniamining.com

Cambridge Mineral Resources
www.cambmin.co.uk

Corus Group
www.corusgroup.com

Global Recycle
www.globalrecycle.net

Johnson Matthey
www.matthey.com

Metal Bulletin
www.metalbulletin.plc.uk

Rio Tinto
www.riotinto.com

Scottish Geology
www.scottishgeology.com

The Gold Institute
www.goldinstitute.org

The Silver Institute
www.silverinstitute.org

UK Coal plc
www.ukcoal.com

Institute of Minerals, Materials & Mining
www.iom3.org

International Council on Mining & Metals
www.icmm.com

Minerals UK (British Geological Survey)
www.bgs.ac.uk/mineralsuk/home.html

Professional Bodies

Association of Mining Analysts
www.ama.org.uk

modelling agencies

Elisabeth Smith
www.elisabethsmith.co.uk

Elite
www.elitepremier.com

The Look Agency (Glasgow)
www.thelookagency.co.uk

The Model Team (Glasgow)
www.modelteam.co.uk

Models 1
www.models1.co.uk

Scallywags
www.scallywags.co.uk

Scots Models
www.scotsmodels.co.uk

Storm Models
www.stormmodels.com

office supplies & services

3m
www.3m.co.uk

Active Office
www.activeoffice.net

Admin Systems
www.adminsystems.co.uk

Avery Dennison Office Products
www.avery.co.uk

Brian Reynolds
www.brianreynolds.co.uk

Chrystal-Hill
http://chrystal-hill.co.uk

Claire Clifford
www.claire-clifford.co.uk

Clarkes Stationers
www.clarkesonline.co.uk

Conqueror
www.conqueror.com

Contract Furniture UK
www.contractfurnitureuk.com

CPS Mailing Systems
www.cpsscotland.co.uk

Cucumberman
www.cucumberman.com

Euroffice
www.euroffice.co.uk

Filofax
www.filofax.com

Fold Tables
www.foldtables.co.uk

Ikon
www.ikon.com

Kall Kwik
www.kallkwik.co.uk

J McCormick
www.jmccormick.co.uk

McLean Group
www.mcleangroup.co.uk

Mondus
www.mondus.co.uk

Morris Office
www.morrisoffice.co.uk

Mr Office
www.Mr-Office.com

NCR
www.ncr.com

Neat Ideas
www.neat-ideas.com

Northern Light
www.northernlight.co.uk

Office Online
www.office-online.co.uk

Office Shop
www.officeshop.org.uk

Office World
www.officeworld.co.uk

Oyez Straker
www.oyezstraker.co.uk

Paper Plus
www.paperplus.co.uk

Partmaster
www.partmaster.co.uk

Pilot Pens
www.pilotpen.co.uk

Pitney Bowes
www.pitneybowes.com/uk

Prontaprint
www.prontaprint.co.uk

Regus
www.regus.com

Ricoh
www.ricoh.com

Ryman
www.ryman.co.uk

Scotforms (Livingston)
www.scotforms.co.uk

Select Furniture
www.selectfurniture.co.uk

Spicers
www.spicersnet.com

Staples
www.staples.co.uk

The Media Factory
www.tmfsolutions.co.uk

Tibbett & Britten
www.tibbet-britten.com

Viking
www.viking-direct.co.uk

Viking Direct
www.viking-direct.co.uk

Vista Paper
www.vistapapers.co.uk

Visual Services Ltd
www.ednet.co.uk/~visualservices

Waterstons Stationery (Edinburgh)
www.waterstonsstationery.co.uk

Wordflow
www.wordflow.co.uk

Work Place Office
www.workplaceoffice.co.uk

paper & packaging

Abbey Corrugated
www.abbeycorrugated.co.uk

API Foils Ltd
www.api-worldwide.com/home.htm

Arjo Wiggins
www.arjowiggins.com

BPB Recycling
www.bpbrecycling.co.uk

Bunzl
www.bunzl.com

Cullen Packaging
www.cullen-packaging.co.uk

Curtis Fine Papers
www.curtisfinepapers.com

David S Smith
www.davidssmith.com

Inveresk Paper
www.inveresk.co.uk

Jefferson Smurfit
www.smurfit-group.com

John W Hannay & Co
www.hannay.co.uk

Linpac
www.linpac.com

Remade (scottish recycling site)
www.remade.org.uk

Rexam
www.rexam.co.uk

Smith & McLaurin
www.smcl.co.uk

Smith Anderson
www.smithanderson.com

Tetrapak
www.tetrapak.com

Tullis Russell Group
www.tullis-russell.co.uk

UPM-Kymmene
www.upm-kymmene.com

Waste Recycling Group
www.wrg.co.uk

Professional Bodies

Confederation of European Paper Industries
www.cepi.org

Corrugated Packaging Association
www.corrugated.org.uk

European Organisation on Packaging & the Environment
www.europen.be

National Association of Paper Merchants
www.napm.org.uk

National Packaging Council
www.natpack.org.uk

Paper Federation of Great Britain
www.paper.org.uk

pharmaceutical

3M
www.3m.com

Abbott
www.abbott.com

Allergan
www.allergan.com

Amersham International
www.amersham.co.uk

Asta Medica
www.astamedica.com

AstraZeneca
www.astrazeneca.com

Aventis
www.aventis.com

BASF
www.basf.com

Bayer
www.bayer.com

Bristol Myers Squibb
www.bms.com

Dura
www.durapharm.com

Eli Lilly
www.lilly.com

Fischer
www.dr-fischer.com

Glaxo Wellcome
www.glaxowellcome.com

Hoechst
www.hoechst.com

Johnson & Johnson
www.jnj.com

Medeva
www.medeva.co.uk

Merck
www.merck.com

Monsanto
www.monsanto.com

Novartis
www.novartis.com

Novo Nordisk
www.novo.dk

Nycomed Amersham
www.amersham.co.uk

Organon
www.organon.com

Pfizer
www.pfizer.com

Roche
www.roche.com

Schering-Plough
www.schering-pl.it

Searle
www.searle.com

Shire Pharmaceuticals Group
www.shiregroup.com

SmithKline Beecham
www.sb.com

Solvay
www.solvay.com

Takeda
www.takedapharm.com

UniChem
www.unichem.co.uk

Warner-Lambert
www.warner-lambert.com

printing & publishing

Associated News
www.accociatednewspapers.co.uk

Blackwell
www.blackwellpublishers.co.uk

Bloomsbury
www.bloomsbury.com

Butterworth Heinemann
www.bh.com

Butterworths
www.butterworths.co.uk

Cambridge University Press
www.cup.cam.ac.uk

DC Thomson
www.dcthomson.co.uk

Dorling Kindersley
www.dk.com

Earthscan
www.earthscan.co.uk

Eastern Counties Newspapers
www.ecn.co.uk

Express Newspapers
www.expressnewspapers.co.uk

Ginn
www.ginn.co.uk

Harper Collins
www.harpercollins.co.uk

Heinemann
www.heinemann.co.uk

HMSO
www.hmso.gov.uk

Hodder & Stoughton
www.madaboutbooks.com

Kogan Page
www.kogan-page.co.uk

Macmillan
www.macmillan.co.uk

McGraw-Hill
www.mcgraw-hill.co.uk

Metro
www.metropublishing.com

Miller Freeman
www.mfplc.co.uk

Minerva Press
www.minerva-press.co.uk

News International
www.newscorp.com

Orbit
www.orbitbooks.co.uk

Osborne Books
www.osbornebooks.co.uk

Oxford University Press
www.oup.co.uk

Paragon
www.paragon.co.uk

Pearson
www.pearson.co.uk

Penguin
www.penguin.co.uk

Puffin
www.puffin.co.uk

Random House
www.randomhouse.co.uk

Reed
www.reedbusiness.com

Rough Guides
www.roughguides.com

Simon & Schuster
www.simonsays.co.uk

St. Ives
www.st-ives.co.uk

Sweet & Maxwell
www.smlawpub.co.uk

Thomson
www.thomson.com

Thorsons
www.thorsons.com

Time Warner
www.timeinc.com

Trinity Mirror
www.trinity.plc.uk

Usborne Publishing
www.usborne.com

Wace Group
www.sevenww.co.uk

Western Newspapers
www.westpress.co.uk

Wiley
www.wiley.com

private investigators

Association of British Investigators
www.theabi.org.uk

Carratu
www.carratu.com

Dun & Bradstreet
www.dunandbrad.co.uk

Institute of Professional Investigators
www.ipi.org.uk

International Federation of Associations of Private Investigators
www.i-k-d.com

Nationwide
www.nig.co.uk

professional bodies & associations

Academy of Experts
www.academy-experts.org

Accounting Standards Body
www.asb.org.uk

Advertising Association
www.adassoc.org.uk

Agricultural Engineers Association
www.aea.uk.com

Association of Accounting Technicians
www.aat.co.uk

Association of Chartered Certified Accountants
www.acca.co.uk

Association of Consulting Engineers
www.acenet.co.uk

Association of Corporate Treasurers
www.corporate-treasurers.co.uk

Association of Fundraising Consultants
www.afc.org.uk

Association of International Accountants
www.a-i-a.org.uk

Association of Investment Trust Companies
www.aitc.co.uk

Association of Personal Injury Lawyers
www.apil.com

Association of Private Client Investment Managers & Stockbrokers
www.apcims.org

Association of Qualitative Research Practitioners
www.aqrp.co.uk

Association of Unit Trusts & Investment Funds (AUTIF)
www.investmentfunds.org.uk

British Airline Pilots Association
www.balpa.org.uk

British Association of Professional Draftsmen
www.drafter.co.uk

British Women Pilots' Association
www.bwpa.demon.co.uk

British Women Racing Drivers Club
www.bwrdc.co.uk

Charted Institute of Environmental Health Officers
www.cieh.org.uk/cieh

Chartered Institute of Marketing
www.cim.co.uk

Chartered Institute of Patent Agents
www.cipa.org.uk

Chartered Institute of Public Finance & Accountancy
www.cipfa.org.uk

Chartered Institute of Taxation
www.tax.org.uk

Chartered Institute of Transport
www.citrans.org.uk

European Central Securities Depositories Association
www.ecsda.com

Factors & Discounters Association
www.factors.org.uk

Financial Accounting Standards Board
www.fasb.org

Financial Reporting Council
www.frc.org.uk

Hotel & Catering International Management Association
www.hcima.org.uk

Incorporated Society of British Advertisers
www.isba.org.uk

Institute of Chartered Accountants
www.icaew.co.uk

Institute of Chartered Accountants of Scotland
www.icas.org.uk

Institute of Chartered Engineers
www.ice.org.uk

Institute of Financial Accountants
www.ifa.org.uk

Institute of Internal Auditors
www.iia.org.uk

Institute of Practitioners in Advertising
www.ipa.co.uk

International Federation of Accountants
www.ifac.org

Law Society
www.law-services.org.uk

London Investment Bank Association
www.liba.org.uk

Securities Institute
www.securities-institute.org.uk

Society of Authors
www.writer.org.uk/society

Society of Freelance Editors & Proofreaders
www.sfep.org.uk

Society of Indexers
www.socind.demon.co.uk

Society of Insolvency Practitioners
www.spi.org.uk

Society of Investment Professionals
www.uksip.org

Writers Guild of Great Britain
www.writers.org.uk/guild

professions

Accountants

Acumen Accountants
www.acumen.ltd.uk

Aiton & Co
www.aitonca.com

Alexander Sloan
www.alexandersloan.co.uk

Arthur Andersen
www.arthurandersen.com

Baker Tilly
www.bakertilly.co.uk

BDO Stoy Hayward
www.bdo.co.uk

BKR Haines Watt
www.hwca.com

Blick Rothenberg
www.blickrothenberg.com

Chiene & Tait
www.chiene.co.uk

Deloitte & Touche
www.deloitte-touche.co.uk

Drummond TLG
www.drummond.uk.com

Eagle Consulting
www.eagleconsulting.co.uk

Ernst & Young
www.ey.com

Fraser Williams
www.fraser-williams.com

Gilmour Hamilton & Co
www.gilmour-hamilton.co.uk

Grant Thornton
www.grant-thornton.co.uk

Hacker Young
www.hackeryoung.co.uk

Haines Watts
www.hwca.com

Hamlyns
www.hamlyns.co.uk

Hays Allan
www.haysallan.com

Horwath Clark Whitehill
www.horwathcw.com

Hughes Allen
www.hughes-allen.co.uk

Kidsons Impey
www.kidsons.co.uk

KPMG
www.kpmg.co.uk

Levy Gee
www.levygee.co.uk

Mazars Neville Russell
www.mazars-nr.co.uk

Moores Rowland
www.moores-rowland.co.uk

O'Sullivan Cleary
www.osullivan.co.uk

Pannell Kerr Forster
www.pkf.com

PricewaterhouseCoopers
www.pwcglobal.com

Pritchards
www.pritchardsca.co.uk

RA Woollard
www.woollard.org.uk

Ritson Smith
www.ritson-smith.com

Robson Rhodes
www.robsonrhodes.com

Saint & Co
www.users.globalnet.co.uk/~saintco

Scott Moncrieff
www.scott-moncrieff.com

Tenon Scotland
www.tenongroup.com/home

Tindell Grant & Co
www.tindellgrant.co.uk

Professional Bodies

Association of Authorised Public Accountants
www.accaglobal.com/aapa

Association of Chartered Certified Accountants
www.accaglobal.com

Chartered Institute of Management Accountants
www.cima.org.uk

Chartered Institute of Public Finance & Accountants
www.cipfa.org.uk

European Federation of Accountants
www.fee.be

Institute of Chartered Accountants of England & Wales
www.icaew.co.uk

Institute of Chartered Accountants of Ireland
www.icai.ie

Institute of Chartered Accountants of Scotland
www.icas.org.uk

International Federation of Accountants
www.ifac.org

Scottish Top 10

Andersen
www.arthurandersen.com

Baker Tilly
www.bakertilly.co.uk

BDO Stoy Hayward
www.bdo.co.uk

Deloitte Touche
www.deloitte.co.uk

Ernst & Young
www.ey.com

Horwath Clark Whitehill
www.horwathcw.com

KPMG
www.kpmg.co.uk/kpmg/uk

PKF
www.pkf.co.uk

PricewaterhouseCoopers
www.pwcglobal.com

Architects

3d Architecture
www.3dgroup.co.uk

Andrea Faed Architects
www.andreafaed.co.uk

BDP
www.bdp.co.uk

Benjamin Tindall Architects
www.benjamintindallarchitects.co.uk

Campbell & Arnott
www.campbellandarnott.co.uk

CDA Group
www.cda-group.co.uk

Cochrane MacGregor
www.cmcg.co.uk

Conran & Partners
www.conranandpartners.com

Duffy & Batt
www.sust-concepts.co.uk

Ecology Building Design
www.ecology.co.uk/eclinks1.htm

Ian Springford Architects
www.isarchitects.co.uk

Keppie Design
www.keppiedesign.co.uk

LDN
www.ldn.co.uk

Lee Boyd Architects
www.leeboyd.co.uk

Lightarch
www.lightarch.com

Malcolm Fraser Architects
www.malcolmfraser.co.uk

Murray & Dunlop Architects
www.murraydunloparchitects.com

Oliver Chapman Architects
www.oliverchapmanarchitects.com

Parr Architects
www.parrarchitects.com

Reich & Hall Architects
www.reiachandhall.co.uk

Richard Murphy Architects
www.richardmurphyarchitects.com

RMJM Architects
www.rmjm.com

Simpson & Brown
www.simpsonandbrown.co.uk

Smith Scott Mullan Architects
www.smith-scott-mullan.co.uk

Professional Bodies & Associations

Edinburgh Architectural Association
www.e-a-a.org.uk

Royal Incorporation of Architects in Scotland
www.rias.org.uk

Royal Institute of British Architects
www.architecture.com

Solicitors

Allen & Overy
www.allenovery.com

Baker & McKenzie
www.bakerinfo.com

Barlow Lyde & Gilbert
www.blg.co.uk

Beachcroft Stanleys
www.beachcroft.co.uk

Berwin Leighton
www.berwinleighton.com

Bird & Bird
www.twobirds.com

Brodies
www.brodies.co.uk

Cameron McKenna
www.cmck.com

Clifford Chance
www.cliffordchance.com

Collyer Bristow
www.collyer-bristow.co.uk

Coudert Brothers
www.coudert.com

Davies Arnold Cooper
www.dac.co.uk

Denton Wilde Sapte
www.dentonwildesapte.com

Dibb Lupton Alsop
www.dibbluptonalsop.co.uk

DJ Freeman
www.djfreeman.co.uk

Edge & Ellison
www.edge.co.uk

Eversheds
www.eversheds.com

Fenwick Elliot
www.fenwickelliott.co.uk

Field Fisher Waterhouse
www.ffwlaw.com

Freshfields
www.freshfields.com

Gouldens
www.gouldens.com

Harbottle & Lewis
www.harbottle.co.uk

Herbert Smith
www.herbertsmith.com

Jeffrey Green Russell
www.jgrweb.com

Lawrence Graham
www.lawgram.com

Linklaters
www.linklaters.com

Llewelyn Zietman
www.llz.co.uk

Lovell White Durrant
www.lovellwhitedurrant.com

MacFarlanes
www.macfarlanes.com

Maclay Murray & Spens
www.maclaymurrayspens.co.uk

McGrigor Donald
www.mcgrigors.com

Nabarro Nathanson
www.nabarro.com

Nicholson Graham Jones
www.ngj.co.uk

Norton Rose
www.nortonrose.com

Olswang
www.olswang.co.uk

Paisner & Co
www.paisner.co.uk

Pinsent Curtis
www.pinsent-curtis.co.uk

Shoosmiths
www.shoosmiths.co.uk

Simkins Partnership
www.simkins.com

Simmons & Simmons
www.simmons-simmons.com

Slaughter & May
www.slaughterandmay.com

Taylor Joynson Garrett
www.tjg.co.uk

Theodore Goddard
www.theogoddard.com

real estate

Canary Wharf Group
www.canarywharf.com

Great Portland Estates
www.gpe.co.uk

Land Securities
www.landsecurities.com

Slough Estates
www.sloughestates.com

recruitment

Agencies

Adecco
www.adecco.co.uk

Blue Arrow
www.bluearrow.co.uk

Brook Street
www.brookstreet.co.uk

Hays
www.hays-ap.com

Manpower
www.manpower.co.uk

Michael Page
www.michaelpage.com

Pareto Law
www.paretolaw.co.uk

RCR International
www.rcri.co.uk

Reed
www.reed.co.uk

Select Appointments
www.selectgroup.com

Talisman
www.talismanretail.co.uk

Job Listings

BBC
www.bbc.co.uk/jobs

Big Blue Dog
www.bigbluedog.com

Guardian
www.jobsunlimited.co.uk

Job Hunter
www.jobhunter.co.uk

Monster
www.monster.co.uk

Stepstone
www.stepstone.com

Top Jobs
www.topjobs.net

Total Jobs
www.totaljobs.com

Yahoo! Classifieds
http://uk.classifieds.yahoo.com/uk/emp

retail

Arcadia
www.arcadia.co.uk

ASDA
www.asda.co.uk

Body Shop
www.the-body-shop.com

Boots
www.boots-plc.com

Debenhams
www.debenhams.co.uk

Dixons
www.dixons-group-plc.co.uk

Great Universal Stores
www.gusplc.co.uk

House of Fraser
www.hofbi.co.uk

Iceland
www.iceland.co.uk

J Sainsbury
www.j-sainsbury.co.uk

JJB Sports
www.jjb.co.uk

John Lewis Partnership
www.john-lewis-partnership.co.uk

Kingfisher
www.kingfisher.co.uk

Marks & Spencer
www.marks-and-spencer.com

MFI Furniture
www.mfigroup.co.uk

Morrison Supermarkets
www.morrisons.plc.uk

Next
www.next.co.uk

Safeway
www.safeway.co.uk

Selfridges
www.selfridges.co.uk

Somerfield
www.somerfield.co.uk

Storehouse
www.storehouse.co.uk

Tesco
www.tesco.co.uk

WH Smith
www.whsmithgroup.com

Wolsey
www.wolsey.com

services

Accenture (Andersen Consulting)
www.accenture.com

Association of Exhibition Organisers
www.aeo.org

Avis Europe
www.avis-europe.com

British Franchise Association
www.franchise.org.uk

British Security Association
www.bsia.co.uk

Capita Group
www.capitagroup.co.uk

Chartered Institute of Marketing
www.cim.co.uk

Chartered Institute of Purchasing & Supply
www.cips.org

Christie's International
www.christies.com

Confederation of British Industry
www.cbi.org.uk

De La Rue
www.delarue.com

Federation of Small Business
www.fsb.org.uk

Hays
www.hays-plc.com

Insitute of Export
www.export.org.uk

Photo-Me International
www.photo-me.co.uk

Rentokil
www.rentokil.co.uk

Rentokil Initial
www.rentokil-initial.com

Tempus Group
www.tempusgroup.co.uk

Williams
www.williams-plc.com

shipping & shipbuilding

BP Marine
www.bpmarine.com

Fairplay
www.fairplay.co.uk

Geest Line
www.geestline.co.uk

Harland & Wolff Holdings PLC
www.harland-wolff.com

Harrison Line
www.harrisons.co.uk

Institute of Chartered Shipbrokers
www.ics.org.uk

Maersk Company
www.maersk.co.uk

Medway Ports
www.medwayports.com

Norman Shipping Group
www.norman.co.uk

Port of Kawasaki
www.city.kawasaki.jp/index_e.htm

Port of Antwerp
www.portofantwerp.be

Port of Bordeaux
www.bordeaux-port.fr

Port of Larne
www.portoflarne.co.uk

Port of Liverpool
www.portofliverpool.co.uk

Port of London
www.portoflondon.co.uk

Port of Marseilles
www.marseillesportservices.com

Port of Montreal
www.port-montreal.com

Port of Oostende
www.portofoostende.be

Port of Osaka
www.optc.or.jp

Port of Quebec
www.portquebec.ca

Port of Reykjavik
www.rvk.is/hofnin

Port of Zeebrugge
www.zeebruggeport.be

standards

Food Standards Agency Scotland
www.foodstandards.gov.uk/scotland/

Qualifications & Curriculum Authority
www.qca.org.uk

Qualifications for Industry
www.qfi.co.uk

Scotland the Brand
www.scotlandthebrand.com

Trading Standards
www.tradingstandards.net

stock & commodity exchanges & financial listings

America
www.amex.com

Amsterdam
www.aex.nl

Australia
www.asx.com.au

Baltic Exchange
www.balticexchange.co.uk

Berlin
www.berlinerboerse.de

Bermuda
www.bsx.com

Brussels
www.stockexchange.be

Bucharest
www.bvb.ro

Cayman
www.csx.com.ky

Chicago
www.chicagostockex.com

Dow Jones
www.dowjones.com

EASDAQ
www.easdaq.be

Frankfurt
www.exchange.de

Helsinki
www.hse.fi

Hong Kong
www.sehk.com.hk

International Petroleum Exchange (IPE)
www.ipe.uk.com

Johannesburg
www.jse.co.za

LIFFE
www.liffe.com

Lisbon
www.bvl.pt

London
www.londonstockex.co.uk

London Clearing House
www.lch.co.uk

London Metal Exchange
www.lme.co.uk

Madrid
www.bolsamadrid.es

Montreal
www.m-x.ca

NASDAQ
www.nasdaq.com

New York
www.nyse.com

OPEC
www.opec.org

Paris
www.bourse-de-paris.fr

Stockholm
www.stockholmsborsen.se

Switzerland
www.swx.ch

Taiwan
www.tse.com.tw

Tokyo
www.tse.or.jp

Toronto
www.tse.com

Vancouver
www.vse.ca

Warsaw
www.gpw.com.pl/xml/indexe.xml

telecommunications

AT&T
www.att.com

Breathe
www.breathe.com

British Telecommunications
www.bt.com

Cable & Wireless
www.cwplc.com

COLT Telecom Group
www.colt-telecom.com

Energis
www.energis.co.uk

First Telecom
www.firsttelecom.com

Freeserve
www.freeserve.net

Marconi
www.marconi.com

NTL
www.ntl.com

O2
www.o2.co.uk

One Tel
www.onetel.co.uk

Orange
www.orange.co.uk

Scottish Telecom
www.scottishtelecom.com

T-Mobile
www.t-mobile.co.uk

Telewest Communications
www.telewest.co.uk

Thus
www.thus.net

Virgin Mobile
www.virgin.com/mobile

Vizzavi
www.vizzavi.co.uk

Vodafone
www.vodafone.com

trade unions & associations

Ambulance Service Union
www.asu.org.uk

Amicus – Amalgamated Engineering & Electrical Union (AEEU)
www.aeeu.org.uk

Associated Society of Locomotive Engineers & Firemen
www.aslef.org.uk

Association for Consultants & Trainers
www.act-assn.dircon.co.uk

Association for Information Management
www.aslib.co.uk

Association of Car Fleet Operators
www.acfo.org/resources

Association of College Management
www.acm.uk.com

Association of Direct Labour Organisations
www.adlo.org.uk

Association of European Travel Agents International
www.aeta.co.uk

Association of Independent Tour Operators
www.aito.co.uk

Association of Master Upholsters & Soft Furnishers
www.upholsterers.co.uk

Association of National Tourist Offices
www.tourist-offices.org.uk

Association of Plastic Manufacturers
www.apme.org

Association of Play Industries
www.ipma.uk.com

Association of Residential Letting Agents
www.arla.co.uk

Association of Suppliers to the British Clothing Industry
www.asbci.co.uk

Association of Suppliers to the Furniture Industry
www.asfi.org

Association of University Teachers
www.aut.org.uk

AUT Aberdeen
www.abdn.ac.uk/aut

AUT Dundee
www.tay.ac.uk/aut

AUT Edinburgh
www.eaut.ed.ac.uk

AUT Glasgow
www.gla.ac.uk/Staff/GAUT

AUT St Andrews
www.st-and.ac.uk/~aut

AUT Stirling
www.stir.ac.uk/theuni/stafinfo/aut/AUT.HTM

AUT Strathclyde
www.strath.ac.uk/Other/AUT

Bakers, Food & Allied Workers' Union
www.bfawu.org

BECTU
www.bectu.org.uk

Booksellers Association
www.booksellers.org.uk

British Aerosol Manufacturers Association
www.bama.co.uk

British Air Line Pilots Association
www.balpa.org.uk

British Antique Furniture Restorers Association
www.bafra.org.uk

British Apparel & Textile Confederation
www.mediatex.co.uk/resources/assocs/batc.htm

British Association of Picture Libraries
www.bapla.org.uk

British Contract Furnishing Association
www.bcfa.org.uk

British Furniture Manufacturers
www.bfm.org.uk

British Healthcare Trades Association
www.bhta.com

British Jewellers Association
www.bja.org.uk

British Marine Industries Federation
www.bmif.co.uk

British Office Systems & Stationery Federation
www.bossfed.co.uk

British Printing Industries Federation
www.bpif.org.uk

British Toy & Hobby Association
www.btha.co.uk

Broadcasting Entertainment Cinematograph & Theatre Union (BECTU)
www.bectu.org.uk

Butlers Guild
www.butlersguild.com

Communications Workers Union (CWU)
www.cwu.org

Community & Youth Workers' Union
www.cywu.org.uk

CONNECT
www.connectuk.org

Edinburgh Trade Union Council
www.ccis.org.uk/etuc

Federation of Recruitment & Employment Services
www.fres.co.uk

Federation of the Electronics Industry
www.fei.org.uk

Fire Brigades Union Scotland
www.fbuscotland.co.uk

General Federation of Trade Unions
www.gftu.org.uk

Giftware Association
www.giftware.org.uk

Grain & Feed Trade Association (GAFTA)
www.gafta.com

Graphical Paper & Media Union (GPMU)
www.gpmu.org.uk

Independent Financial Advisers Association (IFA Association)
www.ifaa.org.uk

Independent Publishers Guild
www.ipg.uk.com

Institute of Building Control
www.building-control.org

Institute of Packaging
www.iop.co.uk

Institute of Paper
www.instpaper.org.uk

Institute of Printing
www.instituteofprinting.org

Institute of the Motor Industry
www.motor.org.uk

Institution of Professionals Managers & Specialisyts (IPMS)
www.ipms.org.uk

International Association for the Protection of Industrial Property
www.aippi.org

International Federation of Chemical, Energy, Mine & General Workers Unions
www.icem.org

Iron & Steel Trades Confederation
www.istc-tu.org.uk

Kitchen Specialists Association
www.ksa.co.uk

Knitting, Footwear & Textile Workers (KFAT)
www.kfat.org.uk

Musicians Union
www.musiciansunion.org.uk

Napo
www.napo.org.uk

National Association of Goldsmiths
www.progold.net

National Association of Paper Merchants
www.napm.org.uk

National Association of School Masters Union of Women Teachers (NASUWT)
www.teachersunion.org.uk

National Housing Federation
www.housing.org.uk

National Union of Journalists (NUJ)
www.nuj.org.uk

National Union of Knitwear, Footwear & Apparel Trades
www.kfat.org.uk

National Union of Teachers (NUT)
www.teachers.org.uk

Newspaper Society
www.newspapersoc.org.uk

Periodical Publishers Association
www.ppa.co.uk

Printmakers Council
www.printmaker.co.uk/pmc

Public & Commercial Services Union
www.ptc.org.uk

Scottish Childminding Association
www.childminding.org

Scottish Newspaper Publishers Association
www.snpa.org.uk

Scottish Prison Officers Association
www.poauk.org.uk/about.html

Scottish Trade Union Review
www.scottishreview.com

Scottish Trades Union Congress
www.demon.co.uk/stuc

Screen Printers Association
www.martex.co.uk/screen-printing

Shipbuilders & Shiprepairers Association
www.ssa.org.uk

Tobacco Manufacturers' Association
www.the-tma.org.uk

Transport & General Workers Union
www.tgwu.org.uk

Transport Salaried Staffs Association
www.tssa.org.uk

TUC
www.tuc.org.uk

UK Aromatherapy Practitioners & Suppliers
www.fragrant.demon.co.uk/ukaromas.html

UNIFI
www.unifi.org.uk

Union of Shop, Distributive & Allied Workers (USDAW)
www.usdaw.co.uk

UNISON
www.unison.org.uk

UNISON – Scotland
www.unison-scotland.org.uk

Writers Guild of Great Britain
www.writers.org.uk/guild

transport

Aberdeen Airport
www.baa.com/main/airports/aberdeen

Air France
www.airfrance.co.uk

ARRIVA
www.arriva.co.uk

Associated British Ports
www.abports.co.uk

BAA
www.baa.co.uk

Barra Airport
www.scottishflightguide.co.uk/barraairport.htm

Bearsden & Milngavie Station Taxis
www.stationtaxis.co.uk

British Airways
www.british-airways.com

British European
www.british-european.com

British Midland
www.flybmi.com

Central Highland Taxis, Inverness
www.invernessonline.com/taxis/about.htm

Central Taxis
www.taxis-edinburgh.co.uk

Chamber of Shipping
www.british-shipping.org

City Link
www.citylink.co.uk

Discovery Taxis, Dundee
www.discovery-taxis.co.uk

Dundee Airport
www.angusanddundee.co.uk/convention/airport.cfm

East Dumbartonshire TOA
http://taxis-glasgow.com

Easy Jet
www.easyjet.com

Edinburgh Airport
www.baa.com/main/airports/edinburgh

Eurotunnel
www.eurotunnel.co.uk

FirstGroup
www.firstgroup.com

Glasgow Airport
www.baa.com/main/airports/glasgow

Glasgow Airport Taxis
www.ga-taxis.co.uk

Glasgow Prestiwck Airport
http://glaspres01.uuhost.uk.uu.net

Glasgow Prestwick Taxis & Couriers
www.alanm.com

Glasgow Wide TOA
www.gwtoa.co.uk

GNER
www.gner.co.uk

Go
www.go-fly.com

Go-Ahead
www.go-ahead.com

Highlands & Islands Airports
www.hial.co.uk

Iberia
www.iberia.co.uk

KLM
www.klm.co.uk

Kyle Taxis, Highlands
www.lochalsh.net/taxi

Lloyds Register
www.lr.org

Lothian Buses
www.lothianbuses.co.uk

National Express
www.gobycoach.com

NFC
www.nfc.co.uk

Ocean
www.oceangroup.uk.com

Railtrack
www.railtrack.co.uk

Road Haulage Association
www.rha.net

Ryanair
www.ryanair.com

Scot Airways
www.scotairways.co.uk

Scot Rail
www.scotrail.co.uk

Sea Containers
www.seacontainers.com

Shire Taxis, Abredeen
www.shiretaxis.co.uk

South African Airways
www.saa.co.uk

SPT
www.spt.co.uk

Stagecoach Buses
www.stagecoachbus.com

Stagecoach Holdings
www.stagecoachholdings.com

The Trainline
www.thetrainline.com

Virgin Trains
www.virgintrains.co.uk

US corporations

ABC
www.abc.go.com

AlliedSignal
www.alliedsignal.com

Amerada Hess
www.hess.com

American Electric Power
www.aep.com

American Express
www.americanexpress.com

American Home Products
www.ahp.com

American Standard
www.americanstandard.com

Amoco
www.bpamoco.com

AOL Time Warner
www.aoltimewarner.com

Apple Computer
www.apple.com

AT&T
www.att.com

Bank One
www.bankone.com

BankAmerica Corp.
www.bankamerica.com

Barnes & Noble
www.barnesandnoble.com

Bell Atlantic
www.bell-atl.com

Black & Decker
www.blackanddecker.com

Boeing
www.boeing.com

Budweiser
www.budweiser.com

CBS
www.cbs.com

Cendant
www.cendant.com

Chase Manhattan Corp.
www.chase.com

Chevron
www.chevron.com

Chubb
www.chubb.com

Coca-Cola
www.thecoca-colacompany.com

Colgate-Palmolive
www.colgate.com

Compaq
www.compaq.com

Computer Associates
www.compusa.com

Continental Airlines
www.flycontinental.com

Dell
www.dell.com

Delta Airlines
www.delta-air.com

Dow Chemical
www.dow.com

Du Pont
www.dupont.com

Eastman Kodak
www.kodak.com

Electronic Data Systems
www.eds.com

Eli Lilly
www.lilly.com

Exxon
www.exxon.com

Federal Express
www.fedex.com

Ford Motor
www.ford.com

General Electric
www.ge.com

General Mills
www.generalmills.com

General Motors
www.gm.com

Goodyear
www.goodyear.com

Hershey Foods
www.hersheys.com

Hewlett Packard
www.hp.com

Hilton Hotels
www.hilton.com

Honeywell
www.honeywell.com

IBM
www.ibm.com

Intel
www.intel.com

JC Penney
www.jcpenney.com

Johnson & Johnson
www.jnj.com

JP Morgan
www.jpmorgan.com

Kellogg's
www.kelloggs.com

Kimberly-Clark
www.kimberly-clark.com

Lockheed Martin
www.lmco.com

Manpower
www.manpower.com

McDonald's
www.mcdonalds.com

McGraw-Hill
www.mcgraw-hill.com

Merck
www.merck.com

Merrill Lynch
www.ml.com

Microsoft
www.microsoft.com

Monsanto
www.monsanto.com

Morgan Stanley Dean Witter Discover
www.deanwitterdiscover.com

NBC
www.nbc.com

NCR
www.ncr.com

Nickelodeon
www.nick.com

Occidental Petroleum
www.oxy.com

Paramount Pictures
www.paramount.com

PepsiCo
www.pepsico.com

Pfizer
www.pfizer.com

Pharmacia & Upjohn
www.pharmacia.com

Philip Morris
www.pmdocs.com

Proctor & Gamble
www.pg.com

Quaker Oats
www.quakeroats.com

Reader's Digest Association
www.readersdigest.com

RJR Nabisco Holdings
www.rjrnabisco.com

Rockwell International
www.rockwell.com

Sara Lee
www.saralee.com

Schering-Plough
www.sch-plough.com

Sears Roebuck
www.sears.com

Southwestern Bell
www.sbc.com

Texas Instruments
www.ti.com

Union Carbide
www.unioncarbide.com

Union Pacific
www.up.com

Unisys
www.unisys.com

United Airlines
www.ual.com

United Parcel Service
www.ups.com

United Technologies
www.utc.com

Viacom
www.viacom.com

Wal-Mart
www.wal-mart.com

Walt Disney
www.disney.go.com

Warner-Lambert
www.warner-lambert.com

Whirlpool
www.whirlpool.com

Xerox
www.xerox.com

utilities

British Energy
www.british-energy.com

British Nuclear Fuels
www.bnfl.co.uk

N-Power
www.npower.com

National Grid
www.ngc.co.uk

National Power
www.national-power.com

PowerGen
www.pgen.com

Scottish & Southern Energy
www.scottish-southern.co.uk

Scottish Gas
www.gas.co.uk

Scottish Hydro-Electric
www.hydro.co.uk

Scottish Power
www.scottishpower.plc.uk

Scottish Water
www.esw.co.uk

UK Atomic Energy Authority
www.ukaea.org.uk

Wavegen
www.wavegen.co.uk

children

- cartoon characters
- clubs & activities
- computer games
- days out
- film & television
- games & toys
- homework & revision
- magazines, books & authors
- theatre
- websites

cartoon characters

Asterix
www.asterix.tm.fr

Batman
www.batman.com

Beavis & Butthead
www.beavis-butthead.com

Bugs Bunny
www.cartoonnetwork.com/bugs

Captain America
www.winghead.org

Captain Marvel
http://shazam.imginc.com

Casper
www.harvey.com/comics/04/index.shtml

Daffy Duck
www.cartoonnetwork.com/daffy

Danger Mouse
www.dangermouse.org

Dick Tracy
http://dicktracy.comicspage.com

Dilbert
www.unitedmedia.com/comics/dilbert

Doonsbury
www.doonesbury.com

Felix the Cat
www.felixthecat.com

Flash Gordon
www.kingfeatures.com/comics/fgorgon

Flintstones
http://members.optushome.com.au/webrock

Fred Basset
http://fredbasset.comicspage.com

Garfield
www.garfield.com

Hagar the Horrible
www.kingfeatures.com/comics/hagar

Inspector Gadget
www.inspector-gadget.net

Marmaduke
www.unitedmedia.com/comics/marmaduke

Noggin The Nog
www.nogginthenog.co.uk

Pokemon
http://upnetwork.com

Popeye
www.midwest.net/orgs/ace1

Road Runner
www.itr.qc.ca/~mario/roadrunner.htm

Scooby Doo
www.cartoonnetwork.com/scooby

Simpsons
www.thesimpsons.com

Spiderman
www.kingfeatures.com/comics/spiderman

Teenage Mutant Ninja Turtles
www.ninjaturtles.com

Tom & Jerry
http://tomandjerrythemovie.warnerbros.com

X-men
www.x-men.com

clubs & activities

Achievers International
www.achieversinternational.org

Boys' Brigade
www.boys-brigade.org.uk

British Council
www.britcoun.org

British Youth Council
www.byc.org.uk

Britkid
www.britkid.org

Childrens Society
www.the-childrens-society.org.uk

Connect Youth International
www.connectyouthinternational.com

Crusaders
www.crusaders.org.uk

Duke of Edinburgh Award
www.theaward.org

Envirovision
www.envirovision.org

Girl Guides Association
www.guides.org.uk

Groundswell Project
www.groundswell.org.uk

Information for Young People in the UK
www.youthinformation.com

National Association for Gifted Children
www.nagcbritain.org.uk

National Association for Youth Justice
www.nayj.org.uk

National Association of Clubs for Young People
www.nacyp.org.uk

National Association of Youth Theatres
www.nayt.org.uk

National Children's Bureau
www.ncb.org.uk

National Rounders Association
http://rounders.punters.co.uk

National Youth Agency (UK)
www.nya.org.uk

Ocean Youth Trust
www.oyc.org.uk

Pony Club
www.pony-club.org.uk

Prince's Trust
www.princes-trust.org.uk

Roald Dahl Club
www.roalddahlclub.com

ScoutNet
www.scoutnet.org.uk

Scouts
www.scoutbase.org.uk

Sea Cadets
www.btinternet.com/~sailmaster

Tumbletots
www.tumbletots.com

UK Motor Projects Site
www.motorprojects.org.uk

UK Youth
www.ukyouth.org

Who Cares Trust
www.thewhocarestrust.org.uk

YMCA Scotland
www.ymcascotland.org

Young Scot
www.youngscot.org

Young Voice
www.young-voice.org

Youth Scotland
www.ycs.org.uk

YouthLink Scotland
www.youthlink.co.uk

Youthreach
www.clubi.ie/youthreach

computer games

Console Domain
www.consoledomain.com

Nintendo
www.nintendo.co.uk

PlanIt4Kids.com
www.planit4kids.com

PlayStation
www.playstation-europe.com

PlayStation 2
www.playstation2.com

Sega
www.sega.com

Sega Dreamcast
www.dreamcast-europe.com

days out

Activity Point – days out search facility
www.activitypoint.co.uk

Adventure Island
www.adventureisland.co.uk

Alton Towers
www.alton-towers.co.uk

American Adventure Theme Park
www.adventureworld.co.uk

Argyll Wildlife Park
www.argyllwildlifepark.co.uk

Aviemore Funhouse
www.aviemorefunhouse.co.uk

Babbacombe Model Village
www.babbacombemodelvillage.co.uk

Barry Island Pleasure Park
www.pleasurepark.co.uk

Bekonscot Model Village
www.bekonscot.org.uk

Bingham's Park Farm
www.binghams.co.uk

Blackpool Pleasure Beach
www.bpbltd.com

Blackpool Tower
www.blackpool.gov.uk/tower.htm

Brighton Palace Pier
www.brightonpier.co.uk

Cedarpoint
www.cedarpoint.com

Chessington World of Adventure
www.chessington.co.uk

Crealy Park
www.crealy.co.uk

Deep Sea World
www.deepseaworld.com

Discovery Point
www.rrs-discovery.co.uk

Dome
www.dome2000.co.uk

Drayton Manor
www.draytonmanor.co.uk

Dreamworld Family Entertainment Centre
www.dreamworld.co.uk

Edinburgh Butterfly Farm & Insect World
www.edinburgh-butterfly-world.co.uk

Edinburgh Dungeons
www.thedungeons.com

Edinburgh Zoo
www.edinburghzoo.org.uk

Eureka!
www.eureka.org.uk

Fantasy Island
www.fantasyisland.co.uk

Flambards Village
www.flambards.co.uk

Football World
www.football-world.co.uk

Glasgow Science Centre
www.gsc.org.uk

Glasgow Zoo
www.glasgowzoo.co.uk

Great Yarmouth Pleasure Beach
www.pleasure-beach.co.uk

Harbour Park
www.harbourpark.com

Heron's Brook
www.herons-brook.co.uk

Highland Folk Museum
www.highlandfolk.com

Highland Museum of Childhood
www.hmoc.freeserve.co.uk

Jorvik Viking Centre
www.jorvik-viking-centre.co.uk

Kidsnet
www.kidsnet.co.uk

Kidstravel
www.kidstravel.co.uk

Landmark Centre
www.landmark-centre.co.uk

Lands End
www.landsend-landmark.co.uk

Leault Farm
www.leaultfarm.co.uk

Legoland
www.legoland.co.uk

Lightwater Valley
www.lightwatervalley.co.uk

Loch Insh Watersports
www.lochinsh.com

Loch Morlich Watersports
www.lochmorlich.com

Loudoun Castle
www.loudouncastle.co.uk

Lowther Leisure & Wildlife Park
www.lowtherpark.co.uk

M&D's Scotlands Theme Park
www.scotlandsthemepark.com

Macduff Marine Aquarium
www.marine-aquarium.com

Museum of Childhood Edinburgh
www.cac.org.uk

New Lanark World Heritage Site
www.newlanark.org

Oakwood Park
www.oakwood-leisure.com

Our Dynamic Earth
www.dynamicearth.co.uk

Plan It For Kids
www.planit4kids.com

Pleasure Island
www.pleasure-island.co.uk

Pleasureland
www.pleasureland.uk.com

Raceland (E. Lothian)
www.raceland.co.uk

Racing Karts (Livingston)
www.racingkarts.co.uk

ScotKart (Glasgow)
www.scotkart.co.uk

Scottish Karting
www.scottishkarting.co.uk

Scottish Seabird Centre
www.seabird.org

Secret Bunker St Andrews
www.secretbunker.co.uk

Sensation
www.sensation.org.uk

Shaws Sweet Factory
www.shawsdundee.co.uk

Southend On Sea Pier
www.swine.co.uk

Storybook Glen
www.storybookglenaberdeen.co.uk

Strathspey Steam Railway
www.strathspeyrailway.co.uk

The Big Idea
www.bigidea.org.uk

Thorpe Park
www.thorpepark.co.uk

Verdant Works
www.rrs-discovery.co.uk/verdant

Wicksteed Park
www.wicksteedpark.co.uk

Woolly Mammoth Activities
www.woolly-mammoth.co.uk

film & television

4Learning
www.4learning.co.uk

Angelina Ballerina
www.angelinaballerina.com

Animal Zone
www.bbc.co.uk/animalzone

Antz
www.antz.com

Art Attack
www.artattack.co.uk

Barney
www.barneyonline.com

Batman & Robin
www.batman-robin.com

BBC Schools
www.bbc.co.uk/education/schools

Bill Nye the Science Guy
www.billnye.com

Blue Peter
www.bbc.co.uk/bluepeter

Bob the Builder
www.bobthebuilder.org

Bug's Life
www.abugslife.com

Cartoon Network
www.cartoon-network.co.uk

CBBC
www.bbc.co.uk/cbbc

Channel 4 Schools
www.schools.channel4.com

CITV
www.citv.co.uk

Clangers
www.clangers.co.uk

Close Shave
www.aardman.com/wallaceandgromit/films/acloseshave

Dennis the Menace
www.kingfeatures.com/features/comics/dennis/about.htm

Digimon – The Movie
www.digievolution.net/digimonmovie.shtml

Discovery Channel
www.discovery.com

Disney Channel
www.disneychannel.co.uk

Dr Dolittle 2
www.drdolittle2.com

Dungeons And Dragons
www.seednd.com

Fairy Tale
www.fairytalemovie.com

Flash Gordon
www.kingfeatures.com/comics/flashg.gif

Fox Kids
www.foxkids.co.uk

Garfield
www.garfield.com

Hercules
www.herc.co.uk

Hyperlinks
www.bbc.co.uk/hyperlinks

Kid's Channel
www.kids-channel.co.uk

Little Mermaid
www.thelittlemermaid.com

Live & Kicking
www.bbc.co.uk/kicking

Mighty Morphin' Power Rangers
www.foxkids.com/power_rangers

Mulan
www.mulan.com

Munsters
www.munsters.com

Muppets
www.muppets.com

Muppets from Space
www.muppetsfromspace.com

Newsround
www.bbc.co.uk/newsround

Nickelodeon
www.nick.co.uk

Pingu, Oswald & other HIT Entertainment chracters
www.hitentertainment.com/html/classicChar/classic.asp

PlanIt4Kids.com
www.planit4kids.com

Pokemon the First Movie
www.pokemonthemovie.com

Popeye
www.kingfeatures.com/comics/popeye

Rugrats
www.cooltoons.com/shows/rugrats

Rugrats the Movie
www.nick.com/rugrats.tin

Sabrina the Teenage Witch
www.paramount.com/television/sabrina

Sesame Street
www.sesamestreet.com

Shrek
www.shrek.com

Simpsons
www.thesimpsons.com

Star Trek
www.startrek.com

Star Wars
www.starwars.com

Stuart Little
www.stuartlittle.com

Tarzan
www.tarzan.co.uk

Teddy Bears
www.theteddybears.com

Teletubbies
www.teletubbies.com

The Borrowers
www.britfilms.com/britfilms98/films/features012.html

The Emperor's New Groove
http://disney.go.com/disneypictures/emperorsnewgroove

The Saturday Show
www.bbc.co.uk/cbbc/saturdayshow

Thomas the Tank Engine
www.thomasthetankengine.com

Thunderbirds
www.thunderbirdsonline.co.uk

Tomb Raider
www.tombraidermovie.com

Top of the Pops
www.bbc.co.uk/totp

Toy Story
www.toystory.com

Tweenies
www.bbc.co.uk/education/tweenies

Universal Studios
www.universalstudios.com

Walking with Dinosaurs
www.bbc.co.uk/dinosaurs

Wallace & Gromit
www.aardman.com

Warner Bros
www.kids.warnerbros.com

Wombles
www.mikebatt.com/wombles

X-Men
www.x-men-the-movie.com

Xena Warrior Princess
www.mca.com/tv/xena

games & toys

Action Man
www.actionman.co.ukAirfix Models
www.airfix.com

Barbie
www.barbie.com

Beanie Babies
www.ty.com

Brio
www.brio.co.uk

Cabbage Patch Kids
www.cabbagepatchkids.com

Cluedo
www.cluedo.com

Corgi
www.corgi.co.uk

Crayola
www.crayola.com

Etch-a-sketch
www.etch-a-sketch.com

Fisher Price
www.fisher-price.com

Furbys
www.furbys.co.uk

Hasbro
www.hasbro.com

Hasbro Interactive
www.hasbro-interactive.com

Hornby
www.hornby.co.uk

Knex
www.knex.co.uk

Lego
www.lego.com

Little Tikes
www.rubbermaid.com/littletikes

Matchbox
www.matchboxtoys.com

Mattel
www.mattel.com

Meccano
www.meccano.co.uk

Monopoly
www.monopoly.com

Mr Potato Head
www.mrpotatohead.com

Panini
www.panini.co.uk

PlanIt4Kids.com
www.planit4kids.com

Playmobil
www.playmobil.de

Pokemon
www.pokemon.com

Quadro
www.quadro-toys.co.uk

Scalextric
www.scalextric.co.uk

Scrabble
www.scrabble.com

Si-O(fada)g
www.siogdolls.com

Silly Putty
www.sillyputty.com

Slinky
www.slinkytoys.com

Tomy
www.tomy.co.uk

Toys.com
www.etoys.com

Toyzone
www.toyzone.co.uk

Trivial Pursuits
www.trivialpursuit.com

Young Embroiderers
www.hiraeth.com/ytg

homework & revision

A-levels
www.a-levels.co.uk

Bitesize Revision
www.bbc.co.uk/education/revision

BJ Pinchbeck Homework Helper
www.bjpinchbeck.com

Freeserve Revision
www.freeserve.net/education/examrevision

GCSE Answers
www.gcse.com

GCSE Bitesize Revision
www.bbc.co.uk/education/gcsebitesize

Homework Elephant
www.homeworkelephant.free-online.co.uk

Homework High
www.homeworkhigh.com

Learn
www.learn.co.uk

Learn Free
www.learnfree.co.uk

LineOne Learning
www.lineone.net/learning

Maximus
www.minimus-etc.co.uk

NRICH Primary Maths (University of Cambridge)
www.nrich.maths.org.uk/primary

S-Cool
www.s-cool.co.uk

Schools Online (Science)
www.shu.ac.uk/schools/sci/sol/contents.htm

Thunk.Com
www.thunk.com

Topmarks
www.topmarks.co.uk

magazines, books & authors

Anne Fine
www.annefine.co.uk

Beano
www.beano.co.uk

Beatrix Potter
www.peterrabbit.co.uk

Bright Sparks (Junior Mensa Magazine)
www.mensa.org.uk/mensa/junior/magazine.html

British Arthur Ransome Society
www.arthur-ransome.org

Children's Book Council
www.cbcbooks.org

DC Comics
www.dccomics.com

Dorling Kindersley
www.dk.com

Dr Seuss
www.seussville.com

Enid Blyton
www.blyton.com

Eric Carle
www.eric-carle.com

Flash Gordon
www.kingfeatures.com/comics/fgordon

Girl Talk
www.girl-talk.com

Girl's World
www.agirlsworld.com

Goosebumps
www.scholastic.com/goosebumps

Hagar the Horrible
www.kingfeatures.com/features/comics/hagar/about.htm

HarperCollin's Childrens Books
www.harperchildrens.com

Harry Potter
www.harrypotter.com

Judy Blume
www.judyblume.com

Ladybird Books
www.ladybird.co.uk

Kids Reads
www.kidsreads.com

Marvel Comics
www.marvelcomics.com

Maths Maze
www.mathsyear2000.co.uk

Miffy
www.miffy.co.uk

Mr Men
www.mrmen.net

National Geographic for Kids
www.nationalgeographic.com/kids

Oor Wullie
www.thatsbraw.co.uk

Paddington Bear
www.paddingtonbear.co.uk

Right Start
www.rightstartmagazine.co.uk

Roald Dahl
www.roalddahl.org

Snoopy
www.snoopy.com

Spider Man
www.kingfeatures.com/comics/spiderman

The Broons
www.thatsbraw.co.uk/

Thomas the Tank Engine
www.thomasthetankengine.com

Tintin
www.tintin.be

Watership Down
www.watershipdown.net

Willie Wonka
www.wonka.com

Winnie the Pooh
www.winniethepooh.co.uk

theatre

Mersey Young Peoples Theatre
www.mypt.uk.com

National Association of Youth Theatre
www.nayt.org.uk

Polka Children's Theatre
www.polkatheatre.com

Puppeteers Company
www.puppco.demon.co.uk

QuickSilver
www.ecna.org/qsilver

websites

Alfy
www.alfy.co.uk

AOL UK Kid's Channel
www.aol.co.uk/channels/kids

Ask Jeeves for Kids
www.ajkids.com

Beanie Babies Official Club
www.beaniebabyofficialclub.com

Big Idea
www.bigidea.com

Bonus.com
www.bonus.com

Brain Teaser
www.brain-teaser.com

Bullying
www.bullying.co.uk

Bullying (BBC)
www.bbc.co.uk/education/bully

Carnegie Museum – Discovery Room
www.clpgh.org/cmnh/discovery

ChildLine
www.childline.org.uk

Compuserve Kids
www.compuserve.com/gateway/kids

Cooking for Kids
www.learnfree.co.uk/cookingforkids/html

Disney
www.disney.com

Disney Interactive
www.disney.co.uk/disneyinteractive

EcoKids
www.bytesize.com/ecokids

Enchanted Learning
www.enchantedlearning.com

Eplay
www.eplay.co.uk

European Youth Observatory
www.diba.es/eyo/index.html

Freeserve Revision
www.freeserve.net/education/examrevision

Galaxy Kids
www.galaxykids.co.uk

Homework Elephant
www.homeworkelephant.free-online.co.uk

How Stuff Works
www.howstuffworks.com

IOL Kidz
www.disneyblast.com

Kids' Almanac
www.kids.infoplease.com

Kids' Crosswords
www.kidcrosswords.com

Kids' Domain
www.kidsdomain.com

Kids' Jokes
www.kidsjokes.com

KidsCom
www.kidscom.com

McVities Jaffa Cakes
www.jaffacakes.co.uk

Microsoft Kids
www.microsoft.com/kids

Polly Pocket
www.pollypocket.com

Pooh Corner
www.pooh-corner.com

Pupil Line
www.pupiline.net

Puzzle Up
www.puzzleup.com

RSPCA Kid's Stuff
www.rspca.org.uk/content/kids_stuff.html

Smart as Kids
www.smartazzkids.com

The Big Busy House
www.harperchildrens.com

The Freezone Network
www.freezone.com

The Junction
www.thej.co.uk

The Park
www.oceanfree.net/thepark/flash.html

Theodore's Tugboat
www.cochran.com/theodore

Thunk
www.thunk.com

UTV – Kidzone
www.utv.co.uk/kidzone

Warner Bros Kids' Page
www.kids.warnerbros.com

Yahoo! Games
www.games.yahoo.com

Yahooligans!
www.yahooligans.com

YouthInformation.com
www.youthinformation.com

YouthOrg UK
www.youth.org.uk

Advice

Bullying Online
www.bullying.co.uk

Childline
www.childline.org.uk

Children 1st
www.children1st.org.uk

Children in Scotland
www.childreninscotland.org.uk

Children's Hearing Systems (Youth Justice)
www.childrens-hearings.co.uk

Diabetes UK
www.diabetes.org.uk

Eating Disorders Association
www.edauk.com

Health Education Boards of Scotland
www.hebs.scot.nhs.uk

One Parent Families – Scotland
www.opfs.org.uk

Parent Centre (Dept of Education & Skills)
www.dfes.gov.uk/parents

Parentline
www.children1st.org.uk/parentline

Parentlineplus
www.parentlineplus.org.uk

Parents Online
www.parentsonline.gov.uk

Scottish Dyslexia Trust
www.dyslexia-scotland.org

Scottish Health
www.show.scot.nhs.uk

Stammering
www.stammering.org

Teenadvice Online
www.teenadviceonline.org

Teencancer
www.teencancer.org

The Site
www.thesite.org

Vegetarian Recipes
www.vegkitchen.com

Vegetarian Society
www.vegsoc.org

Young Person's Rights – Scotland
www.article12.org

Your Turn
www.yourturn.net

Educational

Bitesize Revision
www.bbc.co.uk/education/revision

Enchanted Learning
www.enchantedlearning.com

Esat Young Scientist & Technology Exhibition
www.esatys.com

European Schoolnet
www.eun.org

Examteacher.com
www.examteacher.com

Freeserve Revision
www.freeserve.net/education/examrevision

GCSE Guide
www.gcseguide.co.uk

GetNetWise
www.getnetwise.org

Homework Elephant
www.homeworkelephant.co.uk

Homework High
www.4learning.co.uk/apps/homework/index.jsp

How Stuff Works
www.howstuffworks.com

Learning Store
www.learningstore.co.uk

One World
www.oneworld.net

Pupiline
www.pupiline.com

Schools Online (Science)
www.shu.ac.uk/schools/sci/sol/contents.htm

Schoolzone
www.schoolzone.co.uk

Scottish Council for Research in Education
www.scre.ac.uk

TopStudy
www.topstudy.com

Youth Pathways Project
www.15up.com/15

education, training & research

- adult education
- agriculture
- art & architecture
- ballet, drama & music
- books, magazines & websites
- business & law
- colleges
- complementary health
- educational organisations
- hospitality
- medical & dental
- postgraduate & research
- pre-school
- professional associations
- schools
- student bodies & organisations
- tuition & part-time learning
- universities
- veterinary schools

adult education

Adult Learners Gateway
www.dfes.gov.uk/adultlearners/index.shtml

Adult Learning
www.support4learning.org.uk/education/adult.htm

Adult Literacy
www.literacytrust.org.uk

BBC Adult learning
www.bbc.co.uk/learning/adults

National Institute of Adult Continuing Education
www.niace.org.uk

Night Courses
www.nightcourses.com

agriculture

Oatridge, Broxburn
www.oatridge.ac.uk

Royal Agricultural College
www.royagcol.ac.uk

Scottish Agricultural College
www.sac.ac.uk

art & architecture

Architectural Association School of Architecture
www.arch-assoc.org.uk

Architectural Heritage Society of Scotland
www.ahss.org.uk

British Institute of Architectural Technologists
www.biat.org.uk

Courtauld Institute
www.courtauld.ac.uk

Duncan of Jordanstone College of Art, Dundee
www.dundee.ac.uk/main/depts.htm

Edinburgh College of Art
www.eca.ac.uk

Edinburgh Department of Architecture
www.caad.ed.ac.uk

Glasgow College of Building & Printing
www.gcbp.ac.uk

Glasgow School of Art
www.gsa.ac.uk

Hull School of Architecture
www.humber.ac.uk/arc

Institute of Contemporary Art
www.ica.org.uk

London College of Printing
www.linst.ac.uk/lcp

Mackintosh School of Architecture, Glasgow
www.gsa.ac.uk/architecture

National Society for Education in Art & Design
www.nsead.org

National Training Organisation for Arts & Entertainment (Metier)
www.metier.org.uk

Royal College of Art
www.rca.ac.uk

Ruskin School of Drawing & Fine Art
www.ruskin-sch.ox.ac.uk

School of Art History, St.Andrews
www-ah.st-andrews.ac.uk

Scott Sutherland School of Architecture, Aberdeen
www.rgu.ac.uk/sss

Slade
www.ucl.ac.uk/slade

Strathclyde Department of Architecture
www.strath.ac.uk/Departments/Architecture

Surrey Institute of Art & Design
www.surrart.ac.uk

ballet, drama & music

Arts Educational London Schools
www.artsed.co.uk

Associated Board of the Royal Schools of Music
www.abrsm.ac.uk

Birmingham School of Speech & Drama
www.bssd.ac.uk/bssd

Bristol Old Vic Theatre School
www.oldvic.drama.ac.uk

Brit School
www.brit.croydon.sch.uk

British Universities Film & Video Council
www.bufvc.ac.uk

Central School of Speech & Drama
www.cssd.ac.uk

Cygnet Training Theatre (Exeter)
www.drama.ac.uk/cygnet.html

Dance School of Scotland
www.scottishballet.co.uk/school/school.htm

De Montfort University
www.dmu.ac.uk

Drama Centre London
http://dcl.drama.ac.uk

East 15 Acting School
http://east15.ac.uk

Elmhurst School for Dance & Performing Arts
www.elmhurstdance.co.uk

English National Ballet School
www.en-ballet.co.uk/school

Guildhall School of Music & Drama
www.guildhall.drama.ac.uk

Jeremy Whelan
www.jeremy-whelan-acting.com

Lee Strasberg
www.strasberg.com

Liverpool Institute for Performing Arts
www.lipa.ac.uk

Liverpool John Moore's University
www.livjm.ac.uk/university/courses/dance.htm

London Academy of Music & Dramatic Art (LAMDA)
www.lamda.org.uk

London Contemporary Dance School
www.theplace.org.uk/html/nav/edfr.htm

London International Film School
www.lifs.org.uk

Manchester Metropolitan University, School of Theatre
www.artdes.mmu.ac.uk

Mountview Theatre School
www.mountview.ac.uk

National Council for Drama Training
www.ncdt.co.uk

National Film & Television School
www.nftsfilm-tv.ac.uk

North of England College of Dance
www.zebra.co.uk/necd

Northern School of Contemporary Dance
www.nscd.ac.uk

Oxford School of Drama
www.oxford.drama.ac.uk

Queen Margaret College, School of Drama (Edinburgh)
www.drama.ac.uk/queenm.html

Rambert School
www.brunel.ac.uk/faculty/arts/rambert

Roehampton Institute of Dance
www.roehampton.ac.uk/academic/arts&hum/dance/dance.html

Rose Bruford College of Speech & Drama
www.bruford.ac.uk

Royal Academy of Dramatic Art (RADA)
www.rada.org

Royal Academy of Music
www.ram.ac.uk

Royal Ballet School
www.royal-ballet-school.org.uk

Royal College of Music
www.rcm.ac.uk

Royal Northern College
www.rncm.ac.uk

Royal Scottish Academy of Music & Drama
www.rsamd.ac.uk

Trinity College of Music
www.tcm.ac.uk

University of Surrey
www.surrey.ac.uk/dance

Webber Douglas Academy of Dramatic Art
www.drama.ac.uk/webberd.html

Welsh College of Music & Drama
www.welsh.drama.ac.uk

books, magazines & websites

@School
www.atschool.co.uk

Association of Teachers Websites
www.byteachers.org.uk

BBC Education
www.bbc.co.uk/education

BBC Scotland Education
www.bbc.co.uk/scotland/education

Brainwise Scotland
www.brainwise.co.uk

BT Teaching Awards
www.teachingawards.com

Bullying
www.bullying.co.uk

Child Net
www.childnet-int.org

Education Portal
www.educating.cc

Education Show
www.education-net.co.uk

Floodlight
www.floodlight.co.uk

Gabbitas Guide to Independent Schools
www.gabbitas.net

Good Schools Guide
www.goodschoolsguide.co.uk

Guide to UK Boarding Schools
www.boarding-schools.com

Incorporated Association of Preparatory Schools
www.iaps.org.uk

Independent Schools Directory
www.indschools.co.uk

Independent Schools Information Service
www.isis.org.uk

Learn
www.learn.co.uk

Learn Direct Scotland
www.learndirectscotland.com

Maths Maze
www.mathsyear2000.co.uk

National Curriculum
www.dfes.gov.uk/nc

National Grid for Learning
www.ngfl.gov.uk

Nelson Books
www.nelson.co.uk

On Course
www.oncourse.co.uk

Parents Centre
www.dfes.gov.uk/parents

Qualifications & Curriculum Authority
www.qca.org.uk

RM
www.rm.com

School Friend
www.schoolfriend.co.uk

Scottish Qualifications Authority
www.sqa.org.uk

Special Educational Needs
www.dfe.gov.uk/sen

Student Life
www.student-life-magazine.co.uk

Student Loans Company
www.slc.co.uk

Student World
www.student-world.com

Think
www.think.com

Times Educational Supplement
www.tes.co.uk

Times Higher Educational Supplement
www.thesis.co.uk

Times Literary Supplement
www.the-tls.co.uk

Universities UK
www.universitiesuk.ac.uk

business & law

Aberdeen Business School
www.abs.ac.uk

BPP Law School
www.bpp.com

College of Law
www.lawcol.org.uk

Edinburgh Business School
www.ebs.hw.ac.uk

Glasgow School of Law
www.law.gla.ac.uk

London Business School
www.lbs.lon.ac.uk

Manchester Business School
www.mbs.ac.uk

colleges

Aberdeen
www.abcol.ac.uk

Angus
www.angus.ac.uk

Anniesland
www.anniesland.ac.uk

Association of Scottish Colleges
www.ascol.org.uk

Ayr
www.ayrcoll.ac.uk

Banff & Buchan
www.banffbuchan.com

Barony
www.barony.ac.uk

Bells College of Technology
www.a-dc-02.bell.ac.uk/2002/default.htm

Borders
www.borderscollege.ac.uk

Cardonald
www.cardonald.ac.uk

Central College of Commerce
www.centralcollege.co.uk

Clackmannan
www.clacks.ac.uk

Clydebank
www.clydebank.ac.uk

Coatbridge
www.coatbridge.ac.uk

Cumbernauld
www.cumbernauld.ac.uk

Dumfries & Galloway
www.dumgal.ac.uk

Dundee
www.dundeecoll.ac.uk

Edinburgh Telford
www.ed-coll.ac.uk

Elmwood, Cupar
www.elmwood.ac.uk

Falkirk
www.falkirkcollege.ac.uk

Fife
www.fife.ac.uk

Glasgow College of Food Technology
www.gcft.ac.uk

Glenrothes
www.glenrothes-college.ac.uk

Inverness
www.uhi.ac.uk/INVERNESS.HTM

James Watt
www.jameswatt.ac.uk

Jewel & Esk Valley
www.jevc.ac.uk

John Wheatly, Glasgow
www.jwheatley.ac.uk

Kilmarnock
www.kilmarnock.ac.uk

Langside, Glasgow
www.langside.ac.uk

Lauder, Dunfermline
www.lauder.ac.uk

Lews Castle, Stornoway
www.lews.uhi.ac.uk

Moray, Elgin
www.moray.ac.uk

North Glasgow
www.north-gla.ac.uk

North Highland
www.thurso.uhi.ac.uk

Northern College of Education, Aberdeen
www.norcol.ac.uk

Orkney
www.orkney.uhi.ac.uk

Perth
www.perth.ac.uk

Queen Margaret, Edinburgh
www.qmuc.ac.uk

Reid Kerr, Paisley
www.reidkerr.ac.uk/rkc

Sabhal Mor Ostaig, Skye
www.smo.uhi.ac.uk

Shetland
www.shetland.uhi.ac.uk

South Lanarkshire
www.south-lanarkshire-college.ac.uk

Stevenson, Edinburgh
www.stevenson.ac.uk

Stow, Glasgow
www.stow.ac.uk

West Lothian
www.west-lothian.ac.uk

complementary health

Academy of Curative Hypnotherapists
www.ach.co.uk

British College of Naturopathy & Osteopathy
www.bcno.org.uk

British School of Homeopathy
www.homeopathy.co.uk

College of Integrated Chinese Medicine
www.cicm.org.uk

London College of Clinical Hypnosis
www.lcch.co.uk

London College of Traditional Acupuncture & Oriental Medicine
www.lcta.com

Royal College of Speech & Language Therapists
www.rcslt.org

educational organisations

General

Association of Recognised English Language Schools
www.arels.org.uk

Book Trust
www.booktrust.org.uk

Careers Research & Advisory Centre
www.crac.org.uk

Careers Services National Association
www.careers-uk.com

Careers Services Unit
www.prospects.csu.man.ac.uk

Civil Service College
www.open.gov.uk/college/cschome.htm

Community Learning Scotland
www.communitylearning.org

Disability Rights Commission- Education
www.drc-gb.org/drc/campaigns/page431.asp

Education Business Partnership
www.ebp.org.uk

Graduate Careers Services Unit
www.prospects.csu.man.ac.uk

Learning & Teaching Scotland
www.ltscotland.com

Learning & Teaching Support Network
www.ltsn.ac.uk

National Institute of Adult Continuing Education
www.niace.org.uk

National Literacy Trust
www.literacytrust.org.uk

On Course
www.oncourse.co.uk

Scottish Book Trust
www.scottishbooktrust.com

Scottish Council For Research In Education
www.scre.ac.uk

Scottish Education & Training
www.educationukscotland.org

Scottish Further Education Unit
www.sfeu.ac.uk

Society for College, National & University Libraries
www.sconul.ac.uk

University of London Careers Service
www.careers.lon.ac.uk

Young Enterprise Scotland
www.yes.org.uk

Governing Bodies

British Association for Open Learning
www.baol.co.uk

British Council for Education
www.britcoun.org

British Educational Communications & Technology Agency (BECTA)
www.becta.org.uk

Central Council for Education & Training in Social Work
www.ccetsw.org.uk

City & Guilds Institute
www.city-and-guilds.co.uk

General Teaching Council for Scotland
www.gtcs.org.uk

Higher Education Funding Council for Scotland
www.shefc.ac.uk/shefc

National Council for Drama Training
www.ncdt.co.uk

National Council for the Training of Journalists
www.nctj.com

Office for Standards in Education
www.ofsted.gov.uk

Royal Institution of Great Britain
www.ri.ac.uk

Scottish Council for Educational Technology
www.scet.org.uk

Scottish Higher Education Funding Council
www.shefc.ac.uk

Teacher Training Agency
www.teach-tta.gov.uk

Training & Enterprise Councils
www.tec.co.uk

UK Council for Graduate Education
www.warwick.ac.uk/ukcge

hospitality

Scottish Hotel School
www.shs.strath.ac.uk

medical & dental

Aberdeen School of Medicine
www.bms.abdn.ac.uk

Eastman Dental Institute
www.eastman.ucl.ac.uk

Edinburgh School of Medicine
www.mvm.ed.ac.uk

Glasgow Caledonian University
www.fhis.gcal.ac.uk

Glasgow Dental & Medical School
www.gla.ac.uk/schools/dental

University of Aberdeen
www.bms.abdn.ac.uk

postgraduate & research

Association for University Research & Industry Links
www.auril.org.uk

Greenwich Maritime Institute
www.nri.org/gmi

HERO – Higher Education & Research Opportunities in the UK
www.hero.ac.uk

National Foundation for Educational Research
www.nfer.ac.uk

National Postgraduate Committee
www.npc.org.uk

Nuffield Trust
www.nuffieldtrust.org.uk

Research Councils UK
www.research-councils.ac.uk

Roslin Biotechnology Institute
www.roslin.ac.uk

Royal Academy of Engineers
www.raeng.org.uk

Royal Botanical Garden, Edinburgh
www.rbge.org.uk

Royal Institute of International Affairs
www.riia.org

Scholarship Search
www.scholarship-search.org.uk

Society for Research into Higher Education
www.srhe.ac.uk

Society of Antiquaries
www.sal.org.uk

Technology Scotland
www.technologyscotland.org

Tenovus
www.tenovus.org.uk

UK Council for Graduate Education
www.ukcge.ac.uk

pre-school

Montessori Foundation
www.montessori.org

Norland Nanny School
www.norland.co.uk

professional associations

Association of Christian Teachers
www.christian-teachers.org

Association of University Administrators
www.aua.ac.ul

schools

Scottish Primary School page
http://ourworld.compuserve.com/homepages/Webber

Scottish Schools Directory
www.inscotland.com/pages/directory/schools.htm

Independent

American Community Schools
www.acs-england.co.uk

Boarding School Association
www.boarding.org.uk

Gabbitas Guide to Independent Schools
www.gabbitas.net

Girls' Schools Association
www.girls-schools.org.uk

Incorporated Association of Preparatory Schools
www.iaps.org.uk

Independent Schools Directory
www.indschools.co.uk

Independent Schools Information Service
www.isis.org.uk

Scottish Council of Independent Schools
www.scis.org.uk

Public

Ampleforth
www.ampleforth.org.uk

Benenden
www.benenden.kent.sch.uk

Cheltenham College
www.cheltcoll.gloucs.sch.uk

Dulwich College
www.dulwich.org.uk

Eton College
www.etoncollege.com

Gordonstoun
www.gordonstoun.org.uk

King's
www.ksw.org.uk

Manchester Grammar
www.mgs.org

Millfield
www.millfield.somerset.sch.uk

Oundle
www.oundleschool.org.uk

Roedean
www.roedean.co.uk

Rugby
www.rugby-school.co.uk

Shrewsbury
www.shrewsbury.org.uk

St Paul's
www.stpauls.co.uk

Stowe
www.stowe.co.uk

Uppingham
www.uppingham.co.uk

Westminster
www.westminster.org.uk

Winchester College
www.wincoll.ac.uk

Wrekin College
www.wrekin-college.salop.sch.uk

student bodies & organisations

4U Students
www.4u-students.com

Camp America
www.campamerica.co.uk

National Union of Students
www.nus.org.uk

Student Awards Agency for Scotland
www.student-support-saas.gov.uk

Student Buzz
www.studentbuzz.com

Student Life Magazine
www.student-life-magazine.co.uk

Student UK
www.studentuk.com

University & Colleges Admissions Service
www.ucas.ac.uk

tuition & part-time learning

Floodlight
www.floodlight.co.uk

Institut Francais
www.ambafrance.org.uk

Kumon Maths
www.kumon.demon.co.uk

Learn Direct
www.learndirect.co.uk

Lifelong Learning (DfES)
www.lifelonglearning.com

Linguaphone
www.linguaphone.co.uk

National Literacy Trust
www.literacytrust.org.uk

National Organisation for Adult Learning
www.niace.org.uk

Oncourse
www.oncourse.co.uk

University of the Third Age
www.u3a.org.uk

Workers' Educational Association
www.wea.org.uk

universities

Aberdeen
www.abdn.ac.uk

Abertay Dundee
www.abertay.ac.uk

Dundee
www.dundee.ac.uk

Edinburgh
www.ed.ac.uk

Glasgow
www.gla.ac.uk

Glasgow Caledonian
www.gcal.ac.uk

Glasgow School of Art
www.gsa.ac.uk

Glasgow School of Education (St.Andrews College)
www.stac.ac.uk

Heriot-Watt
www.hw.ac.uk

Highlands & Islands
www.uhi.ac.uk

Moray House, School of Education
www.education.ed.ac.uk

Napier
www.napier.ac.uk

Paisley
www.paisley.ac.uk

Queen Margaret University College
www.qmuc.ac.uk

Robert Gordon
www.rgu.ac.uk

St Andrews
www.st-and.ac.uk

Stirling
www.stir.ac.uk

Strathclyde
www.strath.ac.uk

Organisations

Association for Commonwealth Universities
www.acu.ac.uk/

Association of UK Higher Education European Officers
www.heuro.org

UK Universities Course Advisory Service
www.edcasworldwide.com

Universities Scotland
www.universities-scotland.ac.uk

Useful Websites

BUBL Information Service
www.bubl.ac.uk

Graduate UK
www.graduateuk.com

veterinary schools

Bristol
www.bris.ac.uk/depts/vetsci/wel.htm

British Veterinary Nursing Association
www.bvna.org.uk

Cambridge
www.vet.cam.ac.uk

Dublin
www.hermes.ucd.ie/~vetmed

Edinburgh
www.vet.ed.ac.uk

Glasgow
www.gla.ac.uk/acad/facvet

International Veterinary Student's Association
www.ivsa.org

Liverpool
www.liv.ac.uk/vets/vethome.html

Royal College of Veterinary Surgeons (London)
www.rcvs.org.uk

Royal Veterinary College (London)
www.rvc.ac.uk

agriculture •
architecture •
construction •
government •
green issues •
landscape •
preservation •
transport •

environment

agriculture

Country Landowners' Association
www.cla.org.uk

Dalgety Arable
www.dalgety.co.uk

East of England Agricultural Society
www.eastofengland.org.uk

Farmers Weekly Interactive
www.fwi.co.uk

Farmers' Union of Wales
www.fuw.org.uk

Home Grown Cereals Authority
www.hgca.co.uk

Institute for Animal Health
www.iah.bbsrc.ac.uk

Institute of Arable Crops Research
www.res.bbsrc.ac.uk

Institute of Food Research
www.ifrn.bbsrc.ac.uk conscientious

John Innes Centre
www.uea.ac.uk/nrp/jic

Milk Marque
www.milkmarque.com

National Institute of Agricultural Botany
www.niab.com

Royal Agricultural Society
www.rase.org.uk

Royal Bath & West Society
www.bathandwest.co.uk

Royal Highland & Agricultural Society of Scotland
www.rhass.org.uk

Royal Ulster Agricultural Society
www.ruas.co.uk

Royal Welsh Agricultural Society
www.rwas.co.uk

Soil Association
www.earthfoods.co.uk

Tenant Farmers Association
www.tenant-farmers.org.uk

Yorkshire Agricultural Society
www.yas.co.uk

architecture

Archinet
www.archinet.co.uk

Architects Journal
www.constructionplus.co.uk

Architectural Heritage
www.eup.ed.ac.uk/journals/architectural

Architectural Heritage Fund
www.ahfund.co.uk

Architectural Review
www.arplus.com

Architecture Centre, Bristol
www.arch-centre.demon.co.uk

Architecture Foundation
www.architecturefoundation.org.uk

Architecture Week
www.archweek.co.uk

Architecturelink
www.architecturelink.org.uk

Association for Environment Conscious Building
www.aecb.net

Civic Trust
www.civictrust.org.uk

Commission for Architecture & the Built Environment (CABE)
www.cabe.org.uk

Commonwealth Association of Architects
www.archexchange.org

Frank Lloyd Wright
www.wrightplus.com

Guild of Architectural Ironmongers (GAI)
www.martex.co.uk/gai/index.htm

International Union of Architects
www.uia-architectes.org

Pevsner Architectural Guides
www.pevsner.co.uk

RIAS, Scotland
www.rias.org.uk

RIBA Publications
www.ribabookshop.com

Royal Institute of British Architects
www.riba.org

Society of Architectural Historians of Great Britain
www.sahgb.org.uk

Stirling Prize
www.ribaawards.co.uk

Twentieth Century Society
www.c20society.demon.co.uk

World Architecture
www.world-architecture.co.uk

construction

Association of Consulting Engineers
www.acenet.co.uk

Association of Project Management
www.apm.org.uk

BEPAC
www.bepac.dmu.ac.uk

British Construction Industry Awards
www.bciawards.org.uk

Concrete Society
www.concrete.org.uk

Construction Industry Board
www.ciboard.org.uk

Construction Industry Council
www.cic.org.uk

Construction Industry Research & Information Association
www.ciria.org.uk

Energy-Efficient Building Association
www.eeba.org

European Construction Institute
www.eci-online.org

Housing Forum
www.thehousingforum.org.uk

Institution of Civil Engineers
www.ice.org.uk

National Homebuilder Awards
www.nationalhomebuilder.com

Steel Construction Institute
www.steel-sci.org

Urban Design Alliance
www.udal.org.uk

government

Countryside Agency
www.countryside.gov.uk

Countryside Council for Wales
www.ccw.gov.uk

Department of Environment, Transport & the Regions
www.detr.gov.uk

English Nature
www.english-nature.org.uk

Environment Agency Wales
www.environment-agency.wales.gov.uk

GRID – Global Resource Information Database (United Nations)
www.grida.no

Ministry of Agriculture, Fisheries & Food
www.open.gov.uk/maff

National Environment Research Council
www.nerc.ac.uk

National Heritage
www.heritage.gov.uk

Natural Environment Research Council
www.nerc.ac.uk

Royal Commission on Historical Manuscripts
www.hmc.gov.uk

Royal Commission on the Ancient & Historical Monuments of Scotland
www.rcahms.gov.uk

Royal Commission on the Ancient & Historical Monuments of Wales
www.rcahmw.org.uk

Scottish Environment Protection Agency
www.sepa.org.uk

Town & Country Planning Association
www.tcpa.org.uk

green issues

Action for the Environment
www.groundwork.org.uk

British Wind Energy Association
www.bwea.com

Can-Do Community Recycling
www.fraserburgh.org.uk/cando

Centre for Alternative Technology
www.cat.org.uk

Conservation Foundation
www.conservationfoundation.co.uk

Countryside Council for Wales
www.ccw.gov.uk

Countryside Foundation for Education
www.countrysidefoundation.org.uk

Countryside Watch
www.countrysidewatch.co.uk

Earthwatch
www.uk.earthwatch.org

Energy Saving Trust
www.est.org.uk

Friends of the Earth Scotland
www.foe-scotland.org.uk

Game Conservancy Trust
www.game-conservancy.org.uk

Going for Green
www.gfg.iclnet.co.uk

Greenpeace International
www.greenpeace.org

Waste Watch
www.wastewatch.org.uk

landscape

Alliance for Historic Landscape Preservation
www.mindspring.com/~ahlp

Arboricultural Association
www.trees.org.uk

Association of Gardens Trusts
www.btinternet.com/~gardenstrusts

Association of National Park & Countryside Voluntary Wardens
www.naturenet.net/orgs/acvw

Field Magazine
www.thefield.co.uk

Historic Gardens Foundation
www.historicgardens.freeserve.co.uk

International Society of Arboriculture
www.ag.uiuc.edu/~isa

Landscape Design Trust
www.landscape.co.uk

Landscape Institute
www.l-i.org.uk

Moorland Association
www.cla.org.uk/moorland

National Arborist Association
www.natlarb.com

National Countryside Show
www.countrysideshow.co.uk

Royal Forestry Society
www.rfs.org.uk

Rural Development Commission
www.box.argonet.co.uk/rdc

Tree Register
www.tree-register.org

Trees for Life
www.treesforlife.org.uk

preservation

Antiquity Magazine
http://intarch.ac.uk/antiquity

Architectural Heritage Society of Scotland
www.ahss.org.uk

Assemblage Archaeology Journal
www.shef.ac.uk/~assem

Association for Industrial Archaeology
www.twelveheads.demon.co.uk/aia.htm

Association for the Protection of Rural Scotland
www.aprs.org.uk

Association of Archaeological Illustrators & Surveyors
www.aais.org.uk

Association of Local Government Archaeological Officers
www.algao.org.uk

British Archaeology Magazine
www.britarch.ac.uk/ba/ba.html

British Trust for Conservation Volunteers
www.btcv.org.uk

Construction History Society
www.construct.rdg.ac.uk/chs

Council for British Archaeology
www.britarch.ac.uk

Current Archaeology
www.archaeology.co.uk

Ecclesiological Society
www.ecclsoc.org

English Heritage
www.english-heritage.org.uk

European Association of Archaeologists
www.e-a-a.org

Historic Chapels Trust
www.hct.org.uk

Historic Houses Association
www.historic-houses-assn.org

Institute of Field Archaeologists
www.archaeologists.net

Institution of Historic Building Conservation
www.ihbc.org.uk

Landmark Trust
www.landmarktrust.co.uk

Museum of London Archaeology Service
www.molas.org.uk

National Trust for Scotland
www.nts.org.uk

Open Churches Trust
www.merseyworld.com/faith/html_file/octhead.htm

Regeneration Through Heritage
www.bitc.org.uk/rth

RESCUE (British Archaeology Trust)
www.rescue-archaeology.freeserve.co.uk

River Thames Society
www.riverthamessociety.org.uk

Royal Highland Education Trust
www.sfacet.org.uk

Royal Society for Nature Conservation
www.rsnc.org

Society for the Protection of Ancient Buildings
www.spab.org.uk

United Kingdom Institute for Conservation
www.ukic.org.uk

York Archaeological Trust
www.pastforward.co.uk

transport

Environmental Transport Association
www.eta.co.uk

Sustrans
www.sustrans.org.uk

food & drink

- breweries
- chefs
- clubs & associations
- famous brands
- fast food
- food & drink online
- food marketing
- magazines & websites
- manufacturers
- professional bodies
- restaurants & bars
- state agencies
- supermarkets
- trade associations
- whisky
- wine

breweries

Abbey Ales
www.abbeyales.co.uk

Amstel
www.amstel.com

Badger
www.breworld.com/badger

Bass Ale
www.bassale.com

Beamish Brewery
www.aardvark.ie/beamish

Beck's
www.becks-beer.com

Blacksheep
www.blacksheep.co.uk

Boddingtons
www.boddingtons.com

Brains
www.sabrain.co.uk

Budweiser
www.budweiser.com

Budweiser Budvar
www.budweiser.cz

Caffrey's
www.caffreys.ie

Carlsberg
www.carlsberg.co.uk

Cobra
www.cobrabeer.com

Corona
www.corona.com

Dos Equis
www.dosx.com

Duvel
www.duvel.be

Felinfoel
www.felinfoel-brewery.com

Foster's
www.fostersbeer.com

Freedom
www.freedombrew.com

Fuller's
www.fullers.co.uk

Grolsch
www.grolsch.com

Guinness
www.guinness.ie

Harp
www.iol.ie/~ange/harp.htm

Heineken
www.heineken.com

Holsten
www.holsten.de

HP Bulmer
www.bulmer.com

JD Wetherspoon
www.jdwetherspoon.co.uk

Kronenbourg
www.k1664.co.uk

Labatt's
www.labatt.com

Marston's
www.breworld.com/marstons

Merrydown
www.merrydown.plc.uk

Miller Lite
www.millerlite.com

Molson
www.molson.com

Morland
www.morland.co.uk

Morrells
www.morrells.co.uk

Murphy's Beer
www.murphysbeers.com

Newcastle Brown
www.broonale.co.uk

Ridleys
www.ridleys.co.uk

Rolling Rock
www.rollingrock.co.uk

Ruddles
www.ruddles.co.uk

Scrumpy Jack
www.scrumpyjack.com

Shepherd Neame
www.shepherd-neame.co.uk

Singha
www.singha.com

Society of Independent Brewers
www.siba.co.uk

Strongbow
www.strongbow.com

Thwaites
www.thwaites.co.uk

Vaux Breweries
www.vaux-breweries.co.uk

Woodfordes
www.woodfordes.co.uk

Wychwood Brewery
www.wychwood.co.uk

Young's
www.youngs.co.uk

Scottish

Arran Brewery
www.arranbrewery.co.uk

Atlas Brewery
www.atlasbrewery.com

Beers Scotland.com
www.beers-scotland.co.uk

Belhaven Brewery
www.belhaven.co.uk

Black Isle Brewery
www.blackislebrewery.com

Bridge of Allen Brewery
www.lugton.co.uk/index.html

Broughton Ales
www.broughtonales.co.uk

Cairngorm Brewery
www.cairngormbrewery.com

Caledonian Brewery
www.caledonian-brewery.co.uk

Eglesbrech Brewery
www.behindthewall.co.uk/micro.htm

Fisherrow Brewery
www.fisherrow.co.uk

Forth Brewery
www.forthbrewery.com

Fyfe Brewing Co
www.e-fife.com/harbourbar/fyfebrewingco.htm

Heather Ale
www.heatherale.co.uk

Hebridean Brewery
www.hebridean-brewery.co.uk

Houston Brewery
www.houston-brewing.co.uk

Inveralmond Brewery
www.inveralmond-brewery.co.uk

Isle of Skye Brewery
www.skyebrewery.demon.co.uk

Kelburn Brewery
www.kelburnbrewery.com

Maclay Thistle
www.maclay.com

Moulin Brewery
www.pitlochryhotels.co.uk/moulinhotel

Orkney Brewery
www.orkneybrewery.co.uk

Scottish & Newcastle
www.scottish-newcastle.com

Sulwath Brewers
www.sulwathbrewers.co.uk

Tennent's
www.interbrew.com

Traquair Brewery
www.traquair.co.uk/beer.html

Valhalla Brewery
www.valhallabrewery.co.uk

chefs

Ainsley Harriott
www.bbc.co.uk/food/celebritychefs/harriott.shtml

Albert Roux
www.albertroux.co.uk

Andrew Fairlie
www.taste-of-scotland.com/andrew-fairlie.html

Anton Mosiman
www.mosiman.com

Clarissa Dickson Wright
www.bbc.co.uk/food/celebritychefs/wright.shtml

Craft Guild of Chefs
www.chefpoint.co.uk

Delia Smith
www.deliaonline.com

Federation of Chefs – Scotland
www.scottishchefs.com

Gary Rhodes
www.bbc.co.uk/food/celebritychefs/rhodes.shtml

Jamie Oliver
www.jamieoliver.net

Keith Floyd
www.keithfloyd.co.uk

Lindsay Bareham
www.thisislondon.com/lindsaybareham

Martin Wishart
www.martin-wishart.co.uk

Nick Nairn
www.bbc.co.uk/food/celebritychefs/nairn.shtml

Raymond Blanc
www.manoir.co.uk

clubs & associations

British Meat
www.meatmatters.com

British Nutrition Foundation
www.nutrition.org.uk

CAMRA (Campaign for Real Ale)
www.camra.org.uk

Campaign for Real Food
www.thecarf.co.uk

Campden & Chorleywood Food Research Association
www.campden.co.uk

Chilled Food Association
www.chilledfood.org

Chocolate Society
www.chocolate.co.uk

Circle of Wine Writers
www.circleofwinewriters.org

Federation of Scottish Chefs
www.scottishchefs.com

Food Additives & Ingredients Association
www.faia.org.uk

Foods of Scotland
www.foodsofscotland.co.uk

Guild of Food Writers
www.gfw.co.uk

National Association of Farmers Markets
www.farmersmarkets.net

National Pork Producers Council
www.nppc.org

Pizza, Pasta & Italian Food Association
www.jwfidler.co.uk/main/papa.htm

Scottish Farmers Markets Association
www.scottishfarmersmarkets.co.uk

Scottish Food & Drink
www.scottishfoodanddrink.com

Slow Food Association
www.slowfood.com

Soil Association
www.soilassociation.org.uk

Speciality Foods
www.speciality-foods.com

Vegan Society
www.vegansociety.com

Vegetarian Friends
www.vegetarianfriends.com

Vegetarian Society
www.vegsoc.org

Wholesome Food Association
www.wholesomefood.org

famous brands

Absolut Vodka
www.absolutvodka.com

After Eights
www.aftereights.co.uk

Anchor Foods
www.anchorfoods.com

Asian Home Gourmet
www.asianhomegourmet.com

Bacardi
www.bacardi.com

Bahlsen
www.bahlsen.co.uk

Baileys
www.baileys.com

Baxters
www.baxters.co.uk

Beefeater
www.beefeater.co.uk

Ben & Jerry's
www.benjerry.co.uk

Bendicks of Mayfair
www.bendicks.co.uk

Bensons Crisps
www.bensons-crisps.co.uk

Birds Eye Walls
www.birdseye.com

Blue Dragon
www.bluedragon.co.uk

Boaters Coffee
www.boaters.co.uk

Boost
www.boost.co.uk

Brannigans
www.brannigans.co.uk

Budweiser
www.budweiser.com

Buitoni
www.buitoni.co.uk

Cadbury's
www.cadbury.co.uk

Campbell's
www.campbellsoup.com

Captain Morgan Rum
www.rum.com

Celebrations
www.celebrations365.com

Chiltern Hills
www.chilternhills.co.uk

Clipper Teas
www.clipper-teas.com

Coca Cola
www.cocacola.com

Courvoisier
www.courvoisier.com

Creme Egg
www.cremeegg.co.uk

Crunchie
www.crunchie.co.uk

Cuervo
www.cuervo.com

Culpeper
www.culpeper.co.uk

Danepak
www.danepak.co.uk

Danone
www.danone.com

Delifrance
www.delifrance.com

Douwe Egberts
www.douwe-egberts.co.uk

Dr Pepper
www.drpepper.com

Drambuie
www.drambuie.co.uk

Evian
www.evian.com

Finlandia Vodka
www.finlandia-vodka.com

Fishermans Friends
www.fishermansfriend.co.uk

Fresh Food Company
www.freshfood.co.uk

Frosties
www.frosties.co.uk

Fyffes
www.fyffes.com

Gerber Foods
www.gerberfoods.com

Godiva
www.godiva.com

Gourmet World
www.gourmet-world.co.uk

Grahams Port
www.grahams-port.com

Grand Marnier
www.grand-marnier.com

Haagen Dazs
www.haagen-dazs.com

Haribo
www.haribo.com

Harmonie
www.harmonie.co.uk

Harveys of Bristol
www.harveysbc.com

Heinz
www.heinz.co.uk

Homepride
www.homepride.co.uk

Horizon Foods
www.horizonfoods.com

Hula Hoops
www.hulahoops.co.uk

I Can't Believe It's Not Butter
www.tasteyoulove.com

Irn Bru
www.irn-bru.co.uk

Jaffa Cakes
www.jaffacakes.co.uk

Jelly Belly
www.jellybelly.com

Jersey Royals
www.jerseyroyals.co.uk

Kellogg's
www.kelloggs.co.uk

Kenco
www.kencocoffee.co.uk

Kerrygold
www.kerrygold.co.uk

Kinder Surprise
www.kindersurprise.co.uk

Kit-Kat
www.kitkat.co.uk

Kraft
www.kraftfoods.com

Lavazza
www.lavazza.com

Lift
www.lifttea.co.uk

Loch Fyne
www.loch-fyne.com

Lucozade
www.lucozade.co.uk

Mackies
www.mackies.co.uk

Malibu
www.malibu-rum.com

Mars
www.mars.com

Mini Heroes
www.miniheroes.co.uk

Moet & Chandon
www.moet.com

Moy Park
www.moypark.co.uk

Muller
www.muller.co.uk

Natco Spices
www.natco-foods.co.uk

Nescafe
www.nescafe.co.uk

Nesquik
www.nesquik.co.uk

Nestle
www.nestle.co.uk

Nimble
www.nimblebread.co.uk

Nutrasweet
www.nutrasweet.com

Old Speckled Hen
www.oldspeckledhen.co.uk

Olivetum Olive Oil
www.olivetum.com

Peperami
www.peperami.com

Pepsi
www.pepsi.co.uk

Pernod-Ricard
www.pernod-ricard.fr

Perrier
www.perrier.com

Pillsbury
www.pillsbury.com

Plymouth Gin
www.plymouthgin.com

Poppets
www.poppets.com

Primebake
www.primebake.co.uk

Pro Plus
www.proplus.co.uk

Quaker Oats
www.quakeroatmeal.com

Quorn
www.quorn.com

Rank Hovis
www.rankhovis.co.uk

Remy Martin
www.remy.com

Ridgways
www.ridgways.co.uk

Rivella
www.rivella.co.uk

Rombouts
www.rombouts.co.uk

Ryvita
www.ryvita.co.uk

Sara Lee
www.saraleebakery.com

Schwartz Herbs
www.schwartz.co.uk

Schweppes
www.schweppes.com

Sharwood's
www.sharwoods.com

Silver Spoon
www.silverspoon.co.uk

Slush Puppy
www.slushpuppy.co.uk

Smint
www.smint.co.uk

Smirnoff
www.smirnoff.com

Snickers
www.snickers.com

Southern Comfort
www.southerncomfort.com

Spam
www.spam.com

St Ivel
www.st-ivel.co.uk

Sunny Delight
www.sunnyd.co.uk

Sweet Factory
www.sweet-factory.com

Sweet'N Low
www.sweetnlow.com

Tango
www.tango.co.uk

Tate & Lyle
www.tate-lyle.co.uk

Thorntons
www.thorntons.co.uk

Tia Maria
www.tiamaria.co.uk

Tiptree
www.tiptree.com

Tizer
www.tizer.co.uk

Twinings Tea
www.twinings.co.uk

Twix
www.twix.com

Typhoo
www.typhoo.com

Uncle Ben's
www.unclebens.com

Unigate
www.unigate.plc.uk

United Biscuits
www.unitedbiscuits.co.uk

Utterly Butterly
www.utterly-butterly.co.uk

Van den Bergh Foods
www.vdbfoods.co.uk

Vichy
www.vichy.com

Virgin Cola
www.virgincola.co.uk

Volvic
www.volvic.co.uk

Walkers
www.walkers.co.uk

Wensleydale
www.wensleydale.co.uk

Whittard of Chelsea
www.whittard.com

Whitworths
www.whitworths.co.uk

Whole Earth
www.earthfoods.co.uk

Wotsits
www.wotsits.co.uk

Wrigley's
www.wrigley.com

Yakult
www.yakult.co.uk

Yeo Valley
www.yeo-organic.co.uk

Yogz
www.yogz.com

fast food

1st Pizza Direct (Inverness)
www.1stpizzadirect.co.uk

Burger King
www.burgerking.co.uk

Deliverance
www.deliverance.co.uk

Domino's Pizza
www.dominos.co.uk

Dunkin' Donuts
www.dunkindonuts.com

Four-in-One
www.fourinone.co.uk

Harry Ramsdens
www.harryramsdens.co.uk

KFC
www.kfc.co.uk

Kinness Fry Bar (St Andrews)
www.kfb-standrews.co.uk

Little Chef
www.little-chef.co.uk

McDonald's
www.mcdonalds.co.uk

Menu 2 Menu
www.menu2menu.com

Menus R Us
www.menusrus.net/Scotland.html

Perfect Pizza
www.perfectpizza.co.uk

Pizza Hut
www.pizzahut.co.uk

Pret A Manger
www.pret.com

Roadchef
www.roadchef.com

Room Service
www.roomservice.co.uk

Starbucks
www.starbucks.com

Subway
www.subway.co.uk

Wimpy
www.wimpyburgers.co.uk

Yo Sushi
www.yosushi.com

food & drink online

Betty's By Post (Harrogate)
www.bettysbypost.com

Bottoms Up
www.bottomsup.co.uk

Fortnum & Mason
www.fortnumandmason.co.uk

Harrods
www.harrods.com

Heinz Direct
www.heinz-direct.co.uk

Jane Asher Party Cakes
www.jane-asher.co.uk

Last Orders.com
www.lastorders.com

Le Gourmet Francais
www.gourmet2000.co.uk

Oddbins
www.oddbins.co.uk

Organics Direct
www.organicsdirect.com

Paxton & Whitfield
www.cheesemongers.co.uk

Price Offers
www.priceoffers.co.uk

Real Meat Company
www.realmeat.co.uk

Selfridges
www.selfridges.co.uk

Threshers
www.thresherwineshop.co.uk

Vegnet
www.vegnet.co.uk

Victoria Wine
www.victoriawine.co.uk

Whittards of Chelsea
www.whittard.com

Wine Cellar
www.winecellar.co.uk

food marketing

Associated British Meat
www.abm.org.uk

British Egg Information Service
www.britegg.co.uk

British Meat
www.britishmeat.org.uk

British Potato Council
www.potato.org.uk

Food from Britain
www.foodfrombritain.com

National Dairy Council
www.milk.co.uk

Pub Guide
www.william-reed.co.uk/magazines/
s_publife.html

Real Beer
http://realbeer.com

Scottish Food & Drink
www.scottishfoodanddrink.com

Tea Council
www.tea.co.uk

magazines & websites

Adlib
www.adlib.ie

BBC Food & Drink
www.bbc.co.uk/foodanddrink

Brewer
www.breworld.com/the_brewer

British Food Journal
www.mcb.co.uk/bfj.htm

Carlton Food Network
www.cfn.co.uk

Checkout Ireland
www.checkout.ie

Classicwhiskey.com
www.classicwhiskey.com

Consumers' Association of Ireland
www.consumerassociation.ie

Cooking Light
www.cookinglight.com

Decanter.com
www.decanter.com

Drinkwine.com
www.drinkwine.com

Dublin Drinking
www.dublindrinking.com

Eat@Home
www.eatathome.ie

Epicurious
www.epicurious.com

Fifth Sense
www.fifthsense.com

Food & Wine
www.foodandwine.ie

Food & Wine.net
www.foodandwine.net

Gourmet Ireland
www.gourmetireland.com

The Grocer
www.foodanddrink.co.uk

Ireland Guide
www.ireland-guide.com

Irish Pub Guide
www.irishpubguide.ie

IrishFood.com
www.irishfood.com

JustFood.com
www.justfood.com

Oz Clarke
www.ozclarke.com

Pub Guide
www.licensee.co.uk

Taste of Scotland
www.tasteofscotland.co.uk

VegDining
www.vegdining.com

Wine Spectator
www.winespectator.com

Wine Today
www.winetoday.com

manufacturers

International

Absolut Vodka
www.absolutvodka.com

Bacardi
www.bacardi.com

Ben & Jerry.s
www.benjerry.co.uk

Birds Eye
www.birdseye.com

Blue Dragon
www.bluedragon.co.uk

Boost
www.boost.co.uk

Buitoni
www.buitoni.co.uk

Campbell's
www.campbellsoup.com

Capri-Sun
www.capri-sun.com

Cheerios
www.cheerios.com

Chiquita
www.chiquita.com

Coca-Cola
www.coca-cola.co.uk

Crunchie
www.crunchie.co.uk

Cuisine de France
www.cuisinedefrance.co.uk

Danepak
www.danepak.co.uk

Danone
www.danonegroup.com

Del Monte
www.delmonte.com

Delifrance
www.delifrance.com

Dolmio
www.dolmio.com

Douwe Egberts
www.douwe-egberts.co.uk

Dr Pepper
www.drpepper.com

Drambuie
www.drambuie.co.uk

Dunkin Donuts
www.dunkindonuts.com

Evian
www.evian.com

Frosties
www.tonythetiger.com

Fyffes
www.fyffes.com

Gerber Foods
www.gerberfoods.com

Grand Marnier
www.grand-marnier.com

Haribo
www.haribo.com

Havana Club
www.havana-club.com

Heinz
www.heinz.com

Hellmann's/Bestfoods
www.bestfoods.com

Hula Hoops
www.hulahoops.co.uk

Häagen Dazs
www.haagen-dazs.com

Jack Daniel's
www.jackdaniels.co.uk

Jim Beam
www.jimbeam.com

Kellogg's
www.kelloggs.co.uk

Kenco
www.kencocoffee.co.uk

Kinder Surprise
www.kindersurprise.co.uk

KitKat
www.kitkat.co.uk

Knorr
www.unilever.co.uk/ourbrands/brand_knorr.html

Kraft
www.kraftfoods.com

Lucozade
www.lucozade.com

M&Ms
www.m-ms.com

Mars
www.mars.com

Moët & Chandon
www.moet.com

Monini
www.monini.com

Müller
www.muller.co.uk

Nabisco
www.chipsahoy.com

Nestlé
www.nestle.com

Nutella
www.nutella.it

Nutrasweet
www.nutrasweet.com

Nutri-Grain
www.nutri-grain.com

Old El Paso
www.oldelpaso.com

Peperami
www.peperami.com

Pepsi
www.pepsi.co.uk

Perrier
www.perrier.com

Pop Tarts
www.poptarts.com

Pringles
www.pringles.com

Provamel
www.provamel.co.uk

Quaker Oats
www.quakeroatmeal.com

Quorn
www.quorn.com

Ragu
www.ragu.com

Red Bull
www.redbull.com

Ryvita
www.ryvita.co.uk

Sara Lee
www.saraleebakery.com

Schwartz Herbs
www.schwartz.co.uk

Schweppes
www.cadburyschweppes.com

Sharwood's
www.sharwoods.com

Silver Spoon
www.silverspoon.co.uk

Smirnoff
www.smirnoff.com

Snapple
www.snapple.com

Snickers
www.snickers.com

Southern Comfort
www.southerncomfort.com

St Ivel
www.st-ivel.co.uk

Sunny Delight
www.sunnyd.com

Sweet'N Low
www.sweetnlow.com

Thorntons
www.thorntons.co.uk

Tropicana
www.tropicana.com

Twix
www.twix.com

Uncle Ben's
www.unclebens.com

Vegimite
www.vegemite.com.au

Walkers
www.walkers.co.uk

Weetabix
www.weetabix.co.uk

Whole Earth
www.earthfoods.co.uk

Wrigley's
www.wrigley.com

Yogz
www.yogz.com

Scottish

A P Jess
www.apjess.co.uk

Alex Dalgetty (Bannocks & Black Buns)
www.galashiels.bordernet.co.uk/alexdalgetty

Arbroath Fisheries
www.arbroath-smokie.co.uk

Ardtaraig Fine Foods
www.ardtaraigfinefoods.co.uk

Ashers Bakery
www.ashers-bakery.co.uk

Aulds the Bakers
www.aulds.co.uk

Barr's Irn Bru
www.irn-bru.co.uk

Baxters
www.baxters.co.uk

Brodies of Edinburgh
www.brodies1867.co.uk

Caledonian Curry
www.caledoniancurry.co.uk

Capaldi's Ice-Cream
www.capaldis.co.uk

Creeside Smokery
www.creeside.co.uk/smokedsalmon.htm

Dean's of Huntly
www.deans.co.uk

Deeside Spring Water
www.deesidespringwater.co.uk

Donald Russell
www.donaldrusselldirect.com

Duncans of Deeside (Shortbread)
www.nettrak.co.uk/houseofcaledonia/duncans_of_deeside.htm

Edinburgh Preserves
www.edinburgh-preserves.com

Eskside Bakery
www.esksidebakery.co.uk

G&G Sinclair
www.thejamkitchen.com

Gaffney Confectionery
www.gaffneyconfectionery.co.uk

Galloway Smokehouse
www.gallowaysmokehouse.co.uk

Gillies Fine Foods
www.gilliesfinefoods.co.uk

Gleneagles Water
www.highland-spring.com/the_company/gleneagles.asp

Grants
www.grantshaggis.com

Great Glen Fine Foods
www.greatglenfinefoods.co.uk

Haggis Hunt!
www.haggishunt.com

Heather Hills Honey
www.heather-hills.com

Highland Spring
www.highlandspring.com

I J Mellis
www.ijmellischeesemonger.co.uk

Inverawe Smokehouse
www.smoked-salmon.co.uk

Isabella's Preserves
www.isabellaspreserves.co.uk

Keltic Seafare
www.kelticseafare.com

Kinvara Smokery
www.kinvarasmokedsalmon.com

Krystal-Klear Soft Drinks
www.krystal-klear.com

Lawson of Speyside
www.lawson-of-speyside.com

Loch Fyne Oysters
www.loch-fyne.com

Macdonald's Smoked Produce
www.smokedproduce.co.uk

Mackay's
www.mackays.com

Mackie's Ice Cream
www.mackies.co.uk

Macphie of Glenbervie
www.macphie.com

Macsween's
www.macsween.co.uk

Mathiesons Fine Foods
www.mathiesons.co.uk

McKean's
www.scottishhaggis.co.uk

McLelland & Co
www.mclelland.co.uk

Miele's Ice-Cream
www.mieles.co.uk

Moniack Highland Wineries
www.moniackcastle.co.uk

Nardini's Ice-Cream
www.nardini.co.uk

Natural Mineral Water Information Service
www.naturalmineralwater.org

Orkney Quality Food & Drink
www.oqfd.co.uk

Orkney Shellfish
www.shellfish.co.uk

Paterson Arran
www.paterson-arran.com

Pettigrews of Kelso
www.pettigrews.com

Purely Scottish
www.purelyscottish.com

Rannoch Smokery
www.rannochsmokery.co.uk

Renshaw Scott
www.renshawscott.co.uk

S Luca Ice-Cream
www.s-luca.co.uk

Salar Smokery
www.salar.co.uk

Shetland Smokehouse
www.shetlandsmokehouse.co.uk

Simmers-Nairns Biscuits
www.simmers-nairns.com

Simply Organic
www.simplyorganic.co.uk

Strathmore Mineral Water
www.matthewclark.co.uk/brands/strathmore.shtml

Tombuie Smokehouse
www.tombuie.com

Walkers Shortbread
www.walkers-shortbread.co.uk

Wicken Fen Vegetarian Foods
www.wickenfen.co.uk

William Sword Bakers
www.williamsword.co.uk

Williamson Fruit
www.williamsonfruit.co.uk

professional bodies

Brewers & Licensed Retailers Association of Scotland
www.blras.org

British Beer & Pubs Association
www.beerandpub.com

British Society of Baking
www.bsb.org.uk

Cask Marque
www.cask-marque.co.uk

English Wine Producers
www.englishwineproducers.com

FSA Mineral Water List
www.foodstandards.gov.uk/foodindustry/42877

National Association of Master Bakers
www.masterbakers.co.uk

Natural Mineral Water Information Service
www.naturalmineralwater.org

Scottish Association of Master Bakers
www.samb.co.uk

Scottish Food & Drink
www.scottishfoodanddrink.com

Society of Independent Brewers
www.siba.co.uk

restaurants & bars

Aquarium
www.theaquarium.co.uk

Balls Brothers
www.ballsbrothers.co.uk

Bank
www.bankrestaurant.co.uk

Belgo
www.belgo-restaurants.co.uk

Benihana
www.benihana.co.uk

Bibendum
www.bibendum.co.uk

Blue Elephant
www.blueelephant.com

Blue Print Café
www.conran.co.uk/restaurants/blueprint

Café Rouge
www.caferouge.co.uk

Cantina Del Ponte
www.conran.co.uk/restaurants/cantina

The Ceilidh Place (Highland)
www.theceilidhplace.com

The Cellar (Fife)
www.theaa.com/restaurants/5653.html

Chez Gerard
www.sante-gcg.com/chezgerard/chez-home.html

Corney & Barrow
www.corney-barrow-winebars.co.uk

Cringletie House Hotel (Borders)
www.cringletie.com

Cromlix House (Stirling)
www.cromlixhouse.com

The Cross (Highland)
www.thecross.co.uk

Fashion Café
www.fashion-cafe.com

Fatty Arbuckle's
www.fatty-arbuckles.co.uk

Fish!
www.fishdiner.co.uk

Football Football
www.footballfootball.com

Greenhouse
www.capital-london.net/greenhouse/index.html

Greywalls (E Lothian)
www.greywalls.co.uk

Hard Rock Café
www.hardrock.com

Harry Ramsden's
www.harryramsdens.co.uk

Isle of Eriska Hotel (Argyll)
www.eriska-hotel.co.uk

Jazz Café
www.jazzcafe.co.uk

Le Pont de la Tour
www.conran.co.uk/restaurants/lepont

Leith's
www.leiths.com

Loch Fyne Seafood
www.loch-fyne.com

Loch Melfort Hotel
www.lochmelfort.co.uk

Moshi Moshi
www.moshimoshi.co.uk

Nando's Chickenland UK
www.nandos.co.uk

Offshore
www.offshore.co.uk

The Peat Inn (Fife)
www.thepeatinn.co.uk

People's Palace
www.capital-london.net/peoples-palace/index.html

Pharmacy
www.outpatients.co.uk

Pizza Express
www.pizzaexpress.co.uk

Pizza Hut
www.pizzahut.com

Planet Hollywood
www.planethollywood.com

Porters
www.porters.uk.com

Prism
www.prismrestaurant.com

Rainforest Café
www.rainforestcafe.com

Red Fort
www.redfort.co.uk

Ritz
www.theritzhotel.co.uk/restaurant

Rock Garden
www.rockgarden.co.uk

Rules
www.rules.co.uk

Sardis
www.sardis.com

Savoy Grill
www.savoy-group.co.uk/savoy/dining/savoy_grill.html

Scarista House (Harris)
www.scaristahouse.com

Silver Darling (Aberdeen)
www.webcafe.co.uk/Restaurants/Seafood/Silver_Darling/silver_darling.html

Sticky Fingers
www.stickyfingers.co.uk

The Three Chimneys (Skye)
www.threechimneys.co.uk

Veeraswamy
www.veeraswamy.com

Wagamama
www.wagamama.com

Waterfront (Oban)
www.waterfront-restaurant.co.uk

Waterside Inn
www.waterside-inn.co.uk

Wiltons
www.wiltons.co.uk

Yo! Sushi
www.yosushi.co.uk

Edinburgh

The Atrium
www.atriumrestaurant.co.uk

Dubh Prais
www.bencraighouse.co.uk

Duck's
http://ducks.co.uk

Edinburgh Restauranteurs Association
www.edinburghrestaurants.co.uk

Forth Floor
www.harveynichols.com

Haldanes
www.haldanesrestaurant.com

Henderson's
www.hendersonsofedinburgh.co.uk

Howies
www.howies.uk.com

The Hub
www.eif.co.uk/thehub

Martin Wishart
www.martin-wishart.co.uk

Martins
www.edinburghrestaurants.co.uk/martins.html

Merchants
www.merchantsrestaurant.co.uk

Skippers
www.skippers.co.uk

Stac Polly
www.stacpolly.com

Tapas Tree
www.tapastree.co.uk

The Tower
www.tower-restaurant.com

Valvona & Crolla
www.valvonacrolla.co.uk

The Vintners Rooms
www.thevintnersrooms.demon.co.uk

Waterfront
www.edinburgh-waterfront.com

The Witchery
www.thewitchery.com

Glasgow

Bouzy Rouge
www.bouzy-rouge.com

Frango
www.frangorestaurant.co.uk

Gamba
www.gamba.co.uk

Glasgow Restauranteurs Association
www.bestglasgowrestaurants.com

Groucho St Judes
www.saintjudes.com

Malmaison
www.malmaison.com

Mussel Inn
www.mussel-inn.com

Nairns
www.nairns.co.uk

Papingo
www.papingo.co.uk

Stravaigin
www.stravaigin.com

Ubiquitous Chip
www.ubiquitouschip.co.uk

Guide

AA Restaurant Guide
www.theaa.com/restaurants

The List (restaurant listings)
www.list.co.uk

The Oracle (restaurant search)
http://theoracle.co.uk

Which Guides
www.which.net

state agencies

Department of Environment, Food & Rural Affairs (DEFRA)
www.defra.gov.uk

Food Standards Agency
www.foodstandards.gov.uk

Health & Safety Executive & Scottish Executive
www.hse.gov.uk/scotland/scordat.htm

Scottish Executive Agriculture & Food
www.scotland.gov.uk/whatwedo.asp

World Food Safety Organisation
www.worldfoodsafety.org

supermarkets

Aldi
www.aldi-stores.co.uk

Asda
www.asda.co.uk

Budgens
www.budgens.co.uk

Co-op
www.co-op.co.uk

Iceland
www.iceland.co.uk

Londis
www.londis.co.uk

Marks & Spencer
www.marksandspencer.com

Morrisons
www.morrisons.plc.uk

Safeway
www.safeway.co.uk

Sainsburys
www.jsainsbury.co.uk

Savacentre
www.savacentre.co.uk

Somerfield
www.somerfield.co.uk

Spar
www.spar.co.uk

Tesco
www.tescodirect.com

Waitrose
www.waitrose.co.uk

trade associations

Allied Brewers Traders Association
www.breworld.com/abta

Brewers & Licensed Retailers Association
www.blra.co.uk

Brewers' & Maltsters' Guild of Ireland
www.dublinbrewing.com/excise.html

British Potato Council
www.potato.org.uk

British Sandwich Association
www.martex.co.uk/bsa

Catering Equipment Distributors Association
www.ceda.co.uk

Consortium of Caterers & Administration in Education
www.fairtry.ndirect.co.uk/ccaeduc

Federation of Bakers
www.bakersfederation.org.uk

Food & Drink Federation
www.fdf.org.uk

Gin & Vodka Association of Great Britain
www.ginvodka.org

Hygiene Mark
www.hygienemark.com

Institute of Brewing
www.breworld.com/iob

Institute of Food Research
www.ifrn.bbsrc.ac.uk

Institute of Food Science & Technology
www.ifst.org

International Association of Culinary Professionals
www.iacp-online.org

International Brewers' Guild
www.breworld.com/brewersguild

International Food Information Council
http://ific.org/food

National Association of Catering Butchers
www.haighs.com/nacb.htm

National Association of Master Bakers
www.masterbakers.co.uk

National Farmers' Union
www.nfu.org.uk

National Federation of Fish Friers
www.federationoffishfriers.co.uk

National Pasta Association
www.ilovepasta.org

National Soft Drink Association
www.nsda.org

Restaurant Association
www.ragb.co.uk

Scotch Whisky Association
www.scotch-whisky.org.uk

Traidcraft Exchange
www.traidcraft.co.uk

Worshipful Company of Bakers
www.bakers.co.uk

whisky

Aberlour
www.aberlour.co.uk

Adelphi Distillery
www.highlandtrail.co.uk

Allied Domecq
www.allieddomecqplc.com

Ardbeg
www.ardbeg.com

Arran Whisky
www.arranwhisky.com

Ballantines
www.ballantines.com

Bowmore
www.bowmorescotch.com

Chivas
www.chivas.com

Cragganmore
www.scotch.com

Cutty Sark
www.cutty-sark.com

Dalwhinnie
www.scotch.com

Dew of Ben Nevis
www.bennevisdistillery.com

Dewar's Scotch Whisky
www.dewars.com

Douglas Laing & Co
www.douglaslaing.com/main.htm

Edradour
www.edradour.co.uk

Edrington Group
www.edringtongroup.com

Famous Grouse
www.famousgrouse.com

Glen Moray
www.glenmoray.com

Glen Ord
www.glenord.com

Glencoe
www.bennevisdistillery.com

Glenfarclas
www.glenfarclas.co.uk

Glenfiddich
www.glenfiddich.com

Glengoyne
www.glengoynedistillery.co.uk

Glenkinchie
www.scotch.com

Glenlivet
www.glenlivet.com

Glenmorangie
www.glenmorangie.com

Glenturret
www.glenturret.com

Gordon & MacPhail
www.gordonandmacphail.com

Green Spot
www.mitchellandson.com/features/greenspt.htm

Highland Park
www.highlandpark.co.uk

Ian Mcleod & Co
www.ianmacleod.com

International Whisky Co Ltd
www.royalsilk.com

Inverhouse Distillery
www.inverhouse.com

Islay
www.islaywhisky.com

Islay Whisky Society
www.islaywhiskysociety.com

J & B
www.jbscotch.com

Jack Daniels
www.jackdaniels.co.uk

Jameson
www.jameson.ie

Jim Beam
www.jimbeam.com

Johnnie Walker
www.smws.com

Kyndal
www.kyndal.co.uk

Lagavulin
www.scotch.com

Laphroaig
www.laphroaig.com

Macallan
www.themacallan.com

Midleton
www.classicwhiskey.com/distilleries/midleton.htm

Morrison Bowmore
www.morrisonbowmore.co.uk

North British Distillery Co
www.northbritish.co.uk

Oban
www.scotch.com

Pernod Ricard
www.pernod-ricard.com

Scotch Malt Whisky Society
www.smws.com

Scotch Whisky.com
www.scotchwhisky.com

Scotch Whisky Heritage Centre
www.whisky-heritage.co.uk

Seagram
www.seagram.com

Southern Comfort
www.southerncomfort.com

Talisker
www.scotch.com

Tullamore Dew
www.tullamore-dew.org

Whisky Magazine
www.whiskymag.com

Whisky Directory
www.scotlandonline.com/heritage/heritage_whisky.cfm

Whisky Shop
www.whiskyshop.com

wine

Berry Bros & Rudd
www.berry-bros.co.uk

Bodegas Faustino
www.bodegasfaustino.com

Bordeaux Direct
www.bordeauxdirect.co.uk

Bordeaux Index
www.bordeauxindex.com

Consort Connoisseur Wine Storage
www.wine-cellars-uk.co.uk

Cranwick
www.cranwick.com

Everywine
www.everywine.co.uk

Forth Wines
www.matthewclark.co.uk/forth_wines/welcome.shtml

Front Page Wines
www.frontpagewines.com

Haddows
www.victoriawine.co.uk/htm/haddows.htm

Hardys
www.hardys-wines.com

Institute of Masters of Wine
www.masters-of-wine.org

International Wine & Food Society
www.brodie.co.uk/iwfs/frames_main.htm

International Wine Challenge
www.intwinechallenge.co.uk

iWine
www.iwine.com

Jacobs Creek
www.jacobscreek.com

Laithwaites
www.laithwaites.co.uk

Laytons
www.laytons.co.uk

Leinster Merchant Wines
www.merchantwines.com

Lindemans
www.lindemans.co.uk

Matthew Clark
www.matthewclark.co.uk

Oddbins
www.oddbins.com

Orgasmic Wines
www.orgasmicwines.com

Portman Group
www.portman-group.org.uk

The Wine Society
www.thewinesociety.com

Victoria Wine
www.victoriawine.co.uk

Vinopolis
www.vinopolis.co.uk

Virgin Wines
www.virginwines.com

Waverley Vintners
www.waverley-direct.co.uk

Wine & Spirit Association
www.wsa.org.uk

Wine Development Board of Ireland
www.wineboard.com

Wine Lovers Page
www.wineloverspage.com

Wine Pages
www.wine-pages.com

Wine Today
www.winetoday.com

Winefiles
www.winefiles.org

Wineraks
www.wineraks.co.uk

Wonderful Wine
www.wonderful-wines.co.uk

- armed forces
- embassies
- foreign government
- international organisations
- law
- legal institutions abroad
- monarchy
- overseas territories & crown dependencies
- political parties
- post offices
- pressure groups
- professional associations
- research councils
- scottish executive
- scottish parliament
- UK government

armed forces

Air Training Corps (ATC)
www.aircadets.org/site

Army Records Office
www.army.mod.uk/contacts/divisions/records.htm

British Army
www.army.mod.uk

RAF Careers
www.raf-careers.com

Royal Air Force
www.raf.mod.uk

Royal Air Forces Association
www.rafa.org.uk

Royal Auxillary Air Force
www.rauxaf.mod.uk

Royal Marines
www.royal-marines.mod.uk

Royal Navy
www.royal-navy.mod.uk

Royal Navy Careers
www.royal-navy.mod.uk/careers

Territorial Army
www.army.mod.uk/ta

embassies

British Embassies Abroad

Australia
www.uk.emb.gov.au

Azerbaijan
www.britishembassy.az

Bahrain
www.ukembassy.gov.bh

Bangladeshi
www.ukinbangladesh.org

Belgium
www.british-embassy.be

Brunei
www.britain-brunei.org

Bulgaria
www.british-embassy.bg

Cameroon
http://britcam.org

Canada
www.bis-canada.org

Chilean
www.britemb.cl

Cyprus
www.britain.org.cy

Czech Republic
www.britain.cz

Denmark
www.britishembassy.dk

Ecuadorian
www.britembquito.org.ec

European Union
http://ukrep.fco.gov.uk

Fiji
www.ukinthepacific.bhc.org.fj

Finland
www.ukembassy.fi

France
www.amb-grandebretagne.fr

Germany
www.britischebotschaft.de

Greece
www.british-embassy.gr

Hong Kong
www.britishconsulate.org.hk

Hungarian
www.britishembassy.hu

India
www.ukinindia.org

Indonesia
www.britain-in-indonesia.or.id

Israel
www.britemb.org.il

Italy
www.britain.it

Japan
www.gate-uk.co.jp/embassy

Jordan
www.britain.org.jo

Korean Republic
www.britain.or.kr

Latvian
www.britain.lv

Lebanon
www.britishembassy.org.lb

Lithuanian
www.britain.lt

Malaysian
www.britain.org.my

Mexico
www.embajadabritanica.com.mx

Netherlands
www.britishembassy.org.nl

New Zealand
www.brithighcomm.org.nz

Norway
www.britain.no

Pakistan
http://britainonline.org.pk

Poland
www.britishembassy.pl

Romanian
www.britain.ro

Russian Federation
www.britemb.msk.ru

Singapore
www.britain.org.sg

Slovak Republic
www.britemb.sk

Slovenia
www.british-embassy.si

South Africa
www.britain.org.za

Sweden
www.britishembassy.com

Switzerland
www.britain-in-switzerland.ch

Taiwan
www.btco.org.tw

Thailand
www.britishemb.or.th

Tunisia
www.british-emb.intl.tn

Turkish
www.britishembassy.org.tr

Turkmenistan
www.britishembassytm.org.uk

Ukraine
www.britemb-ukraine.net

United Arab Emirates
www.britain-uae.org

United Nations
www.ukun.org

USA
www.britainusa.com

Uzbekistan
www.britain.uz

Venezuela
www.britain.org.ve

Vietnam
www.uk-vietnam.org

Foreign Embassies & Consulates in the UK

Algerian
www.personal.u-net.com/~consalglond

American
www.usembassy.org.uk

Antiguan
www.antigua-barbuda.com

Argentinian
www.argentine-embassy-uk.org.uk

Australian
www.australia.org.uk

Austrian
www.bmaa.gv.at/embassy/uk

Belarussian
www.belemb.freeserve.co.uk

Belgian
www.belgium-embassy.co.uk

Brazilian
www.brazil.org.uk

Canadian
www.canada.org.uk

Chilean
www.echileuk.demon.co.uk

Chinese
www.chinese-embassy.org.uk

Colombian
www.colombia.uklatino.com

Costa Rican
www.embcrlon.demon.co.uk

Czech
www.czech.org.uk/political.htm

Danish
www.denmark.org.uk

Egyptian
www.egypt-embassy.org.uk

Estonian
www.estonia.gov.uk

Ethiopian
www.ethioembassy.org.uk

Finnish
www.finemb.org.uk

French
www.ambafrance.org.uk

German
www.german-embassy.org.uk

Hungarian
http://dspace.dial.pipex.com/huemblon

Icelandic
www.iceland.org.uk

Indian
www.hcilondon.org

Iranian
www.iran-embassy.org.uk

Israeli
www.israel-embassy.org.uk

Italian
www.embitaly.org.uk

Jamaican
www.jhcuk.com

Japanese
www.embjapan.org.uk

Jordanian
www.jordanembassyuk.gov.jo

Kazakh
www.kazakhstan-embassy.org.uk

Krygyz Republic Embassy
www.kyrgyz-embassy.org.uk

Lithuanian
www.users.globalnet.co.uk/~lralon

Luxembourg
www.luxembourg.co.uk

Mexican
www.embamex.co.uk

New Zealand
www.newzealandhc.org.uk

Norwegian
www.norway.org.uk

Peruvian
www.peruembassy-uk.com

Philippines
www.philemb.demon.co.uk

Polish
www.poland-embassy.org.uk

Portuguese
www.portembassy.gla.ac.uk

Romanian
www.embassyhomepage.com/romania

Royal Napelese
www.nepembassy.org.uk

Royal Netherlands
www.netherlands-embassy.org.uk

Russian
www.britemb.msk.ru

Saudi Arabian
www.saudiembassy.org.uk/index2.htm

Singaporean
www.mfa.gov.sg/london

Slovak Republic
www.slovakembassy.co.uk

Slovenian
www.embassy-slovenia.org.uk

South African
www.southafricahouse.com

Spanish
www.spanishembassy.org.uk

Sri Lankan
http://ourworld.compuserve.com/homepages/lanka

Swedish
www.swedish-embassy.org.uk

Swiss
www.swissembassy.org.uk

Tanzanian
www.tanzania-online.gov.uk

Thai
www.thaiconsul-uk.com

Turkish
www.turkishembassy-london.com

Venezuelan
www.venezlon.demon.co.uk

Yemenese
http://users.pgen.net/embassy/yemen.htm

foreign government

Albanian
http://mininf.gov.al/shqip/default.asp

Algerian
www.gga.dz/dwww/english

Andorran
www.andorra.ad/govern

Angolan
www.angola.org

Antigua & Bermuda
www.antigua-barbuda.org

Argentinian
www.senado.gov.ar

Armenia
www.gov.am

Australian
www.fed.gov.au

Australian Parliament
www.aph.gov.au

Austrian
www.parlinkom.gv.at

Azerbaijan
www.president.az

Bahamas
www.bahamas.com

Bahrain
www.bahrain.gov.bh

Bangladeshi
www.bangladeshgov.org

Barbadan
www.barbados.gov.bb

Belarussian
www.president.gov.by/eng

Belgian
www.belgium.fgov.be

Belize
www.belize.gov.bz

Benin
www.nationbynation.com/Benin/Gov.html

Bhutan
www.kingdomofbhutan.com

Bolivian
www.congreso.gov.bo

Bosnia & Herzegovina
www.parlamentfbih.gov.ba

Botswanan
www.gov.bw

Brazilian
www.brasil.gov.br

British Virgin Islands
www.bvi.gov.vg

Brunei
www.brunet.bn

Bulgarian
www.na.acad.bg

Burkina Faso
www.primature.gov.bf

Burundi
www.burundi.gov.bi

Cambodian
www.cambodian-parliament.org

Cameroon
www.camnet.cm/celcom/homepr.htm

Canadian
www.canada.gc.ca

Chilean
www.presidencia.cl

Chinese
www.gov.cn

Colombian
www.gobiernoenlinea.gov.co

Congo (Republic)
www.photius.com/wfb2000/countries/congo_republic_of_the/congo_republic_of_the_government.html

Cook Islands
www.cook-islands.gov.ck

Costa Rican
www.casapres.go.cr

Cote D'Ivoire
www.pr.ci

Croatian
www.sabor.hr

Cuban
www.cubagov.cu

Cypriot
www.pio.gov.cy

Czech
www.vlada.cz

Danish
www.folketinget.dk

Djibouti
www.education.dj

Dominican
www.presidencia.gov.do

Dutch
www.parlement.nl

Ecuador
www.ec-gov.net

Egyptian
www.presidency.gov.eg

El Salvador
www.casapres.gob.sv

Estonian
www.vm.ee/eng

Ethiopian
www.ethiopar.net

Federated States of Micronesia
http://fsmgov.org/ngovt.html

Fiji
www.fiji.gov.fj

Finnish
http://virtual.finland.fi

French
www.assemblee-nat.fr

Gabon
www.senat-gabon.org

Gambian
www.gambia.com

Georgian
www.presidpress.gov.ge

German
www.government.de

German (Parliament)
www.bundesregierung.de

Ghana
www.ghana.gov.gh

Greek
www.mpa.gr

Guatemala
www.congreso.gob.gt

Guinea
www.guinee.gov.gn

Haitian
www.mdnhaiti.org

Honduras
www.congreso.gob.hn

Hong Kong
www.info.gov.hk

Hungarian
www.mkogy.hu

Icelandic
www.althingi.is

Indian
http://alfa.nic.in

Indian Government
www.indiagov.org

Indonesian
www.dpr.go.id

Iranian
www.president.ir

Iraqi
www.uruklink.net/naoi

Irish
www.irlgov.ie

Israeli
www.info.gov.il

Israeli (Foreign Affairs)
www.israel.org

Italian
http://english.camera.it

Jamaican
www.cabinet.gov.jm

Japanese
www.kantei.go.jp

Jordanian
www.arab.net/jordan/jn_national.htm

Kazakhstan
www.president.kz

Kenyan
www.kenyaweb.com/government

Korean
www.assembly.go.kr

Krygyzstan
www.gov.kg

Kuwaiti
www.kna.org.kw

Latvian
www.mfa.gov.lv

Lebanese
www.lp.gov.lb

Liberian
www.liberiaemb.org

Libya
www.arab.net/libya/la_national.htm

Liechtenstein
www.photius.com/wfb1999/liechtenstein/liechtenstein_government.html

Lithuanian
www.lrvk.lt

Luxembourg
www.chd.lu

Macedonian
www.gov.mk

Madagascar
www.assemblee-nationale.mg

Malaysian
www.parlimen.gov.my

Maldives
www.presidencymaldives.gov.mv

Maltese
www.gov.mt

Mauritanian
www.mauritania.mr

Mauritius
http://ncb.intnet.mu/govt

Mexican
www.senado.gob.mx

Moldova
www.moldova.md

Mongolian
www.pmis.gov.mn

Morocco
www.pm.gov.ma

Mozambique
www.mozambique.mz

Namibia
www.op.gov.na

New Zealand
www.govt.nz

Nicaragua
www.asamblea.gob.ni

Nigerian
www.nopa.net

Norwegian
www.stortinget.no

Omani
www.omanet.com

Pakistani
www.pak.gov.pk/govt

Palestinian
www.pna.net

Panamanian
www.presidencia.gob.pa

Paraguay
www.nationbynation.com/Paraguay/Gov.html

Peruvian
www.congreso.gob.pe

Philippino
www.asiadragons.com/philippines/government_and_politics

Polish
www.poland.pl

Portuguese
www.parlamento.pt

Qatar
www.gov.qa

Romanian
www.guv.ro

Russian
www.gov.ru

Russian (Parliament)
www.duma.ru

Rwanda
www.rwanda1.com/government

Samoan
www.asg-gov.com

Saudi Arabian
www.saudinf.com

Senegalese
www.primature.sn

Sierra Leonian
www.sierra-leone.gov.sl

Singaporean
www.gov.sg

Slovakian
www.government.gov.sk

Slovenian
www.dz-rs.si

South African
www.polity.org.za

South Korean
www.cwd.go.kr

Spanish
www.la-moncloa.es

Sri Lankan
www.priu.gov.lk

St Kitts & St Nevis
www.interknowledge.com/stkitts-nevis/index.html

Swaziland
www.swazi.com/government

Swedish
www.sweden.gov.se

Swiss
www.admin.ch

Tanzanian
www.tanzania.go.tz

Thai
www.parliament.go.th

Togan
www.republicoftogo.com

Trinidad & Tobagan
www.ttparliament.org

Tunisian
www.ministeres.tn

Turkish
www.tbmm.gov.tr

Turkish Cypriot
www.cm.gov.nc.tr

Uganda
www.parliament.go.ug

Ukranian
www.rada.kiev.ua

United Arab Emirates
www.uae.gov.ae

Uruguayan
www.parlamento.gub.uy

USA – Congress
www.congress.org

USA – House of Representatives
www.house.gov

USA – Senate
www.senate.gov

USA – White House
www.whitehouse.gov

Uzbekistani
www.gov.uz

Vatican
www.vatican.va

Venezuelan
www.parlamento.gov.ve

Yemenite
www.yemeninfo.gov.ye

Yugoslavian
www.gov.yu

Zambian
www.statehouse.gov.zm

Zimbabwe
www.gta.gov.zw

international organisations

African Union (formerly OAU)
www.africa-union.org

Amnesty International
www.amnesty.org

Arctic Council
www.arctic-council.org

Commonwealth
www.tcol.co.uk

Council of Europe
www.coe.fr

Council of Europe
www.coe.int

EU
www.europa.eu.int

European Central Bank
www.ecb.int

European Commission
www.europa.eu.int

European Court of Justice
www.curia.eu.int/en

European Investment Bank
www.eib.eu.int

European Monetary Union
www.europeanmovement.ie/emu.htm

European Parliament
www.europarl.eu.int

European Trade Union Confederation
www.etuc.org

European Union
www.europa.eu.int

G8
www.g7.utoronto.ca

Human Rights Watch
www.hrw.org

Institute of World Politics
www.iwp.edu

Inter American Commission on Human Rights
www.oas.org

International Atomic Agency
www.icao.int

International Crisis Group
www.intl-crisis-group.org

International Maritime Organisation
www.imo.org

International Monetary Fund
www.imf.org

International Red Cross
www.icrc.org

NATO
www.nato.int

Organisation for Economic Co-operation & Development (OECD)
www.oecd.org

Organisation of American States
www.oas.org

Organisation of Petroleum Exporting Countries (OPEC)
www.opec.org

Red Cross
www.icrc.org

Royal Commonwealth Society
www.rcsint.org

Smithsonian Institution
www.si.edu

UN
www.un.org

UNICEF (United Nations Children's Fund)
www.unicef.org

Union of International Associations
www.uia.org/website.htm

United Nations
www.un.org

World Bank
www.worldbank.org

World Health Organisation
www.who.int

World Meteorological Organisation
www.wmo.ch

World Trade Organisation
www.wto.org

law

Advisory, Conciliation & Arbitration Service
www.acas.org.uk

Avocates
www.advocates.org

Civil Justice Council
www.civiljusticecouncil.gov.uk

Court of Session
www.scotcourts.gov.uk/session/session.htm

Criminal Cases Review Commission
www.ccrc.gov.uk

Criminal Justice System
www.criminal-justice-system.gov.uk

Crown Office
www.crownoffice.gov.uk

Edinburgh Public Defender
www.pdso.demon.co.uk

Employment Appeal Tribunal
www.employmentappeals.gov.uk

European Court of Human Rights
www.echr.coe.int

European Court of Justice
http://europa.eu.int/cj/en

High Court of Justiciary
www.scotcourts.gov.uk/justiciary/justiciary.htm

House of Lords (Court)
www.parliament.the-stationery-office.co.uk/pa/ld/ldjudinf.htm

International Bar Association
www.ibanet.org

International Court of Justice
www.icj-cij.org

Law Society of Scotland
www.lawscot.org.uk

Magistrates' Association
www.magistrates-association.org.uk

Scottish Courts Service
www.scotcourts.gov.uk

Scottish Human Rights Centre
www.scottishhumanrightscentre.org.uk

Scottish Law Online
www.scottishlaw.org.uk

Serious Fraud Office
www.sfo.gov.uk

Sheriff Courts
www.scotcourts.gov.uk/html/sheriff.htm

Society for Computers & Law
www.scl.org

Youth Justice Board
www.youth-justice-board.gov.uk

legal institutions abroad

Australia
www.fedcourt.gov.au

Brazil
www.trt10.gov.br

Canada
www.courts.gov.bc.ca

Croatia
www.croadria.com/zupsudbj

Egypt
www.us.sis.gov.eg/online/html/ol0412a.htm

Hong Kong
www.info.gov.hk/index_e.htm

India
www.supremecourtofindia.com

Ireland
www.local.ie/society_and_government/government/law

Israel
www.court.gov.il

Japan
www.courts.go.jp

Jordan
www.nic.gov.jo/gid/constitution

Kenya
www.statehousekenya.go.ke

Korea
www.scourt.go.kr/menu_eng.html

Malaysia
www.mahkamah.gov.my

Mexico
http://info.juridicas.unam.mx

New Zealand
www.courts.govt.nz

Pakistan
www.pakistanbiz.com/pakistan/judiciary.html

Phillipines
www.supremecourt.gov.ph

Singapore
www.gov.sg/judiciary/supremect

South Africa
www.concourt.gov.za/constitution

Turkey
www.turkey.org/politics/p_judici.htm

USA
www.uscourts.gov

monarchy

Crown Estate
www.crownestate.co.uk

Queens Gallery, Hollyroodhouse
www.royal.gov.uk/output/Page623.asp

The Queens Gallery
www.royal.gov.uk/output/Page1208.asp

The Royal Mews
www.royal.gov.uk/output/page556.asp

Royal Family

Diana, Princess of Wales (Obituary)
www.royal.gov.uk/output/page151.asp

HM Queen Elizabeth
www.royal.gov.uk/output/page412.asp

HM Queen Elizabeth, Queen Mother (Obituary)
www.royal.gov.uk/output/page1011.asp

HRH Duke of York
www.royal.gov.uk/output/page416.asp

HRH Earl of Wessex
www.royal.gov.uk/output/page417.asp

HRH Prince of Wales
www.royal.gov.uk/output/page415.asp

HRH Prince Philip, Duke of Edinburgh
www.royal.gov.uk/output/page413.asp

HRH Princess Alexandra
www.royal.gov.uk/output/page424.asp

HRH Princess Margaret (Obituary)
www.royal.gov.uk/output/page948.asp

HRH Princess Royal
www.royal.gov.uk/output/page418.asp

TRH Duke & Duchess of Kent
www.royal.gov.uk/output/page422.asp

TRH Princess Alice, Duchess of Gloucester & the Duke & Duchess of Gloucester
www.royal.gov.uk/output/page420.asp

Royal Palaces

Balmoral
http://www.royal.gov.uk/output/page560.asp

Buckingham Palace
www.royal.gov.uk/output/page555.asp

Frogmore House
www.royal.gov.uk/output/page558.asp

Kensington Palace
www.royal.gov.uk/output/page563.asp

Sandringham House
www.royal.gov.uk/output/page561.asp

St James's Palace
www.royal.gov.uk/output/page562.asp

The Palace of Holyroodhouse
www.royal.gov.uk/output/page559.asp

Windsor Castle
www.royal.gov.uk/output/page557.asp

overseas territories & crown dependencies

Anguilla
www.gov.ai

British Virgin Islands
www.britishvirginislands.com

Cayman Islands
www.gov.ky

Falklands Islands Government
www.falklands.gov.fk

Gibraltar
www.gibraltar.gov.gi

Isle of Man Government
www.gov.im

Pitcairn Islands
http://users.iconz.co.nz/pitcairn

St Helena
www.sainthelena.gov.sh

Turks & Caicos Islands
www.tcimall.tc/Government

political parties

Scottish Conservative Party
www.scottishtories.org.uk

Scottish Labour Party
www.scottishlabour.org.uk

Scottish Socialist Party
www.scottishsocialistparty.org

Communist Party
www.myspace.co.uk/cp-of-britain

Conservative Party
www.tory.org.uk

Democratic Unionist Party, Northern Ireland
www.dup.org.uk

Green Party, England & Wales
www.greenparty.org.uk

Green Party, Scotland
www.scottishgreens.org.uk

Green Party, Wales
www.walesgreenparty.org.uk

Labour Party
www.labour.org.uk

Liberal Democratic Party
www.libdems.org.uk

Natural Law Party
www.natural-law-party.org.uk

Plaid Cymru, Wales
www.plaid-cymru.wales.com

Progressive Unionist Party
www.pup.org

Scottish Liberal Democratic Party
www.scotlibdems.org.uk

Scottish Nationalist Party
www.snp.org.uk

Sinn Fein, Northern Ireland
www.sinnfein.ie

Social & Democratic Labour Party, Northern Ireland
www.sdlp.ie

Socialist Party
www.socialistparty.org.uk

Ulster Unionist Party
www.uup.org

Foreign

African National Congress, South Africa
www.anc.org.za

Christian Democratic Party
www.cda.nl

Communist Party, Russian Federation
www.geocities.com/CapitolHill/Lobby/3198

Communist Party, USA
www.cpusa.org

Democratic Party, Australia
www.democrats.org.au

Democratic Party, USA
www.democrats.org

International Socialist Organisation
www.internationalsocialist.org

Labour Party, Australia
www.alp.org.au

Labour Party, New Zealand
www.labour.org.nz

Labour Party, Norway
www.politicalresources.net/no-dna.htm

Liberal Democratic Party, Japan
www.jimin.or.jp/jimin/english

Liberal Party, Australia
www.liberal.org.au

Liberal Party, Canada
www.liberal.ca

National Congress, India
www.indiancongress.org

National Party, New Zealand
www.national.org.nz

Nationalist Party, Vietnam
www.vietquoc.com

People's Party, Pakistan
www.ppp.org.pk

Reform Party
www.reformparty.org

Republican Movement, Australia
www.republic.org.au

Republican Party, Ireland
www.fiannafail.ie

Republican Party, USA
www.rnc.org

Social Democratic Party, Germany
www.spd.de

United Democratic Front, Nigeria
www.udfn.com

United National Party, Sri Lanka
www.lanka.net/lisl2/yellow/unp

post offices

Consignia
www.consignia.com

Guernsey
http://post-office.guernsey.net

Ireland
www.anpost.ie

Isle of Man
www.gov.im/postoffice

Jersey
www.jerseypost.com

Post Office
www.postoffice.co.uk

Post Office Counters
www.postoffice-counters.co.uk

Royal Mail
www.royalmail.co.uk

pressure groups

Adam Smith Institute
www.adamsmith.org

Amnesty International
www.amnesty.org.uk

ASH
www.ash.org.uk

Association of British Counties
www.abcounties.co.uk

Association of British Drivers
www.abd.org.uk

Bruges Group
www.eurocritic.demon.co.uk

Campaign Against Censorship of the Internet in Britain
www.liberty.org.uk/cacib

Campaign for an English Parliament
www.englishpm.demon.co.uk

Campaign for Dark Skies
www.dark-skies.freeserve.co.uk

Campaign for Freedom of Information
www.cfoi.org.uk

Campaign for Nuclear Disarmament (CND)
www.cnduk.org

Campaign for Press & Broadcasting Freedom
www.cpbf.org.uk

Campaign for Safe E-Commerce Legislation
www.stand.org.uk

Campaign for Shooting
www.foresight-cfs.org.uk

Charter 88
www.charter88.org..uk

Country Landowners Association
www.cla.org.uk

Countryside Alliance
www.countryside-alliance.org

Crimestoppers
www.crimestoppers-uk.org

Democracy Movement
www.democracy-movement.org.uk

Electoral Reform Society
www.electoral-reform.org.uk

Euro Know
www.euro-know.org

Fabian Society
www.fabian-society.org.uk

Fireworks Safety Campaign
www.fireworksafety.co.uk

Free Britain
www.freebritain.co.uk

Friends of the Earth
www.foe.co.uk

Going for Green
www.goingforgreen.org.uk

Greenpeace International
www.greenpeace.org

Independence for Scotland
www.forscotland.com

League Against Cruel Sports
www.league.uk.com

Liberty (National Council for Civil Liberties)
www.liberty-human-rights.org.uk

National Pure Water Association
www.npwa.freeserve.co.uk

Portman Group
www.portman-group.org.uk

Privacy International
www.privacyinternational.org

Searchlight
www.s-light.demon.co.uk

Silent Majority
www.silentmajority.co.uk

UK Independence Party
www.independenceuk.org.uk

Vegetarian Society
www.vegsoc.org

Voluntary Euthanasia Society
www.ves.org.uk

professional associations

Association of Directors of Social Services
www.adss.org.uk

Association of First Division Civil Servants
www.fda.org.uk

research councils

Biotechnology & Biological Sciences
www.bbsrc.ac.uk

Council for the Central Laboratory
www.cclrc.ac.uk

Economic & Social
www.esrc.ac.uk

Engineering & Physical Sciences
www.epsrc.ac.uk

Medical
www.mrc.ac.uk

Natural Environment
www.nerc.ac.uk

Particle Physics & Astronomy
www.pparc.ac.uk

scottish executive

Education & Young People
www.scotland.gov.uk/pages/news/dept.aspx?id=1

Enterprise, Transport & Lifelong Learning
www.scotland.gov.uk/pages/news/dept.aspx?id=2

Environment & Rural Development
www.scotland.gov.uk/pages/news/dept.aspx?id=6

Finance & Public Services
www.scotland.gov.uk/pages/news/dept.aspx?id=3

First Minister
www.scotland.gov.uk/pages/news/dept.aspx?id=10

Health & Community Care
www.scotland.gov.uk/pages/news/dept.aspx?id=4

Justice
www.scotland.gov.uk/pages/news/dept.aspx?id=5

Scottish Executive
www.scotland.gov.uk

Social Justice
www.scotland.gov.uk/pages/news/dept.aspx?id=7

Tourism, Culture & Sport
www.scotland.gov.uk/pages/news/dept.aspx?id=8

scottish parliament

Annual Reports
www.scottish.parliament.uk/parl_bus/annreps.html

Bills
www.scottish.parliament.uk/parl_bus/legis.html

Business Bulletin
www.scottish.parliament.uk/agenda_and_decisions/forth.html

Committees
www.scottish.parliament.uk/official_report/cttee.html

Constituencies & Regions
www.scottish.parliament.uk/msps/region.html

Educational Resources
www.scottish.parliament.uk/ypt/resources.html

Factfiles
www.scottish.parliament.uk/welcoming_you/factfiles.html

Members of the Scottish Parliament
www.scottish.parliament.uk/msps/ministers020501.htm

Official Report of Parliament
www.scottish.parliament.uk/official_report/meeting.html

Outstanding Motions
www.scottish.parliament.uk/agenda_and_decisions/outmot.htm

Parliamentary Procedure
www.scottish.parliament.uk/parl_bus/proced.html

Petitions
www.scottish.parliament.uk/parl_bus/petitions.html

Scottish Parliament
www.scottish.parliament.uk

UK government

Government Agencies

Advisory, Conciliation & Arbitration Service
www.acas.org.uk

Air Accident Investigation Branch
www.open.gov.uk/aaib

Arts Council
www.artscouncil.org.uk

Audit Commission
www.audit-comm.gov.uk

Benefits Agency
www.dss.gov.uk/ba

British Council
www.britcoun.org

British Railways Board
www.brb.gov.uk

British Trade International
www.brittrade.com

British Waterways Board
www.british-waterways.org

Central Computer & Telecommunications Agency (CCTA)
www.ccta.gov.uk

Central Office of Information
www.coi.gov.uk

Centre for Policy Studies
www.cps.org.uk

Charity Commission
www.charity-commission.gov.uk

Child Support Agency
www.dss.gov.uk/csa

Citizens' Charter
www.open.gov.uk/charter

Commission for Architecture & the Built Environment (CABE)
www.cabe.org.uk

Commission for Racial Equality
www.cre.gov.uk

Commonwealth War Graves Commission
www.cwgc.org

Communicable Disease Surveillance Centre
www.who.int/emc

Companies House
www.companieshouse.gov.uk

Contributions Agency
www.dss.gov.uk/ca

Crafts Council
www.craftscouncil.org.uk

Crown Prosecution Service (CPS)
www.cps.gov.uk

Data Protection Register
www.dpr.gov.uk

Design Council
www.design-council.org.uk

Driver & Vehicle Licensing Agency (DVLA)
www.dvla.gov.uk/welcome.htm

Driving Standards Agency (DSA)
www.dsa.gov.uk

Employment Service
www.employmentservice.gov.uk

Enterprise Zone
www.enterprisezone.org.uk

Equal Opportunities Commission
www.eoc.org.uk

Forestry Commission of Great Britain
www.forestry.gov.uk

Government Communications Headquarters (GCHQ)
www.gchq.gov.uk

Government Information Service
www.open.gov.uk

Health & Safety Executive
www.hse.gov.uk

Highways Agency
www.highways.gov.uk

HM Customs & Excise
www.hmce.gov.uk

HM Land Registry
www.landreg.gov.uk

HM Prison Service
www.hmprisonservice.gov.uk

HM Stationery Office
www.hmso.gov.uk

HM Treasury Euro Site
www.euro.gov.uk

Housing Corporation
www.housingcorp.org.uk

Inland Revenue
www.inlandrevenue.gov.uk

Insolvency Service
www.insolvency.gov.uk

Institute for Fiscal Studies
www.ifs.org.uk

Law Commission
www.lawcom.gov.uk

Local Government Association
www.lga.gov.uk

Medical Devices Agency
www.medical-devices.gov.uk

Medicines Control Agency
www.mca.gov.uk

MI5
www.mi5.gov.uk

Museums & Galleries Commission
www.cornucopia.org.uk

National Association of Citizens Advice Bureaux
www.nacab.org.uk

National Audit Office
www.nao.gov.uk

National Criminal Intelligence Service
www.ncis.co.uk

National Disability Council
www.disability-council.gov.uk

National Grid for Learning
www.ngfl.gov.uk

National Health Service
www.nhs50.nhs.uk

National Institute for Social Work
www.nisw.org.uk

National Playing Fields Association
www.npfa.co.uk

National Rivers Authority
www.highway57.co.uk

New Deal
www.newdeal.gov.uk

Occupational Pensions Regulatory Authority
www.opra.gov.uk

Office of Technology
www.ost.gov.uk

Official Publications
www.ukop.co.uk

Ordnance Survey
www.ordsvy.gov.uk

Parliamentary Monitoring & Information Service
www.pamis.gov.uk

Passport Agency
www.ukpa.gov.uk

Planning Inspectorate
www.planning-inspectorate.gov.uk

Post Office
www.postoffice.co.uk

Public Record Office
www.pro.gov.uk

Royal Mint
www.royalmint.com

Stationery Office
www.tso.co.uk

Teacher Training Agency
www.teach-tta.gov.uk

Trade UK
www.tradeuk.com

Trading Standards Central
www.tradingstandards.gov.uk

Transport for London
www.transportforlondon.gov.uk

United Kingdom Hydrographic Office
www.hydro.gov.uk

Vehicle Inspectorate
www.via.gov.uk

Women's National Commission
www.thewnc.org.uk

Government Departments

Cabinet Office
www.cabinet-office.gov.uk

Crown Estates
www.crownestate.co.uk

Culture, Media & Sport
www.culture.gov.uk

Education & Skills
www.dfes.gov.uk

Environment, Transport & the Regions
www.detr.gov.uk

Foreign & Commonwealth Office
www.fco.gov.uk

Health
www.doh.gov.uk

HM Treasury
www.hm-treasury.gov.uk

Home Office
www.homeoffice.gov.uk

International Development
www.dfid.gov.uk

Ministry of Agriculture, Fisheries & Food
www.defra.gov.uk

Ministry of Defence
www.mod.uk

National Heritage
www.heritage.gov.uk

Social Security
www.dss.gov.uk

Trade & Industry
www.dti.gov.uk

Local Government

Aberdeen
www.aberdeencity.gov.uk

Aberdeenshire
www.aberdeenshire.gov.uk

Adur
www.adur.co.uk

Alnwick
www.northumberland.com/NEP/alnwick-haldimand_19.htm

Amber Valley
http://public.ambervalley.gov.uk

Anglesey
www.anglesey.gov.uk

Angus
www.angus.gov.uk

Antrim
www.antrim.gov.uk

Ards
www.ards-council.gov.uk

Argyll & Bute
www.argyll-bute.gov.uk

Armagh
www.armagh.gov.uk

Arun
www.arun.gov.uk

Ashfield
www.ashfield.gov.uk

Ashford
www.ashford.gov.uk

Aylesbury
www.aylesburyvaledc.gov.uk

Babergh
www.babergh-south-suffolk.gov.uk

Ballymoney
www.ballymoney.gov.uk

Banbridge
www.banbridge.com

Banbury
www.banburytown.co.uk

Barking & Dagenham
www.barking-dagenham.gov.uk

Barnet
www.barnet.gov.uk

Barnsley
www.barnsley.gov.uk

Barrow-in-Furness
www.barrowbc.gov.uk

Basildon
www.basildon.gov.uk

Basingstoke
www.basingstoke.gov.uk

Bassetlaw
www.bassetlaw.gov.uk

Bath
www.bathnes.gov.uk

Bedford
www.bedford.gov.uk

Bedfordshire
www.bcclgis.gov.uk

Belfast
www.belfastcity.gov.uk

Berwick-upon-Tweed
www.berwick-upon-tweed.gov.uk

Bexley
www.bexley.gov.uk

Birmingham
www.birmingham.gov.uk

Blaby
www.blaby.gov.uk

Blackburn
www.blackburn.gov.uk

Blackpool
www.blackpool.gov.uk

Blyth Valley
www.blythvalley.gov.uk

Bolsover
www.bolsover.gov.uk

Bolton
www.bolton.gov.uk

Boston
www.boston.gov.uk

Bournemouth
www.bournemouth.gov.uk

Bracknell Forest
www.bracknell-forest.gov.uk

Bradford
www.bradford.gov.uk

Braintree
www.locallife.co.uk/braintree/government.asp

Breckland
www.breckland.gov.uk

Brent
www.brent.gov.uk

Brentwood
www.brentwood-council.gov.uk

Bridgend
www.bridgend.gov.uk

Brighton & Hove
www.brighton-hove.gov.uk

Bristol
www.bristol-city.gov.uk

Broadland
www.broadland.gov.uk

Bromley
www.bromley.gov.uk

Bromsgrove
www.bromsgrove.gov.uk

Broxbourne
www.broxbourne.gov.uk

Broxtowe
www.broxtowe.gov.uk

Buckinghamshire
www.buckscc.gov.uk

Burnley
www.burnley.gov.uk

Bury
www.bury.gov.uk

Caerphilly
www.caerphilly.gov.uk

Calderdale
www.calderdale.gov.uk

Cambridge
www.cambridge.gov.uk

Cambridgeshire
www.camcnty.gov.uk

Camden
www.camden.gov.uk

Cannock
www.cannockchasedc.gov.uk

Canterbury
www.canterbury.gov.uk

Caradon
www.caradon.gov.uk

Cardiff
www.cardiff.gov.uk

Carlisle
www.carlisle-city.gov.uk

Carmarthenshire
www.carmarthenshire.gov.uk

Carrick
www.carrick.gov.uk

Carrickfergus
www.carrickfergus.org

Castle Morpeth
www.castlemorpeth.gov.uk

Castlereagh
www.castlereagh.gov.uk

Ceredigion
www.ceredigion.gov.uk

Chard
www.chard.gov.uk

Charnwood
www.charnwoodbcgov.uk

Chelmsford
www.chelmsfordbcgov.uk

Cheltenham
www.cheltenham.gov.uk

Cherwell
www.cherwell-dc.gov.uk

Cheshire
www.cheshire.gov.uk

Chester
www.chestercc.gov.uk

Chester le Street
www.chester-le-street.gov.uk

Chesterfield
www.chesterfieldbc.gov.uk

Chicester
www.chichester.gov.uk

Chiltern
www.chiltern.gov.uk

Christchurch
www.christchurch.gov.uk

Clackmannan
www.clacs.gov.uk

Colchester
www.colchester.gov.uk

Coleraine
www.colerainebc.gov.uk

Congleton
www.congleton.gov.uk

Conwy
www.conwy.gov.uk

Cookstown
www.cookstown.gov.uk

Copeland
www.copelandbc.gov.uk

Cornwall
www.cornwall.gov.uk

Corporation of London
www.cityoflondon.gov.uk

Cotswold
www.cotswold.gov.uk

Coventry
www.coventry.gov.uk

Craigavon
www.craigavon.gov.uk

Craven
www.cravendc.gov.uk

Crawley
www.crawley.gov.uk

Crewe & Nantwich
www.crewe-nantwich.gov.uk

Croydon
www.croydon.gov.uk

Cumbria
www.cumbria.gov.uk

Dacorum
www.dacorum.gov.uk

Darlington
www.darlington.gov.uk

Daventry
www.daventrydc.gov.uk

Denbighshire
www.denbeighshire.gov.uk

Derby
www.derby.gov.uk

Derbyshire
www.derbyshire.gov.uk

Derbyshire Dales
www.derbeyshiredaes.gov.uk

Derry
www.derrycity.gov.uk

Derwentside
www.derwentside.gov.uk

Devizes
www.devizes-tc.gov.uk

Devon
www.devon-cc.gov.uk

Doncaster
www.doncaster.gov.uk

Dorset
www.dorset-cc.gov.uk

Dover
www.dover.gov.uk

Down
www.downdc.gov.uk

Dudley
www.dudley.gov.uk

Dumfries & Galloway
www.dumgal.gov.uk

Dunbarton
www.west-dunbarton.gov.uk

Dundee
www.dundeecity.gov.uk

Dungannon
www.dungannon.gov.uk

Durham (City)
www.durhamcity.gov.uk

Durham (County)
www.durham.gov.uk

Ealing
www.ealing.gov.uk

Easington
www.easington.gov.uk

East Ayrshire
www.east-ayrshire.gov.uk

East Devon
www.east-devon.gov.uk

East Dorset
www.eastdorsetdc.gov.uk

East Dunbartonshire
www.e-dunbarton.org.uk

East Grinstead
www.egnet.co.uk/egtc

East Hampshire
www.easthants.gov.uk

East Hertfordshire
www.eastherts.gov.uk

East Lindsey
www.e-lindsey.gov.uk

East Lothian
www.eastlothian.gov.uk

East Northamptonshire
www.east-northamptonshire.gov.uk

East Renfrewshire
www.eastrenfrewshire.gov.uk

East Riding
www.east-riding-of-yorkshire.gov.uk

East Sussex
www.eastsussexcc.gov.uk

Eastbourne
www.eastbourne.org/council

Eastleigh
www.eastleigh.gov.uk

Eden
www.eden.gov.uk

Edinburgh
www.edinburgh.gov.uk

Elmbridge
www.elmbridge.gov.uk

Enfield
www.enfield.gov.uk

Epping Forest
www.eppingforestdc.gov.uk

Epsom
www.epsom-ewell.gov.uk

Erewash
www.erewash.gov.uk

Essex
www.essexcc.gov.uk

Exeter
www.exeter.gov.uk

Falkirk
www.falkirk.gov.uk

Fareham
www.fareham.gov.uk

Felixstowe
www.felixstowe.gov.uk

Fenland
www.fenland.gov.uk

Fermanagh
www.fermanagh.gov.uk

Fife
www.fife.gov.uk

Flintshire
www.flintshire.gov.uk

Forest Heath
www.forest-heath.gov.uk

Forest of Dean
www.fdean.gov.uk

Fylde
www.fylde.gov.uk

Gateshead
www.gatesheadmbc.gov.uk

Gedling
www.gedling.gov.uk

Glasgow
www.glasgow.gov.uk

Gloucester
www.glos-city.gov.uk

Gloucestershire
www.gloscc.gov.uk

Godalming
www.godalming-tc.gov.uk

Gosport
www.gosport.gov.uk

Gravesham
www.gravesham.gov.uk

Great Yarmouth
www.great-yarmouth.gov.uk

Greater London Assembly & Mayor of London
www.london.gov.uk

Greenwich
www.greenwich.gov.uk

Guildford
www.guildford.gov.uk

Gwynedd
www.gwynedd.gov.uk

Hackney
www.hackney.gov.uk

Halton
www.halton-borough.gov.uk

Hambleton
www.hambleton.gov.uk

Hammersmith & Fulham
www.lbhf.gov.uk

Hampshire
www.hants.gov.uk

Harborough
www.harborough.gov.uk

Haringey
www.haringey.gov.uk

Harlow
www.harlow.gov.uk

Harrogate
www.harrogate.gov.uk

Harrow
www.harrow.gov.uk

Hart
www.hart.gov.uk/dc

Hartlepool
www.hartlepool.gov.uk

Hastings
www.hastings.gov.uk

Havant
www.havant.gov.uk

Havering
www.havering.gov.uk

Herefordshire
www.herefordshire.gov.uk

Hertfordshire
www.hertscc.gov.uk

Hertsmere
www.hertsmere.gov.uk

High Peak
www.highpeak.gov.uk

Highland
www.highland.gov.uk

Hillingdon
www.hillingdon.gov.uk

Horsham
www.horsham.gov.uk

Hounslow
www.hounslow.gov.uk

Huntingdonshire
www.huntsdc.gov.uk

Hyndburn
www.hyndburnbc.gov.uk

Ipswich
www.ipswich.gov.uk

Isle of Wight
www.isleofwight.gov.uk

Islington
www.islington.gov.uk

Jersey
www.jersey.gov.uk

Kennet
www.kennet.gov.uk

Kensington & Chelsea
www.rbkc.gov.uk

Kent
www.kent.gov.uk

Kerrier
www.kerrier.gov.uk

Kettering
www.kettering.gov.uk

Kings Lynn & West Norfolk
www.west-norfolk.gov.uk

Kingston-upon-Hull
www.hullcc.gov.uk

Kingston-upon-Thames
www.kingston.gov.uk

Kirklees
www.kirkleesmc.gov.uk

Knowsley
www.knowsley.gov.uk

Lambeth
www.lambeth.gov.uk

Lancashire
www.lancashire.gov.uk

Lancaster
www.lancaster.gov.uk

Larne
www.larne.com

Leeds
www.leeds.gov.uk

Leicester
www.leicester.gov.uk

Leicestershire
www.leics.gov.uk

Lewes
www.lewes.gov.uk

Lewisham
www.lewisham.gov.uk

Lichfield
www.lichfield.gov.uk

Lincoln
www.lincoln-info.org.uk

Lincolnshire
www.lincolnshire.gov.uk

Lisburn
www.lisburn.gov.uk

Litchfield
www.litchfield.gov.uk

Liverpool
www.liverpool.gov.uk

Londonderry
www.derrycity.gov.uk

Luton
www.luton.gov.uk

Macclesfield
www.macclesfield.gov.uk

Magherafelt
www.magherafelt.gov.uk

Maidstone
www.digitalmaidstone.co.uk

Maldon
www.maldon.gov.uk

Manchester
www.manchester.gov.uk

Mansfield
www.mansfield.gov.uk

Medway
www.medway.gov.uk

Melton
www.melton.gov.uk

Mendip
www.mendip.gov.uk

Merthyr Tydfil
www.merthyr.gov.uk

Merton
www.merton.gov.uk

Mid Bedfordshire
www.midbeds.gov.uk

Mid Devon
www.middevon.gov.uk

Mid Suffolk
www.mid-suffol-dc.gov.uk

Mid-Sussex
www.midsussex.gov.uk

Middlesbrough
www.middlesbrough.gov.uk

Midlothian
www.midlothian.gov.uk

Milton Keynes
www.miltonkeynes.gov.uk

Mole Valley
www.mole-valley.gov.uk

Monmouthshire
www.monmouthshire.gov.uk

Moray
www.moray.gov.uk

Moyle
www.moyle-council.org

Neath Port Talbot
www.neath-porttalbot.gov.uk

New Forest
www.nfdc.gov.uk

Newark
www.newark.gov.uk

Newcastle-under-Lyme
www.newcastle-staffs.gov.uk

Newcastle-upon-Tyne
www.newcastle.gov.uk

Newham
www.newham.gov.uk

Newport
www.newport.gov.uk

Newtonabbey
www.newtonabbey.gov.uk

Norfolk
www.norfolk.gov.uk

North Ayrshire
www.north-ayrshire.gov.uk

North Cornwall
www.ncdc.gov.uk

North Devon
www.northdevon.gov.uk

North Dorset
www.north-dorset.gov.uk

North Down
www.north-down.gov.uk

North East Derbyshire
www.ne-derbyshire.gov.uk

North East Lincolnshire
www.nelinks.gov.uk

North Hertfordshire
www.nhdc.gov.uk

North Kesteven
www.oden.co.uk

North Lanarkshire
www.northlan.gov.uk

North Lincolnshire
www.northlincs.gov.uk

North Norfolk
www.north-norfolk.gov.uk

North Shropshire
www.nshropshire.gov.uk

North Somerset
www.n-somerset.gov.uk

North Tyneside
www.northtyneside.gov.uk

North Warwickshire
www.warwickshire.gov.uk

North West Leicestershire
www.nwleicsdc.gov.uk

North Wiltshire
www.northwilts.gov.uk

North Yorkshire
www.northyorks.gov.uk

Northampton
www.northampton.gov.uk

Northamptonshire
www.northamptonshire.gov.uk

Northumberland
www.northumberland.gov.uk

Norwich
www.norwich.gov.uk

Nottingham
www.nottinghamcity.gov.uk

Nottinghamshire
www.nottscc.gov.uk

Oadby
www.oadby-wigston.gov.uk

Oldham
www.oldham.gov.uk

Oxford
www.oxford.gov.uk

Oxfordshire
www.oxfordshire.gov.uk

Pembrokeshire
www.pembrokeshire.gov.uk

Pendle
www.pendle.gov.uk

Penwith
www.penwith.gov.uk

Perth & Kinross
www.pkc.gov.uk

Peterborough
www.peterborough.gov.uk

Plymouth
www.plymouth.gov.uk

Poole
www.poole.gov.uk

Portsmouth
www.portsmouthcc.gov.uk

Powys
www.powys.gov.uk

Preston
www.preston.gov.uk

Reading
www.reading.gov.uk

Redbridge
www.redbridge.gov.uk

Redcar & Cleveland
www.redcar-cleveland.gov.uk

Redditch
www.redditchbc.gov.uk

Reigate & Banstead
www.reigate-banstead.gov.uk

Renfrewshire
www.renfrewshire.gov.uk

Rhondda-Cynon-Taff
www.rhondda-cynon-taff.gov.uk

Ribble Valley
www.ribblevalley.gov.uk

Richmond
www.richmond.gov.uk

Richmondshire
www.richmondshire.gov.uk

Rochdale
www.rochdale.gov.uk

Rochester-upon-Medway
www.rochester.gov.uk

Rochford
www.rochford.gov.uk

Rother
www.rother.gov.uk

Rotherham
www.rotherham.gov.uk

Runnymede
www.runnymede.gov.uk

Rushcliffe
www.rushcliff.gov.uk

Rushmore
www.rushmore.gov.uk

Rutland
www.rutland.gov.uk

Ryedale
www.ryedale.gov.uk

Salford
www.salford.gov.uk

Salisbury
www.salisbury.gov.uk

Sandwell
www.sandwellmbc.broadnet.co.uk

Scarborough
www.scarborough.gov.uk

Scottish Borders
www.scotborders.gov.uk

Sedgefield
www.sedgefield.gov.uk

Sefton
www.sefton.gov.uk

Selby
www.selby.gov.uk

Sevenoaks
www.sevenoaks.gov.uk

Sheffield
www.sheffield.gov.uk

Shepway
www.shepway.gov.uk

Shetland Islands
www.shetland.gov.uk

Shrewsbury & Atchham
www.shrewsbury-atcham.gov.uk

Shropshire
www.shropshire-cc.gov.uk

Slough
www.slough.gov.uk

Solihull
www.solihull.gov.uk

Somerset
www.somerset.gov.uk

South Ayrshire
www.south-ayrshire.gov.uk

South Bedfordshire
www.southbeds.gov.uk

South Buckinghamshire
www.southbucks.gov.uk

South Cambridgeshire
www.scambs.gov.uk

South Gloucestershire
www.southglos.gov.uk

South Hams
www.south-hams-dc.gov.uk

South Holland
www.sholland.gov.uk

South Kesteven
www.skdc.com

South Lanarkshire
www.southlanarkshire.gov.uk

South Norfolk
www.south-norfolk.gov.uk

South Northamptonshire
www.southnorthants.gov.uk

South Oxfordshire
www.southoxon.gov.uk

South Ribble
www.south-ribblebc.gov.uk

South Shropshire
www.southshropshire.gov.uk

South Somerset
www.southsomerset.gov.uk

South Staffordshire
www.sstaffs.gov.uk

South Tyneside
www.s-tyneside-mbc.gov.uk

Southampton
www.southampton.gov.uk

Southend-on-Sea
www.southend.gov.uk

Southwark
www.southwark.gov.uk

Spelthorne
www.spelthorne.gov.uk

St Albans
www.stalbans.gov.uk

St Edmundsbury
www.stedmundsbury.gov.uk

St Helens
www.sthelens.gov.uk

Stafford
www.staffordbc.gov.uk

Staffordshire
www.staffordshire.gov.uk

Sterling
www.sterling.gov.uk

Stevenage
www.stevenage.gov.uk

Stockport
www.stockportmbc.gov.uk

Stockton-on-Tees
www.stockton-bc.gov.uk

Stoke-on-Trent
www.stoke.gov.uk

Strabane
www.strabanedc.org.uk

Stroud
www.stroud.gov.uk

Suffolk
www.suffolkcc.gov.uk

Sunderland
www.sunderland.gov.uk

Surrey
www.surreycc.gov.uk

Surrey Heath
www.surreyheath.gov.uk

Sutton
www.sutton.gov.uk

Swale
www.swale.gov.uk

Swansea
www.swansea.gov.uk

Swindon
www.swindon.gov.uk

Tameside
www.tameside.gov.uk

Tamworth
www.tamworth.gov.uk

Tandridge
www.tandridgedc.gov.uk

Taunton Deane
www.tauntondeane.gov.uk

Teesdale
www.teesdale.gov.uk

Teignbridge
www.teignbridge.gov.uk

Telford & Wrekin
www.telford.gov.uk

Tendring
www.tendringdc.gov.uk

Test Valley
www.testvalley.gov.uk

Tewkesbury
www.tewkesburybc.gov.uk

Thannet
www.thannet.gov.uk

Three Rivers
www.3rivers.gov.uk

Thurrock
www.thurrock.gov.uk

Tonbridge & Malling
www.tmbc.gov.uk

Torbay
www.torbay.gov.uk

Torfaen
www.torfaen.gov.uk

Torridge
www.torridge.gov.uk

Tower Hamlets
www.towerhamlets.gov.uk

Trafford
www.trafford.gov.uk

Tunbridge Wells
www.tunbridgewells.gov.uk

Tynedale
www.tynedale.gov.uk

Uttlesford
www.uttlesford.gov.uk

Vale of Glamorgan
www.valeofglamorgan.gov.uk

Vale Royal
www.valeroyal.gov.uk

Wakefield
www.wakefield.gov.uk

Walsall
www.walsall.gov.uk

Waltham Forest
www.lbwf.gov.uk

Wandsworth
www.wandsworth.gov.uk

Wansbeck
www.wansbeck.gov.uk

Warrington
www.warrington.gov.uk

Warwickshire
www.warwickshire.gov.uk

Watford
www.watford.gov.uk

Waveney
www.waveney.gov.uk

Waverley
www.waverley.gov.uk

Wealden
www.wealden.gov.uk

Wear Valley
www.wearvalley.gov.uk

Wellingborough
www.wellingborough.gov.uk

Welwyn Hatfield
www.welhat.gov.uk

West Berkshire
www.westberks.gov.uk

West Devon
www.wdbc.gov.uk

West Dorset
www.westdorset-dc.gov.uk

West Dunbartonshire
www.west-dunbarton.gov.uk

West Oxfordshire
www.westoxon.gov.uk

West Sussex
www.westsussex.gov.uk

West Wiltshire
www.west-wiltshire-dc.gov.uk

Western Isles
www.w-isles.gov.uk

Westminster
www.westminster.gov.uk

Weymouth & Portland
www.weymouth.gov.uk

Wigan
www.wiganmbc.gov.uk

Wiltshire
www.wiltshire.gov.uk

Winchester
www.winchester.gov.uk

Windsor & Maidenhead
www.rbwm.gov.uk

Wirral
www.wirral.gov.uk

Woking
www.woking.gov.uk

Wokingham
www.wokingham.gov.uk

Wolverhampton
www.wolverhampton.gov.uk

Worcester
www.cityofworcester.gov.uk

Worcestershire
www.worcestershire.gov.uk

Worthing
www.worthing.gov.uk

Wrexham
www.wrexham.gov.uk

Wychavon
www.wychavon.gov.uk

Wycombe
www.wycombe.gov.uk

Wyre
www.wyrebc.gov.uk

Wyre Forest
www.wyreforestdc.gov.uk

York
www.york.gov.uk

Parliament

General Election
www.election.co.uk

House of Commons
www.parliament.uk/commons/hsecom.htm

House of Lords
www.parliament.uk/about_lords/about_lords.cfm

Isle of Man
www.tynwald.isle-of-man.org.im

Northern Ireland Assembly
www.ni-assembly.gov.uk

Parliament
www.parliament.uk

Scottish Parliament
www.scottish.parliament.uk

Scottish Parliament Live
www.scottishparliamentlive.com

States of Jersey
www.jersey.gov.uk

Welsh Assembly
www.wales.gov.uk

- agencies
- ancillary services
- animal health
- complementary
- dentistry
- government agencies
- health boards
- hospitals & services (private)
- hospitals, clinics & nhs trusts
- journals, magazines & websites
- medicine & surgery
- nursing & midwifery
- pharmacy
- psychiatry & psychology
- research
- vision

agencies

Association of British Healthcare Industries
www.abhi.org.uk

Health Education Board for Scotland
www.hebs.scot.nhs.uk

Independent Healthcare association
www.iha.org.uk

Institute of Health Service Management
www.ihm.org.uk

Medical Devices Agency
www.medical-devices.gov.uk

Medicines Control Agency
www.open.gov.uk/mca

NHS Confederation
www.nhsconfed.net

Scotland Healthcare System
www.scotlandhealth.org

Scotland's Health At Work
www.shaw.uk.com

Scotland's Public Health Union
www.unison-scotland.org.uk

Scottish Health on the Web
www.show.scot.nhs.uk

ancillary services

Anthony Nolan Bone Marrow Trust
www.anthonynolan.com

Association of Professional Ambulance Personnel
www.apap.org.uk

British Association of Emergency Medical Technicians
www.baemt.org.uk

British Blood Transfusion Service
www.bbts.org.uk

British Healthcare Trade Association
www.bhta.com

British Organ Donor Society
www.argonet.co.uk/body

British Safety Council
www.britishsafetycouncil.co.uk

British Toxicology Society
www.bts.org

Carers National Association
www.carersuk.demon.co.uk

Health Education Authority
www.hea.org.uk

Health Education Board for Scotland
www.hebs.scot.nhs.uk

Hospital Broadcasting Association
www.nahbo.demon.co.uk

Institute of Food Science & Technology
www.ifst.org

Interstitial Cystitis Support group
www.interstitialcystitis.co.uk

Medical Advisory Services for Travellers Abroad (MASTA)
www.masta.org

National Association of Health Authorities & Trusts
www.nahat.net

National Blood Service
www.bloodnet.nbs.nhs.uk

Nursing Homes Registry
www.nursinghomes.co.uk

Royal Institute of Public Health & Hygiene
www.riphh.org.uk

Scottish National Blood Transfusion Service
www.showscot.nhs.uk/snbts

Welsh Blood Transfusion Service
www.welsh-blood.org.uk

animal health

British Equine Veterinary Association
www.beva.org.uk

British Homoeopathic Veterinary Association
www.hom-inform.org

British Small Animal Veterinary Association
www.bsava.ac.uk

British Veterinary Association
www.bva.co.uk

British Veterinary Nursing Association
www.bvna.org.uk

National Office of Animal Health
www.noah.demon.co.uk

Royal College of Veterinary Surgeons
www.rcvs.org.uk

Scottish Veterinary Dental Partnership
www.scottishvetdental.co.uk

Society of Practising Veterinary Surgeons
www.spvs.org.uk

Veterinary Medicines Directorate
www.open.gov.uk/vmd

complementary

Academy of Curative Hypnotherapists
www.ach.co.uk

Alexander Technique
www.ati.com

Aromazones
www.aromazones.com

Association of Reflexologists
www.aor.org.uk

Bach Flower Essences
www.nelsonbach.com/bachessences

British Acupuncture Council
www.acupuncture.org.uk

British Chiropractic Association
www.chiropractic-uk.co.uk

British Dietetic Association
www.vois.org.uk/bda

British Homoeopathic Library
www.hom-inform.org

British Medical Acupuncture Society
www.medical-acupuncture.co.uk

British Naturopathic Society
www.naturopaths.org.uk

British Osteopathic Association
www.osteopathy.org

British Reflexology Association
www.britreflex.co.uk

British School of Homeopathy
www.homeopathy.co.uk

Canadian Chiropractic Association
www.ccachiro.org

Chartered Society of Physiotherapy
www.csphysio.org.uk

College of Integrated Chinese Medicine
www.cicm.org.uk

Feng Shui Society
www.fengshuisociety.org.uk

Foundation for Traditional Chinese Medicine
www.ftcm.org.uk

General Chiropractic Council
www.gcc-uk.org

Guild of Complementary Practioners
www.gcpnet.com

Hale Clinic
www.haleclinic.com

Harvest Clinic Glasgow
www.harvestclinic.co.uk

Health Kinesiology
www.subtlenergy.com

Herb Society
www.herbsociety.co.uk

Homeopathy World
www.hom-inform.org

Hypnotherapy Society
www.hypnotherapysociety.com

International Chiropractors Association
www.chiropractic.org

International Federation of Aromatherapists
www.ifa.org.

National Institute of Ayurvedic Medicine
www.niam.com

Osteopathic Information Service
www.osteopathy.org.uk

Pets as Therapy
www.petsastherapy.org

Register of Chinese Herbal Medicine
www.rchm.co.uk

Reiki Association
www.reikiassociation.org.uk

Royal College of Speech & Language Therapists
www.rcslt.org

Shiatsu Society
www.shiatsu.org

Society of Chiropodists & Podiatrists
www.feetforlife.org

Society of Teachers of the Alexander Technique
www.stat.org.uk

Synergy Scotland
www.synergy-health.co.uk

Transcendental Meditation Scotland
www.tmscotland.org

Trepanation Trust
www.trepanation.com

dentistry

British Dental Association
www.bda-dentistry.org.uk

British Dental Health Foundation
www.dentalhealth.org.uk

British Dental Trade Association
www.bdta.org.uk

British Endodontic Society
www.derweb.ac.uk/bes

British Homeopathic Dental Association
www.bhda.org

British Society for Restorative Dentistry
www.derweb.ac.uk/bsrd

British Society of Dentistry for the Handicapped
www.bsdh.org.uk

Denplan
www.denplan.co.uk

Dental Anxiety & Phobia Association
www.healthyteeth.com

Dental Net UK
www.dentalnetuk.com

Dental Practice Board
www.dentanet.org.uk

General Dental Council
www.gdc-uk.org

National Dentists Directory
www.nationaldirectories.net

National Radiological Protection Board
www.nrpb.org.uk

government agencies

Association of British Healthcare Industries
www.abhi.org.uk

Institute of Health Service Management
www.ihm.org.uk

Medical Devices Agency
www.medical-devices.gov.uk

Medicines Control Agency
www.open.gov.uk/mca

NHS Confederation
www.nhsconfed.net

health boards

Argyll & Clyde
www.show.scot.nhs.uk/achb

Ayrshire & Arran
www.show.scot.nhs.uk/aahb

Borders
www.show.scot.nhs.uk/bhb

Dumfries & Galloway
www.show.scot.nhs.uk/dghb

Fife
www.show.scot.nhs.uk/fhb

Grampian
www.show.scot.nhs.uk/ghb

Greater Glasgow
www.show.scot.nhs.uk/gghb

Highland
www.show.scot.nhs.uk/hhb

Lothian
www.lothianhealth.scot.nhs.uk

Orkney
www.show.scot.nhs.uk/ohb

Shetland
www.show.scot.nhs.uk/shb

hospitals & services (private)

Companies

BMI Healthcare
www.bmihealth.co.uk

BUPA
www.bupa.co.uk

Essential Health Private medical Insurance
www.pmi-scot.co.uk

Nuffield Hospitals
www.nuffieldhospitals.org.uk

Partnerships in Care
www.partnershipsincare.co.uk

PPP Healthcare
www.ppphealthcare.co.uk

Surgicare
www.surgicare.co.uk

Scottish Hospitals & Clinics

Bon Secours, Glasgow
www.bonsecours.org/gbritain_glasgow.htm

Castle Craig Hospital, Peebles (Addiction treatment)
www.castlecraig.co.uk

Fernbrae Hospital, Dundee
www.fernbraehospital.co.uk

Glasgow Nuffield Hospital
www.nuffieldhospitals.org.uk

HCI, Glasgow
www.hci.co.uk

Rosshall Hospital, Glasgow
www.rosshall.com

UK Hospitals & Clinics

Cromwell, London
www.cromwell-hospital.co.uk

HCA international, London Based Hospital Group
www.columbiahealthcare.co.uk

London Clinic
www.lonclin.co.uk

London Radiosurgical Centre
www.radiosurgery.co.uk

Medishield Private Healthcare Assistance
www.medishield.co.uk

Private Healthcare UK
www.privatehealth.co.uk

hospitals, clinics & NHS trusts

Aberdeen Royal Infirmary
www.abdn-royal.com

Fife Acute Hospitals Trust
www.show.scot.nhs.uk/faht

Fife Primary Care Trust
www.show.scot.nhs.uk/fpct

Forth Valley Care Trust
www.show.scot.nhs.uk/nhsfv

Forth Valley Health Information
www.show.scot.nhs.uk/fvlhc

Grampian Primary Care Trust
www.gpct.org.uk

Grampian University Hospitals Trust
www.show.scot.nhs.uk/guh

Greater Glasgow Primary care Trust
www.show.scot.nhs.uk/ggpct

Lothian University Hospitals Trust
www.show.scot.nhs.uk/rie

Royal Infirmary of Edinburgh
www.show.scot.nhs.uk/rie

South Ayrshire Hospitals Trust
www.show.scot.nhs.uk/saht

South Glasgow University Hospitals Trust
www.show.scot.nhs.uk/sguht

Southern General Hospital, Glasgow
www.general-hospital.co.uk

Specialist Health Product Trade Association
www.hfma.co.uk

Wishaw General Hospital, Lanarkshire
www.show.scot.nhs.uk/wishaw

NHS

Aberdeen Royal Infirmary
www.abdn-royal.com

Addenbrooke's
www.addenbrookes.org.uk

Alder Hey Children's
www.alderhey.org.uk

Ashworth
www.nhsconfed.net/ashworth/index.htm

Belfast Royal Hospitals
www.royalhospital.ac.uk

Blackpool Victoria
www.cyberscape.co.uk/bvhaps

Bolton Hospice
www.boltonhospice.org

City Hospital, Birmingham
www.cityhospital.org.uk

Dartford & Gravesham
www.general-hospital.co.uk

Elizabeth Garrett Anderson
www.uclh.org/ega

Great Ormond Street
www.gosh.org.uk

Heatherwood & Wexham Park Hospitals
www.hwph-tr.fsnet.co.uk

Hope University
www.hop.man.ac.uk

Hospital for Tropical Diseases
www.uclh.org/htd

Leicester Royal Infirmary
www.lri.org.uk

Lifespan Healthcare
www.lifespan.org.uk

Middlesbrough General
www.southtees.northy.nhs.uk

Middlesex
www.uclh.org/mdx

Moorfields
www.moorfields.org.uk

National Hospital for Neurology & Neurosurgery
www.uclh.org/nat

North Riding Infirmary
www.southtees.northy.nhs.uk

North Staffs Acute Psychiatric Unit
www.general-hospital.co.uk

Poole
www.poolehos.org

Queen Victoria, East Grinstead
www.queenvic.demon.co.uk

Royal Bournemouth
www.rbh.org.uk

Royal Brompton
www.rbh.nthames.nhs.uk

Royal Buckinghamshire
www.royalbucks.co.uk

Royal Infirmary of Edinburgh
www.show.scot.nhs.uk/rie

Royal Marsden
www.royalmarsden.org

Royal United Hospital Bath
www.ruh-bath.swest.nhs.uk

South Cleveland
www.southtees.northy.nhs.uk

Southampton University Hospitals
www.wcu.heartbeat.co.uk/section1/html1/wcus1ti.htm

Southern General, Glasgow
www.general-hospital.co.uk

St Andrews Group
www.stah.org

Swindon
www.general-hospital.co.uk

UCL Hospitals
www.uclh.org

UCL Obstetric
www.uclh.org/obs

University College
www.uclh.org/uch

University Hospital of Wales
www.nhsconfed.net/universityhospitalofwales

Private

Betty Ford Center
www.bettyfordcenter.org

BMI Healthcare
www.bmihealth.co.uk

Bristol Cancer Help Centre
www.bristolcancerhelp.org

BUPA
www.bupa.co.uk

Cromwell
www.cromwell-hospital.co.uk

London Clinic
www.lonclin.co.uk

London Radiosurgical Centre
www.radiosurgery.co.uk

Marie Stopes Health Clinics
www.mariestopes.org.uk

Mayo Clinic
www.mayo.edu

Nuffield
www.nuffieldhospitals.org.uk

Partnerships in Care
www.partnershipsincare.co.uk

PPP Healthcare
www.ppphealthcare.co.uk

PPP/Columbia
www.columbiahealthcare.co.uk

Priory
www.thepriory-hospital.co.uk

St Martin's Healthcare
www.stmartins-healthcare.co.uk

Surgicare
www.surgicare.co.uk

journals, magazines & websites

British Journal of General Practice
www.rcgp.org.uk/publicat/journal

British Journal of Healthcare Management
www.markallengroup.com/bjhcm.htm

British Journal of Nursing
www.markallengroup.com/publish/medical/bjn

British Medical Journal
www.bmj.com

British Nursing News
www.nurse-nurses-nursing.com/bnno.html

Evidence-Based Nursing
www.bmjpg.com/data/ebn.htm

Health Centre
www.healthcentre.org.uk

Health Service Journal
www.hsj.co.uk

Hospital Doctor
www.health-news.co.uk

Journal of Community Nursing
www.jcn.co.uk

Journal of Neonatal Nursing
www.bizjet.com/jnn

Journal of Public Health Medicine
www.oup.co.uk/pubmed

Journal of the British Acupuncture Council
www.acupuncture.org.uk/ejom

Lancet
www.thelancet.com

Medic Direct
www.medicdirect.co.uk

Medisearch
www.medisearch.co.uk

Medscape
www.medscape.com

Net Doctor
www.netdoctor.co.uk

NHS Digest
www.nhsdigest.org

NHS Direct
www.nhsdirect.nhs.uk

Nursing Standard
www.nursing-standard.co.uk

Nursing Times
www.nursingtimes.net

Organising Medical Network Information
www.omni.ac.uk

Patient Information Publications
www.patient.org.uk

Portfolio of British Nursing
www.british-nursing.com

Positive Health
www.positivehealth.com

Practice Nursing
www.markallengroup.com/publish/medical/pn/index.htm

Pulse
www.epulse.co.uk

Reuters Health Information
www.reutershealth.com

Scottish Health Directory
www.scottishhealthdirectory.com

Scottish Health Information Network
www.shinelib.org.uk

medicine & surgery

American Medical Association
www.ama-assn.org

Anatomical Society
www.anatsoc.org.uk

Association of Clinical Pathologists
www.pathologists.org.uk

Association of Operating Department Practitioners
www.aodp.org

Association of Police Surgeons
www.apsweb.org.uk

British Association of Accident & Emergency Medicine
www.baem.org.uk

British Association of Paediatric Surgeons
www.baps.org.uk

British Association of Plastic Surgeons
www.baps.co.uk

British Fertility Society
www.britishfertilitysociety.org.uk

British Geriatrics Society
www.bgs.ord.uk

British Medical Association
www.bma.org.uk

British Psychological Society
www.bps.org.uk

British Society for Immunology
www.immunology.org

Centre for Medicines Research
www.cmr.org

Chartered Institute of Environmental Health
www.cieh.org.uk

Clinical Standards Board for Scotland
www.clinicalstandards.org

Clinical Trial Managers Association
www.ctma.org.uk

Diana, Princess of Wales Centre for Reproductive Medicine
www.powc.org

General Medical Council
www.gmc-uk.org

Health Technology Board for Scotland
www.htbs.co.uk

Hospital Consultants & Specialists Association
www.hcsa.com

Institute of Child Health
www.ich.bpmf.ac.uk

Medical Defence Union
www.the-mdu.com

Medical Protection Society
www.mps.org.uk

Medical Research Council
www.mrc.ac.uk

National Institute for Clinical Excellence
www.nice.org.uk

National Sports Medicine Institute
www.nsmi.org.uk

NHS Primary Care Group Alliance
www.nhsalliance.org

Physiological Society
www.physoc.org

Royal College of Anaesthetists
www.rcoa.ac.uk

Royal College of General Practitioners
www.rcgp.org.uk

Royal College of Obstetricians & Gynaecologists
www.rcog.org.uk

Royal College of Pathologists
www.rcpath.org

Royal College of Physicians & Surgeons Glasgow
www.gla.ac.uk/External/RCPS

Royal College of Physicians, Edinburgh
www.rcpe.ac.uk

Royal College of Surgeons, Edinburgh
www.rcsed.ac.uk

Royal College of Surgeons, England
www.rcseng.ac.uk

Royal Society of Medicine
www.roysocmed.ac.uk

nursing & midwifery

Active Birth Centre
www.activebirthcentre.com

Association for Improvements in Maternity Services
www.aims.org.uk

Association of Radical Midwives
www.radmid.demon.co.uk

British Nursing Agencies
www.nursing-list.com

British Nursing Association
www.bna.co.uk

English National Board for Nursing, Midwifery & Health Visiting
www.enb.org.uk

Federation of Independent Nursing Agencies
www.fina-nursing.com

Florence Nightingale Foundation
www.florence-nightingale-foundation.org.uk

Foundation of Nursing Studies
www.fons.org

In-flight Nurses Association
www.gmb.dircon.co.uk/ifna

Infection Control Nurses Association
www.icna.co.uk

National Association of Theatre Nurses UK
www.natn.org.uk

National Board for Nursing, Midwifery & Health Visiting for Northern Ireland
www.n-i.nhs.uk/nbni

National Board of Nursing, Midwifery & Health Visiting in Scotland
www.nbs.org.uk

National HIV Nurses Association
www.fons.org/nhivna

NHS Nursing
www.doh.gov.uk/nursing.htm

Royal College of Nursing
www.rcn.org.uk

Royal College of Nursing Scotland
www.rcnscotland.org

Scottish National Board for Nursing, Midwifery & Health Visiting
www.nbs.org.uk

United Kingdom Central Council for Nursing, Midwifery & Health Visiting
www.ukcc.org.uk

Welsh National Board for Nursing, Midwifery & Health Visiting
www.wnb.org.uk

pharmacy

Association of the British Pharmaceutical Industry
www.abpi.org.uk

Boots Pharmacists' Association
http://omnisbpa.members.beeb.net

British Association of European Pharmaceutical Distributors
www.api.org.uk

British Pharmacopoeia
www.pharmacopoeia.org.uk

European Agency for the Evaluation of Medicinal products
www.eudra.org

Medicines Control Agency
www.open.gov.uk/mca/mcahome.htm

National Pharmaceutical Association
www.npa.co.uk

Pharmaceutical Journal
www.pharmj.com

Royal Pharmaceutical Society of Great Britain
www.rpsgb.org.uk

Scottish Pharmaceutical General Council
www.spgc.org.uk

United Kingdom Medicines Information Pharmacists Group
www.druginfozone.org

psychiatry & psychology

Association of Psychological Therapists
www.apt.uk.com

British Association for Behavioural & Cognitive Psychotherapies
www.babcp.org.uk

British Association of Psychotherapists
www.bap-psychtherapy.org

British Psychological Society
www.bps.org.uk

Institute of Mental Health
www.imhl.com

Institute of Psychiatry
www.iop.kcl.ac.uk

Institute of Psychotherapy & Social Studies
www.ipss.dircon.co.uk

Manchester Institute of Psychotherapy
www.mcpt.co.uk

Scottish Dementia Network
www.dementianetwork.org

United Kingdom Council for Psychotherapy
www.psychotherapy.org.uk

research

AIDS Education & Research Trust
www.avert.com

Applied Vision Association
www.dmu.ac.uk/ava

Canadian Neuro-Optic Research Institute
www.cnri.edu

Medical Research Council (Brain Sciences Unit)
www.mrc-cbu.cam.ac.uk

RAFT Institute
www.raft.ac.uk

Society for the Study of Fertility
www.ssf.org.uk

Tenovus
www.tenovus.org.uk

vision

Medical

British Contact Lens Association
www.bcla.org.uk

British Ophthalmic Anaesthesia Society
www.boas.org

CIBAVision
www.cibavision.co.uk

College of Optometrists
www.college-optometrists.org

Scottish Sensory Centre
www.ssc.mhie.ac.uk

Opticians

20/20 Opticians
www.20-20.co.uk

Boots Opticians
www.bootsopticians.co.uk

David Clulow
www.davidclulow.com

Dolland & Aitchison
www.danda.co.uk

Eye Clinic
www.eye-clinic.co.uk

Optical Express
www.opticalexpress.co.uk

Specsavers
www.specsavers.com

Vision Express
www.visionexpress.co.uk

Zeiss Direct
www.zeiss-direct.co.uk

help!

- ambulance services
- breakdown services
- charities & helplines
- consumer problems
- fire & rescue services
- funeral services
- police
- watchdogs & ombudsmen

ambulance services

Ambulance Service Association
www.ambex.co.uk

Scottish Ambulance Service
www.scottishambulance.com

St John's Ambulance Brigade
www.sja.org.uk

breakdown services

AA
www.theaa.co.uk

Britannia Rescue
www.britanniarescue.com

Direct Line Breakdown
www.directline.com

Green Flag
www.greenflag.co.uk

National Breakdown
www.nationalbreakdown.com

NCI breakdown cover
www.ncionline.co.uk

RAC
www.rac.co.uk

charities & helplines

Animals

Animal Aid
www.animalaid.org.uk

Animal Health Trust
www.aht.org.uk

Animal Rescue
www.animalrescue.org.uk

Animal Samaritans
www.animalsamaritans.org.uk

AnimalKind
www.netcomuk.co.uk/~jcox

Battersea Dogs Home
www.dogshome.org

Blue Cross
www.thebluecross.org.uk

Brigitte Bardot Foundation
www.fondationbrigittebardot.fr/uk

British Horse Society
www.bhs.org.uk

Care for the Wild International
www.careforthewild.org.uk

Cats Protection League
www.cats.org.uk

Dian Fossey Gorilla Fund
www.gorillas.org

Donkey Sanctuary
www.thedonkeysanctuary.org.uk

International Animal Rescue
www.iar.org.uk

International Fund for Animal Welfare
www.ifaw.org

International League for the Protection of Horses
www.ilph.org

National Anti-Vivisection Society
www.navs.org

National Canine Defence League
www.ncdl.org.uk

National Pet Week
www.nationalpetweek.org.uk

PDSA
www.pdsa.org.uk

Royal Society for the Prevention of Cruelty to Animals (RSPCA)
www.rspca.org.uk

Royal Society for the Protection of Birds (RSPB)
www.rspb.org.uk

Save the Rhino
www.savetherhino.co.uk

Scottish Society for the Prevention of Cruelty to Animals
www.scottishspca.org

VIVA
www.viva.org.uk

World Society for the Protection of Animals
www.wspa.org.uk

World Wildlife Fund UK
www.wwf.org.uk

Children

Action Group
www.actiongroup.org.uk

Adoption Information Line
www.adoption.org.uk

Association for Families who have Adopted from Abroad
www.afaa.mcmail.com

Barnado's
www.barnados.org.uk

British Agencies for Adoption & Fostering
www.baaf.org.uk

Child Accident Prevention Trust
www.capt.org.uk

Childline
www.childline.org.uk

Children in Need
www.bbc.co.uk/cin

Children With Aids
www.cwac.org

Children's Society
www.the-childrens-society.org.uk

Contact a Family
www.cafamily.org.uk

Families Need Fathers
www.fnf.org.uk

First Cheque 2000
www.firstcheque2000.org.uk

Fostering Information Line
www.fostering.org.uk

Gingerbread
www.gingerbread.org.uk

Kidscape
www.kidscape.org.uk

Mensa Foundation for Gifted Children
www.mfgc.org.uk/mfgc

Missing Kids
www.missingkids.co.uk

National Association of Toy & Leisure Libraries
www.natll.org.uk

National Society for the Prevention of Cruelty to Children (NSPCC)
www.nspcc.org.uk

NCH
www.nch.org

NCH Action for Children
www.nchafc.org.uk

No Limits Sports Club For Children with Special Needs
www.agurney.demon.co.uk/nolimits

Ocean Youth Trust Scotland
www.oytscotland.org.uk

PACT
www.pactcharity.co.uk

Partners in Play
www.partnersinplay.org.uk

Royal Scottish Society for the Prevention of Cruelty to Children (Children 1st)
www.children1st.org.uk

Save the Children
www.savethechildren.org.uk

Scottish Childminding Association
www.childminding.org

Variety Club of Great Britain
www.varietyclub.org.uk

Community

General

Action for Victims of Medical Accidents
www.avma.org.uk

Addaction
www.addaction.org.uk

Age Concern
www.ace.org.uk

Alcoholics Anonymous
www.aa-uk.org.uk

British Association for Counselling
www.counselling.co.uk

Business in the Community
www.bitc.org.uk

Centrepoint
www.centrepoint.org.uk

Church Action on Poverty
www.church-poverty.org.uk

Citizens Advice Bureau
www.adviceguide.org.uk

Comic Relief
www.comicrelief.org.uk

Community Transport Association
www.communitytransport.com

Crisis
www.crisis.org.uk

Diana Memorial Fund
www.theworkcontinues.org

English-Speaking Union
www.esu.org

Foyer Federation
www.foyer.net

Gamblers Anonymous
www.gamblersanonymous.org.uk

Give As You Earn
www.giveasyouearn.org

Help the Aged
www.helptheaged.org.uk

Leonard Cheshire Foundation
www.leonard-cheshire.org

National Lotteries Charities Board
www.nclb.org.uk

Neighbourhood Watch
www.nwatch.org.uk

Nuffield Trust
www.nuffieldtrust.org.uk

Prince's Trust
www.princes-trust.org.uk

Relate
www.relate.org.uk

Rotary International
www.rotary.org

Royal National Institute for Deaf People (RNID)
www.rnid.org.uk

Royal National Institute for the Blind (RNIB)
www.rnib.org.uk

Royal National Lifeboat Institution (RNLI)
www.rnli.org.uk

Royal Society for the Prevention of Accidents (ROSPA)
www.rospa.co.uk

Salvation Army
www.salvationarmy.org.uk

Samaritans
www.samaritans.org.uk

Shelter
www.shelter.org.uk

UK Firework Safety
www.eig.org.uk/fws

UK National Workplace Bullying Advice Line
www.successunlimited.co.uk

Unison
www.unison.org.uk

VSO
www.vso.org.uk

Women's Aid
www.womensaid.org.uk

Community – Scotland

Abbeyfield Scotland (Elderly Aid)
www.scotland.abbeyfield.com

Apex (Jobs for Ex-offenders)
www.apexscotland.org.uk

Citizens Advice Scotland
www.cas.org.uk

Common Knowledge, Glasgow
www.ckglasgow.org.uk

Community Self Build, Scotland
www.selfbuild-scotland.org.uk

Cornerstone Community Care
www.cornerstone.org.uk

Energy Action Scotland
www.eas.org.uk

Family Mediation Scotland
www.familymediationscotland.org.uk

Highland Advice & Information Network
www.hain.org.uk

Lloyds TSB Foundation for Scotland
www.ltsbfoundationforscotland.org.uk

Narcotics Anonymous
www.nascotland.org

Quarriers Care
www.quarriers.org.uk

Rehab Scotland
www.rehab.ie/scotland

Scotland Against Drugs
www.sad.org.uk

Scottish Refugee Council
www.scottishrefugeecouncil.org.uk

The Thistle Foundation
www.thistle.org.uk

Victim Support Scotland
www.victimsupportsco.demon.co.uk

Young Women's Centre (Dundee)
www.youngwomenscentre.org.uk

Education

Book Trust
www.booktrust.org.uk

British Association for Open Learning
www.baol.co.uk

British Dyslexia Association
www.bda-dyslexia.org.uk

Careers Services National Association
www.careers-uk.com

Raleigh International
www.raleighinternational.org

Scottish Book Trust
www.scottishbooktrust.com

Environmental – Scotland

Friends of the Earth, Scotland
www.foe-scotland.org.uk

John Muir Trust
www.jmt.org

Scottish Environmental Link
www.scotlink.org

Working for Environmental Community Action Now
www.wecan.org.uk

Health

General

Ability
www.ability.org.uk

Action against Breast Cancer
www.aabc.org.uk

Action for Cancer Trust
www.actionforcancertrust.com

Action for ME
www.afme.org.uk

Action for Tinnitus Research
www.tinnitus-research.org

Action on Pre-eclampsia
www.apec.org.uk

Alcohol Concern
www.alcoholconcern.org.uk

Alcoholics Anonymous
www.alcoholics-anonymous.org

Alzheimer's Association
www.alz.org

Alzheimer's Disease Society
www.alzheimers.org.uk

Anorexia & Bulimia Care
www.anorexiabulimiacare.co.uk

Anthony Nolan Bone Marrow Trust
www.anthonynolan.com

Arachnoiditis Trust
www.arachnoiditistrust.org

Arthritis Care
www.arthritiscare.org.uk

Association for International Cancer Research
www.aicr.org.uk

Association for Post-Natal Illness
www.apni.org

Association for Spina Bifida & Hydrocephalus
www.asbah.org

Bliss
www.bliss.org.uk

Bob Champion Cancer Trust
www.bobchampion.org.uk

Breast Cancer Campaign
www.bcc-uk.org

Breast Clinic
www.thebreastclinic.com

British Acoustic Neuroma Association
www.ukan.co.uk/bana

British Cardiac Society
www.cardiac.org.uk

British Diabetic Association
www.diabetes.org.uk

British Epilepsy Association
www.epilepsy.org.uk

British Heart Foundation
www.bhf.org.uk

British Red Cross
www.redcross.org.uk

Cancer Bacup
www.cancerbacup.org.uk

Cancer Research Fund
www.crc.org.uk

Centre for Recovery from Drug & Alcohol Abuse
www.recovery.org.uk

CJD Foundation
www.cjdfoundation.org

Council for Disabled Children
www.ncb.org.uk/cdc

Crusaid
www.crusaid.org.uk

Depression Alliance
www.gn.apc.org/da

Diabetes Insight
www.diabetic.org.uk

Disability Now
www.disabilitynow.org.uk

Disabled Living Foundation
www.atlas.co.uk/dlf

Down's Syndrome Association
www.dsa-uk.com

Ectopic Pregnancy Trust
www.ectopic.org.uk

Enuresis Resource & Information Centre
www.eric.org.uk

Epilepsy Research Foundation
www.erf.org.uk

Glaucoma Research Foundation
www.glaucoma.org

Institute for the Study of Drug Dependency
www.isdd.co.uk

King's Fund
www.kingsfund.org.uk

Leukaemia Research Fund
www.leukaemia-research.org.uk

Macmillan Relief
www.macmillan.org.uk

Marie Curie Cancer Care
www.mariecurie.org.uk

Mencap
www.mencap.org.uk

Meningitis Research Foundation
www.meningitis.org.uk

Mind
www.mind.org.uk

Miscarriage Association
www.the-ma.org.uk

Multiple Births Foundation
www.multiplebirths.org.uk

Multiple Sclerosis Society
www.mssociety.org.uk

Muscular Dystrophy Campaign
www.muscular-dystrophy.org

NACC
www.nacc.org.uk

National Addiction Centre
www.netline.co.uk/nac

National AIDS Trust
www.nat.org.uk

National Association for Premenstrual Syndrome
www.pms.org.uk

National Asthma Campaign
www.asthma.org.uk

National Autistic Society
www.nas.org.uk

National Back Pain Association
www.backpain.org

National Deaf Children's Society
www.ndcs.org.uk

National Endometriosis Society
www.endo.org.uk

National Fertility Association
www.issue.co.uk

National Kidney Research Fund
www.nkrf.org.uk

National Meningitis Trust
www.meningitis-trust.org.uk

National Osteoporosis Society
www.nos.org.uk

Northern Ireland Chest, Heart & Stroke Association
www.nichsa.com

Nuffield Trust
www.nuffieldtrust.org

Paralinks
www.paralinks.net

Primary Immunodeficiency Association
www.pia.org.uk

Prostate Cancer
www.prostate-cancer.org.uk

Reach
www.reach.org.uk

Roy Castle Lung Cancer Foundation
www.roycastle.org

Scope
www.scope.org.uk

SIDS – Foundation
www.sids.org.uk/fsid

Stillbirth & Neonatal Death Society
www.uk-sands.org

Stroke Association
www.stroke.org.uk

Terence Higgins Trust
www.tht.org.uk

World Federation of Haemophilia
www.wfh.org

Health – Scotland

Action on Smoking & Health (Scotland)
www.ashscotland.org.uk

Alzheimer Scotland, Action on Dementia
www.alzscot.org

Cancer Awareness in Scotland
www.cancerawareness.org.uk

Capability Scotland
www.capability-scotland.org.uk

Chest, Heart & Stroke Scotland
www.chss.org.uk

Deaf Connections
www.deafconnections.co.uk

Deafblind Scotland
www.deafblindscotland.org.uk

Healthy Gay Scotland
www.hgscotland.org.uk

Operation Heart Start
www.heartstart.org

St. Andrew's Ambulance Association
www.firstaid.org.uk

Overseas Development

Action Aid
www.oneworld.org/actionaid

Afghanaid
www.afghanaid.org.uk

Amnesty International
www.amnesty.org

Book Aid International
www.bookaid.org

Care International
www.care.org

Christian Aid
www.christian-aid.org.uk

Globalaid
www.globalaid.co.uk

Oxfam
www.oxfam.org.uk

Red Cross
www.redcross.org.uk

Scottish International Relief
www.charitiesdirect.com/charity2/ch014052.htm

Sight Savers
www.sightsavers.org

The Tibet Society
www.tibetsociety.com

Voluntary Organisations

Edinburgh Voluntary Organisations Council
www.evoc.org.uk

Learning Link Scotland
www.learninglinkscotland.org.uk

Scottish Council for Voluntary Organisations
www.scvo.org.uk

Scottish Council for Voluntary Services
www.cvsscotland.org.uk

Shared Care Scotland
www.sharedcarescotland.com

consumer problems

The Advertising Standards Authority
www.asa.org.uk

British Standards Institution
www.bsi.org.uk

British Weights & Measures Association
www.british-weights-and-measures-association.co.uk

The Complainer
www.complainer.co.uk

Consumer Gateway (DTI)
www.consumer.gov.uk

Consumers in Europe Group
www.ceg.co.uk

European Agency of Information on Consumer Affairs
www.euro-conso.org

Local Authorities Co-ordinating Body on Food & Trading Standards
www.lacots.org.uk

National Association of Citizens Advice Bureaux
www.nacab.org.uk

Office of Fair trading
www.oft.gov.uk

Scottish Consumer Council
www.scotconsumer.org.uk

Scottish Trading Standards
www.scotss.org.uk

Trading Standards Office
www.tradingstandards.gov.uk

Watchdog
www.bbc.co.uk/watchdog

fire & rescue services

British Fire Service
www.fire.org.uk

Coastguard Agency
www.coastguard.gov.uk

Fire Brigade Union
www.fbu.org.uk

International Rescue Corps
www.ps2.com/irc

Maritime & Coastguard Agency
www.mcagency.org.uk

Mountain Rescue
www.mra.org

Mountain Rescue Committee of Scotland
www.mrc-scotland.org.uk

Royal Naval Lifeboat Institution
www.rnli.org.uk

Scottish Avalanche Information Service
www.sais.gov.uk

Scottish Fire Brigades
www.fire.org.uk/scotland

funeral services

British Institute of Embalmers
www.bie.org.uk

Co-operative Funeral Services
www.funeral-services.co.uk

National Association of Memorial Masons
www.namm.org.uk

Society of Allied & Independent Funeral Directors
www.saif.org.uk

police

General

Association of Police Authorities
www.apa.police.uk

British Transport Police
www.btp.police.uk

Interpol
www.interpol.com

Ministry of Defence Police
www.mod.uk/mdp

National Crime Squad
www.nationalcrimesquad.police.uk

Scottish Police Force
www.scottish.police.uk

UK Atomic Energy Constabulary
www.ukaea.org.uk/ukaeac

Regional

Central Scotland Police
www.centralscotland.police.uk

Dumfries & Galloway Constabulary
www.dumfriesandgalloway.police.uk

Fife Constabulary
www.fife.police.uk

Grampian Police
www.grampian.police.uk

Lothian & Borders Police
www.lbp.police.uk

Northern Constabulary
www.northern.police.uk

Strathclyde Police
www.strathclyde.police.uk

Tayside Police
www.tayside.police.uk

watchdogs & ombudsmen

Adjudicator's Office
www.open.gov.uk/adjoff/index.htm

Adult Learning Inspectorate
www.ali.gov.uk

Advertising Standards Authority
www.asa.org.uk

Banking Ombudsman
www.obo.org.uk

Broadcasting Standards Commission
www.bsc.org.uk

Data Protection Registrar
www.dataprotection.gov.uk

Drinking Water Inspectorate
www.dwi.detr.gov.uk

Estate Agents Ombudsman
www.oea.co.uk

Health Service Ombudsman
www.ombudsman.org.uk

Independent Complaints Reviewer to HM Land Registry
www.icrev.demon.co.uk/icrbook.htm

Independent Television Commission
www.itc.org.uk

Insurance Ombudsman Bureau
www.theiob.org.uk

Jasper Griegson (The Complainer)
www.complainer.co.uk

Local Government Ombudsman
www.open.gov.uk/lgo

Northern Ireland Ombudsman
www.ombudsman.nics.gov.uk

OFFER (Electricity)
www.open.gov.uk/offer

Office for the Supervision of Solicitors
www.lawsociety.org.uk

Office of Fair Trading
www.oft.gov.uk

OFGAS (Gas)
www.ofgas.gov.uk

OFSTED (Teaching)
www.open.gov.uk/ofsted

OFTEL (Telecommunications)
www.oftel.org

OFWAT (Water)
www.open.gov.uk/ofwat

Parliamentary & Health Service Ombudsman
www.ombudsman.org.uk

Press Complaints Commission
www.pcc.org.uk

Radio Authority
www.radioauthority.org.uk

Rail Users' Consultative Committees
www.rail-reg.gov.uk/rucc

Scottish Legal Services Ombudsman
www.slso.org.uk

Scottish Water
www.esw.co.uk

hobbies & leisure

- astrology
- ballooning
- birds & bird watching
- boating
- bodybuilding
- bridge
- chess
- climbing
- collecting
- cookery
- country pursuits
- dancing
- fishing
- flying
- football
- gambling
- games
- gardening
- genealogy
- handicrafts
- homebrew
- horseriding
- karting
- metal detecting
- miscellaneous clubs & associations
- models
- motorsport
- music
- outdoor pursuits
- pets
- photography

astrology

About Astrology
http://astrology.about.com

Astrologer's Perspective
www.anastrologersperspective.com

Astrology Association of Great Britain
www.astrologer.com/aanet

Astrology Online
www.astrology-online.com

Astrology World
www.astrology-world.com

British Astrological & Psychic Society
www.bapsoc.co.uk

Faculty of Astrology Studies
www.astrology.org.uk

Johnathan Cainer
www.cainer.com

Paul Wade
www.astrologywizard.com/homepage.htm

Russell Grant
www.russellgrant.com

Scottish Astrological Association
www.lunatica.fsnet.co.uk

ballooning

Adventure Balloons
www.adventureballoons.co.uk

Alba Ballooning
www.albaballooning.co.uk

Balloons over Britain
www.balloonsoverbritain.co.uk

British Association of Balloon Operators
www.babo.org.uk

Hot Air Ballooning
www.launch.net

Virgin Challenger
www.challenger.virgin.net

birds & bird watching

African Bird Club
www.africanbirdclub.org

Association of Field Ornithologists
www.afonet.org

Bird On!
http://birdcare.com/birdon

Bird Trip & Tours
www.birdwatch.co.uk

Birding Scotland
www.birdingscotland.org.uk

Birds of Britain
www.birdsofbritain.co.uk

Birdwatch Magazine
www.birdwatch.co.uk

Birdwatch.net
www.birdwatch.net

British Falconers Club
www.britishfalconersclub.co.uk

British Homing World
www.pigeonracing.com

British Ornithologists' Union
www.bou.org.uk

British Trust for Ornithology
www.birdcare.com

Budgerigar Society
www.budgerigarsociety.com

Budgerigar World
www.tuxford.dabsol.co.uk

Conserv@tion Scotland
www.habitat.org.uk/scot.htm

Game Conservancy Trust
www.game-conservancy.org.uk

National Birds of Prey Centre
www.nbpc.co.uk

National Flying Club
www.nationalflyingclub.co.uk

Oriental Bird Club
www.orientalbirdclub.org

Parrot Society UK
www.theparrotsocietyuk.org

Racing Pigeon Magazine
www.racingpigeon.co.uk

Rare Breeding Birds Panel
www.indaal.demon.co.uk/rbbp.html

Royal Pigeon Racing Association
www.rpra-ne.demon.co.uk

RSPB
www.rspb.org.uk

Scottish Ornithologists Club
www.the-soc.fsnet.co.uk

Scottish Wildlife Trust
www.swt.org.uk

UK Parrot Society
www.theparrotsocietyuk.org

Wildfowl & Wetlands Trust
www.wwt.org.uk

boating

Association of Inland Navigation Authorities
www.cam.net.uk/home/aina

Big Blue Boat Shows
www.bigblue.org.uk

Classic Motor Boat Association
www.cmba.classic-marine.co.uk

National Association of Boat Owners
www.nabo.org.uk

Sport Scotland
www.sportscotland.org.uk

Canoeing

British Canoe Union
www.bcu.org.uk

Scottish Canoe Association
www.scot-canoe.org

Rowing

Amateur Rowing Association
www.ara-rowing.org

FISA (Official World Rowing Site)
www.worldrowing.com

Scottish Amateur Rowing Association
www.scottish-rowing.org.uk

Waterways

Association of Waterways Cruising Clubs
www.penpont.demon.co.uk/awcchp.htm

British Waterways
www.britishwaterways.co.uk

Inland Waterways Association
www.waterways.org.uk

Scottish Waterways
www.scottishcanals.co.uk

UK Waterways Network
www.ukwaterways.net

Yachting

Clyde Yacht Clubs
http://homepages.rya-online.net/cyca

Forth Yacht Clubs
www.fyca.org.uk

Inshore Waters Weather Forecast (Met Office)
www.meto.govt.uk/datafiles/inshore.html

International Sailing Federation
www.sailing.org

Port Edgar Marina
www.portedgar.co.uk

Royal Yachting Association
www.rya.org.uk

RYA Scotland
www.ryascotland.org.uk

Scottish Sailing Institute
http://scottishsailinginstitute.com

UK Sailing Index
www.uksail.com

West Highland Anchorage & Moorings Association
www.whamassoc.org.uk

Yachting & Boating World
www.ybw.com

Yachting Life
www.yachtinglife.co.uk

bodybuilding

Flex Magazine
www.flexonline.com

International Federation of Body Builders
www.ifbb.com

Mens Fitness Magazine
www.mensfitness.com

Muscle & Fitness Magazine
www.muscle-fitness.com

Weider Nutrition
www.weider.ca

bridge

American Contract Bridge League
www.acbl.org

Bridge Today
www.bridgetoday.com/bt

Bridge World
www.bridgeworld.com

Canadian Bridge Federation
www.cbf.ca

English Bridge Union
www.ebu.co.uk

Israeli Bridge Federation
http://tx.technion.ac.il/~herbst/ibf.html

Northern Ireland Bridge Union
www.nibu.co.uk

Pakistan Bridge Federation
http://pbf.port5.com

Scottish Bridge Union
www.sbu.dircon.co.uk

South African Bridge Federation
www.sabf.co.za

Welsh Bridge Union
www.wbu.org.uk

World Bridge Federation
www.bridge.gr

chess

British Chess Federation
www.bcf.ndirect.co.uk

British Chess Magazine
www.bcmchess.co.uk

British Federation of Correspondence Chess
www.wibbly-wobbly.org.uk

Chess Master
www.chessmaster.com

Chess Scotland
www.scottishchess.com

Garry Kasparov
www.clubkasparov.ru

Internet Chess Club
www.chessclub.comurl changed – updated

London Chess Centre
www.chesscentre.com

Scottish Chess Association
www.users.globalnet.co.uk/~sca

Scottish Correspondence Chess Association
www.scottishcca.co.uk

This Week in Chess
www.chess.co.uk

World Chess Federation
www.fide.com

climbing

British Mountain Guides
www.bmg.org.uk

British Mountaineering Council
www.thebmc.co.uk

Mountain Rescue
www.mra.org

Mountain Sports Guide
www.mtn.co.uk

Mountaineering Council for Scotland
www.mountaineering-scotland.org.uk

Rockface
www.rockface.co.uk

Scottish Mountaineering Club
www.smc.org.uk/smc

Three Peaks Challenge
www.netdesktop.co.uk/3peaks

collecting

Cards

Cartophilic Society of Great Britain
www.cardclubs.ndirect.co.uk

International Playing Card Society
www.pagat.com/ipcs

Trade Card Collector's Association
www.tradecardcollectors.com

Coins

British Association of Numismatic Societies
www.coinclubs.freeserve.co.uk

Coin Dealer Directory
www.numis.co.uk

Coin News
www.coin-news.com

Coins & Antiquities Magazine
www.coins-and-antiquities.co.uk

Royal Numismatic Society
www.users.dircon.co.uk/~rns/index.html

Spink & Son
www.spink-online.com

World of Money
www.thebritishmuseum.ac.uk/worldofmoney

Miscellaneous

Airfix Collectors Club
www.djairfix.freeserve.co.uk

Antiquarian Horological Society
www.ahsoc.demon.co.uk

Armourer Magazine
www.armourer.u-net.com

Association of Bottled Beer Collectors
http://ourworld.compuserve.com/homepages/john_mann/abbchome.htm

British Matchbox Label & Booklet Society
www.studenter.hb.se/~match/bml&bs

British Watch & Clock Collectors Association
www.timecap.co.uk

UK Sucrologists Club
www.uksucrologistclub.org.uk

Stamps

Association of First Day Cover Collectors
www.gbfdc.co.uk

Association of Scottish Philatelic Societies
www.scottishphilately.co.uk

British Aerophilatelic Federation
www.btinternet.com/~baef

British Library Philatelic Collections
www.bl.uk/collections/philatelic

GB Philatelic Society
www.gbps.org.uk/

Hallmark Group
www.hallmark-group.co.uk

National Philatelic Society
www.ukphilately.org.uk/nps

National Postal Museum
www.royalmail.co.uk/athome/stamps/museum.htm

Philatelic Societies of the World
www.philatelicsociety.com

Philatelic Traders' Society
www.philatelic-traders-society.co.uk

Post Office
www.postoffice.co.uk

Robin Hood Stamp Company
www.robinhood-stamp.co.uk

Royal Mail
www.royalmail.com

Royal Philatelic Society London
www.rpsl.org.uk

Scot Stamps
www.scotstamps.co.uk

Stanley Gibbons
www.stanleygibbons.co.uk

The Great Britain Philatelic Society
www.gbps.org.uk

UK Philatelic Museums & Libraries
www.gs.dial.pipex.com/museum3.htm

UK Philately
www.ukphilately.org.uk

UK Stamp Fairs
www.stampdiary.com

cookery

Allrecipes.com
www.allrecipes.com

Ballymaloe Cookery School
www.ballymaloe-cookery-school.ie

BBC Food & Drink
www.bbc.co.uk/foodanddrink

Edinburgh School of Food & Wine
www.cookerycompany.com

Fresh Food Cookbook
www.freshfood.co.uk/cookbook

Gourmet World
www.gourmetworld.co.uk

Leith's School of Food & Wine
www.leiths.com

Mosiman Academy
www.mosiman.com

Recipe World
www.recipe-world.com

Royal Thai Cookery School
www.rtsca.com

Tante Marie Cookery School
www.tantemarie.co.uk

UK Cookery Directory
www.uk-cookerydirectory.co.uk

Wendy Barrie's Scottish Cookery Portal
www.wendybarrie.co.uk

country pursuits

British Association for Shooting & Conservation
www.basc.org.uk

British Falconers Club
www.users.zetnet.co.uk/bfc

British Field Sports Society
www.bfss.org

CLA Game Fair
www.countrypursuits.co.uk/cla.htm

Clay Pigeon Shooting Association
www.cpsa.co.uk

Countryside Alliance
www.countryside-alliance.org

Countrysports
www.countrysports.co.uk

Field Magazine
www.thefield.co.uk

Masters of Drag & Bloodhounds Association
www.users.globalnet.co.uk/~dhwallis/mdha.html

National Association of Regional Game Councils
www.iol.ie/~nargc

National Association of Specialist Anglers
www.cygnet.co.uk/ukfw/nasa

Shooting Gazette
www.countrypursuits.co.uk

Sportsman's Association (SAGBNI)
www.sportsmans-association.org

UK Practical Shooting Association
www.ukpsa.co.uk

dancing

Ballroom Dancing Times
www.dancing-times.co.uk

DanceSport UK
www.dancesport.uk.com

Imperial Society of Teachers of Dancing (ISTD)
www.istd.org.uk

International Dance Sport Federation
www.idsf.net

International Dance Teachers Association (IDTA)
www.idta.co.uk

fishing

Angling Magazine
www.anglemag.freeserve.co.uk

Angling News
www.angling-news.co.uk

Bankside Fishing Tackle
www.banksidefishing.co.uk

Coarse Fishing in the Highlands
http://nnh.co.uk/highland-coarse

Countryside Alliance
www.countryside-alliance.net

Fish & Fly Magazine
www.fishandfly.co.uk

Fishing in Scotland
www.fishing-uk-scotland.com

Fishing the Fly
www.fishingthefly.co.uk

Fishing UK
www.fishing.co.uk

Fishing World
www.fishing.org

Fishing.co.uk
www.fishing.co.uk

Fly Dressers' Guild
www.the-fdg.org

Fly Fishing UK
www.flyfishuk.com

Flytyer
www.flytyer.co.uk

Gardner
www.gardnertackle.co.uk

Go-Fishing
www.go-fishing.co.uk

Glasgow Angling Centre
www.fishingmegastore.com

Grayling Society
www.graylingsociety.org

Harrisons Rods
www.harrisonrods.co.uk

Maver
www.maver.co.uk

National Federation of Anglers
www.fire.org.uk/nfa

RMC Angling
www.rmcangling.co.uk

Salmon & Trout Association
www.salmon-trout.org

Scottish Anglers National Association (SANA)
www.sana.org.uk

Scottish Angling Information
www.premier-pages.co.uk/angling

Scottish Federation for Coarse Angling
www.sfca.co.uk

Sea Anglers Conservation Network
www.anglenet.co.uk

Specialist Anglers Conservation Group
www.anglersnet.co.uk/sacg

UK Angling Guide
http://uk-fishing.com

UK Fly Fishing & Tyers Federation
www.fly-fisherman.org.uk

Where-to-Fish
www.where-to-fish.com

flying

Aeroclub
www.aeroclub.net

Aircrew Association – Saltire Branch
www.aircrew-saltire.org

Airspace Magazine
www.raes.org.uk

British Hang Gliding & Para Gliding Association
www.bhpa.co.uk

British Microlight Aircraft Association
www.avnet.co.uk/bmaa

Denham Aerodrome
www.egld.com

Kite Club of Scotland
www.kcos.net

Kite Society of Great Britain
www.thekitesociety.org.uk

Military Airshows in the UK
www.militaryairshows.co.uk

Museum of Flight
www.nms.ac.uk/flight

Ormond Flying Club
www.ormandflyingclub.com

Pilot Magazine
www.pilotweb.co.uk

RAF Kinloss
www.kinloss-raf.co.uk

RAF Leuchars
www.leuchars.raf.mod.uk

RAF Lossiemouth
www.fly.to/raflossie

Red Arrows
www.deltaweb.co.uk/reds

Royal Aeronautical Society
www.raes.org.uk

Scottish Aviation Project
www.aviationscotland.org.uk

Scottish Flying Schools & Clubs Directory
www.flyingzone.co.uk/flyingschools/scotland/scotlandfs.htm

Scottish Hang Gliding & Para Gliding Federation
www.flyingscot.f9.co.uk

World Air Sports Federation
www.fai.org

football

All the Teams
www.alltheteams.co.uk

Amateur Football League
www.soccerbot.com/afl

FIFA
www.fifa.com

The Football Association
www.the-fa.org

Football Forum
www.thefootballforum.co.uk

GAA Online
www.gaa.ie

Ian St John's Soccer Camps
www.soccercamps.co.uk

Scottish Football Association
www.scottishfa.co.uk

Sunday Football League Directory
www.sunday-football.co.uk

UEFA
www.uefa.com

Umbro International Football Festival
www.worldwidesoccer.co.uk

gambling

Blue Sq
www.bluesq.com

Bookie Guide
www.bookieguide.com

British Casino Association
www.british-casinos.co.uk

Casino Choice
www.casinochoice.co.uk

City Index
www.cityindex.co.uk

Complete Casino Gaming & Gambling Directory
www.casinocity.com

First Betting
http://firstbetting.com

Football Data
www.football-data.co.uk

Gamblers Anonymous
www.gamblersanonymous.org.uk

Gamblershouse
www.gamblershouse.com

Greyhound Racing Board
www.thedogs.co.uk

IG Index
www.igindex.co.uk

Jockey Club
www.thejockeyclub.co.uk

Ladbrokes
www.ladbrokes.co.uk

Littlewoods Pools
www.littlewoods-pools.co.uk

Mecca Bingo Online
www.meccabingo.com

MyBetting
www.mybetting.co.uk

National Lottery
www.national-lottery.co.uk

Paddy Power
www.paddypower.com

Perfect Racing System
www.theperfectracingsystem.co.uk

Rank Leisure
www.rank.com

Scottish Horse Racing
www.scottishracing.co.uk

Soccer Tips for Free
www.soccertips4free.co.uk

Soccer Winners
www.soccerwinners.com

Sporting Index
www.sportingindex.com

Stanley Racing
www.stanleyleisure.com

Surfabet
www.surfabet.com

Tipsters Exposed
www.tipstersexposed.com

Toals Bookmakers
www.toals.co.uk

Tote
www.tote.co.uk

Turf Club
www.turfclub.ie

UK Betting
www.ukbetting.com

Victor Chandler
www.victorchandler.com

William Hill
www.williamhill.co.uk

Zetters
www.zetters.co.uk

games

About Board Games
http://boardgames.about.com

Bridge Club Live
www.bridgeclublive.com

British Isles Backgammon Association
www.cottagewebs.co.uk/biba

Games Workshop
www.games-workshop.com

Loquax
www.loquax.co.uk

Monopoly
www.monopoly.com

Scottish Bridge Union
www.sbu.dircon.co.uk

Scrabble
www.scrabble.com

Trivial Pursuit
www.trivialpursuit.com

gardening

Atco
www.atco.co.uk

BBC Ground Force
www.bbc.co.uk/groundforce

BBC Home Front in the Garden
www.bbc.co.uk/homefrontgarden

Birstall Garden Centre
www.birstall.co.uk

Black & Decker Online
www.blackanddecker.com

Chelsea Flower Show
www.rhs.org.uk/chelsea

Crocus
www.crocus.co.uk

Cyclamen Society
www.cyclamen.org

The Eden Project
www.edenproject.com

Florajac's
www.florajacs.co.uk

Flower & Plant Association
www.flowers.org.uk

Flymo
www.flymo.co.uk

Garden
www.igarden.co.uk

Garden History Society
www.gardenhistorysociety.org

Garden Links
www.gardenlinks.ndo.co.uk

Garden Seeker
www.gardenseeker.com

Garden Visit
www.gardenvisit.com

Gardeners' World
www.gardenersworld.beeb.com

Gardening 365
www.oxalis.co.uk

Gardening Scotland
www.gardeningscotland.com

Gardening-uk
www.gardening-uk.com

Greenfingers.com
www.greenfingers.com

Hampton Court Palace Flower Show
www.rhs.org.uk/hamptoncourt

Hampton Court Palace Flower Show
www.rhs.org.uk/hamptoncourt

Hartland
www.hartland.co.uk

Hayter
www.hayter.co.uk

Herb Society
www.herbsociety.co.uk

Heritage Seed Library
www.hdra.org.uk

International Bulb Society
www.bulbsociety.com

Landscape Trust
www.landscape.co.uk

Levington
www.levington.co.uk

Miracle-Gro Online
www.miraclegro.com

National Garden
www.garden.org

National Gardens Scheme
www.ngs.org.uk

National Herb Centre
www.herbcentre.co.uk

New Eden
www.neweden.co.uk

Organic Gardening
www.organicgardening.com

Permaculture Association
www.permaculture.co.uk

Qualcast
www.qualcast.co.uk

Royal Caledonian Horticultural Society
www.rchs.fsnet.co.uk

Royal Horticultural Society
www.rhs.org.uk

Royal Horticultural Society Shop
www.grogro.com

Royal National Rose Society
www.roses.co.uk

Scottish Allotments & Garden Society
www.sags.org.uk

Scottish Rock Garden Club
www.srgc.org.uk

Secretts
www.secretts.co.uk

Spear & Jackson
www.spear-and-jackson.com

Van Tubergen
www.vantubergen.co.uk

Wildflower Page
www.habitat.org.uk/wildflwr.htm

genealogy

Ancestral Scotland
www.ancestralscotland.com

Ancestry Research
www.ancestors.co.uk

Association of Scottish Genealogists & Record Agents
www.asgra.co.uk

British Heraldic Archive
www.kwtelecom.com/heraldry

Burke's Peerage & Landed Gentry
www.burkes-landed-gentry.com

Family Records
www.familyrecords.gov.uk

Family Records Centre
www.pro.gov.uk/about/frc

Family Tree Magazine
www.family-tree.co.uk

Federation of Family History Societies
www.ffhs.org.uk

Gathering of the Clans
www.tartans.com

Gendex Genealogical Index
www.gendex.com

Genealogical Services Directory
www.genealogical.co.uk

Genealogy
www.genealogy.org

General Register Office for Scotland
www.gro-scotland.gov.uk

GENUKI, UK & Ireland Genealogy
www.genuki.org.uk

Institute of Heraldic & Genealogical Studies
www.ihgs.ac.uk

Mormons Family Search
www.familysearch.org

NamesUK
www.namesuk.com

National Archives of Ireland
www.nationalarchives.ie

National Archives of Scotland
www.nas.gov.uk

National Library of Scotland
www.nls.uk

Northern Ireland Statistics & Research Agency
www.nisra.gov.uk

Origins
www.origins.net

Public Record Office
www.pro.gov.uk

Scotland's People (Official Govt Site)
www.scotlandspeople.gov.uk

Scottish Archive Network
www.scan.org.ukurl changed – updated

Scottish Association of Family History Societies
www.safhs.org.uk

Scottish Clans
www.scotclans.com

Scottish Genealogy Society
www.scotsgenealogy.com

Scottish Roots
www.scottish-roots.co.uk

Society of Genealogists
www.sog.org.uk

handicrafts

Association of Guilds of Weavers, Spinners & Dyers
www.wsd.org.uk

Bead Society of Great Britain
http://members.delphi.com/britishbeads

Calligraphy & Lettering Arts Society
www.clas.co.uk

Ceramics Monthly
www.ceramicsmonthly.org

Classic Stitch
www.classicstitch.co.uk

Colour Craft Needlework
www.colour-craft.com

County Needlecraft
www.countyneedlecraft.com

Craft UK
www.craft-fair.co.uk

Crafts Council
www.craftscouncil.org.uk

Crochet Design
www.crochet.co.uk

Embroiderers' Guild
www.embroiderersguild.org.uk

Glass Art Society
www.glassart.org

Guild of Silk Painters
www.silkpainters-guild.co.uk

Hobbycraft
www.hobbycraft.co.uk

Homecrafts
www.homecrafts.co.uk

Husqvarna
www.husqvarnastudio.co.uk

International Feltmakers Association
www.antel.demon.co.uk/ifa/ifa.htm

Knitting Now
www.knittingnow.com

Knitting Today
www.knittingtoday.com

Lace Guild
www.laceguild.demon.co.uk

Lace Magazine
www.lacemagazine.com

Marquetry Society
www.marquetry.org

Popular Crafts
www.popularcrafts.com

Quick & Easy Cross Stitch
www.futurenet.com/futureonline/magazines

Quilters' Guild of the British Isles
www.quiltersguild.org.uk

Quilting Directory
www.quiltingdirectory.co.uk

Rowan
www.rowanyarns.co.uk

Royal School of Needlework
www.royal-needlework.co.uk

Scottish Borders Crafts Association
www.scottishborderscraftsassociation.org.uk

Scottish Women's Rural Institute
www.swri.org.uk

Society of Scribes & Illuminators
www.calligraphy.org

Stoll UK
www.stolluk.co.uk

UK Cross Stitch Club
www.crossstitch.org

UK Stained Glass News
www.stainedglassnews.co.uk

Vogue Knitting
www.vogueknitting.com

homebrew

Breworld
www.breworld.com

Craft Brewing Association
www.breworld.com/cba

EDME
www.edme.com

horseriding

Association of British Riding Schools
www.equiworld.net/abrs

Ayr Riding Club
www.ayrridingclub.co.uk

British Driving Society
www.britishdrivingsociety.co.uk

British Equestrian Trade Association
www.beta-uk.org

British Horse Society
www.bhs.org.uk

British Horse Society Scotland
www.bhsscotland.org.uk

British Show Jumping Association
www.bsja.co.uk

Dalkeith Park Equestrian Club
www.dpec.org.uk

Edinburgh Polo Club
www.eteamz.com/edinburghpolo

Endurance Horse & Pony Society
www.ehps.org.uk

Fife Riding Club
www.fife-riding-club.co.ukurl changed – updated

Flower Hill
www.flowerhill.neturl changed – updated

Gleneagles Equestrian Centre
www.gleneagles.com/activities/activities_html/equestrian.html

Horse & Pony Sales
www.horseandponysales.co.uk

Horsetrace
www.horsetrace.com

Mounted Games Association (Scotland)
www.mgascotland.co.uk

Muirmill International Equestrian Centre
www.muirmill.com

Pony Club
www.pony-club.org.uk

Scothorse
www.sport-horses.org

Scottish Carriage Driving Association
www.scda.co.uk

Scottish Equestrian Association
www.houstonhousehorsetrials.co.uk/sea2

Scottish Equestrian Magazine
www.thescottishequestrian.co.uk

Scottish Horse Riding Holiday Centre
http://home.freeuk.com/scotequi/frameset.htm

Scottish Polo
www.scotpolo.org.uk

Side Saddle Association
www.equiworld.com/ssa

Trekking & Riding Society of Scotland
www.ridinginscotland.com

UK Saddlery
www.uksaddlery.com

World of Horses
www.worldofhorses.co.uk

karting

Association of British Kart Clubs
www.karting.co.uk/abkc

Association of Racing Kart Schools
www.arks.co.uk

British Superkart Association
www.superkart.mcmail.com

Challenge 2000
www.kartchallenge.com

Daytona
www.daytona.co.uk

UK Karting
www.karting.co.uk

metal detecting

C Scope
www.cscope.co.uk

Detecnicks
www.detecnicks.co.uk

Federation of Independent Detectorists
www.detectorists.net

National Council for Metal Detecting
www.ncmd.freeserve.co.uk

UK Detector Net
www.ukdetectornet.co.uk

miscellaneous clubs & associations

Association of Woodturners of Great Britain
www.woodturners.co.uk

Boys' Brigade
www.boys-brigade.org.uk

British Council
www.britishcouncil.org

British Model Flying Association
www.bmfa.org

British Youth Council
www.byc.org.uk

Country Gentleman's Association
www.thecga.co.uk

Elgar Society
www.elgar.org

English Pool Association
www.epa.org.uk

Girl Guides
www.girlguides.org.uk

Gunpowder Plot Society
www.gunpowder-plot.org

Historical Model Railway Society
www.hmrs.org.uk

Hovercraft Club of Great Britain
www.hovercraft.org.uk

International Freemasonry
www.london-lodges.org/masonlinks.htm

Lighthouse Society of Great Britain
www.lsgb.co.uk

London Underground Railway Society
www.lurs.org.uk

Mensa
www.mensa.org

National Association of Youth Theatres
www.nayt.org.uk

National Federation of Young Farmers Clubs
www.nfyfc.org.uk

Paintball Zone
www.paintballzone.demon.co.uk

Radio Society of Great Britain
www.rsgb.org

Red Cross
www.redcross.org.uk

Rotaract Club
www.rotaract.org.uk

Royal British Legion
www.britishlegion.org.uk

Scottish Centre for Active Citizenship
www.communitylearning.org/scac.asp

Scottish Women's Rural Institute
www.swri.org.uk

Scottish Youth Hostel Association
www.syha.org.uk

Scouts Association
www.scouts-scotland.org.uk

Stagweb
www.stagweb.co.uk

Tai Chi Union of Great Britain
www.taichiunion.com

United Kingdom Radio Society
www.ukrs.org

Women's Institute
www.nfwi.org.uk

Womens Royal Voluntary Service (WRVS)
www.wrvs.org.uk

YMCA
www.ymca.org.uk

Youth Clubs UK
www.youthclubs.org.uk

Youth Hostelling Association
www.yha.org.uk

Youth UK
www.youth.org.uk

Youthlink Scotland
www.youthlink.co.uk

models

Airfix
www.airfix.co.uk

Ballantynes of Walkerburn
www.ballantynes-walkerburn.com

Beatties
www.beatties.net

British Electric Flight Association
www.befa007.freeserve.co.uk

British Model Flying Association
www.bmfa.org

British Model Soldier Society
www.btinternet.com/~model.soldiers

Corgi
www.corgi.co.uk

Hannants
www.hannants.co.uk

Historical Model Railway Society
www.hmrs.org.uk

Hornby
www.hornby.co.uk

Model Planes@about.com
http://miniatures.about.com

Model Yachting Association
www.ukmya.mcmail.com

Scalextric
www.scalextric.co.uk

Scottish Aeromodellers Association
www.saaweb.org.uk

Scottish Fishing Boat Models
www.lemur.demon.co.uk/boats.htm

Tri-ang Model Railways
www.tri-ang.co.uk

Weavermodels
www.weavermodels.co.uk

motorsport

BMW
www.bmw.co.uk

British Motor Racing Circuits
www.bmrc.co.uk

British Motorcycle Club
www.bemsee.co.uk

British Motorcyclists Federation
www.bmf.co.uk

Caledonia Harley Club
www.dchne16.demon.co.uk

Classic Racing Motorcycle Club
www.crmc.co.uk

European Touring Car Championship
www.eurostc.com

FIA
www.fia.com

Find-a-motorbike
www.findamotorbike.co.uk

The Grid
www.thegrid.co.uk

Harley-Davidson
www.harley-davidson.co.uk

Honda
www.honda.co.uk

Internet BSA Club
www.geocities.com/MotorCity/Speedway/6046

Knockhill Racing Circuit
www.knockhill.com

Motor Cycle Industry Association
www.mcia.co.uk

Motor Cycle News
www.motorcyclenews.com

Motor Cycle World Magazine
www.motorcycleworld.co.uk

Motor Sports Association
www.msauk.org

Piaggio
www.piaggio.com

Promotorsport
www.promotorsport.co.uk

Rally Pages
www.rallypages.com

Royal Scottish Automobile Club
www.rsacmotorsport.co.uk

Scottish Motor Racing Club
www.smrc-uk.com

Scottish Motorsport
www.scottishmotorsport.com

Scottish Motorsport Marshalls Club
www.smmc.org.uk

Suzuki
www.suzuki.co.uk

Triumph
www.triumph.co.uk

Triumph Owners Motorcycle Club
www.tomcc.demon.co.uk

TVR
www.tvr-eng.co.uk

Vespa
www.vespa.com

Wheelife
www.wheelife.co.uk

Yamaha
www.yamaha-motor.co.uk

music

Akai
www.akai.com

Association of Blind Piano Tuners
www.uk-piano.org/abpt

Banks Music Publications
www.banksmusicpublications.cwc.net

Bluthners
www.bluthers.co.uk

Boosey & Hawkes
www.boosey.com

British Flute Society
www.bfs.org.uk

Chamberlain Music
www.chamberlainmusic.com

Chappells
www.uk-piano.org/chappell

Fender
www.fender.com

Gibson
www.gibson.com

Kemble Pianos
www.uk-piano.org/kemble

Marshall Amplification
www.marshallamps.com

Premier Percussion
www.premier-percussion.com

Sheet Music Direct
www.sheetmusicdirect.com

Steinway
www.steinway.com

Yamaha
www.yamaha-music.co.uk

outdoor pursuits

British Holiday & Home Parks Association
www.ukparks.com

British Orienteering Federation
www.cix.co.uk/~bof

British Walking Federation
www.bwf-ivv.org.uk

Camping & Caravanning Club
www.campingandcaravanningclub.co.uk

Camping & Outdoor Leisure Association
www.cola.org.uk

Camping UK Directory
www.camping.uk-directory.com

Caravan Club
www.caravanclub.co.uk

Compass Sport Magazine
www.compasssport.com

Cotswold Outdoor
www.cotswold-outdoor.co.uk

Duke of Edinburgh's Award Scheme
www.theaward.org

English Lakeland Ramblers
www.ramblers.com

Fell Runners Association
www.fellrunner.org.uk

Field & Trek
www.field-trek.co.uk

International Orienteering Federation
www.orienteering.org

National Caving Association
www.nca.org.uk

National Trails
www.nationaltrails.gov.uk

Ordnance Survey
www.ordsvy.gov.uk

Ramblers Association
www.ramblers.org.uk

Caving

Caving
www.caving.org.uk

National Caving Association
www.nca.org.uk

Country Sports

Association of Deer Management Groups
www.deer-management.co.uk

British Association for Shooting & Conservation
www.basc.org.uk

CKD Finalyson Hughes
www.sport.ckdfh.co.uk

Country Land & Business Association
www.cla.org.uk

Hotbarrels
www.hotbarrels.com

Scottish Countryside Access Network
www.scottishcountrynet.org

Scottish Countryside Alliance
www.scottishcountrysidealliance.org

Scottish Gamekeepers Association
www.scottishgamekeepers.co.uk

Diving

Dive Sites on West Coast
www.geministorm.co.uk/dive.htm

PADI International
www.padi.co.uk

Puffin Dive Centre
www.puffin.org.uk

Scot Dive Magazine
www.mounthigh.co.uk/scotdive

Scottish Association for Country Sports
www.sacs.org.uk

Scottish Dive Centre
www.scottishdivecentre.co.uk

Scottish Diving Charters
www.scottishdivingcharters.co.uk

Scottish Diving Magazine
www.arcl.ed.ac.uk/scotfed/scotdive/sdhome.htm

Scottish Diving Medicine
www.sams.ac.uk/sdm/home.htm

Scottish Sub-aqua Club
www.scotsac.com

Scoutscroft Dive Centre
www.divescoutscroft.freeserve.co.uk

Equipment

9feet
www.9feet.com

Altberg Boots
www.altberg.co.uk

Blacks
www.blacks.co.uk

Cotswold Outdoor
www.cotswold-outdoor.co.uk

Field & Trek
www.field-trek.co.uk

Mountain Equipment
www.mountain-equipment.co.uk

Outdoor Megastore
www.outdoormegastore.co.uk

Scuba Booty
www.scubabooty.co.uk

Slioch
www.slioch.co.uk

Tiso
www.tiso.ws

Mountain Biking

Bike Magic
www.bikemagic.com

CTC
www.ctc.org.uk

Glasgow Mountain Bike Club
www.gmbc.supanet.com

International Mountain Bike Association
www.imba.com

Mountain Bike Instruction
www.mountainbikeinstruction.co.uk

Mountain Biking UK
www.mountainbikinguk.co.uk

MTB Britain
www.mtbbritain.co.uk

MTB Routes
www.mtbroutes.com

Scottish Cycling
www.scottishcycling.org

Trail Cyclists Association
www.trailquest.co.uk

Mountaineering

Boots Across Scotland
www.bootsacrossscotland.org.uk

British Mountain Guides
www.bmg.org.uk

British Mountaineering Council
www.thebmc.co.uk

Great Outdoor Recreation Pages
www.gorp.com

Mountain Bothies Association
www.mountainbothies.org.uk

Mountain Leader Training Board
www.mltb.org

Mountain Rescue Committee of Scotland
www.mrc-scotland.org.uk

Mountaineering Council of Scotland
www.mountaineering-scotland.org.uk

Munro Magic
www.munromagic.com

The Munro Society
http://munrosociety.org.uk

Ordnance Survey
www.ordsvy.gov.uk

Ramblers Association
www.ramblers.org.uk

Scottish Avalanche Information Service
www.sais.gov.uk

Scottish Mountaineering Club
www.smc.org.uk

Scottish Orienteering Association
www.scottish-orienteering.org

Scottish Rights of Way & Access Society
www.scotways.com

Walking Wild
www.walkingwild.com

Parachuting

British Parachute Association
www.bpa.org.uk

Paragon Sky Diving
www.paragonskydiving.20m.com

Scottish Sports Parachute Association
www.dundeecity.gov.uk/orgs/orx0671.htm

Sky Dive St Andrews
www.skydivestandrews.co.uk

Skydive
http://skydivewww.com

pets

Cats

Cat World
www.catworld.co.uk

Cats Protection League
www.cats.org.uk

Feline Advisory Bureau
www.fabcats.org

Supreme Cat Show
www.chace.demon.co.uk

Whiskas Cat Food
www.petsource.com/whiskas

Dogs

Associated Sheep, Police & Army Dog Society
www.aspads.org.uk

Battersea Dogs Home
www.dogshome.org

Border Collie Trust
www.bctgb.freeserve.co.uk

British Dog Breeders Council
www.k9netuk.com/bdbc

Canine World
www.canineworld.com

Council of Docked Breeds
www.cdb.org

Crossbreed & Mongrel Club
www.crossbreed.freeserve.co.uk

Crufts
www.crufts.org.uk

Dog Club UK
www.dogclub.co.uk

Dogs Online
www.dogsonline.co.uk

Dogs Today
www.lightwave.co.uk/dogs-today

Dogs Worldwide
www.dogsworldwide.com

Fanciers Breeder Referral List
www.breedlist.com

K9 Directory
www.k9directory.co.uk

Kennel Club
www.the-kennel-club.org.uk

National Canine Defence League
www.ncdl.org.uk

National Dogsitters
www.dogsit.com

National Puppy Register
www.findapup.net

Pedigree Petfoods
www.petcat.co.uk

Fish

British Aquatic Resource Centre
www.cfkc.demon.co.uk

British Cichlid Association
www.bca.zetnet.co.uk

British Killifish Association
www.bka.freeuk.com

British Koi Keepers' Society
www.bkks.co.uk

Practical Fishkeeping
www.aquarist.net/pfk

General

Animail
www.animail.co.uk

British Dragonfly Society
www.dragonflysoc.org.uk

British House Rabbit Association
www.houserabbit.co.uk

Donkey Sanctuary
www.thedonkeysanctuary.org.uk

Insect World
www.insect-world.com

National Fancy Rat Society
www.nfrs.org

National Gerbil Society
www.gerbils.co.uk

National Hamster Council
www.hamsters-uk.org

Parrot Paradise
www.parrots-paradise.co.uk

Pedigree Petfoods
www.pets-pantry.co.uk/
complete_foods_from_pedigree_pet.htm

Pet Cover
www.petcover.com

Petmad
www.petmad.com

Pet Plan Insurance
www.petplan.co.uk

Pet Planet
www.petplanet.co.uk

Pets At Home
www.petsathome.com

Pets Direct UK
www.petsdirectuk.com

Pets on Holiday
www.pets-on-holiday.com

Pets Pyjamas.com
www.pets-pyjamas.co.uk

Rabbits Online
www.rabbitsonline.com

Rabbits UK
www.cs.cf.ac.uk/rabbits

Reptilian Online
www.reptilian.co.uk

RSPCA
www.rspca.org.uk

Scottish Dogs Online
www.scotdogs.com

Scottish Parrot Mart
www.scottishparrotmart.cjb.net

Scottish SPCA
www.scottishspca.org

Serpents Magazine
www.serpents.co.uk

Turtle World
www.downey288.freeserve.co.uk

UK Feathers
www.ukfeathers.co.uk

UK Reptiles Online
www.ukreptiles.com

Vivarium Magazine
www.thevivarium.freeserve.co.uk

Yahoo! Pets
http://pets.yahoo.com

photography

Association of Photographers
www.the-aop.org

British Institute of Professional Photography
www.bipp.com

Digital Photography Review
www.dpreview.com

George Logan
www.scottish-photography.co.uk

Photosites UK
www.photosites.co.uk

Photoworkshops
www.photoworkshops.co.uk

Scottish Photography
www.scottishphotography.com

Scottish Viewpoint Photolibrary
www.scottishviewpoint.com

Source Magazine
www.sourcemagazine.demon.co.uk

Sue Anderson's Island Focus
www.islandfocus.co.uk

theRowan
www.therowan.com

Cameras & Equipment

Agfa
www.agfa.co.uk

Canon
www.canon.co.uk

Casio
www.casio.co.uk

Contax
www.contax.com

Epson
www.epson.com

Fuji Film
www.fujifilm.com

Kodak
www.kodak.co.uk

Konica
www.konica.com

Leica
www.leica-camera.com

Minolta
www.minolta.co.uk

Nikon
www.nikon.co.uk

Olympus
www.olympus-europa.com

Panasonic
www.panasonic.com

Pentax
www.pentax.co.uk

Polaroid
www.polaroid.com

Ricoh
www.ricoh-cameras.co.uk

Rollei
www.rollei.com

Samson
www.samson.com

Sigma
www.sigma-aldrich.com

Yashica
www.yashica.com

Magazines & Websites

Amateur Photography UK
www.amphot.co.uk

British Journal of Photography
www.bjphoto.demon.co.uk

Centre for Photographic Art
www.photography.org

Classic Camera
www.marriott.u-net.com/ccm.htm

Focus
www.focus-online.com

Royal Photographic Society
www.rps.org

UK Amateur Photograph
www.amphot.co.uk

Which Camera?
www.whichcamera.co.uk

information sources

encyclopaedias

Britannica
www.britannica.co.uk

Catholic Encyclopaedia
www.newadvent.org/cathen

Encarta
www.encarta.msn.com

Encyclopedia
www.encyclopedia.com

Grolier
www.grolier.com

Hutchinson
www.bt-ern.co.uk/helicon

Probert
www.probert-encyclopaedia.co.uk

gaelic sites

Acair Books (Publishers)
www.acairbooks.com

An Gàidheal Ùr (Gaelic Newspaper)
www.an-gaidheal-ur.co.uk

BBC Alba
www.bbc.co.uk/scotland/alba

Bith Beò ann an Gaidhlig (Gaelic Career Opportunities)
www.bithbeo.org.uk

Cànan Limited (Gaelic Publishers)
www.canan.co.uk

CLI (Gaelic Learners Association)
www.gaelic.net/cli

Comann nam Parant (Gaelic Parents Site)
www.parant.org.uk

Comataidh Craolaidh Gaidhlig (Gaelic Broadcasting Committee)
www.ccg.org.uk

Comunn na Gàidhlig (Gaelic Development Agency)
www.cnag.org.uk

Fèisean nan Gàidheal (Gaelic Festivals Association)
www.feisean.org

Gaelic Book Council
www.gaelicbooks.net

Gaelic Society of Inverness
www.gsi.org.uk

Gàidhlig Online
www.gaeliconline.co.uk

Ministerial Advisory Group on Gaelic
www.magog.org.uk

Proiseact nan Ealan (National Gaelic Arts Agency)
www.gaelic-arts.com

Proiseact Thiriodh (Tiree Project)
www.tiriodh.ed.ac.uk

Royal National Mod
www.the-mod.co.uk

Sabhal Mòr Ostaig (Gaelic College, Isle of Skye)
www.smo.uhi.ac.uk

Stòrlann Nàiseanta na Gàidhlig (National Gaelic Educational Resource Centre)
www.storlann.co.uk

Tobar an Dualchais (National Gaelic Archive)
www.smo.uhi.ac.uk/dualchas

UK Committee of European Bureau for Lesser Used Languages
www.eblul.org.uk

libraries

National

British Library
www.bl.uk

National Library Catalogues Worldwide
www.library.uq.edu.au/ssah/jeast

National Library of Scotland
www.nls.uk

Public

Aberdeenshire Council Libraries
http://opac.aberdeenshire.gov.uk/www-bin/alis

Argyll & Bute Libraries
www.argyll-bute.gov.uk/couninfo/dev2d.htm

Angus Council Libraries
www.angus.gov.uk/history/libraries

Borders Council Libraries
www.scottishborders.gov.uk/libraries

Clackmannanshire Libraries
www.clacksweb.org.uk/dyna/library

Dumfries & Galloway Libraries
www.dumgal.gov.uk/services/depts/comres/library

Dundee City Libraries
www.dundeecity.gov.uk/nrd

East Ayrshire Libraries
www.east-ayrshire.gov.uk/comleilib

Edinburgh City Libraries
www.edinburgh.gov.uk/libraries

Glasgow City Libraries
www.glasgow.gov.uk/html/council/dept/cls/body.htm

Highland Council Libraries
www.highland.gov.uk/educ/default.htm

Moray Council Libraries
www.moray.org/Education/libraries.htm

North Ayrshire Libraries
www.ers.north-ayrshire.gov.uk

North Lanarkshire Libraries
www.nll.org

Perth & Kinross Libraries
www.pkc.gov.uk/library

South Ayrshire Libraries
www.south-ayrshire.gov.uk/libraries

Stirling Libraries
www.stirling.gov.uk/libraries

West Lothian Libraries
www.wlonline.org/main/frames~1~34~0.htm

Western Isles Libraries
www.w-isles.gov.uk/w-isles/library

Scottish Resources

Scottish Academic Library Serials
http://edina.ed.ac.uk/salser

Scottish Confederation of University & Research Libraries
http://scurl.ac.uk

Scottish Cultural Resources Access Network
www.scran.ac.uk

Scottish Library Association
www.slamit.org.uk

Slainte – Scottish Libraries Information
www.slainte.org.uk

University Libraries

Aberdeen University Library
www.abdn.ac.uk/diss/library

Abertay University Library
http://iserv.tay.ac.uk

Cambridge University Library
www.lib.cam.ac.uk

Dundee University Library
www.dundee.ac.uk/library

Edinburgh University Library
www.lib.ed.ac.uk

Glasgow University Library
www.lib.gla.ac.uk

Harvard University Library
http://hul.harvard.edu

Heriot Watt University Library
www.hw.ac.uk/library

LSE Library
www.lse.ac.uk/library

Oxford University Libraries
www.lib.ox.ac.uk

St Andrews University Library
www-library.st-and.ac.uk

Stirling University Library
www.library.stir.ac.uk/libs

Strathclyde University Library
www.lib.strath.ac.uk

maps

3D Atlas Online
www.3datlas.com

Alba Cartographic
www.albacartographic.demon.co.uk

Association for Geographic Information (AGI)
www.agi.org.uk

British Cartographic Society
www.cartography.org.uk

British Geological Survey
www.bgs.ac.uk

Committee of the National Mapping Agencies of Europe
www.cerco.org

Edinburgh University Geography Dept.
www.geo.ed.ac.uk/home/scotland/maps.html

Geography Network
www.geographynetwork.com

Harvey
www.harveymaps.co.uk

Mapblast
www.mapblast.com

Multi-purpose European Ground-Related Information Network
www.megrin.org

Multimap
www.multimap.com

National Map Centre (UK)
www.mapstore.co.uk

Ordnance Survey
www.ordsvy.gov.uk

Shell Geostar
www.shellgeostar.com

Society of Cartographers
www.soc.org.uk

Stanfords
www.stanfords.co.uk

Street Map
www.streetmap.co.uk

museums

Edinburgh City Council Museums
www.cac.org.uk

Glasgow Museums (unofficial)
www.g3web.co.uk/glasgow_museums

MuseumNet
www.museums.co.uk

Museums & Galleries Commission
www.museums.gov.uk

National Galleries of Scotland
www.nationalgalleries.org

National History Museum
www.nhm.ac.uk

National Museums of Scotland
www.nms.ac.uk

Scottish Museums Council
www.scottishmuseums.org.uk

news

BBC
www.bbc.co.uk/news

CNN
www.cnn.com

IRN
www.irn.co.uk

ITN
www.itn.co.uk

News Unlimited
www.newsunlimited.co.uk

NewsNow
www.newsnow.co.uk

PA News
www.pa.press.net

PR Newswire
www.prnewswire.com

Reuters
www.reuters.com

Sky
www.sky.com/news

Tass
www.tass.ru/english

Teletext
www.teletext.co.uk

Universal Press Syndicate
www.uexpress.com

news agencies

AFP Asia
www.asia.dailynews.yahoo.com

AP World
www.newsday.com

CNN
www.cnn.com

Emerald News Media
www.btinternet.com/~emeraldnews

IRN
www.irn.co.uk

ITN
www.itn.co.uk

News Unlimited
www.newsunlimited.co.uk

Newshound
www.nuzhound.com

NewsNow
www.newsnow.co.uk

PA News
www.pa.press.net

PR Newswire
www.prnewswire.com

Reuters
www.reuters.com

Sky
www.sky.com/news

Tass
www.tass.ru/english

Teletext
www.teletext.co.uk

Universal Press Syndicate
www.uexpress.com

UPI/AFP
www.drudgereport.com

newspapers

Scottish Media Monitor – Directory
www.scottishmediamonitor.com/links.cfm

Foreign

Asahi Shinbun (Japan)
www.asahi.com/english

Budapest Sun (Hungary)
www.centraleurope.com

China Times (Taiwan)
www.chinatimes.com.tw/english

Copenhagen Post (Denmark)
www.cphpost.dk

Cyprus News (Cyprus)
www.cynews.com

Daily Star (Bangaladesh)
www.dailystarnews.com

Daily Star (Lebanon)
www.dailystar.com.lb

East African Standard (Kenya)
www.eastandard.net

Express (Tanzania)
www.theexpress.com

Gibraltar Chronicle (Gibraltar)
www.gibnet.com/chron

Good Morning (Belgium)
www.yweb.com/goodmorningnews

Guardian (Nigeria)
www.ngrguardiannews.com

Hellenic Star (Greece)
www.hellenicstar.net

Herald (Pakistan)
www.xiber.com

Hindu (India)
www.the-hindu.com

Hollywood Reporter (USA)
www.hollywoodreporter.com

Hurriyet (Turkey)
www.hurriyet.com.tr

Indonesian Observer (Indonesia)
www.indoexchange.com/indonesian-observer

International Herald Tribune (USA)
www.iht.com

Iran Daily (Iran)
www.iran-daily.com

Irish News (Eire)
www.irishnews.com

Island (Sri Lanka)
www.island.lk

Jerusalem Post (Israel)
www.jpost.co.il

Jordon Times (Jordon)
www.arabia.com

Korea Herald (Korea)
www.koreaherald.co.kr

Kurier (Austria)
www.kurier.at

Kuwait Times (Kuwait)
www.paaet.edu.kw/ktimes

Los Angeles Times (USA)
www.latimes.com

Middle East Times (Egypt)
www.metimes.com

Monitor (Uganda)
www.africanews.com/monitor

Nation (Thailand)
www.nationgroup.com

Nederlander (Holland)
www.netherlander.com

Norway Post
www.norwaypost.no

Paris Match
www.parismatch.com

Peoples Daily (China)
http://english.peopledaily.com.cn/index.htm

Philippine Star (Philippines)
www.philstar.com

Pravda (Russia)
www.pravda.ru

Saigon Times (Vietnam)
www.saigon-news.com

South China Morning Post (Hong Kong)
www.scmp.com

Times of India (India)
www.timesofindia.com

WOZA (South Africa)
www.woza.co.za

Zaobao (Singapore)
www.zaobao.com

International

Belfast Telegraph
www.belfasttelegraph.co.uk

Irish Independent
www.independent.ie

Irish Times
www.ireland.com

New York Times
www.nytimes.com

USA Today
www.usatoday.com

Wall Street Journal
www.wsj.com

Washington Post
www.washingtonpost.com

Local

Aberdeen & District Independent
www.aberdeen-indy.co.uk

Aberdeen Evening Express
www.thisisnorthscotland.co.uk

Aberdeen Press & Journal
www.thisisnorthscotland.co.uk

Argyllshire Advertiser
www.argyllshireadvertiser.co.uk

Ayrshire Post
www.inside-scotland.co.uk/ayrshire/post

Blairgowrie Advertiser
www.inside-scotland.co.uk/perthshire/index.html

Business am
www.businessam.co.uk

Border Telegraph
www.bordertelegraph.com

Dundee Courier
www.thecourier.co.uk

Dundee Evening Telegraph
www.dcthomson.co.uk/mags/tele

Dundee Weekly News
www.dcthomson.co.uk/mags/weekly

Edinburgh Echo
www.edinburghecho.co.uk

Edinburgh Evening News
www.edinburghnews.com

Falkirk Herald
www.falkirkherald.co.uk

Glasgow Evening Times
www.eveningtimes.co.uk

Greenock Telegraph
www.greenocktelegraph.co.uk

The Herald
www.theherald.co.uk

Kilmarnock Standard
www.inside-scotland.co.uk

Northern Scot
www.northern-scot.co.uk

Oban Times
www.obantimes.co.uk

Orcadian
www.orcadian.co.uk

Scottish & Universal Newspapers
www.inside-scotland.co.uk

Sunday Post
www.sundaypost.com

Shetland News
www.Shetland-news.co.uk

Shetland Today
www.shetlandtoday.uk

Tweeddale Press (Lothian & Borders titles)
www.tweeddalepress.co.uk

West Highland Free Press
www.whfp.com

National

Daily Express
www.express.co.uk

The Daily Record
www.dailyrecord.co.uk

Daily Telegraph
www.telegraph.co.uk

Financial Times
www.ft.com

Guardian
www.guardian.co.uk

Jewish Telegraph
www.jewishtelegraph.com

Mirror
www.mirror.co.uk

Observer
www.observer.co.uk

Racing Post
www.racingpost.co.uk

Scotland on Sunday
www.scotlandonsunday.com

The Scotsman
www.scotsman.com

Sun
www.thesun.co.uk

Sunday Herald
www.sundayherald.com

Sunday Times
www.sunday-times.co.uk

Telegraph
www.telegraph.co.uk

The Times
www.the-times.co.uk

The Week
www.theweek.co.uk

Professional Bodies

European Newspaper Publishers Association
www.enpa.be

Press Association
www.pa.press.net

Scottish Newspaper Publishers Association – Weekly Press
www.snpa.org.uk

Society of Editors
www.ukeditors.com

opinion polls

Audit Bureau of Circulation
www.abc.org.uk

British Market Research Association
www.bmra.org.uk

Gallup
www.gallup.com

ICM
www.icmresearch.co.uk

Mintel.com
www.mintel.co.uk

Mori
www.mori.com

NOP
www.nop.co.uk

phone numbers

BT Online Phonebook
www.bt.com/phonenetuk

Eircom
www.eircom.ie-new

Phonenumbers.net
www.phonenumbers.net

Telephone Code Changes
www.numberchange.org

Thomson Directories
www.thomweb.co.uk

UK PhoneBook
www.ukphonebook.com

World Telephone Directories on the Web
www.teldir.com

Yellow Pages
www.yell.co.uk

professional bodies & associations

European Newspaper Publishers Association
www.enpa.be

Press Association
www.pa.press.net

Society of Editors
www.ukeditors.com

reference

British Geological Survey
www.bgs.ac.uk

Jane's
www.janes.com

National Statistics Online
www.statistics.gov.uk

Oxford English Dictionary
www.oed.com

Roget's Thesaurus
www.thesaurus.com

Scottish Collections Network
http://scone.strath.ac.uk/service/index.cfm

Scottish Genealogy Society
www.scotsgenealogy.com

Scottish Tourist Board
www.visitscotland.com

Statistics at the Scottish Executive
www.scotland.gov.uk/stats

The Life Search Project
www.thelifesearchproject.org.uk

Community Portal

Ayrshire E-Communities
www.e-ayrshire.co.uk

Craigmillar
www.craignet.org.uk

North Edinburgh
www.northedinburgh.org

Pentland
www.pentlandcom.com

South Edinburgh
www.southedinburgh.net

West Edinburgh
www.westedinburgh.net

Online Directories

Border Net
www.bordernet.co.uk

BUBL
http://bubl.ac.uk

Electric Scotland
www.electricscotland.com

Hi-ways
www.hi-ways.org

Kelly's Guide
www.kellysonline.net

Rampant Scotland
www.rampantscotland.com

Scotland.org
www.scotland.org

UK 250
www.uk250.com

UK Online
www.ukonline.net

weather

BBC Weather Centre
www.bbc.co.uk/weather

ITN
www.itn.co.uk/weather

Met Office
www.metoffice.com

Online Weather
www.onlineweather.com

Weather Call
www.weathercall.co.uk

Weather Channel UK
www.weather.co.uk

World Meteorological Organisation
www.wmo.ch

living

- cars
- dating agencies
- disability
- family life
- hairdressers, beauty salons & image consultants
- health & fitness
- home life
- magazines & websites
- military associations
- motorcycles
- new age
- religion
- retirement
- weddings

cars

Accessories & Repairs

Allmake Motor Parts
www.allmakemotorparts.co.uk

Alpine Electronics
www.alpine1.com

Audioseek
www.audioseek.com

Autogas UK
www.autogas.co.uk

Autoglass
www.autoglass.co.uk

Britax
www.britax.co.uk

Bygone Era
www.bygone-era.com

Car Parts World
www.carpartsworld.co.uk

Car Roof Racks
www.car-roofracks.co.uk

Continental Tyres
www.conti.de

Cooper Tyre & Rubber Company
www.coopertire.com

Duckworth
www.duckworth.co.uk

Elite Registrations
www.elite-registrations.co.uk

Ferodo
www.ferodo.co.uk

Ferodo Brake Tech
www.ferodobraketech.com

Finelist
www.finelist.co.uk

Fleet Support Group
www.fsguk.com

Global Registrations
www.globalreg.co.uk

Halfords
www.halfords.co.uk

Hammerite
www.hammerite-automotive.com

KAGE
www.kage.ltd.uk

Kenwood
www.kenwood-electronics.co.uk

Kwik-Fit
www.kwik-fit.com

Michelin
www.michelin.com

Motor Sports Online Store
www.mso.net

Motor World
www.motor-world.co.uk

Motorola
www.motorola.com

National Tyre Distributors Association
www.ntda.co.uk

National Tyres
www.national.co.uk

Need For Speed
www.needforspeed.co.uk

New Reg Personalised Registration Numbers
www.reg.co.uk

Parts Direct
www.partsdirect.co.uk

Pirelli
www.pirelli.co.uk

RAC Trackstar
www.ractrackstar.com

Registration Transfers
www.regtransfers.co.uk

Roaduser
www.roaduser.co.uk

S-Link Design
www.slinkdesign.co.uk

Tracker
www.tracker-network.co.uk

Trafficmaster
www.trafficmaster.co.uk

Tyre Trade News
www.tyretradenews.co.uk

Tyresave
www.tyresave.co.uk

UK Registrations
www.reg.co.uk

Unipart
www.unipart.co.uk

Buying, Selling & Auctions

Autobytel
www.autobyteluk.com

Autofinder
www.autofinder.net

British Car Auctions Group
www.bca-group.com

Car Exchange
www.thecarexchange.co.uk

Car World
www.carworld.co.uk

Fish4 Cars
www.fish4cars.co.uk

Jam Jar Cars
www.jamjar.com

Lex Retail
www.lexretail.co.uk

Motor Auction Consortium
www.carworld.co.uk/auction/mac.htm

National Car Auctions
www.carworld.co.uk/auction/nca.htm

Scottish Car Auctions
www.scottishcarauctions.co.uk

Shotts Motor Auction
www.shotts-auction.co.uk

Tins
www.tins.co.uk

UK Motor Vehicle Auctions
www.auctions.co.uk/cars

Driving Schools

BSM
www.bsm.co.uk

Institute of Advanced Motoring
www.iam.org.uk

Motor Schools Association
www.msagb.co.uk

UK Learner Drivers
www.learners.co.uk

Magazines & Websites

Auto Exchange
www.autoexchange.co.uk

Auto Express
www.autoexpress.co.uk

Auto Trader
www.autotrader.co.uk

Auto Wired
www.autowired.co.uk

Autobytel
www.autobytel.co.uk

Autofinder
www.autofinder.net

Automobile
www.hartlana.co.uk

Automotive Body Repair News
www.abrn.com

Automotive Online
www.automotive-online.com

BBC Top Gear
www.topgear.com

BMW Car
www.bmwcarmagazine.com

British Car Auctions
www.bca-group.com

British Car Links
www.britishcarlinks.com

Car
www.carmagazine.co.uk

CarNet
www.carnet.co.uk

Classic Car Directory
www.classicdirect.co.uk

Classic Car World
www.classiccarworld.co.uk

Classic Motor
www.classicmotor.co.uk

Drive
www.drive.com

Fleet NewsNet
www.fleetnewsnet.co.uk

Fleet NewsNet
www.automotive.co.uk

Haynes
www.haynes.co.uk

Learner Drivers UK
www.learners.co.uk

Max Power
www.maxpower.co.uk

MG Enthusiast
www.mgcars.org.uk/mgmag

Motor World
www.motor-world.co.uk

Motoring UK
www.motoring-uk.co.uk

MotorTrader
www.motortrader.co.uk

Parkers Online
www.carmagazine.co.uk

Power On Wheels
www.power-on-wheels.co.uk

ShopQ
www.shopq.co.uk

Top Gear
www.topgear.beeb.com

Tyre Trade News
www.tyretradenews.co.uk

Tyres-Online
www.tyres-online.co.uk

WhatCar?
www.whatcar.co.uk

Which? – Motoring
www.which.net/motoring

World Off Road
www.worldoffroad.com

Manufacturers

AC
www.accars.co.uk

Alfa Romeo
www.alfaromeo.com

Aston Martin
www.astonmartin.com

Audi
www.audi.co.uk

Bentley
www.rolls-royceandbentley.co.uk

BMW
www.bmw.co.uk

Bristol
www.bristolcars.co.uk

Cadillac
www.cadillaceurope.com

Caterham
www.caterham.co.uk

Chevrolet
www.chevrolet.com

Chrysler
www.chrysler.co.uk

Citroen
www.citroen.co.uk

Daewoo
www.daewoo.com

Dennis Group
www.dennis-group.co.uk

Ferrari
www.ferrari.com

Fiat
www.fiat.co.uk

Ford
www.ford.co.uk

General Motors
www.gm.com

Honda
www.honda.co.uk

Hyundai
www.hyundai-car.co.uk

Isuzo
www.isuzo.co.uk

Jaguar
www.jaguar.com/uk

Jeep
www.jeep.co.uk

Jensen
www.jensen-motors.co.uk

Kia
www.kia.com

Lamborghini
www.lamborghini.it

Land Rover
www.landrover.co.uk

Lexus
www.lexus.co.uk

London Taxi
www.london-taxis.co.uk

Lotus
www.lotuscars.co.uk

Maserati
www.maserati.com

Mazda
www.mazda.co.uk

Mercedes Benz
www.mercedes-benz.co.uk

MG
www.mgcars.com

Mini
www.mini.co.uk

Mitsubishi
www.mitsubishi-cars.co.uk

Morgan
www.morgan-motor.co.uk

Nissan
www.nissan.co.uk

Opel
www.opel.com

Peugeot
www.peugeot.co.uk

Porsche
www.porsche.com

Proton
www.proton.co.uk

Renault
www.renault.co.uk

Rolls Royce
www.rolls-royceandbentley.co.uk

Rover
www.rovercars.com

Saab
www.saab.co.uk

SEAT
www.seat.com

Skoda
www.skoda-auto.com

Ssang Yong
www.ssangyong.co.kr/english/index.html

Subaru
www.subaru.co.uk

Suzuki
www.suzuki.co.uk

Toyota
www.toyota.co.uk

TVR
www.tvr-eng.co.uk

Vauxhall
www.vauxhall.co.uk

Volkswagen
www.vw.co.uk

Volvo
www.volvocars.volvo.co.uk

Westfield
www.westfield-sportscars.co.uk

Owners' Clubs

Aston Martin
www.amoc.org

Jensen
www.british-steel.org

Rolls Royce
www.rroc.org

Petrol

Electrical Vehicles UK
www.evuk.co.uk

Esso
www.esso.co.uk

Mobil
www.mobil.co.uk

Shell
www.shell.com

Texaco
www.texaco.co.uk

TotalFinaElf
www.totalfinaelf.com

Registrations

DVLA personalised
www.dvla-som.co.uk

Elite Registrations
www.elite-registrations.co.uk

Global Registrations
www.globalreg.co.uk

NewReg Personalised Numbers
www.reg.co.uk

Number Net
www.numbernet.co.uk

Registration Transfers
www.regtransfers.co.uk

dating agencies

Dateline
www.dateline.co.uk

Dating Agencies UK
www.dating-agencies-uk.co.uk

Drawing Down the Moon
www.drawingdownthemoon.co.uk

Executive Club
www.thematchmaker.co.uk

Online Dating Services
www.online-dating-services.co.uk

Pearmatch
www.pearmatch.co.uk

Sarah Eden Introductions
www.sara-eden.co.uk

Sirius
www.clubsirius.com

disability

Shaw Trust
www.shaw-trust.org.uk

family life

Advisory Centre For Education
www.ace-ed.org.uk

Anti-bullying Network
www.antibullying.net

Association of Breastfeeding Mothers
http://home.clara.net/abm

BBC Parenting Resource
www.bbc.co.uk/education/health/parenting

Child of Achievement
www.childofachievement.co.uk

Children's legal Centre
www2.essex.ac.uk/clc

Community Hygiene Concern
www.chc.org

Families Need Fathers
www.fnf.org.uk

Family Planning Association
www.fpa.org.uk

La Leche (Breastfeeding) League
www.lalecheleague.org

National Childbirth Trust
www.nct-online.org

One Parent Families Scotland
www.opfs.org.uk

Parent News
www.parents-news.co.uk

Parent Soup
www.parentsoup.com

Parentline
www.parentlineplus.org.uk

Serene
www.our-space.co.uk/serene.htm

hairdressers, beauty salons & image consultants

Andrew Collinge Hairdressing
www.andrewcollinge.com

Charles Worthington
www.cwlondon.com

Daniel Galvin
www.daniel-galvin.co.uk

Elizabeth Arden Red Door Salons
www.reddoorsalons.com

House of Colour
www.houseofcolour.co.uk

Jo Hansford
www.johansford.co.uk

National Hairdressers Federation
www.the-nhf.org

Toni & Guy
www.toniandguy.co.uk

Vidal Sassoon
www.vidalsassoon.co.uk

health & fitness

Body Friendly Healthy Holidays
www.bodyfriendly.co.uk

British Naturist Society
www.british-naturist.org.uk

British Wheel of Yoga
www.bwy.org

Cambridge Diet
www.cambridge-diet.co.uk

Cannons Health Clubs
www.cannons-health-clubs.co.uk

Champneys
www.central-chamber.co.uk

David Lloyd Leisure
www.davidlloydleisure.co.uk

Esporta
www.esporta.co.uk

Forestmere Health Farm
www.forestmere.co.uk

Greens Health & Fitness
www.greensonline.co.uk

Gym User
www.gymuser.co.uk

Harbour Club
www.harbourclub.co.uk

Henlow Grange Health Farm
www.henlowgrange.co.uk

Holmes Place
www.holmesplace.co.uk

Ivy Court Fitness Clubs
www.ivycourt.com

Nirvana Spa
www.nirvana-spa.co.uk

Pilates Foundation
www.pilatesfoundation.com

Pilates.co.uk
www.pilates.co.uk

Roundlewood Health Spa, Perthshire
www.roundelwood.org.uk

Scotland (Lothian Region) Health & Fitness Club Directory
www.lothian.health-club.net

Scotland (Strathclyde Region) Health & Fitness Club Directory
www..health-club.net/strathclyde.htm

Slimming World
www.slimming-world.co.uk

Sopwell House
www.sopwellhouse.co.uk

Tai Chi Union
www.taichiunion.com

Weightwatchers
www.weightwatchers.com

Yoga Scotland
www.yogascotland.org.uk

Yoga Village UK
www.yogauk.com

home life

Cleaning & Laundry

Corby Press
www.corbypress.com

Fairy
www.fairynonbio.co.uk

Finish
www.finish.co.uk

Persil
www.persil.co.uk

Scotchcare
www.scotchcare-services.co.uk

Servicemaster residential Cleaning
www.servicemaster.co.uk

Sketchley
www.sketchley.co.uk

White Knight
www.white-knight.co.uk

Estate Agents

Bradford & Bingley
www.bb-ea.co.uk

Bushells
www.bushells.com

Chancellors
www.chancellors.co.uk

Chestertons
www.chestertons.co.uk

CityLet
www.citylet.com

Cluttons
www.cluttons.com

Connells
www.connells.co.uk

Copping Joyce
www.coppingjoyce.co.uk

Drivers Jonas
www.djonas.co.uk

Easier
www.easier.co.uk

Egerton
www.egertonproperty.co.uk

Felicity J Lord
www.fjlord.co.uk

Foxtons
www.foxtons.co.uk

Friend & Falcke
www.friendandfalcke.co.uk

General Accident
www.gaproperty.co.uk

Goldschmidt Howland
www.goldschmidt-howland.co.uk

Haart
www.haart.co.uk

Hamptons
www.hamptons.co.uk

Humberts
www.humberts.co.uk

Jackson-Stops & Staff
www.jackson-stops.co.uk

John D Wood
www.johndwood.co.uk

King Sturge
www.kingsturge.co.uk

Knight Frank
www.knightfrank.co.uk

London Property Guide
www.londonpropertyguide.co.uk

London Property News
www.lpn.co.uk

Mclean Forth
www.mcleanforth.com

National Homes Network
www.nhn.co.uk

National Property Register
www.national-property-register.co.uk

Richard Ellis
www.richardellis.co.uk

Savills
www.fpdsavills.co.uk

Spicer McColl
www.spicer.co.uk

Strettons
www.strettons.co.uk

Strutt & Parker
www.struttandparker.co.uk

Winkworth
www.winkworth.co.uk

Heating

Baxi Heating
www.baxi.com

British Gas
www.gas.co.uk

Calor Gas
www.calorgas.co.uk

CORGI
www.corgi-gas.com

Energy Saving Trust
www.est.org.uk

Energy Shop
www.energyshop-plc.co.uk

Gleaner Oil & Gas
www.gleaner.co.uk

Potterton
www.potterton.co.uk

Robinson Willey
www.robinson-willey.co.uk

Scottish Hydro-electric
www.hydro.co.uk

Thermsaver
www.thermsaver.co.uk

Valor
www.valor.co.uk

House Builders

Alfred McAlpine
www.alfred-mcalpine.co.uk

Antler Homes
www.antlerhomes.co.uk

Anville Homes
www.anvilleconstruction.co.uk

Ashwood Homes
www.ashwoodhomes.co.uk

Banner Homes
www.banner-homes.co.uk

Barratt Homes
www.ukpg.co.uk/barratt

Beechwood Homes
www.beechwood.co.uk

Bellway
www.bellway.co.uk

Bewley Homes
www.bewley.co.uk

Bloor Homes
www.bloorhomes.com

Bryant Homes
www.bryant.co.uk

Builders Directory
www.whotouse.co.uk

Builders In Scotland
www.buildersinscotland.com

Charles Church
www.charles-church.co.uk

Construction Confederation
www.constructionconfederation.co.uk

Country Life
www.countrylife.demon.co.uk

Countryside Residential
www.countrysideresidential.co.uk

Crownwood Developments
www.crownwooddevelopments.co.uk

David Wilson Homes
www.dwh.co.uk

Fairview
www.fairview.co.uk

Fordy Homes
www.fordyhomes.co.uk

Gainsborough
www.gainsbc.co.uk

George Wimpey
www.wimpey.co.uk

Goldcrest Homes
www.goldcresthomes.plc.uk

Hazelmere
www.hazelmerehomes.co.uk

House Builders Federation
www.hbf.co.uk

John Fleming
www.johnfleming.co.uk

Laing
www.laing.co.uk

Linden Homes
www.lindenhomes.co.uk

McAlpine
www.alfred-mcalpine.co.uk

McLean Homes
www.wimpey.co.uk/mclean

National Federation of Builders
www.builders.org.uk

National Housebuliders Council (NHBC)
www.nhbc.co.uk

Persimmon Homes
www.persimmon.plc.uk

Rialto Homes
www.rialtohomes.co.uk

Robertson Residential
www.robertson.co.uk

St James Homes
www.stjameshomes.co.uk

Tarmac
www.tarmac.co.uk

Taylor Woodrow
www.taywood.co.uk

Thirlstone Home Development
www.thirlstone.co.uk

Ward Homes
www.ward-homes.co.uk

Westbury Homes
www.westbury-homes.co.uk

Wilcon
www.wilcon.co.uk

Wimpey Homes
www.wimpey.co.uk

Housekeeping

GH Institute
www.goodhousekeeping.co.uk

Online Property sites

Asserta Home
www.assertahome.com

Farm Property Scotland
www.farmspropertyscotland.com

Highland Homefinders
www.highlandhomefinders.co.uk

Market Place
www.marketplace.co.uk

National Homes Network Independent
www.nhn.co.uk

National Property Register
www.national-property-register.co.uk

Property Finder
www.propertyfinder.co.uk

Property Scotland
www.property-scotland.com

Property Window Directory
www.propertywindow.com

S1 Homes
www.s1homes.com

Professional Bodies & Trade Associations

Advisory Service (Windows & Conservatories)
www.advisoryservice.co.uk

Archinet
www.archinet.co.uk

Association of Electrical & Mechanical Trades
www.aemt.co.uk

Association of Master Upholsterers & Soft Furnishers
www.upholsters.co.uk

British Standards Institute
www.bsi.org.uk

British Water
www.britishwater.co.uk

British Woodworkers Federation
www.bwf.org.uk

Chartered Institute of Building
www.ciob.org.uk

Confederation of Roofing Contractors
www.corc.co.uk

Construction Employers Federation
www.cefni.co.uk

CORGI (Gas Installers)
www.corgi-gas.com

Electricity Association
www.electricity.org.uk

Engineering Council UK
www.engc.org.uk

Federation of Environmental Trade Associations
www.feta.co.uk

Federation of Master Builders
www.fmb.org.uk

Glass & Glazing Federation
www.ggf.org.uk

Guild of Architectural Ironmongers
www.martex.co.uk/gai

Housebuilders Federation
www.hbf.co.uk

Incorporated Society of Valuers & Auctioneers
www.isva.co.uk

Institute of Plumbing
www.plumbers.org.uk

Institution of Structural Engineers
www.istructe.org.uk

Motor Schools Association
www.msagb.co.uk

National Association of Estate Agents
www.naea.co.uk

National Federation of Builders
www.builders.org.uk

National Hairdressers Federation
www.the-nhf.org

National Housebuliders Council (NHBC)
www.nhbc.co.uk

Replacement Window Advisory Service
www.ggf.org.uk

Royal Incorporation of Architects in Scotland
www.rias.org.uk

Royal Institute of British Architects
www.architecture.com

Royal Institution of Chartered Surveyors
www.rics.org.uk

Scottish Timber Trade association
www.stta.org.uk

Water UK
www.water.org.uk

Removals & Storage

Aardvark Self Storage
www.avk.co.uk

Abbey Self-Storage
www.abbey-self-storage.co.uk

Ace Removals
www.ace-removals.co.uk

All Trans overseas
www.alltrans.co.uk

Anglo Pacific overseas
www.anglopacific.co.uk

Association of Relocation Agents
www.relocationagents.com

Baggage Express
www.baggage-express.com

Bishops Move
www.bishops-move.co.uk

British Association of Removers
www.barmovers.com

Capital Movers
www.capital-worldwide.com

Cargo Forwarding International
www.cargoforwarding.co.uk

European Removals
www.europeanremovals.com

Federation of International Removers
www.fidi.com

Gerard Removers
www.gerardremovers.co.uk

House Removals.com
www.houseremovals.com

Interpac
www.interpac.co.uk

Mac Pac
www.mac-pac.co.uk

Moves
www.moves.co.uk

National Guild Of Removers
www.ngrs.org.uk

Pickfords
www.pickfords.co.uk

Teacrate
www.teacrate.com

Transeuro
www.transeuro.com

Safety & Security

Ability Security Systems
www.ability-security.co.uk

ADT
www.adt.co.uk

AG Securities
www.agsecurities.co.uk

Banham
www.banham.com

Bates Alams
www.batesalarms.co.uk

Child Accident Prevention Trust
www.capt.org.uk

DTI Home Safety Network
www.dti.gov.uk/homesafetynetwork

Health & Safety Executive
www.open.gov.uk/hse/hsehome.htm

Ingersoll
www.nt-architectural-products.co.uk

Institute for Home Safety
www.homesafe.org.uk

Local Homewatch
www.localhomewatch.co.uk

National Inspection Council for Electrical Installation Contracting
www.niceic.org.uk

Neighbourhood Watch
www.neighbourhoodwatch.net

Royal Society for the Prevention of Accidents
www.rospa.co.uk

Safety Systems & Alarm Inspection Board
www.ssaib.co.uk

Secom
www.secom-plc.com

Utilities

Amerada
www.amerada.co.uk

British Energy
www.british-energy.com

British Gas
www.gas.co.uk

Centrica
www.centrica.co.uk

Eastern Energy
www.easternenergy.co.uk

Eastern Group
www.eastern.co.uk

London Electricity
www.london-electricity.co.uk

MEB
www.meb.co.uk

National Grid
www.ngc.co.uk

National Power
www.national-power.com

North West Water
www.nww.co.uk

Northern Ireland Electricity
www.nie.co.uk

Scottish Hydro-Electric
www.hydro.co.uk

Scottish Nuclear
www.snl.co.uk

ScottishPower
www.scottishpower.co.uk

Servowarm
www.servowarm.co.uk

Severn Trent
www.severn-trent.com

South West Water
www.swwater.co.uk

Sutton & East Surrey Water
www.waterplc.com

SWALEC
www.swalec.com

Transco
www.transco.uk.com

Wessex Water
www.wessexwater.plc.uk

Yorkshire Utilities
www.yorkutil.syol.com

magazines & websites

All About Parents
www.allaboutparents.com

Antiques Trade Gazette
www.atg-online.com

Baby Directory
www.babydirectory.com

Babyworld
www.babyworld.co.uk

BBC Good Homes
www.goodhomes.beeb.com

Beeb.com
www.beeb.com

Beme
www.beme.com

Big Issue
www.bigissue.com

Charlotte Street
www.charlottestreet.com

Cosmopolitan
www.cosmomag.com

Country Life
www.countrylife.co.uk

Docklands & City
www.docklandsandcity.com

Elle
www.ellemag.com

Esquire
www.esquiremag.com

FHM
www.fhm.co.uk

Glamour
www.glamourmagazine.co.uk

Good Housekeeping
www.goodhousekeeping.co.uk

GQ
www.gq-magazine.co.uk

Handbag.com
www.handbag.com

Hello!
www.hello-magazine.co.uk

House & Garden
www.houseandgarden.co.uk

House Beautiful
http://housebeautiful.women.com/hb

Internet Advisor
www.netadvisor.co.uk

Jewish Online
www.jewishonline.org.uk

Jewish.net
www.jewish.net

Kitchen Specialists Association
www.ksa.co.uk/consumer

Kitchens, Bedrooms & Bathrooms Magazine
www.dmg.co.uk/kbbmag

Life
www.pathfinder.com/life

Loaded
www.loaded.co.uk

Magazine Shop
www.magazineshop.co.uk

Maxim
www.maximmag.com

Men's Health
www.menshealth.com

Mother & Baby
www.motherandbaby.co.uk

National Enquirer
www.nationalenquirer.com

New Woman
www.newwomanonline.co.uk

Parent News
www.parents-news.co.uk

Playboy
www.playboy.com

Private Eye
www.private-eye.co.uk

Readers' Digest
www.readersdigest.co.uk

Shout
www.dcthomson.co.uk/mags/shout

Spectator
www.spectator.co.uk

Tatler
www.tatler.co.uk

Totally Jewish
www.totallyjewish.com

UFO
www.ufomag.co.uk

Vanity Fair
www.vanityfair.co.uk

Viz
www.viz.co.uk

Vogue
www.vogue.co.uk

Web User
www.web-user.co.uk

World of Interiors
www.worldofinteriors.co.uk

Zoom
www.zoom.co.uk

Scottish

Caledonia
www.caledonia-magazine.com

Highlander Web
www.highlanderweb.co.uk

Homes & Interiors Scotland
www.homesandinteriorsscotland.com

IC Scotland
www.icscotland.co.uk

Scot Web
www.scotweb.co.uk

Scotland Magazine
www.scotlandmag.com

Scottish Banner
www.scottishbanner.com

Scottish Field
www.scottishfield.co.uk

Scottish Internet
www.tartan-umbrella.com

Scottish Radiance
www.scottishradiance.com

military associations

American Legion
www.legion.org

Army Catering Corps Association
www.regiments.org/milhist/uk/corps/ACC.htm

Bomber Command Historical Society
www.hellzapoppin.demon.co.uk

Far East Prisoners of War
www.fepow.org.uk

Friends of War Memorials
www.war-memorials.com

Home Service Force Association
www.hsf-association.freeserve.co.uk

Officers' Pensions Society
www.officerspensionsoc.co.uk

Radio Officers' Association
www.btinternet.com/~roae

RAF Benevolent Fund
www.raf-benfund.org.uk

Royal Air Forces Association
www.rafa.org.uk

Royal Auxiliary Air Force
www.rauxaf.mod.uk

Royal British Legion
www.britishlegion.org.uk

Royal Canadian Legion
www.legion.ca

Scottish Military Historical Society
www.btinternet.com/~james.mckay/
dispatch.htm

Scottish National War Memorial
www.snwm.org

motorcycles

Autocom
www.autocom.co.uk

Bike Trader Interactive
www.biketrader.co.uk

BMW
www.bmw.co.uk

British Bike Site
www.britishbikesite.co.uk

British Motor Racing Circuits
www.bmrc.co.uk

British Motorcyclists Federation
www.bmf.co.uk

British Speedway Promoters
www.british-speedway.co.uk

BSA Owners' Club UK
www.bsaoc.demon.co.uk

CSM Motorcycle Training
www.csm.uk.com

Ducati
www.ducati.com

Ducati Owners Club GB
http://homepages.enterprise.net/dtempleton

Federation of European Motorcyclists' Associations
www.mag-uk.org/fema/

Harley-Davidson
www.harley-davidson.co.uk

Honda
www.honda.co.uk

Honda Owners Club GB
www.hoc.org.uk

Kawasaki
www.kawasaki.com

Moto Guzzi
www.motoguzzi.it

Moto Guzzi Club GB
http://freespace.virgin.net/motoguzzi.clubgb/

Motorbikes Online
www.motorbikes-online.com

Motorcycle Industry Association
www.mcia.co.uk

Motorcycle News
www.motorcyclenews.com

Motorcycle Sport
www.bikenet.co.uk

Motorcycle UK
www.motorcycle-uk.com

Motorcycle World Magazine
www.motorcycleworld.co.uk

Norton Owners' Club
www.noc.co.uk

Piaggio
www.piaggio.com

Scootering Magazine
www.scootering.com

Scottish Motorcycle Show
www.scottishmotorcycleshow.co.uk

Suzuki
www.suzuki.co.uk

Suzuki Owners Club
www.suzuki-club.co.uk

Triumph
www.triumph.co.uk

Triumph Owners Motorcycle Club
www.tomcc.demon.co.uk

TVR
www.tvr-eng.co.uk

Vespa
www.vespa.com

Yamaha
www.yamaha-motor.co.uk

new age

British Feng Shui Society
www.fengshuisociety.org.uk

Findhorn Foundation, Aberdeen
www.findhorn.org

Foundation for International Spiritual Unfoldment
www.fisu.org

International Centre for Reiki Training
www.reiki.org

Raven Lodge of Shamanism
www.shamana.co.uk

religion

Buddhist

Aukana Training
www.aukana.org.uk

Buddhist Society (UK)
www.thebuddhistsociety.org.uk

Centre for Buddhist Studies
www.bris.ac.uk

Glasgow Buddhist Centre
www.glasgowbuddhistcentre.com

International Zen Association
www.zen-izauk.org

Journal of Buddhist Ethics
http://jbe.gold.ac.uk

Middle Way Journal
www.buddsoc.org.uk/mw.htm

Christian

African Inland Mission
www.aim-us.org

Anglican
www.anglican.org/online

Archbishop of Canterbury
www.archbishopofcanterbury.org

Baptist Church
www.baptist.org.uk

Care for the Family
www.care-for-the-family.org.uk

Carmelite Friars UK
www.carmelite.org

Catholic Church (in England & Wales)
www.tasc.ac.uk/cc

Catholic Church (Scotland)
www.catholic-scotland.org.uk

Christadelphian
www.christadelphian.org.uk

Christian Fellowship Church
www.cfc-net.org

Church of England
www.church-of-england.org

Church of Jesus Christ Latter Day Saints
www.ldscn.com

Church of Scotland
www.cofs.org.uk

Church Society
www.churchsociety.org

Free Church of Scotland
www.freechurch.org

Jehovah's Witnesses
www.watchtower.org

Jesus Army
www.jesus.org.uk

Mennonite Church
www.mennlink.org

Methodist Church
www.methodist.org.uk

Mormonism
www.mormon.net

Order of St Benedict
www.osb.org

Orthodox
www.orthodox.co.uk

Religious Society of Friends (Quakers)
www.quaker.org

Retreat Association
www.retreats.org.uk

Salvation Army
www.salvationarmy.org.uk

Scientology
www.scientology.org.uk

Scripture Union
www.scripture.org.uk

Seventh Day Adventist
www.adventist.org.uk

Unitarian
www.unitarian.org.uk

United Free Church of Scotland
www.ufcos.org.uk

United Pentecostal Church
www.upci.org

Vatican
www.vatican.va

World Council of Churches
www.wcc-coe.org

Hindu

Institute For Applied Spiritual Technology
www.ifast.net

Jay Swaminarayan
www.shreeswaminarayan.org.uk

National Hindu Students Forum
www.nhsf.org.uk

Islamic

Federation of Students Islamic Societies
www.fosis.org.uk

Investigating Islam
www.islamic.org.uk

Islam
www.islamic.org.uk

Islamic Centre England
www.ic-el.org

Islamic Foundation
www.islamic-foundation.org.uk

Islamic Unity Society
www.ius.org.uk

Muslim Council of Britain
www.mcb.org.uk

World Assembly of Muslim Youth
www.wamy.co.uk

Young Muslims UK
www.ymuk.com

Jewish

Holocaust History
www.holocausthistory.net

International Council of Jewish Women
www.icjw.org.uk

Jewish Board of Deputies
www.bod.org.uk

Judaism
www.jewish.co.uk

Maccabi Union
www.maccabi.org.uk

Reform Synagogues
www.refsyn.org.uk

Union of Liberal & Progressive Synagogues
www.ulps.org

Others

Atheist, Agnostic & Humanist
www.abarnett.demon.co.uk/atheism/index.html

Bahai Faith
www.bahai.com

British Humanist Association
www.humanism.org.uk

Church of Scientology
www.scientology.org.uk

Church of the Open Mind
www.hibbert.org.uk

Fountain International
www.fountain-international.org

Hare Krishna UK
www.iskcon.org.uk

International Society for Krishna Consciousness
www.religioustolerance.org/hare.htm

Jediism
www.jediism.org/homepage.html

Order of Bards, Ovates & Druids
www.druidry.org

Pagan Federation
www.paganfed.demon.co.uk

Satanism UK
www.satanism-uk.com

Shinto
www.religioustolerance.org/shinto.htm

Spiritualists' National Union
www.snu.org.uk

Sikh

British Organisation of Sikh Students
www.boss-uk.org

Sikh Arts & Cultural Association
www.saca.co.uk

Sikh Spirit
www.sikhspirit.com

Sikhism UK
www.sikhism.org.uk

retirement

Anchor Homes
www.anchor.org.uk

Association of Retired & Persons over 50
www.arp.org.uk

Too Young to Retire
www.2young2retire.com

weddings

Confetti
www.confetti.co.uk

Guild of Wedding Photographers
www.gwp-uk.co.uk

Highland Wedding Belles
www.highlandweddingbelles.co.uk

Litu Planners
www.litu.com

Pick a Band
www.pickaband.co.uk

Pronuptia
www.pronuptia.co.uk

Scottish Wedding Consultants
www.scottishweddingconsultants.co.uk

Virgin Brides
www.virgin.com

Wedding Service Directory
www.wedding-service.co.uk

Wedding Store UK
www.weddingstore.co.uk

Wedsite Scotland
www.wedsitescotland.com

museums, libraries & information

- encyclopaedias
- history
- libraries
- maps
- museums
- opinion polls & market research
- phone numbers
- professional bodies & associations
- reference
- weather

encyclopaedias

Britannica
www.britannica.co.uk

Encarta
www.encarta.msn.com

Encyclopedia
www.encyclopedia.com

Grolier
www.grolier.com

Hutchinson
www.bt-ern.co.uk/helicon

Probert
www.probert-encyclopaedia.co.uk

history

Anne Frank Educational Trust
www.afet.org.uk

Britannia History
http://britannia.com/history

British Association of Paper Historians
www.baph.freeserve.co.uk

Economic History Society
www.ehs.org.uk

English Civil War Society
http://english-civil-war-society.org/public_html/index.html

English Heritage
www.english-heritage.org.uk

First Empire Magazine
www.firstempire.ltd.uk

Galpin Society
www.music.ed.ac.uk/euchmi/galpin

Historical Association
www.hictory.org.uk

History – BBC Online
www.bbc.co.uk/history

History Today Magazine
www.historytoday.com

Institute of Historical Research
www.ihrinfo.ac.uk

Journal of Design History
www.oup.co.uk/design

Journal of Victorian Culture
www.indiana.edu/~victoria/jvc.html

Local History Magazine
www.local-history.co.uk

Making History (BBC)
www.bbc.co.uk/education/archive/makinghistory

Manorial Society of Great Britain
www.msgb.co.uk

Oral History Society
www.essex.ac.uk/sociology/oralhis.htm

Society for History of Mathematics
www.dcs.warwick.ac.uk/bshm

Society for the Promotion of Roman Studies
www.sas.ac.uk/icls/roman/default.htm

libraries

Aberdeen University Library
www.abdn.ac.uk/library

Balliol College Library
www.balliol.ox.ac.uk/library/library.html

Barbican
www.barbican.co.uk

Bodleian Library, Oxford
www.bodley.ox.ac.uk

British Film Institute National Library
www.bfi.org.uk/nationallibrary

British Library
www.bl.uk

Cambridge University Library
www.lib.cam.ac.uk

Corporation of London Records Office (CLRO)
www.corpoflondon.gov.uk

Edinburgh University Library
http://datalib.ed.ac.uk

John Rylands Library
http://rylibweb.man.ac.uk

Library of Congress
www.loc.gov

London Library
http://webpac.londonlibrary.co.uk

National Archives of Ireland
www.nationalarchives.ie

National Art Library (Victoria & Albert Museum)
www.nal.vam.ac.uk

National Library of Scotland
www.nls.uk

National Library of Wales
www.llgc.org.uk

National Library of Women
www.lgu.ac.uk/fawcett/main.htm

Natural History Museum Library
www.nhm.ac.uk/info/library/index.html

Public Record Office of England & Wales
www.pro.gov.uk

Science Museum Library
www.nmsi.ac.uk/library

maps

3D Atlas Online
www.3datlas.com

Association for Geographic Information (AGI)
www.agi.org.uk

Australian National Mapping Agency
www.auslig.gov.au

British Cartographic Society
www.cartography.org.uk

British Geological Survey
www.bgs.ac.uk

Committee of the National Mapping Agencies of Europe
www.cerco.org

Geomatics Canada
www.geocan.nrcan.gc.ca

Harvey
www.harveymaps.co.uk

Land Information New Zealand
www.linz.govt.nz

Mapblast
www.mapblast.com

Multi-purpose European Ground-Related Information Network
www.megrin.org

Multimap
www.multimap.com

National Map Centre
www.mapstore.co.uk

Ordnance Survey
www.ordsvy.gov.uk

Ordnance Survey Ireland
www.irlgov.ie/osi

Ordnance Survey of Northern Ireland
www.nics.gov.uk/doe/ordnance

Shell Geostar
www.shellgeostar.com

Society of Cartographers
www.soc.org.uk

Stanfords
www.stanfords.co.uk

Street Map
www.streetmap.co.uk

US Geological Survey
www.usgs.gov

museums

Aerospace Museum
www.rafmuseum.org.uk/flat/cosford

Andrew Carnegie Birthplace Museum
www.carnegiemuseum.co.uk

Armed Forces Museum
www.nms.ac.uk

Ashmolean Museum
www.ashmol.ox.ac.uk

Bank of England Museum
www.bankofengland.co.uk

Bass Museum
www.bass-museum.com

Beamish Open Air Museum
www.merlins.demon.co.uk/beamish

Bear Museum, Petersfield
www.bearmuseum.co.uk

Birmingham & Midland Transport Museum
www.bammot.org.uk

Birmingham Railway Museum
www.vintagetrains.co.uk/brm.htm

Black Country Living Museum
www.bclm.co.uk

Bletchley Park
www.bletchleypark.org.uk

Brewers Quay & The Timewalk
www.brewers-quay.co.uk

Bristol City Museum & Art Gallery
www.bristol-city.gov.uk/cgi-bin

Britain At War Experience
www.britain-at-war.co.uk

British Lawnmower Museum
www.dspace.dial.pipex.com/town/square/gf86

British Museum
www.british-museum.ac.uk

British Road Transport Museum
www.mbrt.co.uk

Broadfield House Glass Museum
www.dudley.gov.uk

Bronte Parsonage Museum
www.bronte.org.uk

Brooklands Museum
www.brooklands.org.uk

Cabinet War Rooms
www.iwm.org.uk/cabinet.htm

Caernarfon Air Park
www.users.globalnet.co.uk/~airworld

Cambridge Museum of Technology
www.cam.net.uk/home/steam

Chertsey Museum
www.surreycmc.gov.uk/chermus

Clan Cameron Museum
www.clan-cameron.org/museum.html

Clan Donnachaidh Museum
www.donnachaidh.com

Clink Prison Museum
www.clink.co.uk

Cobbaton Combat Collection
www.cobbatoncombat.co.uk

Cowper & Newton Museum
www.olio.demon.co.uk/cnmhome.html

Creetown Gem & Rock Museum
www.gemrock.net

Cutty Sark
www.cuttysark.org.uk

Design Museum
www.southwark.gov.uk/tourism

Dickens House Museum
www.dickensmuseum.com

Dinosaur Museum
www.dinosaur-museum.org.uk

Discovery Point
www.rrs-discovery.co.uk

Dover Museum
www.designmuseum.org

Dunaskin Open Air Museum
www.dunaskin.org.uk

Eastleigh Museum
www.hants.gov.uk/museum/eastlmus

Eden Camp Modern History Museum
www.edencamp.co.uk

Elgin Museum
www.elginmuseum.demon.co.uk

Elmbridge Museum
www.surrey-online.co.uk

Eureka The Museum For Children
www.eureka.org.uk

Fitzwilliam Museum
www.fitzmuseum.cam.ac.uk

Florence Nightingale
www.florence-nightingale.co.uk

Fort Grey
www.museum.guernsey.net

Freud Museum
www.freud.org.uk

Galleries of Justice
www.galleriesofjustice.org.uk

Geffrye Museum
www.geffrye-museum.org.uk

Gracie Fields Museum
www.rochdale.gov.uk/gracie

Grampian Transport Museum
www.craigandsuttar.co.uk/gtm

Grantown Museum
www.grantown-on-spey.co.uk/museum.htm

Green Howards Regimental Museum
www.greenhowards.org.uk

Gressenhall Norfolk Rural Life Museum
www.museums.norfolk.gov.uk

Hancock Museum
www.ncl.ac.uk/hancock

Haynes Motor Museum
www.haynesmotormuseum.co.uk

Heritage Motor Centre
www.heritage.org.uk

HMS Belfast
www.iwm.org.uk/belfast.htm

HMS Victory
www.flagship.org.uk/victory.htm

HMS Warrior
www.flagship.org.uk/hmswarrior1860.htm

Horniman Museum
www.horniman.demon.co.uk

Hunterian Museum & Art Gallery
www.gla.ac.uk/museum

Imperial War Museum
www.iwm.org.uk

Ironbridge Museum Trust, Telford
www.ironbridge.org.uk

Jane Austen Museum
www.janeaustenmuseum.org.uk

Jersey Museum
www.jerseyheritagetrust.org/museums

Jewish Museum
www.jewishmuseum.org

Kew Bridge Steam Museum
www.kbsm.org

London Toy & Model Museum
www.londontoy.com

London Transport Museum
www.ltmuseum.co.uk

Macclesfield Silk Museum
www.silk-macclesfield.org

Mackintosh House
www.gla.ac.uk/museum/machouse

Maidstone Museum
www.museum.maidstone.gov.uk

Manchester Museum
www.mcc.ac.uk/museum

Manchester Museum of Science & Industry
www.msim.org.uk

Mangapps Farm Railway Museum
www.mangapps.co.uk

Mary Rose
www.maryrose.org

Michael Faraday's Museum
www.ri.ac.uk

Midland Air Museum
www.discover.co.uk/~mam

Museum of Army Flying
www.flying-museum.org.uk

Museum of British Road Transport
www.mbrt.co.uk

Museum of Childhood Memories
www.nwi.co.uk/museumofchildhood

Museum of Classical Archaeology
www.classics.cam.ac.uk/ark.html

Museum of Costume
www.museumofcostume.co.uk

Museum of East Anglian Life
www.suffolkcc.gov.uk/central/meal

Museum of East Asian Art
www.east-asian-art.co.uk

Museum of Garden History
www.museumgardenhistory.org

Museum of London
www.museum-london.org.uk

Museum of Scotland
www.museum.scotland.net

Museum of the History of Science
www.mhs.ox.ac.uk

Museum of the Moving Image
www.bfi.org.uk/momi

Museum of the Royal College of Surgeons
www.rcseng.ac.uk/public/museums.htm

Museum of Welsh Life
www.nmgw.ac.uk

Museums of the Potteries
www.stoke.gov.uk/museums

National Army Museum
www.national-army-museum.ac.uk

National Coal Mining Museum
www.clanvis.com/coalmine

National Maritime Museum
www.nmm.ac.uk

National Motor Museum
www.beaulieu.co.uk

National Museum of Cartoon Art
www.pavilion.co.uk/cartoonet

National Museum of Photography, Film & TV
www.nmpft.org.uk

National Museums & Galleries on Merseyside
www.nmgm.org.uk

National Museums of Scotland
www.nms.ac.uk

National Railway Museum
www.nmsi.ac.uk/nrm

National Tramways Museum
www.tramway.co.uk

National Waterways Museum at Gloucester
www.nwm.org.uk

Natural History Museum
www.nhm.ac.uk

Pitt Rivers Museum, Oxford
www.units.ox.ac.uk/departments/prm

Portland Museum
www.weymouth.gov.uk/portmus.htm

Potteries Museum & Art Gallery
www.stoke.gov.uk/museums/pmag

Ragged School Museum
www.ics-london.co.uk/rsm

River & Rowing Museum
www.rrm.co.uk

Roman Baths Museum
www.romanbaths.co.uk

Royal Airforce Museum
www.rafmuseum.org.uk

Royal Albert Memorial Museum & Art Gallery, Exeter
www.exeter.gov.uk/tourism

Royal Armouries Museum, Leeds
www.armouries.org.uk

Royal Cornwall Museum
www.royalcornwallmuseum.org.uk

Royal Naval Museum
www.flagship.org.uk/rnm.htm

Royal Navy Submarine Museum
www.rnsubmus.co.uk

Royal Ulster Constabulary Museum, Belfast
www.ruc.police.uk

Royal Yacht Britannia
www.royalyachtbritannia.co.uk

Science Museum
www.nmsi.ac.uk

Second World War Experience Centre
www.war-experience.org

Sedgwick Museum of Geology
www.esc.cam.ac.uk

Sherlock Holmes Museum
www.sherlock-holmes.co.uk

Shetland Museum
www.shetland-museum.org.uk

Sikh Museum
www.sikhmuseum.org

Sir John Soane's Museum
www.soane.org

Somerset House
www.somerset-house.org.uk

Southampton Maritime Museum
www.southampton.gov.uk/leisure/visitguide/he.htm

Spitfire & Hurricane Memorial
www.spitfire-museum.com

St Albans Museum
www.stalbans.gov.uk/tourism

St Barbe Museum
www.st-barbe-museum.demon.co.uk

St Helens Transport Museum
www.sthtm.freeserve.co.uk

Tank Museum
www.tankmuseum.co.uk

Techniquest
www.tquest.org.uk

Thackray Medical Museum
www.thackraymuseum.org

Tunbridge Wells Museum
www.tunbridgewells.gov.uk/museum

Verdant Works
www.verdant-works.co.uk

Victoria & Albert Museum
www.vam.ac.uk

Whitby Museum
www.durain.demon.co.uk

Windermere Steamboat Museum
www.steamboat.co.uk

Wordsworth Museum
www.wordsworth.org.uk

Working Silk Museum
www.humphriesweaving.co.uk

York Castle Museum
www.york.gov.uk/heritage/museums

York Dungeon
www.yorkshirenet.co.uk/yorkdungeon

Yorkshire Museum
www.york.gov.uk/heritage/museums/yorkshire

opinion polls & market research

Audit Bureau of Circulation
www.abc.org.uk

British Market Research Association
www.bmra.org.uk

Gallup Organisation
www.gallup.com

Mintel.com
www.mintel.co.uk

Mori
www.mori.com

NOP Research
www.nopres.co.uk

phone numbers

192.com
www.192.com

BT Online Phonebook
www.bt.com/phonenetuk

Business Pages
www.businesspages.co.uk

Phonenumbers.net
www.phonenumbers.net

Telephone Code Changes
www.numberchange.org

Telephone Directories on the Web
www.teldir.com

Thomson Directories
www.thomweb.co.uk

Yellow Pages
www.yell.co.uk

professional bodies & associations

British Association for Information & Library Education & Research
www.bailer.ac.uk

Council for Museums, Archives & Libraries
www.resource.gov.uk

Library & Information Commission
www.lic.gov.uk

Library Association
www.la-hq.org.uk

Museums Association
www.museumsassociation.org

Society of Archivists
www.archives.org.uk

reference

Book Industry Communications
www.bic.org.uk

BUBL Information Service
www.bubl.ac.uk

FTSE
www.ftse.com

Jane's
www.janes.com

Kelly's Guide
www.kellysonline.net

Oxford English Dictionary
www.oed.com

Reference Centre
www.freeserve.net/reference

Roget's Thesaurus
www.thesaurus.com

Scoot
www.scoot.co.uk

Whitakers Almanack
www.whitakersalmanack.co.uk

weather

BBC Weather Centre
www.bbc.co.uk/weather

Belgium
www.meteo.oma.be

France
www.meteo.fr

Germany
www.dwd.de

ITN
www.itn.co.uk/weather

Meteorological Office
www.met-office.gov.uk

Netherlands
www.knmi.nl

Online Weather
www.onlineweather.com

Royal Meteorological Society
www.itu.rdg.ac.uk/rms

Ski Club of Great Britain (Snow Reports)
www.skiclub.co.uk

USA
www.nws.noaa.gov

Weathercall
www.weathercall.co.uk

World Meteorological Organisation
www.wmo.ch

personal finance

- banks & building societies
- credit cards
- ftse 100 companies
- insurance
- investment funds
- investment management
- magazines & websites
- mortgages
- online resource
- professional bodies
- stockbrokers

banks & building societies

3i Group
www.3igroup.com

Abbey National
www.abbeynational.co.uk

Adam & Co
www.adambank.co.uk

Alliance & Leicester
www.alliance-leicester.co.uk

Allied Irish Bank
www.aib.ie

Banc Cymru
www.bankofwales.co.uk

Bank of England
www.bankofengland.co.uk

Bank of Ireland
www.bank-of-ireland.co.uk

Bank of Scotland
www.bankofscotland.co.uk

Bank of Wales
www.bankofwales.co.uk

BankNet
www.mkn.co.uk/bank

Barclaycard
www.barclaycard.co.uk

Barclays Bank
www.barclays.co.uk

Bath
www.bibs.co.uk

Beneficial Bank
www.bankbeneficial.com

Birmingham Midshires
www.birmingham-midshires.co.uk

Bradford & Bingley
www.bradford-bingley.co.uk

Bristol & West
www.bristol-west.co.uk

Brittania Building Society
www.britannia.co.uk

Cahoot
www.cahoot.com

Cambridge
www.cambridge-building-society.co.uk

Capital
www.capitalbank.co.uk

Capital One UK
www.capitalone.co.uk

Cash Centres
www.cashcentres.co.uk

Cater Allen (Isle of Man)
www.caterallen-bank.com

Cater Allen Private Bank
www.caterallen.co.uk

Cazenove & Co
www.cazenove.co.uk

Cheltenham & Gloucester
www.cheltglos.co.uk

Chesham
www.cheshambsoc.co.uk

Citibank
www.citibank.com/uk

Clydesdale Bank
www.cbonline.co.uk

Co-operative Bank
www.co-operativebank.co.uk

Committee of Scottish Clearing Banks
www.scotbanks.org.uk

Coutts
www.coutts.com

Darlington
www.darlington.co.uk

Direct Line
http://uk.directline.com

Dunfermline Building Society
www.dunfermline-bs.co.uk

Ecology Building Society
www.ecology.co.uk

ECU
www.ecu.co.uk/group

Egg Savings
www.egg.com

Express Finance
www.express-finance.co.uk

Fidelity Investments
www.fidelity.co.uk

First Active
www.firstactive.co.uk

First Direct
www.firstdirect.com

First Trust
www.ftbni.co.uk/ft

First-e
www.first-e.com

Fleming
www.fleming.co.uk/premier

Forexia
www.forexia.com

Franklin Templeton
www.templeton.ca

Goldfish
www.goldfish.co.uk

Granville
www.granville.co.uk

Grindlays
www.pb.grindlays.com

Halifax
www.halifax.co.uk

Hambros
www.hambrosbank.com

Hamilton Direct Bank
www.hdb.co.uk

Hays
www.hays-banking.co.uk

HFC
www.hfcbank.co.uk

Home & Capital Trust
www.homecapital.co.uk

HSBC Bank
www.hsbc.co.uk

ICC
www.icc.ie

Intelligent Finance
www.if.com

Internet Savings
www.imbd.com

JP Morgan Fleming Asset Management
www.jpmorganfleming.com

Jyske
www.jbpb.com

Lambeth
www.lambeth.co.uk

Leeds & Holbeck
www.leeds-holbeck.co.uk

Leek
www.leek-united.co.uk

Legal & General
www.landg.com

Lloyds TSB
www.lloydstsb.co.uk

Lombard
www.lombard.co.uk/banking

Market Harborough
www.mhbs.co.uk

Marsden
www.marsdenbs.co.uk

National Savings & Investments
www.nsandi.com

Nationwide
www.nationwide.co.uk

NatWest
www.natwest.co.uk

Northern
www.northern-bank.co.uk

Northern Rock
www.northernrock.co.uk

Norwich & Peterborough
www.npbs.co.uk

Personal Loan Corporation
www.loancorp.co.uk

Prudential
www.pru.co.uk

Rea Brothers
www.reabrothers.co.uk

Royal Bank of Canada (Channel Islands)
www.royalbankci.com

Royal Bank of Scotland
www.rbs.co.uk

Royal Bank of Scotland – Financial Markets
www.rbsmarkets.com

Sainsbury's Bank
www.sainsburysbank.co.uk

Save & Prosper
www.prosper.co.uk

Scotia Capital
www.scotiacapital.com

Scottish Building Society
www.scottishbldgsoc.co.uk

Scottish Financial Enterprise
www.sfe.org.uk

Secure Trust
www.securetrustbank.com

Skipton
www.skipton.co.uk

Smile
www.smile.co.uk

Staffordshire
www.staffordshirebuildingsociety.co.uk

Standard
www.sbl.co.uk

Standard Life Bank
www.standardlifebank.com

Stroud & Swindon
www.stroudandswindon.co.uk

Sunbank
www.sunbank.co.uk

Teachers
www.teachersbs.co.uk

Triodos Bank
www.triodos.co.uk

Ulster Bank
www.ulsterbank.com

Universal
www.universal.uk.com

Virgin Direct
www.virgin-direct.co.uk

Virgin One
www.virginone.com

Woolwich
www.woolwich.co.uk

Yorkshire
www.ybs.co.uk

Yorkshire Bank
www.ybonline.co.uk

credit cards

Advanta
www.rbsadvanta.co.uk

American Express
www.americanexpress.co.uk

Barclaycard
www.barclaycard.co.uk

Capital One
www.capitalone.co.uk

CharityCard
www.charitycard.org

Diners Club
www.dinersclub.com

Football Club Credit Cards
www.footballcard.co.uk

Goldfish
www.goldfish.com

LINK Interchange Network
www.link.co.uk

Marbles
www.marbles.com

Mastercard
www.mastercard.com

MBNA
www.mbna.com

People's Bank
www.peoples.com/ukcreditcards

Scottish Widows
www.scottishwidows.co.uk

Switch
www.switch.co.uk

VISA
www.visa.com

ftse 100 companies

3i Group
www.3igroup.com

Abbey National
www.abbeynational.co.uk

Alliance & Leicester
www.alliance-leicester.co.uk

Allied Domecq
www.allieddomecqplc.com

Amvescap
www.amvescap.com

Asda
www.asda.co.uk

Associated British Foods
www.abf.co.uk

AstraZeneca
www.astrazeneca.com

BAA
www.baa.co.uk

Bank of Scotland
www.bankofscotland.co.uk

Barclays
www.barclays.co.uk

Bass
www.bass.co.uk

Billiton
www.billiton.com

BOC
www.boc.com

Boots
www.boots-plc.com

BP Amoco
www.bpamoco.com

British Aerospace
www.bae.co.uk

British Airways
www.british-airways.com

British Energy
www.british-energy.com

British Gas
www.bgplc.com

British Telecom
www.bt.com

BSkyB
www.sky.co.uk

Cable & Wireless
www.cwplc.com

Cadbury Schweppes
www.cadburyschweppes.com

Carlton
www.carltonplc.co.uk

Centrica
www.centrica.co.uk

CGU
www.cgu-insurance.net

Colt
www.colt-telecom.co.uk

Compass
www.compass-group.com

Daily Mail
www.dmgt.co.uk

Diageo
www.diageo.com

Dixons
www.dixons-group-plc.co.uk

Emap
www.emap.com

EMI
www.emigroup.com

Energis
www.energis.co.uk

GEC
www.gec.com

GKN
www.gknplc.com

Glaxo Wellcome
www.glaxowellcome.co.uk

Granada
www.granada.co.uk

Guardian Royal Exchange
www.gre-group.com

GUS
www.gusplc.com

Halifax
www.halifax.co.uk

Hanson
www.hansonplc.com

Hays
www.hays.co.uk

HSBC
www.hsbcgroup.com

ICI
www.ici.com

Imperial Tobacco
www.imperial-tobacco.com

Invensys
www.btrsiebe.com

Kingfisher
www.kingfisher.co.uk

Ladbroke
www.ladbrokegroup.com

Land Securities
www.propertymall.com/landsecurities

Legal & General
www.landg.com

Lloyds TSB
www.lloydstsb.co.uk

Marks & Spencer
www.marks-and-spencer.co.uk

Misys
www.misys.co.uk

National Grid
www.ngc.co.uk

National Power
www.national-power.com

NatWest
www.natwestgroup.com

Norwich Union
www.norwichunion.co.uk

Orange
www.uk.orange.net

P & O
www.p-and-o.com

Pearson
www.pearson.com

Powergen
www.pgen.com

Prudential
www.prudentialcorporation.com

Railtrack
www.railtrack.co.uk

Reckitt & Colman
www.reckittandcolman.com

Rentokil Initial
www.rentokil-initial.com

Reuters
www.reuters.com

Rio Tinto
www.riotinto.com

Rolls Royce
www.rolls-royce.com

Royal & Sun Alliance
www.royalsunalliance.co.uk

Royal Bank of Scotland
www.royalbankscot.co.uk

Sainsburys
www.j-sainsbury.co.uk

Schroders
www.schroders.co.uk

Scottish & Newcastle
www.scottish-newcastle.com

Scottish & Southern Energy
www.scottish-southern.co.uk

Scottish Power
www.scottishpower.plc.uk

Securicor
www.securicor.com

Sema
www.semagroup.com

Severn Trent
www.severn-trent.com

Shell
www.shell.com

Smith Kline Beecham
www.sb.com

Smiths Industries
www.smiths-industries.com

South African Breweries
www.sab.co.za

Stagecoach
www.stagecoachholdings.com

Standard Chartered
www.standard.com

Telewest
www.telewest.co.uk

Tesco
www.tesco.co.uk

Thames Water
www.thames-water.com

Unilever
www.unilever.com

United News & Media
www.unm.com

United Utilities
www.unitedutilities.com

Vodafone
www.vodafone.co.uk

Whitbread
www.whitbread.co.uk

Woolwich
www.woolwich.co.uk

WPP
www.wpp.com

insurance

A1 Insurance
www.a1insurance.co.uk

AA Insurance
www.aainsurance.co.uk

Abacus Direct
www.abacusdirect.co.uk

Abbey Online
www.abbey-online.co.uk

Admiral
www.admiral-insurance.co.uk

Allied Dunbar Assurance
www.allieddunbar.co.uk

AMP Pearl
www.amp-online.co.uk

Anglia Countrywide
www.anglia-countrywide.co.uk

Aviva Group
www.aviva.com

AXA
www.axa.co.uk

Britannic Assurance
www.britannic.co.uk

BUPA
www.bupa.co.uk

Canada Life
www.canadalife.com

Carquote
www.carquote.co.uk

Central Direct
www.central-insurance.co.uk

CGU
www.cgu-direct.co.uk

Chubb
www.chubb.com

Churchill
www.churchill.co.uk

Co-operative Insurance Society
www.cis.co.uk

Columbus
www.columbusdirect.co.uk

Commercial Union
www.commercialunion.co.uk

Cornhill
www.cornhill.co.uk

County
www.county-insurance.co.uk

DAS Legal Expenses
www.das.co.uk

Denplan
www.denplan.co.uk

Dial Direct
www.ddirect.co.uk

Direct
www.digs.co.uk

Direct Line Insurance
www.directline.com

Eagle Star
www.eaglestar.co.uk

EasyCover
www.easycover.com

Elephant
www.elephant.co.uk

Endsleigh
www.endsleigh.co.uk

Equitable Life
www.equitable.co.uk

General Accident
www.ga.co.uk

Guardian
www.gre.co.uk

Heath Group
www.heathgroup.com

Hibernian Group
www.hibernian.ie

Hiscox
www.hiscox.com

Hogg Robinson
www.hoggrobinson.com

Home Quote
www.home.quote.co.uk

The Insurance Club
www.insuranceclub.co.uk

Insurance Wide
www.insurancewide.com

InterSure
www.intersure.co.uk

Ironsure
www.ironsure.com

Lancaster
www.lancaster-ins.co.uk

Legal And General
www.legal-and-general.co.uk

Lloyds of London
www.lloyds.com

MCM Group
www.mcmgroup.co.uk

Midland Direct
www.midlanddirect.co.uk

National Mutual
www.nationalmutual.co.uk

NFU Mutual
www.nfumutual.co.uk

Norwich Union
www.norwich-union.co.uk

Old Mutual
www.oldmutual.com

Pearl
www.pearl.co.uk

Pet Plan
www.petplan.co.uk

PolicySure
www.policysure.com

PPP/Columbia
www.columbiahealthcare.co.uk

Preferential
www.preferential.co.uk

Preferred Direct
www.pdinsure.co.uk

Privilege Cars
www.privilege.co.uk

Prospero Direct
www.prospero.co.uk

Prudential – Corporate
www.prudential.co.uk

Prudential – Retail
www.pru.co.uk

RAC
www.rac.co.uk

Royal & Sun Alliance Group
www.royal-and-sunalliance.com

Royal Liver
www.royal-liver.com

Royal Sun Alliance
www.royalsunalliance.co.uk

Saga
www.saga.co.uk

Scottish Amicable
www.scottishamicable.com

Scottish Provident
www.scotprov.co.uk

Scottish Widows
www.scottishwidows.co.uk

Screentrade
www.screentrade.co.uk

Sedgwick Group
www.sedgwick.com

Skandia Life
www.skandia.co.uk

Sportscover
www.sportscover.co.uk

Standard Life – Group
www.standardlife.com

Standard Life – Retail
www.standardlife.co.uk

Sun Life of Canada
www.sunbank.co.uk

Swinton
www.swinton.co.uk

Swiss Life (UK)
www.swisslife.co.uk

Trade Indemnity
www.tradeindemnity.com

UK Friendly
www.ukfriendly.co.uk

Western Provident
www.wpahealth.co.uk

Willis Corroon Group
www.williscorroon.com

Winterthur Life
www.winterthur-life.co.uk

Wise Money
www.wisemoney.com

Woolwich Insurance Services
www.woolwich-insurance.co.uk

World Cover Direct
www.worldcover.co.uk

World Trekker
www.worldtrekker.com

Worldwide Travel
www.wwtis.co.uk

Zurich
www.zurich.com

Zurich – Retail
www.zurich.co.uk

Professional Bodies

Association of British Insurers
www.abi.org.uk

British Insurers Brokers' Association
www.biba.org.uk

Chartered Institute of Loss Adjusters
www.cila.co.uk

Life Insurance Association
www.lia.co.uk

investment funds

Aberdeen Asset Management
www.aberdeen-asset.com

Aberdeen Unit Trust Managers
www.aberdeen-knowhow.com

ABN AMRO Asset Management
www.invweek.co.uk/abn

AIB Asset Management
www.aibgovett.com

Baring Asset Management
www.baring-asset.com

Capel Cure Sharp
www.capelcuresharp.co.uk

Cazenove Fund Management
www.cazenove.co.uk/cfm

City of London Investment Group
www.citlon.co.uk

Credit Suisse Asset Management
www.csamfunds.co.uk

Edinburgh Fund Managers
www.edfd.com

Ely Fund Managers
www.ely.uk.com

Fidelity
www.fidelity.co.uk

Finsbury Asset Management
www.finsbury-asset.co.uk

Flemings
www.fleming.co.uk

Foreign & Colonial
www.fandc.co.uk

Framlington
www.framlington.com

Friends Provident
www.friendsprovident.co.uk

Gartmore Investment Management
www.gartmore.iii.co.uk

Gerrard Group
www.gerrard.com

Global Asset Management
www.ukinfo.gam.com

GNI Fund Management
www.gnifm.com

Henderson
www.henderson.co.uk

Herald Investment Management
www.heralduk.com

Hill Samuel
www.hillsamuel.co.uk

INVESCO
www.invesco.co.uk

Investec Guinness Flight
www.investecguinnessflight.com

ISA Shop
www.isa-shop.co.uk

ITS Investment Trusts
www.itsonline.co.uk

Jupiter
www.jupiteronline.co.uk

M&G Group
www.mandg.co.uk

Mercury Asset Management
www.mam.com/uksite

National Savings
www.nationalsavings.co.uk

Norwich Union
www.norwich-union.co.uk

Perpetual Investment
www.perpetual.co.uk

Pictet Group
www.pictet.com

Pinnacle
www.allmortgages.co.uk

PPM UK
www.ppm-uk.com

Premier Asset Management
www.premierfunds.co.uk

Royal Skandia
www.royalskandia.com

Sabre Fund Management
www.sabrefund.com

Save & Prosper
www.prosper.co.uk

Schroders
www.schroder.co.uk

Scottish Amicable
www.scottishamicable.com

Scottish Investment Trust
www.sit.co.uk

Scottish Life International
www.sli.co.im

Scottish Mutual International
www.smi.ie

Scottish Provident
www.scotprov.co.uk

Scottish Value Management
www.scottish-value.co.uk

Threadneedle Investments
www.threadneedle.co.uk

Virgin
www.virginisa.com

investment management

Aberdeen Asset Management
www.aberdeen-asset.com

Baillie Gifford
www.bailliegifford.com

Brittanic Asset Management
www.britannicasset.com

Edinburgh Fund Managers Group
www.edfd.com

Franklin Templeton
www.franklintempleton.co.uk

Martin Currie
www.martincurrie.com

Scottish Equity Partners
www.sep.co.uk

Scottish Mutual
www.scottishmutual.co.uk

Scottish Widows Investment Partnership
www.swipartnership.com

magazines & websites

Bloomberg
www.bloomberg.com

Business Money
www.business-money.com

CAROL
www.carol.co.uk

Citywatch
www.citywatch.co.uk

Direct Debit
www.directdebit.co.uk

Egg-Free Zone
www.eggfreezone.com

Euromoney Online
www.euromoney.com

Hemmington Scott
www.hemscott.co.uk

Interactive Investor International
www.iii.co.uk

International Fund Investment
www.ifiglobal.com

Investment & Pensions Europe
www.ipeurope.co.uk

Investment Trust Newsletter
www.trustnews.co.uk

Investors Chronicle
www.investorschronicle.co.uk

Investors Internet Journal
www.iij.co.uk

Line One Money Zone
www.lineone.net/moneyzone

Money Money Money
www.moneymoneymoney.co.uk

Moneyweb
www.moneyweb.co.uk

MoneyWorld UK
www.moneyworld.co.uk

Motley Fool
www.fool.co.uk

Mrs Cohen
www.mrscohen.com

Offshore Investor
www.offshore-investor.com

Pensions World
www.pensionsworld.co.uk

Quicken.com
www.quicken.com

TheStreet.co.uk
www.thestreet.co.uk

mortgages

Charcol Online
www.charcol.co.uk

Chase De Vere
www.cdvmortgage.co.uk

The Finance Centre
www.tfcmortgages.co.uk

Finance Tracker
www.financetracker.ltd.uk

Home & Capital Trust
www.homecapital.co.uk

Inter-Alliance
www.interalliance.co.uk

John Charcol
www.johncharcol.co.uk

Midlands Insurance Services
www.midlandsinsurance.freeserve.co.uk

The Money Centre
www.themoneycentre.co.uk

Money Supermarket
www.moneysupermarket.com

Moneynet
www.moneynet.co.uk

Mortgage Alliance
www.magreen.demon.co.uk

Mortgage & Loan Group
www.mortgageandloangroup.co.uk

Mortgage Help Desk UK
www.mortgage.u-net.com

Mortgage Intelligence
www.mortgage-intelligence.co.uk

Mortgage Shop
www.mortgage-shop.co.uk

Mortgage Talk
www.mortgagetalk.co.uk

MTS Mortgage Company
www.mtsmortgage.co.uk

Royal & SunAlliance Investments
www.rsa-investments.co.uk

UK Mortgages Guide
www.ukmortgagesguide.co.uk

UK Mortgages Online
www.ukmortgagesonline.com

online resource

Banks.com Directory
www.banks.com

Datastream
www.datastream.com

Dow Jones
www.dowjones.com

Financial Times
http://news.ft.com/home/uk

Find-an-adviser
www.find-an-adviser.co.uk

FTSE
www.ftse.com

O & A Currency Exchange
www.oanda.com/convert/classic

S&P Funds Service
www.funds-sp.com/win/en/Index.jsp

Thomas Cook Foreign Exchange
www.fx4business.com

professional bodies

Arson Prevention Bureau
www.arsonpreventionbureau.org.uk

Association of British Insurers
www.abi.org.uk

Association of Consulting Actuaries
www.aca.org.uk

Association of Independent Financial Advisers
www.aifa.net

Association of Private Client Investment Managers & Stockbrokers
www.apcims.co.uk

Association of Unit Trusts & Investment Funds
www.investmentfunds.org.uk

British Bankers' Association
www.bankfacts.org.uk

British Insurance & Investment Brokers Association
www.biiba.org.uk

British Venture Capital Association
www.bvca.co.uk

Building Societies Association
www.bsa.org.uk

Cambridge Building Society
www.cambridge-building-society.co.uk

Chartered Insurance Institute
www.cii.co.uk

Cornhill Direct
www.cornhilldirect.co.uk

Council of Mortgage Lenders
www.cml.org.uk

Countryside
www.cwide.co.uk

Credit Card Research Group
www.ccrg.org.uk

Finance Scotland
www.financescotland.com

Financial Services Authority
www.sib.co.uk

Financial Services Consumer Panel
www.fs-cp.org.uk

Financial Watch
http://finance.wat.ch

Gartmore Investment
www.gartmore.iii.co.uk

Guernsey Financial Services Commission
www.gfsc.guernseyci.com

HM Treasury
www.hm-treasury.gov.uk

IMRO
www.imro.co.uk

Independent Financial Advisers Association
www.ifaa.org.uk

Institute of Actuaries
www.actuaries.org.uk

Insurance Institute of London
www.iilondon.co.uk

International Risk Institute
http://riskinstitute.ch

International Underwriting Association of London
www.iua.co.uk

Investment Managers Association
www.investmentfunds.org.uk

Investors Compensation Scheme (ICS)
www.the-ics.org.uk

Jersey Financial Services Commission
www.jerseyfsc.org

Liverpool Victoria Friendly Society
www.lvbestbond.co.uk

Loss Prevention Council
www.lpc.co.uk

M&G Group
www.mandg.co.uk

Mercury Asset Management
www.mam.com

National Association of Bank & Insurance Customers
http://freespace.virgin.net/bank.help

National Association of Pension Funds
www.napf.co.uk

United Kingdom Shareholders' Association
www.uksa.org.uk

United Kingdom Shareholders' Association (Scotland)
http://members.aol.com/uksascot

The World Bank
www.worldbank.org

stockbrokers

Barclays Stockbrokers
www.barclays-stockbrokers.com

Brewin Dolphin
www.brewin.co.uk

Capel-Cure Sharp
www.capelcuresharp.co.uk

Cazenove & Co
www.cazenove.co.uk

Charles Schwab Europe
www.schwab-worldwide.com

Charles Stanley & Co
www.charles-stanley.co.uk

CMC Group
www.cmcplc.com

Credit Suisse First Boston de Zoete & Bevan
www.csamfunds.co.uk

Durlacher Corporation
www.durlacher.co.uk

E*TRADE United Kingdom
www.etrade.co.uk

Edward Jones
www.edwardjones.com

European Stockbrokers
www.europeanstockbrokers.co.uk

GNI
www.gni.co.uk

Greig Middleton
www.greigmiddleton.co.uk

James Brearley & Sons
www.jbrearley.co.uk

Killik & Co.
www.killik.co.uk

Mercury Asset Management
www.mercury-asset-management.co.uk

Rudolf Wolff
www.rwolff.com

Salomon Smith Barney
www.sbil.co.uk

Selftrade
www.selftrade.co.uk

TD Waterhouse
www.tdwaterhouse.co.uk

- afghanistan
- andorra
- angola
- argentina
- australia
- austria
- bangladesh
- belgium
- belize
- bolivia
- botswana
- brazil
- britain
- bulgaria
- cambodia
- cameroon
- canada
- caribbean
- channel islands
- chile
- china
- comoros island
- costa rica
- croatia
- cuba
- cyprus
- czech republic
- denmark
- ecuador
- egypt
- estonia
- falkland islands
- finland
- france
- gambia
- germany
- ghana
- gibralatar
- greece
- guatemala
- hungary
- iceland
- india
- indonesia
- iran
- ireland
- israel
- italy
- japan
- jordan
- kenya
- korea
- kuwait
- laos
- latvia
- lebanon

- liechtenstein
- lithuania
- luxembourg
- madagascar
- malawi
- malaysia
- maldives
- malta
- mauritius
- mexico
- monaco
- morocco
- mozambique
- myanmar
- namibia
- nepal
- netherlands
- new zealand
- norway
- pacific islands
- pakistan
- peru
- philippines
- poland
- portugal
- puerto rico
- romania
- russia
- samoa
- senegal
- serbia
- seychelles
- singapore
- slovakia
- slovenia
- solomon islands
- south africa
- spain
- sri lanka
- sweden
- switzerland
- tahiti
- taiwan
- tanzania
- thailand
- tibet
- tonga
- tunisia
- turkey
- uganda
- ukraine
- united arab emirates
- uruguay
- usa
- venezuela
- vietnam
- web cams: views of scotland
- zambia
- zimbabwe

afghanistan

Tourist Information

Afghanistan
www.geocities.com/afghanistan_ca/Tourist.html

andorra

Andorra
www.turisme.ad/angles

angola

Angola
www.angola.org

Towns & Cities

Luanda
www.luanda.com

argentina

Tourist Information

Argentina
www.info.gov.ar

Towns & Cities

Buenos Aires
www.gba.gov.ar

Mar Del Plata
www.argenet.com.ar/emtur

australia

Tourist Information

National Tourist Office
www.australia-online.com

Towns & Cities

Canberra
www.nationalcapital.gov.au

Melbourne
www.melbourne.vic.gov.au

Sydney
www.sydney.visitorsbureau.com.au

Victoria
www.tourism.vic.gov.au

austria

Graz
www.graztourism.at

Innsbruck
www.tiscover.com/innsbruck

Klagenfurt
www.info.klagenfurt.at

Salzburg
www.salzburginfo.at

Vienna
http://info.wien.at

bangladesh

Tourist Information

Bangladesh
www.bangladesh.com

Towns & Cities

Dhaka
www.dhaka.com

belgium

Tourist Information

National Tourist Office
www.belgium-tourism.com

Towns & Cities

Antwerp
www.antwerpen.be

Bruges
www.brugge.be

Brussels
www.brussel.irisnet.be

Gent
www.gent.be

Ostend
www.oostende.be

belize

Tourist Information

Belize Tourism Board
www.travelbelize.org

bolivia

Bolivia Tourism
www.bolivia-tourism.com

botswana

Botswana Tourism
www.gov.bw/tourism/index_f.html

brazil

Brazil
www.brazilinfo.com

Towns & Cities

Brasilia
www.geocities.com/TheTropics/3416/

Rio de Janeiro
www.governo.rj.gov.br

Sao Paulo
www.saopaulo.sp.gov.br

britain

Castles

Ackergill Tower
www.ackergill-tower.co.uk

Adverikie Castle
www.adverikie.com

Affleck Castle
www.monikie.org.uk/affcastl.htm

Alnwick Castle
www.alnwickcastle.com

Amhuinnsuidhe Castle
www.castles.org/Chatelaine/AMHUINN.HTM

Ardvreck Castle
www.castles.org/Chatelaine/ARDVRECK.HTM

Balfour Castle
www.castles.org/Chatelaine/BALFOUR.HTM

Ballindalloch Castle
www.ballindallochcastle.co.uk

Balmoral Castle
www.balmoralcastle.com

Baltersan
http://ourworld.compuserve.com/homepages/Baltersan/index.htm

Barr Castle
www.kirkburn.com/castlelevan/nearby/castles/barr/barr.htm

Blackcraig Castle
www.ladyjill.com/blackcraigsite.html

Blair Castle
www.castles.org/Chatelaine/BLAIR.HTM

Blairquhan Castle
www.scottishcastles-info.co.uk/blairquhan

Brodick Castle
www.castles.org/Chatelaine/BRODICK.HTM

Brodie Castle
www.castles.org/Chatelaine/BRODIE.HTM

Buchanan Castle
www15.pair.com/buchanan/clancast.htm

Caerlaverock Castle
www.aboutscotland.com/caer/caer.html

Caisteal Maol
www.castles.org/Chatelaine/MAOL.HTM

Calgary Castle
www.calgary-castle.com

Carbisdale Castle
www.carbisdale.org

Castle Levan
www.kirkburn.com/castlelevan

Castle Menzies
www.menzies.org

Castle of Park
www.castleofpark.net

Castle Stuart
www.castlestuart.com

Castle Tioram
www.tioram.org.uk

Cawdor Castle
www.castles.org/Chatelaine/CAWDOR.HTM

Craighall Castle
www.craighall.co.uk

Craignethan Castle
www.clydevalley.co.uk/craignethan/index.htm

Dalhousie Castle
www.dalhousiecastle.co.uk

Delgatie Castle
www.delgatiecastle.com

Dirleton Castle
www.maybole.org/history/castles/dirleton.htm

Dornoch Castle
www.dornochcastle.com

Drumlanrig Castle
www.heritageontheweb.co.uk/drumlan/index.htm

Dundas Castle
www.dundascastle.co.uk

Dunderave Castle
www.dunderavecastle.co.uk

Dundonald Castle
www.royaldundonaldcastle.co.uk

Dunduff Castle
www.dunduff.com/

Dunnottar Castle
www.castles.org/Chatelaine/dunnottar

Duns Castle
www.dunscastle.co.uk

Duntrune Castle
www.duntrune.com

Dunvegan Castle
www.castles.org/Chatelaine/DUNVEGAN.HTM

Dupplin Castle
www.aboutscotland.co.uk/perth/dupplin.html

Edinburgh Castle
http://lynn.efr.hw.ac.uk/EDC/guide/edincas.html

Eilean Donan Castle
www.castles.org/Chatelaine/EDC/e-donan.htm

Falkland Palace
www.nts.org.uk/falkland.html

Fenton Tower
www.fentontower.co.uk

Findlater Castle
www.findlater.org.uk/Castle.htm

Forbes Castle
www.castle-forbes.demon.co.uk

Fordyce Castle
www.fordycecastle.co.uk

Fyvie Castle
www.nts.org.uk/fyvie.html

Glamis Castle
www.great-houses-scotland.co.uk/glamis

Glenapp Castle
www.glenappcastle.com

Glengarry Castle
www.glengarry.net

Guide to Scottish Castles
www.castles.org

Haggs Castle
www.pollokshields.demon.co.uk/haggscastle.html

Huntly Castle
www.castles.org/Chatelaine/HUNTLY.HTM

Inverlochy Castle
www.inverlochy.co.uk

Kames Castle
www.kames-castle.co.uk

Kelburn Castle
www.kelburncastle.com/castle.html

Kellie Castle
www.nts.org.uk/kellie.html

Kilchurn Castle
http://libby.withnall.com/kilchurn.htm

Kilmartin Castle
www.kht.org.uk/kilmartin/sites/castle2.html

Kincardine Castle
www.kincardinecastle.com

Kinfauns Castle
www.kinfaunscastle.co.uk

Kinlochaline Castle
http://macinnes.org/kinlochaline.html

Lauriston Castle
www.edinburgh.gov.uk/CEC/Recreation/Leisure/Data/Lauriston_Castle/Lauriston_Castle.html

Leslie Castle
www.celticcastles.com/castles/leslie

Lochdoon Castle
www.maybole.org/history/sketches/spratt/lochdoon.htm

Loudoun Castle
www.loudouncastle.co.uk

Luffness Castle
www.luffnesscastle.co.uk

Merchiston Castle
www.mcsch.org.uk

Minard Castle
www.minardcastle.com

Mugdock Castle
www.mugdock-country-park.org.uk

Murthly Castle
www.scottishcastles-info.co.uk/murthly

Myres Castle
www.scottishcastles-info.co.uk/myres

Newark Castle
www.inverie.com

Pitfichie Castle
www.scottishcastles-info.co.uk/pitfichie

Pitsligo Castle
www.rosehearty.co.uk/around/castle.htm

Rothesay Castle
www.castles.org/Chatelaine/ROTHESAY.HTM

Rumgally House
www.sol.co.uk/r/RUMGALLY

Sinclair Castle
http://members.tripod.co.uk/Girnigoe/sinclaircastle.html

Skelmorlie Castle
www.skelmorliecastle.com

Skibo Castle
www.carnegieclub.co.uk

Slains Castle
www.dch-design.com/CLAN_HAY/CASTLES/Old_Slains.html

Stirling Castle
www.undiscoveredscotland.co.uk/stirling/stirlingcastle/

Strathaven Castle
http://clyde-valley.com/strathaven

Strome Castle
www.nts.org.uk/strome.html

Sundrum Castle
www.sundrumcastle.com

Tarbet Castle
www.tarbertlochfyne.com/thistory/tcastle/index.html

Thirlestane Castle
www.thirlestanecastle.co.uk

Torrisdale Castle
www.torrisdalecastle.freeserve.co.uk

Traquair Castle
www.traquair.co.uk

Tullibote Castle
www.tulbol.demon.co.uk/monc/tullibote-castle.htm

Tulloch Castle
www.tullochcastle.co.uk

Urquhart Castle
www.castles.org/Chatelaine/URQUHART.HTM

Venlaw
www.venlaw.co.uk

Wedderburn
www.wedderburn-castle.co.uk

Historic Railways

Alford Valley
www.alford.org.uk/avr.htm

Bo'ness & Kinneil Railway
www.srps.org.uk/railway/home.html

Flying Scotsman
www.flyingscotsman.com

Mull Rail
www.holidaymull.org/rail/Welcome.html

National Railway Museum
www.nmsi.ac.uk/nrm/html/home_pb/menu.htm

Orient Express
www.orient-expresstrains.com

Queen of Scots
www.queenofscots.co.uk

Royal Scotsman
www.royalscotsman.com

Strathspey Steam Railway
www.btinternet.com/~strathspey.railway

Monuments, Churches & Historic Buildings

Baden Powell House
www.scoutbase.org.uk

Cathedrals in Scotland
www.britainexpress.com/scotland/cathedrals

Dunblane Cathedral
www.dunblanecathedral.org.uk

Glasgow Cathedral
www.glasgowcathedral.org.uk

Great Houses of Scotland
www.great-houses-scotland.co.uk

Hadrian's Wall
www.hadrians-wall.org

Historic Royal Palaces
www.hrp.org.uk

Houses of Parliament
www.parliament.uk

Kilmartin House
www.kht.org.uk

Oban Cathedrals
www.oban-church.org.uk

Royal Commission on the Ancient & Historical Monuments of Scotland
www.rcahms.gov.uk

Scott Monument
www.ebs.hw.ac.uk/EDC/guide/pst.html

St Andrews Cathedral, Aberdeen
http://cathedral.aberdeen.anglican.org

St Andrews Cathedral, Dundee
www.geocities.com/standrewscathedral

St Andrews Cathedral, Inverness
www.inverness-cathedral.org.uk

St Andrews Cathedral, St Andrews
www.aboutbritain.com/StAndrewsCathedral.htm

St Giles Cathedral
www.royalmile.com/info/stgiles.htm

St Machar Cathedral
www.stmachar.com

St Marys Cathedral
www.scotland.anglican.org/aboutus_general_cathedrals.html

St Pauls Cathedral, Dundee
www.stpaulscathedraldundee.org

Wallace Monument
www.stirling.co.uk/attractions/wallace.htm

Parks & Gardens

Ardnaseig Gardens
www.robbins-associates.co.uk/gardens/locate.htm

Armadale Castle Gardens
www.highlandconnection.org/cdltgardens.html

Branklyn Gardens
www.nts.org.uk/branklyn.html

Broughton House Garden
www.nts.org.uk/broughton.html

Castle Kennedy Gardens
www.ukattraction.com/southern-scotland/castle-kennedy.htm

Cluny House
www.aberfeldycottages.co.uk/Attractions.htm#cluny

Crarae Gardens
www.robbins-associates.co.uk/gardens/locate.htm

Crathes Castle & Gardens
www.nts.org.uk/crathes.html

Dawyck Botanic Garden
www.rbge.org.uk/intro/dawyck.htm

Drum Castle & Gardens
www.nts.org.uk/drum.html

Edinburgh Royal Botanic Garden
www.rbge.org.uk

Edzell Castle
www.carnoustie.org/visit/cas.htm

Finlaystone Country Estate
www.finlaystone.co.uk

Glasgow Botanic Gardens
www.zoos.bizland.com/botanicalgardens.htm

Greenbank Garden
www.nts.org.uk/greenbank.html

Hill of Tarvit Mansionhouse & Garden
www.nts.org.uk/hill.html

Inveresk Lodge Garden
www.nts.org.uk/inveresk.html

Leith Hall & Garden
www.nts.org.uk/leith.html

Logan Botanic Garden
www.rbge.org.uk/intro/logan.htm

Mertoun Gardens
http://muses.calligrafix.co.uk/dryburgh/mertoun.html

Mount Stuart House
www.mountstuart.com/

Pitmedden Garden
www.nts.org.uk/pitmedden.html

Pitmuies House & Garden
www.carnoustie.org/visit/gard3.htm

Pollok Country Park
www.nts.org.uk/pollok.html

Princes Street Gardens
www.ebs.hw.ac.uk/EDC/guide/pst.html

St Andrews Botanic Garden
www.st-and.ac.uk/standrews/botanic

Younger Botanica Garden
www.rbge.org.uk/intro/younger.htm

Regions

About Scotland
www.aboutscotland.com

Angus
www.angus.gov.uk

Ayrshire
www.mcintyre.demon.co.uk/local/locality.htm

Edinburgh & Lothians
www.edinburgh.org

Fort William & Lochabar
www.visit-fortwilliam.co.uk

Hebrides
www.hebrides.com

Highlands of Scotland
www.host.co.uk

Isle of Bute
www.isle-of-bute.com

Isle of Skye
www.skye.co.uk

Orkney
www.orknet.co.uk/tourism

Tourist Attractions

BBC Experience
www.bbc.co.uk/experience

Blair Drummond Safari Park
www.safari-park.co.uk

Deep Sea World
www.deepseaworld.com

Dynamic Earth
www.dynamicearth.co.uk

Edinburgh Dungeons
www.thedungeons.com

Edinburgh Ghost Tours
www.witcherytours.com

Glasgow Science Centre
www.gsc.org.uk

Landmark Centre
www.landmark-centre.co.uk

Original Bus Tour Company
www.theoriginaltour.com

Peoples Palace
www.glasgow.gov.uk/html/about/palace/palace.htm

Royal Yacht Brittania
www.royalyachtbritannia.co.uk

RRS Discovery
www.rrs-discovery.co.uk

Tourist Information

24 Hour Museum
www.24hourmuseum.org.uk

Blue Badge Guides
www.blue-badge.org.uk

British Hotel Reservations Centre
www.bhrc.co.uk

British Tourist Authority
www.visitbritain.com

Edinburgh & Lothians Tourist Board
www.edinburgh.org

Good Guide to Britain
www.goodguides.com

Highlands of Scotland Tourist Board
www.host.co.uk

Information Britain
www.information-britain.co.uk

Perthshire Tourist Board
www.perthshire.co.uk

Scottish Tourist Board
www.holiday.scotland.net

Visit Scotland
www.visitscotland.com

Towns & Cities

Aberdeen
www.aberdeencity.gov.uk/acc/default.asp

Aberfoyle
www.aberfoyle.co.uk

Arbroath
www.arbroath.org.uk

Aviewmore
www.aviemore.org

Ayr
www.ayr-web.co.uk

Dunblane
www.dunblaneweb.co.uk

Dundee
www.dundeecity.gov.uk

Dunfermline
www.dunfermlineonline.net

Edinburgh
www.edinburghonline.org.uk

Elgin
www.elginscotland.org

Falkirk
www.falkirkweb.co.uk

Fort William
www.fort-william.net

Galashiels
www.galashiels.bordernet.co.uk

Glasgow
www.glasgow.gov.uk

Grantown on Spey
www.grantown-on-spey.co.uk

Gretna Green
www.gretnagreen.com

Hawick
www.hawick.org.uk

Inverness
www.inverness-scotland.com

John O'Groats
www.visitjohnogroats.com

Kelso
www.hawick.org.uk

Melrose
www.melrose.bordernet.co.uk

Perth
www.therealperth.com

St Andrews
www.saint-andrews.co.uk

Stirling
www.stirling.gov.uk

bulgaria

Tourist Information

Bulgaria
www.tourism-bulgaria.com

cambodia

Cambodia
www.tourismcambodia.com

cameroon

Cameroon
www.compufix.demon.co.uk/camweb

Towns & Cities

Doula
www.douala.com

canada

Regions

Alberta
www.travelalberta.com

British Columbia
www.hellobc.com

Manitoba
www.gov.mb.ca/splash.html

New Brunswick
www.tourismnewbrunswick.ca

Newfoundland & Labrador
www.gov.nf.ca/tourism

Northwest Territories
www.northernfrontier.com

Nova Scotia
http://destination-ns.com

Nunavut
www.nunatour.nt.ca

Ontario
www.ontario-canada.com

Prince Edward Island
www.peiplay.com

Quebec
www.tourisme.gouv.qc.ca

Saskatchewan
www.sasktourism.com

Toronto
www.tourism-toronto.com

Yukon
www.touryukon.com

Tourist Information

Canada
www.travelcanada.ca

caribbean

Antigua
www.antigua-barbuda.com

Bahamas
www.bahama.com

Bermuda
www.bermudatourism.com

Cayman Islands
www.caymanislands.ky

Dominican Republic
www.budgettravel.com/dominicanrepublic.htm

Grenada
www.grenada.org

Jamaica
www.jamaicatravel.com

Puerto Rico
www.prtourism.com

St Kitts & Nevis
www.interknowledge.com/stkitts-nevis

St Vincent & The Grenadines
www.stvincentandgrenadines.com

Trinidad & Tobago
www.visittnt.com

channel islands

Alderney
www.alderney.gov.gg

Guernsey
www.guernseymap.com/tourism.htm

Jersey
www.jtourism.com

chile

Chile Travel Information
www.chile-travel.com

Towns & Cities

Santiago
www.municipal.cl

china

Tourist Information

China
www.cnto.org

China Internet Information Center
www.china.org.cn

Hong Kong
www.hkta.org

National Administration for Cultural Heritage
www.nach.gov.cn

Towns & Cities

Beijing
www.beijing.gov.cn/english/index.htm

Shanghai
www.shanghai.gov.cn/english/index.htm

comoros island

Tourist Information

Comoros
www.iblgroup.com/tourisminternational/comoros

costa rica

Costa Rica
www.tourism-costarica.com

croatia

Croatian Government
www.hr

Croatian National Tourist Board
www.htz.hr

cuba

Cuba
www.cubatravel.cu

cyprus

Cyprus
www.cyprustourism.org

Turkish Republic of Northern Cyprus
www.trncwashdc.org

Towns & Cities

Limassaol
www.limassolmunicipal.com.cy

Nicosia
www.nicosia.org.cy

czech republic

Tourist Information

Czech Republic Tourism
http://cz.avisit.com

Towns & Cities

Prague
www.pis.cz/a

denmark

Regions

Copenhagen
http://copenhagen.now.dk/english.html

Greenland
www.greenland-guide.gl

Tourist Information

National Tourist Office
www.dt.dk

ecuador

Ministry of Tourism
www.vivecuador.com

Towns & Cities

Quito
www.quito.gov.ec

egypt

Tourist Information

State Information Service
www.sis.gov.eg

Towns & Cities

Alexandria
www.alexandria2000.com

estonia

Tourist Information

Estonia
www.visitestonia.com

falkland islands

Falkland Islands
www.tourism.org.fk

finland

Finland
www.mek.fi

Towns & Cities

Helsinki
www.helsinki.fi

Oulu
www.oulutourism.fi

france

Regions

Brittany
www.brittanytourism.com

Tourist Attractions

Disneyland, Paris
www.disneylandparis.com

Tourist Information

National Tourist Office
www.franceguide.com

Towns & Cities

Bordeaux
www.bordeaux-tourisme.com

Cannes
www.ville-cannes.fr

Cote d'Azur
www.cr-paca.fr

Courchevel
www.courchevel.com

La Rochelle
www.ville-larochelle.fr

Lyon
www.lyon-france.com

Nice
www.nice-coteazur.org

Paris
www.paris-france.org

gambia

Tourist Information

Gambia
www.gambia.com

germany

National Tourist Office
www.gnm.de

Towns & Cities

Berlin
www.berlin.de

Bonn
www.bonn.de

Cologne
www.cologne.de

Frankfurt
www.frankfurt-online.de

Munich
www.muenchen.de

Nuremberg
www.nuernberg.de

Stuttgart
www.stuttgart.de

ghana

Tourist Information

Ghana
www.ghana.com/republic

Towns & Cities

Accra
www.accra.com

gibralatar

Gibraltar
www.gibraltar.gov.gi

greece

Greece
www.gnto.gr

Towns & Cities

Athens
www.visitathensga.com

guatemala

Tourist Information

Guatemala
www.guatemala.travel.com.gt

hungary

National Tourist Office
www.hungarytourism.hu

Towns & Cities

Budapest
www.budapest.hu

iceland

Tourist Information

National Tourist Office
www.icetourist.is

Towns & Cities

Reykjavik
www.tourist.reykjavik.is

india

Regions

Assam
http://assamgovt.nic.in

Himachal Pradesh
http://himachal.nic.in

Jammu & Kashmir
www.jammu-kashmir-facts.com

Punjab
http://punjabgovt.nic.in

Rajasthan
www.rajgovt.org

Uttar Pradesh
www.upindia.org

West Bengal
www.westbengal.gov.in

Tourist Information

India
www.indiatouristoffice.org

Towns & Cities

Delhi
http://delhigovt.nic.in

Goa
www.nic.in/goa

Gujarat
www.gujaratindia.com

Kolkata
www.calmanac.org/cmcnew/netfilm/shockfilm.htm

Mumbai
www.mumbainet.com

indonesia

Tourist Information

Bali
www.indonesia-tourism.com

Indonesia
www.indonesia-tourism.com

iran

Iran
http://itto.org

ireland

National Tourist Office
www.shamrock.org

Towns & Cities

Cork
www.corkcoco.com

Donegal
www.donegal.ie

Dublin
www.visitdublin.com

Galway
www.galwaycoco.ie

Kerry
www.kerrycoco.ie

Limerick
www.limerickcorp.ie

Waterford
www.waterfordcorp.ie

israel

Tourist Information

Israel
www.infotour.co.il

Towns & Cities

Haifa
www.haifa.gov.il

Jerusalem
www.jerusalem.muni.il

Tel-Aviv
www.tel-aviv.gov.il

italy

Regions

Sicily
www.bestofsicily.com

Tourist Information

National Tourist Office
www.enit.it

Towns & Cities

Florence
www.florence.ala.it

Milan
www.ils-milano.it/milano_attractions.htm

Rome
www.comune.roma.it

Venice
www.veniceworld.com

japan

Tourist Information

Japan
www.jnto.go.jp

Towns & Cities

Hiroshima
www.city.hiroshima.jp/index-E.html

Okinawa
www.virtualokinawa.com

Osaka
www.city.osaka.jp/english

Sapporo
www.global.city.sapporo.jp

Tokyo
www.chijihonbu.metro.tokyo.jp/english/index.htm

Yokohama
www.city.yokohama.jp/indexE.html

jordan

Tourist Information

Jordan
www.see-jordan.com

kenya

Kenya
www.kenyatourism.org

Towns & Cities

Nairobi
www.kenyaweb.com/vnairobi

korea

Tourist Information

Korea
www.knto.or.kr

Towns & Cities

Seoul
www.metro.seoul.kr

kuwait

Tourist Information

Kuwait
www.kuwait-info.org

laos

Laos
www.visit-laos.com

latvia

Latvia
www.latviatourism.lv

lebanon

Lebanon
www.lebanon-tourism.gov.lb

Towns & Cities

Beirut
www.bse.com.lb

liechtenstein

Tourist Information

Liechtenstein
www.news.li/touri/index.htm

Towns & cities

Schaan
www.schaan.li

Vaduz
www.vaduz.li

lithuania

Tourist Information

Lithuania
www.tourism.lt

luxembourg

Luxembourg
www.luxembourg.co.uk

Towns & Cities

Beaufort
www.beaufort.lu

Grosbous
www.grosbous.lu

Larochette
www.larochette.lu

Luxembourg City
www.luxembourg-city.lu/touristinfo

madagascar

Tourist Information

Madagascar
www.tourisme-madagascar.com

malawi

Malawi
www.maform.malawi.net

malaysia

Malaysia
www.tourism.gov.my

Towns & Cities

Kuala Lumpur
www.klse.com.my

maldives

Tourist Information

Maldives
www.visitmaldives.com

malta

Malta
www.tourism.org.mt

mauritius

Mauritius
www.mauritius.net

mexico

Mexico
www.mexico-travel.com

Towns & Cities

Acapulco
www.acapulco.com

Cancun
www.cancun.com

Mexico City
www.mexicocity.com.mx/mexcity.html

monaco

Tourist Information

Monaco
www.monaco.mc

Towns & Cities

Monte-Carlo
www.monaco.monte-carlo.mc

morocco

Tourist Information

Morocco
www.mincom.gov.ma

mozambique

Mozambique
www.mozambique.mz/turismo/eindex.htm

myanmar

Myanmar
www.find-our-community.net/region/Eastern_Asia/Burma_map.htm

namibia

Namibia
www.dea.met.gov.na

Towns & Cities

Swakopmund
www.horizon.fr/namibia/ainfoswakopmund.html

Windhoek
www.windhoekcc.org.na

nepal

Tourist Information

Nepal
www.welcomenepal.com

netherlands

National Tourist Office
www.goholland.co.uk

Towns & Cities

Amsterdam
www.visitamsterdam.nl

Arnhem
www.arnhem.nl

Eindhoven
www.eindhoven.nl

Groningen
www.groningen.nl

Hague
www.denhaag.nl

Leiden
www.leiden.nl

Maastricht
www.maastricht.nl

Rotterdam
www.stadhuis.rotterdam.nl

Tilburg
www.tilburg.nl

Utrecht
www.utrecht.nl

Venlo
www.venlo.nl

new zealand

Tourist Information

New Zealand
www.nz.com

Towns & Cities

Auckland
www.akcity.govt.nz

Christchurch
www.ccc.govt.nz

Gisborne
www.gisborne.govt.nz

Rotorua
www.rotoruanz.com

Wellington
www.wcc.govt.nz

norway

Tourist Information

National Tourist Office
www.norway.org.uk

Towns & Cities

Oslo
www.virtualoslo.com

pacific islands

Tourist Information

Fiji
www.fiji-online.com.fj

Solomon Islands
www.solomons.com

Tahiti
www.tahiti-tourisme.com

pakistan

Pakistan
www.tourism.gov.pk

Towns & Cities

Karachi
www.karachi.com/

peru

Tourist Information

Peru
www.peru.org.pe

philippines

Philippines
www.tourism.gov.ph

poland

Poland
www.polandtour.org

portugal

Portugal
www.portugal.org

Towns & Cities

Faro
www.cm-faro.pt

Lisbon
www.cm-lisboa.pt

puerto rico

Tourist Information

Puerto Rico
www.gotopuertorico.com

romania

Romania
www.rotravel.com/hotlinks/other.htm

Towns & Cities

Bucharest
www.bucharest.com

russia

Tourist Attractions

Russian National Museums
www.museum.ru

Tourist Information

Russia
www.russia-travel.com

Towns & Cities

Moscow
www.moscowcity.com

St Petersburg
www.stpete.org

samoa

Tourist Information

Samoa
www.visitsamoa.ws

senegal

Senegal
www.senegal-tourism.com

serbia

Serbia
www.serbia-info.com/ntos

seychelles

Seychelles
www.destinationplanner.com/africa/seychelles/tourist_information.html

singapore

Singapore
www.visitsingapore.com

slovakia

Slovakia
www.slovakiatourism.sk

slovenia

Slovenia
www.slovenia-tourism.si

solomon islands

Tourism Council of the South Pacific
www.towd.com/search.cgi?isindex=Tourism+Council+of+the+South+Pacific&ref=

south africa

National Tourist Office
http://satour.com

Towns & Cities

Cape Town
www.ctcc.gov.za

Durban
www.durban.gov.za

Johannesburg
www.joburg.org.za

Pietermaritzburg
www.pmbcc.gov.za

Pretoria
www.pretoria.co.za

spain

Tourist Information

Spain
www.tourspain.co.uk

Towns & Cities

Barcelona
www.bcn.es

Bilbao
www.bilbao.net

Cadiz
www.cadizayto.es

Madrid
www.munimadrid.es

Palma
www.a-palma.es

Seville
www.sevilla.org

Toledo
www.diputoledo.es

Valencia
www.ayto-valencia.es

sri lanka

Tourist Information

Sri Lanka
www.lanka.net/ctb

sweden

Culture Net
www.kulturnat.org

SwedNet
www.swetourism.org.uk

Towns & Cities

Gothenburg
www.goteborg.com

Malmo
www.malmo.com

Stockholm
www.radiosweden.com

switzerland

Tourist Information

Switzerland
www.myswitzerland.com

Towns & Cities

Basel
www.baseltourismus.ch

Geneva
www.geneva-tourism.ch

Zurich
www.zurichtourism.ch

tahiti

Tourist Information

Tahiti
www.tahiti-tourisme.com

taiwan

Taiwan
www.tbroc.gov.tw

tanzania

Regions

Zanzibar
www.zanzibar.net

Tourist Information

Tanzania
www.tanzania-online.gov.uk/tourism/tourism.html

thailand

Thailand
www.tourismthailand.org

tibet

Tibet
www.tibet.com

tonga

Tonga
www.vacations.tvb.gov.to

tunisia

Tunisia
www.tourismtunisia.co.uk

turkey

Turkey
www.turkey.org/turkey

Towns & Cities

Ankara
www.ankara-bel.gov.tr

Istanbul
www.ibb.gov.tr

uganda

Tourist Information

Uganda
www.ugandaweb.com

ukraine

Ukraine
www.ukremb.com

united arab emirates

Dubai
http://dubaitourism.co.ao

uruguay

Uruguay
www.turismo.gub.uy

USA

Go-United States
www.go-unitedstates.com

Massachusetts
www.mass-vacation.com

Orlando
www.go2orlando.com

Texas
www.traveltex.com

Utah
www.utah.com

Towns & Cities

Austin
www.ci.austin.tx.us

Boston
www.ci.boston.ma.us

Chicago
www.ci.chicago.il.us

Dallas
www.dallascityhall.com

Denver
www.denvergov.org

Detroit
www.ci.detroit.mi.us

Honolulu
www.co.honolulu.hi.us

Houston
www.ci.houston.tx.us

Las Vegas
www.ci.las-vegas.nv.us

Los Angeles
www.ci.la.ca.us

Memphis
www.ci.memphis.tn.us

Miami
www.ci.miami.fl.us

Minneapolis St Paul
www.ci.minneapolis.mn.us

New York
www.ci.nyc.ny.us

Philadelphia
www.phila.gov

Salt Lake City
www.ci.slc.ut.us

San Francisco
www.ci.sf.ca.us

Seattle
www.ci.seattle.wa.us

St Louis
http://stlouis.missouri.org

venezuela

Tourist Information

Venezuela
www.venezuela.com

vietnam

Vietnam
www.vietnamtourism.com

Towns & Cities

Hanoi
www.hanoitravel.com

web cams: views of scotland

Assynt, Quinag
www.scotsman.com/webcams.cfm

Assynt, Suilven
www.scotsman.com/webcams.cfm

Ben Lui
www.scotsman.com/webcams.cfm

Ben Nevis & Lochaber
www.lochaber.com/neviscam

Buchanan Street, Glasgow
www.camvista.com/scotland/glasgow/buchst.php3

Calton Hill
www.scotsman.com/webcams.cfm

Central Edinburgh
www.scotsman.com/webcams.cfm

Cullin Hills, Skye
www.camvista.com/scotland/scenic/skye.php3

Drumochter
www.scotsman.com/webcams.cfm

Edinburgh
www.scotlandonline.com/communicate/communicate_ecards_send.cfm?camera_id=12&site_id=10&category_id=1

Edinburgh Castle
www.camvista.com/scotland/edinburgh/ecastle.php3

Forth Rail Bridge
www.camvista.com/scotland/edinburgh/rail.php3

Gleneagles Golf Course
www.scotsman.com/webcams.cfm

Hibernian Football Club
www.scotsman.com/webcams.cfm

Holyrood Park
www.scotsman.com/webcams.cfm

Inverness Castle
www.camvista.com/scotland/highlands/icastle.php3

Kintail
www.scotsman.com/webcams.cfm

Kylesku
www.scotsman.com/webcams.cfm

Lawers Dam
www.scotsman.com/webcams.cfm

Loch Cluanie
www.scotsman.com/webcams.cfm

Loch Garry
www.scotsman.com/webcams.cfm

Loch Lomond
www.camvista.com/scotland/scenic/lomond.php3

Loch Ness Surface
www.scotlandonline.com/communicate/communicate_ecards_send.cfm?camera_id=11&site_id=10&category_id=1

Loch Ness Underwater
www.scotlandonline.com/communicate/communicate_ecards_send.cfm?camera_id=14&site_id=10&category_id=1

Oban
www.camvista.com/scotland/highlands/oban.php3

Princes Street Gardens
www.scotsman.com/webcams.cfm

Royal Mile
www.camvista.com/scotland/edinburgh/royalmile.php3

Scottish Parliament
www.camvista.com/scotland/edinburgh/scotparl.php3

St Andrews Golf Course
www.scotlandonline.com/communicate/communicate_ecards_send.cfm?camera_id=13&site_id=10&category_id=1

Stac Pollaidh East Top
www.scotsman.com/webcams.cfm

Sunset in Assynt
www.scotsman.com/webcams.cfm

Tantallon Castle
www.scotsman.com/webcams.cfm

Torridon
www.scotsman.com/webcams.cfm

zambia

Tourist Information

Zambia
www.zambiatourism.com

Towns & Cities

Lusaka
www.africa-insites.com/zambia/travel/Cities/lusaka.htm

zimbabwe

Tourist Information

Zimbabwe
www.tourismzimbabwe.co.zw

science & nature

- astronomy & space
- botanic gardens
- conservation
- general science
- magazines & websites
- nature & conservation
- societies & institutions
- species re-introductions
- wildlife & animals
- zoos, wildlife parks & aquaria

astronomy & space

Aberdeen Planetarium
www.abcol.ac.uk/planetarium

Astronomical Society of Edinburgh
www.astronomyedinburgh.org

Astronomical Society of Glasgow
www.astronomicalsocietyofglasgow.org.uk/SAG.htm

Astronomy
www.astronomy.com

Astronomy for Kids
www.dustbunny.com/afk

Astronomy Now
www.astronomynow.com

British Astronomical Association
www.cam.ac.uk/~baa

British Astronomical Society
www.ast.cam.ac.uk/~baa

British National Space Centre
www.bnsc.gov.uk

Buzz Aldrin
www.buzzaldrin.com

Campaign for Dark Skies
www.dark-skies.freeserve.co.uk

Consortium for European Research on Extragalactic Surveys
www.jb.man.ac.uk/~ceres1

European Space Agency
www.esrin.esa.it

Greenwich Mean Time
http://greenwichmeantime.com

Hubble Telescope
www.stsci.edu

International Astronomical Union
www.intastun.org

International Meteor Organisation
www.imo.net

Institute for Astronomy (Edinburgh)
www.roe.ac.uk/ifa

Jodrell Bank
www.jb.man.ac.uk

Kennedy Space Centre
www.ksc.nasa.gov

NASA
www.nasa.gov

National Space Science Centre
www.nssc.co.uk

Royal Astronomical Society
www.ras.org.uk

Royal Observatory, Edinburgh
www.roe.ac.uk

Royal Observatory, Greenwich
www.rog.nmm.ac.uk

Scottish Astronomers Group
http://homepage.ntlworld.com/mark.pollock1/index1.html

Sky at Night
www.bbc.co.uk/skyatnight

Society for Popular Astronomy
www.u-net.com/ph/spa

Starchaser Foundation
www.starchaser.co.uk

State Research Centres of Russian Federation
www.extech.msk.su/src_eng

UK Astronomy Technology Centre (Edinburgh)
www.roe.ac.uk/atc

Virtual Solar System
www.solarsystem.12s.comurl changed – updated

botanic gardens

Aberdeen Botanic Garden
www.abdn.ac.uk/central/vcampus/botanic.hti

Dundee Botanic Gardens
www.dundeebotanicgardens.co.uk

Glasgow Botanic Garden
www.clyde-valley.com/glasgow/botanic.htm

Royal Botanic Gardens
www.rbgkew.org.uk

Royal Botanic Gardens Edinburgh & others
www.rbge.org.uk

St Andrews Botanic Garden
www.st-andrews-botanic.org

conservation

Advisory Committee on Protection of the Sea
www.acops.org

Animal Aid
www.animalaid.org.uk

Atlantic Salmon Trust
www.atlanticsalmontrust.org

Bat Conservation Trust
www.bats.org.uk

Bird Life International
www.birdlife.net

Born Free Foundation
www.bornfree.org.uk

British Deer Society
www.bds.org.uk

British Dragonfly Society
www.dragonflysoc.org.uk

British Hedgehog Preservation Society
www.software-technics.co.uk/bhps

British Wildlife Rehabilitation Council
www.nimini.demon.co.uk/bwrc

Fauna & Flora International
www.ffi.org.uk

Flora Locale
www.floralocale.org

Game Conservancy Trust
www.game-conservancy.org.uk

Hawk & Owl Trust
www.mycenae.demon.co.uk/hawkandowl

International Wildlife Coalition
www.iwc.org

Marine Conservation Society
www.goodbeachguide.co.uk

National Birds of Prey Centre
www.nbpc.co.uk

National Federation of Badger Groups
www.nfbg.org.uk

National Seal Sanctuary
www.sealsanctuary.co.uk

Nature Conservation Bureau
www.naturebureau.co.uk

Orangutan Foundation UK
www.orangutan.org.uk

Parrot Line
www.parrotline.org

Rainforest Action Network
www.ran.org

Raptor Conservation
www.raptor.uk.com

Scottish Natural Heritage
www.snh.org.uk

Tusk Force
www.tusk.force.org.uk

Whale & Dolphin Conservation Society
www.wdcs.org.uk

Whale Foundation
www.whale-foundation.org

Wildfowl & Wetlands Trust
www.greenchannel.com/wwt

Wildlife Trust
www.wildlifetrust.org.uk

World Society for the Protection of Animals
www.wspa.org.uk

World Wide Fund for Nature
www.panda.org

WWF International
www.panda.org

WWF UK
www.wwf-uk.org

Young People's Trust for the Environment & Nature Consrevation
www.yptenc.org.uk

general science

The BA – Exploring & Debating Science
www.the-ba.net

Edinburgh International Science Festival
www.sciencefestival.co.uk

European Collaborative for Science, Industry & Technology Exhibitions
http://ecsite.ballou.be/new/index.asp

Foundation for Science & Technology
www.foundation.org.uk

Royal Society
www.royalsoc.ac.uk

Royal Society – Science for All
www.royalsoc.ac.uk/scforall

Satrosphere
www.satrosphere.net

Science Club on the Net
www.scoti.org.uk

Science Engineering & Technology
www.setpointscotland.org.uk

Scottish Science Advisory Committee
www.scottishscience.org.uk

Scottish Science & Technology Network
www.sstn.co.uk

Scottish Science Trust
www.sst.org.uk

Scottish University for Industry
www.scottishufi.co.uk

UK Science Communication Partnership
www.copus.org.uk

Wellcome Trust
www.wellcome.ac.uk

magazines & websites

Alpha Galileo
www.alphagalileo.org

Astronomy
www.astronomy.com

BBC Nature
www.bbc.co.uk/nature

Bioimages
www.bioimages.org.uk

Birds of Britain
www.birdsofbritain.co.uk

Birdwatch
www.birdwatch.co.uk

Chemistry & Industry Magazine
http://enviro.mond.org

Chemistry UK
www.u-net.com/ukchem

Delphi Magazine
www.itecuk.com/delmag

Developers Review
www.itecuk.com/devrev

The Ecologist
www.theecologist.org

Elemental Discoveries
www.camsoft.com/elemental

The Green Directory
www.greendirectory.net

Green Links
www.green-links.co.uk

Journal of Natural History
www.tandf.co.uk/jnls/nah.htm

National Geographic
www.nationalgeographic.com

Nature
www.nature.com

Naturenet
www.naturenet.net

New Civil Engineer
www.nceplus.co.uk

New Electronics
www.neon.co.uk

New Scientist
www.newscientist.co.uk

Physics World
http://physicsweb.org/toc

Planet Ark
www.planetark.org

Science Frontiers
www.science-frontiers.com

Science News
www.sciencenews.org

Science Online
www.scienceonline.org

Scottish Environment News
www.scenes.org.uk

Scottish Environmental Database
http://homepages.ed.ac.uk/eco/env

Stephen Hawking
www.damtp.cam.ac.uk/user/hawking

Tomorrow's World (BBC)
www.bbc.co.uk/tw

UK Environment
www.ukenvironment.org

UK Safari
www.uksafari.com

Walking with Dinosaurs
www.bbc.co.uk/dinosaurs

Wharfe
www.habitat.org.uk

Wildfile
www.wildfile.co.uk

nature & conservation

Cairngorms Partnership
www.cairngorms.co.uk

Do a little, Change a lot
www.dochange.net/environment

Earthwatch
www.uk.earthwatch.org

Exotic Scottish Animals
www.bigcats.org/esa/index.html

Fauna & Flora International
www.fauna-flora.org

Flora Locale
www.floralocale.org

Frontier Conservation
www.frontierprojects.ac.uk

Global Peatland Initiative
www.wetlands.org/projects/GPI/default.htm

Hanson Environment Fund
www.hansonenvfund.org

International Conservation Awareness Network
www.ican21.org.uk

International Mire ConservationGroup
www.imcg.net

International Peat Society
www.peatsociety.fi

Interpret Scotland
www.interpretscotland.org.uk

John Muir Trust
www.jmt.org

Joint Nature Conservation Committee
www.jncc.gov.uk

National Trust
www.ntenvironment.com

National Trust Scotland
www.nts.org.uk

Native Woodland Trust
www.nativewoodtrust.ie

Natural Resources Institute
www.nri.org

Naturenet
www.naturenet.net

Open Spaces Society
www.oss.org.uk

Plant Life
www.plantlife.org.uk

Rainforest Action Network
www.ran.org

Royal Society for Nature Conservation
www.rsnc.org

Scottish Biodiversity Group
www.scotland.gov.uk/biodiversity

Scottish Environment Link
www.scotlink.org

Scottish Environmental Protection Agency
www.sepa.org.uk

Scottish Natural Heritage
www.snh.org.uk

Scottish Raised Bog Project
www.boglife.org

Society for Underwater Exploration
www.underwaterdiscovery.org

Soil Association
www.soilassociation.org

Tree Register
www.tree-register.org

Trees of Time & Place
www.totap.org.uk

United Kingdom Institute for Conservation
www.ukic.org.uk

Waterways Trust
www.thewaterwaystrust.com

Wetlands International
www.wetlands.org

Wise Use of Mires & Peatlands
www.mirewiseuse.com

Woodland Trust
www.woodland-trust.org.uk

World Land Trust
www.worldlandtrust.org

societies & institutions

Amateur Entomologists' Society
www.theaes.org

Association for Science Education
www.ase.org.uk

Association for Women in Science & Engineering
www.awise.org

British Antarctic Survey
www.antartica.ac.uk

British Aquatic Resource Centre
www.cfkc.demon.co.uk

British Association for the Advancement of Science
www.britassoc.org.uk

British Association of Nature Conservationists
www.greenchannel.com/banc

British Bee Keepers Association
www.bbka.demon.co.uk

British Geological Survey
www.bgs.ac.uk

British Horological Institute
www.bhi.co.uk

British Ornithologists' Union
www.bou.org.uk

British Met Office
www.meto.gov.uk

British Trust for Conservation Volunteers
www.btcv.org

British UFO Research Association
www.bufora.org.uk

Central Science Laboratory
www.csl.gov.uk

Cern
www.cern.ch

Council for Science & Technology
www.cst.gov.uk

Countryside Agency
www.countryside.gov.uk

Earthwatch
www.uk.earthwatch.org

Engineering & Physical Sciences Research Council
www.epsrc.ac.uk

English Nature
www.english-nature.org.uk

Fauna & Flora International
www.ffi.org.uk

Field Studies Council
www.field-studies-council.org

Flora Locale
www.floralocale.org

Forensic Science Society
www.demon.co.uk/forensic

Friends of the Earth
www.foe.co.uk

Friends of the Earth Scotland
www.foe-scotland.org.uk

Geological Society
www.geolsoc.org.uk

Greenpeace
www.greenpeace.org

Human Cloning Foundation
www.humancloning.org

Human Genetic Advisory Commission
www.dti.gov.uk/hgac

Independent Cat Society
www.welcome.to/tipcs

Institute for Advancement of Science Technology & Economics
www.iaste.com

Institute of Biology
www.iob.org

Institute of Biomedical Sciences
www.ibms.org

Institute of Broadcast Sound
www.ibs.org.uk

Institute of Hydrology
www.nwl.ac.uk/ih

Isaac Newton Institute
www.newton.cam.ac.uk

Jane Goodall Institute
www.janegoodall.org

Linnean Society of London
www.linnean.org.uk

Mammal Society
www.abdn.ac.uk/mammal

National Bird of Prey Centre
www.appsearch.com/nbpc

National Garden Exhibition Centre
www.clubi.ie/calumet

National Institute of Agricultural Botany
www.niab.com

National NDT Centre
www.aeat.co.uk/ndt

Natural Resources Institute
www.nri.org

Natural Resources Institute Tree Register
www.nri.org

Office of Science & Technology
www.dti.gov.uk/ost

Palaeontological Association
www.nhm.ac.uk/hosted_sites/paleonet/palass

Paleontological Society
www.uic.edu/orgs/paleo

Plantlife
www.plantlife.org.uk

Primate Society of Great Britain
www.psgb.org

Rainforest Action Network
www.ran.org

Roslin Institute
www.ri.bbsrc.ac.uk

Royal Academy of Engineering
www.raeng.org.uk

Royal Botanic Gardens
www.rbgkew.org.uk

Royal Entomological Society
www.royensoc.demon.co.uk

Royal Geographical Society
www.rgs.org

Royal Society
www.royalsoc.ac.uk

Royal Society of Chemistry
www.rsc.org

RSPB
www.rspb.org.uk

Scientists of Global Responsibility
www.sgr.org.uk

Scottish Ornithologists' Club
www.the-soc.org.uk

Scottish Wildlife Trust
www.swt.org.uk

Society for Experimental Biology
www.demon.co.uk/seb

Society for Interdisciplinary Studies
www.knowledge.co.uk/sis

Society for Underwater Exploration
www.underwaterdiscovery.org

The Wildlife Trusts Partnership
www.wildlifetrusts.org

Tree Register
www.tree-register.org

UK Science Park Association
www.ukspa.org.uk

UK Scientific Research Councils
www.physics.gla.ac.uk/~ianm/councils.htm

Uranium Institute
www.uilondon.org

Wildfowl & Wetlands Trust
www.wwt.org.uk

Zoological Society of London
www.zsl.org

species re-introductions

British Wild Boar
www.britishwildboar.org.uk

Invasive Alien Species
www.appliedvegetationdynamics.co.uk/iaapwebsite

Scottish Beavers Network
www.scotsbeavers.org

The Wolf Trust
www.wolftrust.org.uk

wildlife & animals

Amateur Entomologists' Society
www.theaes.org

Birdlife International
www.birdlife.net

Birds Ireland
www.birdsireland.com

British Beekeepers Association
www.bbka.org.uk

British Ornithologists' Union
www.bou.org.uk

Cetacean Research & Rescue Unit
www.crru.org.uk

Friends of the Moray Firth Dolphins
www.loupers.com

Gairloch Marine Life Centre
www.porpoise-gairloch.co.uk

Hebridean Whale & Dolphin Trust
http://whales.gn.apc.org

Hebrides Wildlife
www.wildlifehebrides.com

Jane Goodall Institute
www.janegoodall.org

Mammal Society
www.abdn.ac.uk/mammal

Mammals Trust UK
www.mammalstrustuk.org

National Bird of Prey Centre
www.appsearch.com/nbpc

Northern Ireland Bat Group
www.batgroup.fsnet.co.uk

Primate Society of Great Britain
www.psgb.org

Royal Society for the Prevention of Cruelty to Animals
www.rspca.org.uk

Royal Society for the Protection of Birds
www.rspb.org.uk

Shetland Wildlife
www.wildlife.shetland.co.uk

Whale & Dolphin Conservation Society
www.sea-red.org

Whale Foundation
www.whale-foundation.org

Wildlife News
www.naturalworldtours.co.uk

Wildlifeline
www.wildlifeline.org

WWF International
www.panda.org

Zoological Society of London
www.zsl.org

zoos, wildlife parks & aquaria

Edinburgh Zoo
www.edinburghzoo.org.uk

Glasgow Zoo
http://glasgowzoo.topcities.com

National Sea Life Centre
www.sealife.co.uk

antiques & auctions

Antique Dealers Directory
www.antique-dealers-directory.co.uk

Antiques Roadshow
www.bbc.co.uk/antiques

Antiques Scotland
www.antiques-scotland.com

Antiques Trade Gazette
www.atg-online.com

Association of Art & Antique Dealers (LAPADA)
www.lapada.co.uk

Bonhams
www.bonhams.com

British Horological Institute
www.bhi.co.uk

Christie's
www.christies.com

Daltons Antiques
www.daltons.com

Ebay online auctions
www.ebay.co.uk

Grannie used to have one
www.grannieusedto.co.uk

Lots Road Galleries
www.thesaurus-co.uk/lotsroad

Olympia Fine Art & Antiques Fairs
www.olympia-antiques.co.uk

Philips
www.philips-auctions.com

Portobello Antiques Market
www.portobelloroad.co.uk

QXL.com
www.qxl.com

Ruby Lane Antique Directory
www.rubylane.com

Scottish Antique & Arts Centre
www.scottish-antiques.com

Scottish Web Auction
www.scottishwebauction.com

Sothebys
www.sothebys.com

Stanley Gibbons (stamp collecting)
www.stanleygibbons.com

Wallis & Wallis
www.wallisandwallis.co.uk

beds & bedding

Divine Bedding (Glasgow)
www.divinebedding.co.uk

Dunlopillo
www.dunlopillo.co.uk

Relyon
www.relyon.co.uk

Rest Assured
www.rest-assured.co.uk

Sealy
www.sealyuk.co.uk

Silent Night
www.silentnight.co.uk

Sleep Council
www.sleepcouncil.org.uk

Slumberland
www.slumberland.co.uk

books

Alba Publishing
www.tumpline.co.uk/alba

AlphabetStreet
www.alphabetstreet.co.uk

Amazon
www.amazon.co.uk

Barnes & Noble
www.barnesandnoble.com

BBC Shop
www.bbcshop.com

Blackwell
www.blackwells.co.uk

Bol
www.bol.co.uk

Borders
www.borders.com

CEO Express Bookshop
www.ceoexpress.com

Cook Book Shop
www.cooks-book-shop.co.uk

Dillons
www.dillons.co.uk

Dorling Kindersley
www.dk.com/uk

Express Bookshop
www.bvcd.net/express

Hammicks
www.thebookplace.com

Heffers
www.heffers.co.uk

Internet Bookshop
www.bookshop.co.uk

John Menzies
www.john-menzies.co.uk

John Smith
www.johnsmith.co.uk

Kogan Page
www.kogan-page.co.uk

Penguin
www.penguin.co.uk

Waterstones
www.waterstones.co.uk

WH Smith
www.whsmith.co.uk

World Books
www.worldbooks.co.uk

Zwemmer
www.zwemmer.co.uk

Magazines & Websites

Book 2 Book
www.booktrade.info

The Bookseller
www.thebookseller.com

Scottish Based

Cook Book Shop, Edinburgh
www.cooks-book-shop.co.uk

John Smith
www.johnsmith.co.uk

Scottish Book Trust
www.scottishbooktrust.com

Scottish Publishers Association
www.scottishbooks.org

Second Hand & Antiquarian Scottish booksellers
www.scotbooksmag.demon.co.uk

china, crystal, pottery & glass

China

Chinacraft
www.chinacraft.co.uk

Lladro
http://lladrogib.hypermart.net

Royal Crown Derby
www.royal-crown-derby.co.uk

Royal Doulton
www.royal-doulton.com

Spode China
www.spode.co.uk

Stockwell China
www.stockwellchina.co.uk

Wedgwood
www.wedgwood.co.uk

Crystal

Crystal Images of Strathnairn
www.crystalimages.co.uk

Dartington Crystal
www.dartington.co.uk

Edinburgh Crystal
www.edinburgh-crystal.co.uk

Table Top Company
www.tabletopcompany.com

Waterford Crystal
www.waterford.com

Glass

Caithness Glass
www.caithnessglass.co.uk

Galloway Glass
www.gallowayglass.com

Pottery

Borgh Pottery
www.borgh-pottery.com

Buchan Pottery
www.crieff.co.uk/pottery.html

Edibane Pottery, Isle of Skye
www.edinbane-pottery.co.uk

Highland Stoneware
www.highlandstoneware.com

John Christie, Wood Fired Pottery
www.scotpotter.com

Kilnside Ceramics
www.kilnside.com

Poole Pottery
www.poolepottery.co.uk

Portmeirion Potteries
www.portmeirion.com

Scottish Heritage Ceramics
www.scottish-figurine-decanters.co.uk

Scottish Potters Association
www.scottishpotters.org

Tain Pottery Company
www.tainpottery.co.uk

clothes

Alexandra
www.alexandra.co.uk

Aquascutum
www.aquascutum.co.uk

Armani
www.armaniexchange.com

Artigiano
www.artigiano.co.uk

Austin Reed
www.austinreed.co.uk

Ben Sherman
www.bensherman.co.uk

Benetton
www.benetton.com

Bernini
www.bernini.co.uk

Betty Barclay
www.bettybarclay.co.uk

Boden
www.boden.co.uk

Brooks Brothers
www.brooks-brothers.net

Browns
http://global-m.com/browns/browns.html

Burtons
www.burtonmenswear.co.uk

Caractere
www.vestebene.com

Charles Tyrwhitt
www.ctshirts.co.uk

Ciro Citterio
www.cirocitterio.com

Contessa
www.contessa.org.uk

Coppernob
www.coppernob.com

Cotswold
www.cotswold-outdoor.co.uk

Cotton Moon
www.cottonmoon.co.uk

Cyrillus
www.cyrillus.co.uk

Damart
www.damartonline.co.uk

Diesel
www.diesel.co.uk

DKNY
www.donnakaran.com

Dockers
www.dockers.com

Donaldson
www.donaldson.be

Dorothy Perkins
www.dorothyperkins.co.uk

Dressmart.com
www.dressmart.com

Dunhill'
www.dunhill.com

Eddie Bauer
www.eddiebauer.co.uk

Elvi
www.elvi.co.uk

Empire Stores
www.empirestores.co.uk

Evans
www.evans.ltd.uk

Fat Face
www.fatface.co.uk

Fenn Wright & Manson
www.fwm.co.uk

Frank Usher
www.frankusher.co.uk

Freemans
www.freemans.co.uk

French Connection
www.frenchconnection.com

French Sole
www.frenchsole.com

Gap
www.gap.com

Gap Kids
www.gapkids.com

Georgina von Etzdorf
www.georginavonetzdorf.co.uk

Ghost
www.ghost.ltd.uk

Gianfranco Ferre
www.gianfrancoferre.com

Givenchy
www.givenchy.com

Grattan
www.grattan.co.uk

GUS
www.shoppersuniverse.com

Gymboree
www.gymboree.com

H & M Hennes
www.hm.com

Hackett
www.hackett.co.uk

Harvie & Hudson
www.harvieandhudson.com

Hawkshead
www.hawkshead.com

Henri Lloyd
www.henrilloyd.com

High & Mighty
www.highandmighty.co.uk

Jaeger
www.jaeger.co.uk

James Meade
www.jamesmeade.com

Janet Reger
www.janetreger.com

Kaleidescope
www.kaleidoscope.co.uk

Kays
www.kaysnet.com

Kelsey Tailors
www.kelseytailors.co.uk

Kingshill
www.kingshilldirect.co.uk

L L Bean
www.llbean.com

La Redoute
www.redoute.co.uk

Laetitia Allen
www.laetitiaallenco.uk

Lands' End
www.landsend.co.uk

Laura Ashley
www.laura-ashley.com

Levis
www.eu.levi.com

Liberty
www.liberty-of-london.com

Look Again
www.lookagain.co.uk

Lycra
www.lycra.com

Madhouse
www.madhouse.co.uk

Marks & Spencer
www.marksandspencer.com

Marshalls
www.marshalls.co.uk

Monsoon
www.monsoon.co.uk

Morgan
www.morgan.fr

Moschino
www.moschino.it

Moss Bros
www.mossbros.co.uk

Muji
www.muji.co.uk

Next
www.next.co.uk

Oilily
www.oililyusa.com

Osh Kosh B'Gosh
www.oshkoshbgosh.com

Paul Smith
www.paulsmith.co.uk

Pepe Jeans
www.pepejeans.com

Peruvian Connection
www.peruvianconnection.com

Prada
www.prada.com

Pretty Polly
www.prettypolly.co.uk

Principles
www.principles.co.uk

Pringle
www.pringle-of-scotland.co.uk

QS
www.qsgroup.co.uk

Racing Green
www.racinggreen.co.uk

Ralph Lauren Polo
www.polo.com

Red or Dead
www.redordead.co.uk

Reiss
www.reiss.co.uk

River Island
www.riverisland.com

Scotch Corner
www.scotch-corner.co.uk

Sophia Swire
www.sophiaswire.com

Ted Baker
www.tedbaker.co.uk

Thomas Pink
www.thomaspink.co.uk

Tie Rack
www.tie-rack.co.uk

Timberland
www.timberland.com

Tommy Hilfiger
www.tommypr.com

Top Man
www.topman.co.uk

TopShop
www.tops.co.uk

Van Heusen
www.vanheusendirect.com

Victoria's Secret
www.victoriassecret.com

Virgin Clothing Company
www.virginclothing.co.uk

Wealth of Nations
www.wealthofnations.co.uk

Wonderbra
www.wonderbra.com

Wrangler
www.wrangler.com

Youngs
www.seven.net/youngs

Online shop

Abound
www.shoppersuniverse.com

Armani
www.armaniexchange.com

Artigiano
www.artigiano.co.uk

As Seen on Screen
www.asseenonscreen.com

Ben Sherman
www.bensherman.co.uk

Benetton
www.benetton.com

Bernini
www.bernini.com

Boden
www.boden.co.uk

Brooks Brothers
www.brooks-brothers.net

Burtons
www.burtonmenswear.co.uk

Charles Tyrwhitt
www.ctshirts.co.uk

Contessa
www.contessa.org.uk

Cotton Moon
www.cottonmoon.co.uk

Cotton Traders
www.cottontraders.co.uk

Cyrillus
www.cyrillus.co.uk

Damart
www.damartonline.co.uk

Dorothy Perkins
www.dorothyperkins.co.uk

Eddie Bauer
www.eddiebauer.com

Empire Stores
www.empirestores.co.uk

Evans
www.evans.ltd.uk

Fat Face
www.fatface.co.uk

Fig Leaves
www.figleaves.com

Freemans
www.freemans.co.uk

French Connection UK
www.frenchconnection.co.uk

Grattan
www.grattan.co.uk

Haburi
www.haburi.com

Hawkshead
www.hawkshead.com

Henri Lloyd
www.henrilloyd.com

High & Mighty
www.highandmighty.co.uk

James Meade
www.jamesmeade.com

Janet Reger
www.janetreger.com

Kaleidescope
www.kaleidoscope.co.uk

Kangaroo Poo
www.kangaroo-poo.co.uk

Kays
www.kaysnet.com

Kingshill
www.kingshilldirect.co.uk

L L Bean
www.llbean.com

La Redoute
www.redoute.co.uk

Laden
www.laden.co.uk

Lands' End
www.landsend.co.uk

Laura Ashley
www.laura-ashley.com

Look Again
www.lookagain.co.uk

Madhouse
www.madhouse.co.uk

Marks & Spencer
www.marksandspencer.com

Miss Selfridge
www.missselfridge.co.uk

Peruvian Connection
www.peruvianconnection.com

Pretty Polly
www.prettypolly.co.uk

Sophia Swire
www.sophiaswire.com

Ted Baker
www.tedbaker.co.uk

Thomas Pink
www.thomaspink.co.uk

Tie Rack
www.tie-rack.co.uk

Timberland
www.timberland.com

TopShop
www.tops.co.uk

UK Designer Shop
www.ukdesignershop.com

Victoria's Secret
www.victoriassecret.com

Warehouse
www.warehousefashion.com

Wealth of Nations
www.wealthofnations.co.uk

Scottish Based

Bill Baber Knitwear Design
www.billbaber.com

Campbell Kiltmakers
www.campbellkilts.co.uk

Classic Kilts
www.classickilts.com

Designs On Cashmere
www.scotwebshops.com/cashmere

Donalds Of Crieff Highland wear
www.donaldsons-of-crieff.com

Dressed By Scotland
www.dressedbyscotland.co.uk

Glenshee Woollens
www.glensheewoollens.co.uk

North Ronaldsy Yarn
www.orkneywool.co.uk

Pringle
www.pringle-of-scotland.co.uk

Sexy Tops
www.sexytops.co.uk

Slanj Highlandwear
www.slanj.co.uk

computers & electrical

Dell
www.dell.com

Duracell
www.duracell.com

Ever Ready
www.everready.co.uk

Granada
www.box-clever.com

Hewlett Packard
www.hp.com

Hi-Fidelity
www.hi-fidelity.co.uk

Powerhouse
www.powerhouse-retail.co.uk

Roberts Radios Direct
www.wesellradios.co.uk

Simply
www.simply.co.uk

Tempo
www.tempo.co.uk

Time
www.timecomputers.com

Toshiba
www.toshiba.co.uk

Electrical Retailers

Best Stuff
www.beststuff.co.uk

Comet
www.comet.co.uk

Dixons
www.dixons.co.uk

Granada
www.box-clever.com

Hi-Fidelity
www.hi-fidelity.co.uk

Let's Buy It
www.letsbuyit.com

PC World
www.pcworld.co.uk

Powerhouse
www.powerhouse-retail.co.uk

Roberts Radios Direct
www.wesellradios.co.uk

Simply
www.simply.co.uk

Mobile Phone retailers & Networks

Carphone Warehouse
www.carphonewarehouse.com

Dial-a-phone
www.dialaphone.co.uk

Link
www.the-link.co.uk

Mobile Phone Stores
www.mobile-phone-stores.co.uk

O2
www.o2.co.uk

Orange
www.orange.co.uk

T Mobile
www.t-mobile.co.uk

Virgin Mobile
www.virginmobile.com

Vodafone
www.vodafone.com

Scottish Based

Scottish Electrical Retailers Directory
www.icscotland.co.uk/scotdeal

cosmetics & perfumes

Avon
www.uk.avon.com

BeneFit
www.benefitcosmetics.com

Bobbi Brown
www.bobbibrowncosmetics.com

Body Shop
www.thebodyshop.co.uk

Bonne Bell
www.bonnebell.com

Boots
www.boots.co.uk

Cacharel
www.cacharel.com

Chanel
www.chanel.com

Clarins
www.clarins-paris.com

Clinique
www.clinique.com

Color Me Beautiful
www.colorme.com

Colorlab
www.colorlab-cosmetics.com

Coty
www.cotyshop.com

Cover Girl
www.covergirl.com

Crabtree & Evelyn
www.crabtree-evelyn.com

Culpeper
www.culpeper.co.uk

Dior
www.dior.com

Elizabeth Arden
www.elizabetharden.com

Fragrance Bay
www.fragrancebay.com

Givenchy
www.givenchy.com

Gucci
www.gucci.com

Hard Candy
www.hardcandy.com

Hugo Boss
www.hugo.com

Issey Miyake
www.isseymiyake.com

Jean Paul Gaultier
www.jpgaultier.fr

L'Oreal
www.loreal.com

Lacoste
www.lacoste.com

Lancaster
www.lancaster-beauty.com

Lancome
www.lancome.com

Lush
www.lush.co.uk

Mankind
www.mankindonline.co.uk

Mary Kay
www.marykay.com

Max Factor
www.maxfactor.com

MUM Roll On
www.mum-online.co.uk

Oil of Olay
www.olay.com

Paco Rabanne
www.pacorabanne.com

Profaces
www.profaces.com

Revlon
www.revlon.com

Shiseido
www.shiseido.co.uk

Simply Perfume
www.simplyperfume.com

Sisley
www.sisley.tm.fr

Tommy Hilfiger
www.tommypr.com

Urban Decay
www.urbandecay.com

Yves Saint Laurent
www.yslonline.com

department stores

Aitken & Niven
www.aitken-niven.co.uk

Allders
www.allders.co.uk

Argos
www.argos.co.uk

Bentalls
www.bentalls.co.uk

BHS
www.bhs.co.uk

Debenhams
www.debenhams.co.uk

Fortnum & Mason
www.fortnumandmason.co.uk

Harrods
www.harrods.com

Harvey Nichols
www.harveynichols.com

Home Shopping Channel
www.shop-tv.co.uk

House of Fraser
www.houseoffraser.co.uk

Index
www.indexshop.com

Jenners
www.jenners.com

John Lewis
www.johnlewis.co.uk

Liberty
www.liberty-of-london.com

Littlewoods
www.littlewoods-index.com

Marks & Spencer
www.marksandspencer.com

QVC UK
www.qvcuk.com

Selfridges
www.selfridges.co.uk

Woolworths
www.woolworths.co.uk

flooring

Allied Carpets
www.alliedcarpets.co.uk

Amtico
www.amtico.co.uk

Axminster
www.axminster-carpets.co.uk

Brintons
www.brintons.co.uk

British Wool Marketing Board
www.britishwool.org.uk

Carpet Information Centre
www.carpetinfo.co.uk

Carpetright
www.carpetright.co.uk

Clarkston Carpets, Glasgow
www.clarkstoncarpets.co.uk

Duralay
www.duralay.co.uk

Harris Carpets
www.harriscarpets.co.uk

Marley
www.marley.co.uk

Ryalux
www.ryalux.com

Stoddard
www.stoddardintl.co.uk

Tartan Carpets
www.stevensandgraham.co.uk

Trade Carpets
www.laminatescotland.co.uk

Weston Carpets
www.weston-carpets.co.uk

Wilton
www.wiltoncarpets.com

flowers

Awesome Blossom
www.awesome-blossom.com

Blooms UK
www.blooms.co.uk

Designer Flowers Online
www.designerflowers.org.uk

Florette
www.florette.co.uk

Flowers Direct
www.flowersdirect.co.uk

Global Flower Delivery
www.globalflowerdelivery.com

Interflora
www.interflora.co.uk

Jane Packer
www.jane-packer.co.uk

Paula Pryke
www.paulapryke.co.uk

Teleflorist
www.teleflorist.co.uk

William Hayford
www.william-hayford.co.uk

furniture & upholstery

Andy Thornton, Antique furniture
www.andythorntonltd.co.uk

Chaplins
www.chaplins.co.uk

Conran Shop
www.conran.co.uk

Designers Guild
www.designersguild.com

Domain Furniture
www.domainfurniture.com

Ducal
www.ducal-furniture.co.uk

Durham Pine
wwww.durhampine.com

Ercol
www.ercol.com

Fogarty
www.fogarty.co.uk

G Plan
www.morrisfurniture.co.uk/gplan

Garden Shop
www.thegardenshop.co.uk

General Trading Company
www.general-trading.co.uk

Habitat
www.habitat.net

Hampton & McMurray
www.hamptonandmcmurray.co.uk

Harris Carpets
www.harriscarpets.co.uk

Holding Company
www.theholdingcompany.co.uk

Ikea
www.ikea.com

Indian Ocean Trading Company
www.indian-ocean.co.uk

Iron Bed Company
www.ironbed.co.uk

Kingdom of Leather
www.kingdomofleather.co.uk

Laura Ashley
www.laura-ashley.com

Ligne Roset
www.ligneroset.com

Marks & Spencer
www.marks-and-spencer.co.uk

McCord
www.mccord.uk.com

MFI Homeworks
www.mfi.co.uk

Multiyork
www.multiyork.co.uk

Parker Knoll
www.parkerknoll.co.uk

Purves & Purves
www.purves.co.uk

Scots Pine
www.scotspine.co.uk

Scottish Woodcraft
www.scottishwoodcraft.co.uk

Sharps
www.sharps.co.uk

Shuttle
www.theshuttle-uk.com

SMG Interiors
www.smginteriors.co.uk

Uno
www.uno.co.uk

Wesley Barrell
www.wesley-barrell.co.uk

World of Leather
www.worldofleather.co.uk

gifts

4 Gift Ideas
www.4giftideas.co.uk/salmon.htm

Aristocrat Golf
www.aristocratgolf.co.uk

Classic Scottish Gift Company
www.giftsfromscotland.com

Distinctly British.com
www.distinctlybritish.com

E-treasures
www.etreasures.co.uk

Gifts from Scotland
www.giftsfromscotland.com

Highland Fayre
www.highlandfayre.co.uk

Highland Traveller
www.highlandtraveller.com

Lidianne Cards
www.lidiannecards.co.uk

Proudly Scottish
www.proudlyscottish.com

ScotGold
www.scotgold.com

Scottish Crafts Direct
www.scottishcraftsdirect.com

Scottish Gifts Online
www.scottish-gifts-online.co.uk

Scottish Products Distributors Association
www.scottish-products.com

gifts & stationery

All Occasions
www.alloccasions.co.uk

Birthdays
www.birthdays.co.uk

Cards Galore
www.cardsgalore.com

Charles Letts
www.letts.co.uk

Charles Rennie Mackintosh Store
www.rennie-mackintosh.co.uk

Choc Express
www.chocexpress.com

Clinton Cards
www.clintoncards.co.uk

Find Me a Gift
www.find-me-a-gift.co.uk

Hallmark Cards
www.hallmark.com

Lastminute.com
www.lastminute.com

Links
www.linksoflondon.com

Moon Estates
www.moonestates.com

Paperchase
www.paperchase.co.uk

Papermate
www.papermate.co.uk

Past Times
www.past-times.com

Pen Shop
www.penshop.co.uk

Prince's Trust Shop
www.princestrustshop.co.uk

Red Letter Days
www.redletterdays.co.uk

Smythson of Bond Street
www.smythson.com

Thorntons
www.thorntons.co.uk

Victorinox
www.victorinox.com

Voucher Express
www.voucherexpress.com

WH Smith
www.whsmith.co.uk

Gadgets

Boystuff
www.boysstuff.co.uk

Gadget Shop
www.gadgetshop.com

I Want One of Those
www.iwantoneofthose.com

UK Gadgets
www.ukgadgets.com

Scottish Based

Bonkers Original Gifts
www.bonkers-standrews.co.uk

Caledonia Dreaming
www.caledoniadreaming.net

Cartoonise
www.cartoonise.com

Celtic Shopping Mall
www.celticshoppingmall.com

Charles Letts
www.letts.co.uk

Charles Rennie Mackintosh Store
www.rennie-mackintosh.co.uk

Gifting Online
www.gifting-online.com

Groovy Personalised Chocolate
www.groovychocolate.com

Scotch Corner
www.scotch-corner.co.uk

Scottish Connection Gifts
www.scotsconnection.com

Scottish Gift Store
www.scottishgift.com

Scottish Quality
www.scottishquality.com

Shop Scotland
www.shopscotland.net

Thistle Do Fine
www.thistledofine.com

healthcare, beauty & personal hygiene

Alka Seltzer
www.alka-seltzer.com

BaByliss
www.babyliss.co.uk

Bic
www.bicworld.com

Bioforce
www.bioforce.co.uk

Bodyform
www.bodyform.co.uk

Borealis Skincare
www.borealisskye.co.uk

Braun
www.braun.com

Cibavision
www.cibavision.co.uk

Colgate
www.colgate.com

Denman Brushes
www.denmanbrush.com

Durex
www.durex.com

Gillette
www.gillette.com

Health Store
www.health-store.co.uk

Isle of Skye Soap Company
www.skye-soap.co.uk

Kimberly Clark
www.kimberly-clark.com

L'Oreal
www.loreal.com

Lanes
www.laneshealth.com

Listerine
www.listerine.com

Macleans
www.macleans.co.uk

Nelsons
www.nelsons.co.uk

Nicorette
www.nicorette.co.uk

Nicotinell
www.nicotinell.co.uk

Nivea
www.nivea.co.uk

Nurofen
www.nurofen.com

Oral B
www.oralb.com

Palmers Cocoa Butter
www.palmerscocoabutter.com

Pantene
www.pantene.com

Potter's Herbal Medicines
www.pottersherbals.co.uk

Rennies
www.rennie.co.uk

Scottish Fine Soaps
www.scottishfinesoaps.com

Seven Seas
www.seven-seas.ltd.uk

Slendertone
www.slendertone.co.uk

Solgar
www.solgar.com

Strepsils
www.strepsils.com

Tampax
www.tampax.com

Tisserand
www.tisserand.com

Vitabiotics
www.vitabiotics.com

Wella
www.wella.co.uk

Wilkinson Sword
www.wilkinson-sword.co.uk

home entertainment

Aiwa
www.aiwa.co.uk

Akai
www.akai.com

Alpine
www.alpine-europe.com

Astra
www.ses-astra.com/uk

Bang & Olufsen
www.bang-olufsen.com

Bose
www.bose.com

Hi-Fi Corner
www.hificorner.co.uk

Hitachi
www.hitachi.com

JVC
www.jvc-europe.com

Loud & Clear
www.loud-clear.co.uk

Marantz
www.marrantz.com

Naim
www.naim-audio.com

Panasonic
www.panasonic.co.uk

Phillips
www.phillips.com

Richer Sounds
www.richersounds.com

Russ Andrew's High Fidelity (Edinburgh)
www.russandrews-hifi.co.uk

Sharp
www.sharp.co.uk

Sony
www.sony.com

TAG McLaren Audio
www.tagmclarenaudio.com

Technics
www.technics.com

home improvements & products

Amway
www.amway.com

Anglian Home Improvements
www.anglianhome.co.uk

Aqualisa
www.aqualisa.co.uk

Axminster Power Tools
www.axminster.co.uk

B&Q
www.diy.co.uk

BAC Windows
www.bacwindows.co.uk

Ballingers
www.ballingers.co.uk

Black & Decker
www.blackanddecker.com

Bostik
www.bostik.com

British Stone
www.british-stone.com

Coldshield
www.coldshield.com

Cookson's Tools
www.cooksons.com

Crown
www.crownpaints.co.uk

De Walt
www.dewalt.com

Dolphin
www.dolphin-fitted-bathrooms.co.uk

Draper Tools
www.draper.co.uk

Dulux
www.dulux.co.uk

Duwit
www.duwit.com

Everest
www.everest.co.uk

Expelair
www.expelair.co.uk

Focus Do-it-All
www.focusdoitall.co.uk

Graham & Brown
www.grahambrown.com

Great Mills
www.greatmills.co.uk

Hammerite
www.hammerite.com

Harris
www.lgharris.co.uk

Homebase
www.homebase.co.uk

Ideal Standard
www.ideal-standard.co.uk

Jewson
www.jewson.co.uk

Makita
www.ukindustry.co.uk/makita

Meddings Machine Tools
www.meddings.co.uk

Mica Hardware
www.micahardware.co.uk

National Tile Association
www.nta.org.uk

Osram
www.osram.co.uk

Paint Research Association
www.pra.org.uk

Polycell
www.polycell.co.uk

Potterton
www.potterton.co.uk

Quickgrip
www.quickgrip.com

Rawlplug
www.rawlplug.co.uk

Rytons Building Products
www.rytons.com

Scott & Sargeant
www.scosarg.co.uk

Screwfix
www.screwfix.com

Showerlux
www.showerlux.com

Spring Ram
www.ultrastyl.com

Stanley Tools
www.stanleyworks.com

Stannah Stairlifts
www.stannah.co.uk

Travis Perkins
www.travisperkins.co.uk

Trend
www.trendm.co.uk

Unibond
www.unibond.co.uk

Universal Fittings
www.universal-fittings.co.uk

Vent Axia
www.vent-axia.com

Weatherseal
www.weatherseal.co.uk

Wickes
www.wickes.com

Wilkinsons
www.wilko.co.uk

Organisations

Almost Impartial Guide
www.almostimpartialguide.co.uk

Bathroom Manufacturers Association
www.bathroom-association.org

British Bathroom Council
www.british-bathrooms.org.uk

British Coatings Federation
www.coatings.org.uk

British Stone
www.british-stone.com

House
www.house.co.uk

National Tile Association
www.nta.org.uk

Paint Research Association
www.pra.org.uk

Planning Advice
www.consumer.gov.uk/consumer_web/h_improv.htm

Products

Aqualisa
www.aqualisa.co.uk

Armourcoat
www.armourcoat.co.uk

Black & Decker
www.blackanddecker.com

Bostik
www.bostik.com

Cookson's Tools
www.cooksons.com

Crown
www.crownpaints.co.uk

De Walt
www.dewalt.co.uk

Draper Tools
www.draper.co.uk

Dulux
www.dulux.co.uk

Farrow & Ball
www.farrow-ball.co.uk

Graham & Brown
www.grahambrown.com

Hammerite
www.hammerite.com

Harris
www.lgharris.co.uk

Makita
www.ukindustry.co.uk/makita

Meddings Machine Tools
www.meddings.co.uk

Monkwell
www.monkwell.com

Polycell
www.polycell.co.uk

Potterton
www.potterton.co.uk

Quickgrip
www.quickgrip.com

Rawlplug
www.rawlplug.co.uk

Rytons Building Products
www.rytons.com

Stanley Tools
www.stanleyworks.com

Stannah Stairlifts
www.stannah.co.uk

Trend
www.trendm.co.uk

Unibond
www.unibond.co.uk

Vent Axia
www.vent-axia.com

Weatherseal
www.weatherseal.co.uk

jewellers

Adler
www.adler.ch

Alexanders
www.alexanders-the-jewellers.co.uk

Asprey & Garrard
www.asprey-garrard.com

Bogaert
www.bogaertjewellery.com

Boodle & Dunthorne
www.boodles.co.uk

Cartier
www.cartier.com

De Beers
www.adiamondisforever.com

Ernest Jones
www.ernestjones.co.uk

Goldsmiths
www.goldsmiths.co.uk

Graff
www.graff-uk.com

H Samuel
www.hsamuel.co.uk

Hirsh
www.hirsh.co.uk

Lladro
www.lladro.com

Longines
www.longines.com

N Bloom & Son
www.nbloom.co.uk

Studio Jewellery
www.studiojewellery.com

Theo Fennell
www.theofennell.com

Tiffany
www.tiffany.com

Wright & Teague
www.wrightandteague.com

Scottish Based

Gold Jewellery
www.gold-jewelry.co.uk

Hebridean Jewellery
www.hebridean-jewellery.co.uk

McDonald Crafts
www.mcdonaldcrafts.co.uk

Ortaks
www.ortakshop.com

Scottish Jewellery
www.scottish-jewellery.co.uk

Stores

Alexanders
www.alexanders-the-jewellers.co.uk

Baxters Jewellers
www.baxtersjewellers.com

Ernest Jones
www.ernestjones.co.uk

Flockharts
www.flockharts.com

Goldsmiths
www.goldsmiths.co.uk

H Samuel
www.hsamuel.co.uk

John Park
www.johnpark.co.uk

Marshall Arts Jewellery
www.marshallartsjewellery.com

Theo Fennell
www.theofennell.com

Tiffany
www.tiffany.com

Wright & Teague
www.wrightandteague.com

kitchens & appliances

AEG
www.aeg.com

Aga Rayburn
www.aga-rayburn.co.uk

Atag
www.atag.co.uk

Baumatic
www.baumatic.co.uk

Belling
www.belling.co.uk

Betterwear
www.betterwear.co.uk

Bosch
www.boschappliances.co.uk

Brabantia
www.brabantia.com

Breville
www.breville.co.uk

Cannon
www.cannongas.co.uk

Creda
www.creda.co.uk

Cucina Direct
www.cucinadirect.co.uk

De Dietrich
www.dedietrich.co.uk

Divertimenti
www.divertimenti.co.uk

Dualit
www.dualit.com

Dyson
www.dyson.com

Electrolux
www.electrolux.co.uk

Gaggia
www.gaggia.it

GEC
www.gec.co.uk

Hoover
www.hoover.co.uk

Hotpoint
www.hotpoint.co.uk

Indesit
www.indesit.co.uk

Intoto
www.intoto.co.uk

Lakeland
www.mos.lakelandlimited.co.uk

Le Creuset
www.lecreuset.com

Magnet
www.magnet.co.uk

Miele
www.miele.co.uk

Mitsubishi Electric
www.meuk.mee.com/consumer

Moben
www.moben.co.uk

Moulinex
www.moulinex.co.uk

Neff
www.neff.co.uk

Ocean
www.oceancatalogue.co.uk

Panasonic
www.panasonic.co.uk

Paula Rosa
www.paularosa.com

Philips
www.philips.com

Redring
www.redring.co.uk

Russell Hobbs
www.russell-hobbs.com

Scott & Sargeant Cookshop
www.scottsargeant.com

Servis
www.servis.co.uk

Sheffield Steel
www.made-in-sheffield.com

Siemens
www.siemensappliances.co.uk

Smeg
www.smeguk.com

Stoves
www.stoves.co.uk

Technics
www.technics.co.uk

Tefal
www.tefal.co.uk

Toshiba
www.toshiba.co.uk

Vax
www.vax.co.uk

Whirlpool
www.whirlpool.co.uk

Zanussi
www.zanussi.co.uk

Online Store

Cookers Direct
www.cookers-direct.co.uk

Cucina Direct
www.cucinadirect.co.uk

Divertimenti
www.divertimenti.co.uk

Dyson
www.dyson.com

Easy Buy Appliances
www.easybuyappliances.co.uk

Home Style Kitchens
www.homestylekitchens.co.uk

Scott & Sargeant Cookshop
www.scottsargeant.com

Sheffield Steel
www.made-in-sheffield.com

Ultimate Appliances & Kitchens
www.ultimateappliancesandkitchens.com

Vax
www.vax.co.uk

lighting

Abacus
www.abacus-lighting.com

Anglepoise
www.anglepoise.co.uk

Christopher Wray
www.christopher-wray.com

Institution of Lighting Engineers
www.ile.org.uk

Mathmos
www.mathmos.co.uk

Osram
www.osram.co.uk

luggage

Antler
www.antler.co.uk

Carlton
www.carlton-luggage-direct.com

Go Places
www.goplaces.co.uk

Louis Vuitton
www.vuitton.co.uk

The Luggage Shop
www.luggageshop.co.uk

Samsonite
www.samsonite.com

Tanner Krolle
www.tannerkrolle.com

magazines & websites

Brand Scotland Online Store
www.brandscotland.co.uk

Buy & Sell
www.buyandsell.net

Cyber City shopping
www.ccshop.co.uk

Daltons Weekly
www.daltons.co.uk

Dressmart.com
www.dressmart.com

Electric Scotland
www.electricscotland.com/shopmall.htm

Empire Direct
www.empiredirect.co.uk

Exchange & Mart
www.exchangeandmart.co.uk

Goldfish Guide
www.goldfishguide.com

Jermyn Street
www.jermynstreet.com

Loot
www.loot.com

Proudly Scottish
www.proudlyscottish.com

Shops on the Net
www.sotn.co.uk

ShopSmart
www.shopsmart.com

Which?
www.which.net

markets & malls

Barclaysquare
www.barclaysquare.co.uk

Bicester Village
www.bicester-village.co.uk

Bluewater
www.bluewater.freeserve.co.uk

Central Milton Keynes
www.cmkshop.co.uk

Covent Garden
www.coventgardenmarket.com

Freeport
www.freeportplc.com

Galleria Outlet Centre
www.factory-outlets.co.uk

Glasgow Barrowland
www.glasgow-barrowland.com

Jermyn Street
www.jermynstreet.com

Meadowhall Centre
www.meadowhall.co.uk

Outlet Centres International
www.outletcentres.com

Scottish Farmers Markets
www.scottishfarmersmarkets.co.uk

Shops on the Net
www.sotn.co.uk

ShopSmart
www.shopsmart.com

Whitgift
www.whitgiftshopping.co.uk

mother & baby

Avent
www.avent.co.uk

Babies R Us
www.babiesrus.co.uk

Baby Gap
www.babygap.com

Babycare Direct
www.babycare-direct.co.uk

Bebe Confort
www.bebeconfort.com

Blooming Marvellous
www.bloomingmarvellous.co.uk

Britax
www.britax.co.uk

Bumpsadaisy
www.covent-gardenlife.com/shopping/shops/bumpsadaisy

Chicco
www.chiccousa.com

Cosatto
www.cosatto.com

Formes
www.formes.com

Graco
www.graco.co.uk or www.gracobaby.com

Huggies
www.huggies.com

Johnson's
www.johnsonsbaby.com

JoJo Maman Bebe
www.jojomamanbebe.co.uk

Kid's Window
www.thekidswindow.com

Klippan
www.klippan.co.uk

Land Rover Pushchairs
www.allterrain.co.uk

Mamas & Papas
www.mamasandpapas.co.uk

Mothercare
www.mothercare.com

Nappies Direct
www.nappies-direct.co.uk

National Childbirth Trust
www.nct-online.org

Pampers
www.pampers.com

Pegasus Pushchairs
www.allterrain.co.uk

Popular Baby Names
www.popularbabynames.com

Real Nappy Association
www.realnappy.com

Urchin
www.urchin.co.uk

music, games & video

Alba Vision
www.scotland-info.co.uk/albavision

Blackstar
www.blackstar.co.uk

Blockbuster
www.blockbuster.co.uk

Boxman
www.boxman.co.uk

Britannia Music Club
www.britmusic.co.uk

Carlton Video
www.carltonvideo.co.uk

CD Now
www.cdnow.com

CD Wow
www.cd-wow.com

Computer Exchange
www.cex.co.uk

DVD Direct
www.dvd-uk.com

DVD World
www.dvdworld.co.uk

DVDplus
www.dvdplus.co.uk

Game
www.game-retail.co.uk

Gameplay
www.gameplay.com

Global Video
www.globalvideo.co.uk

HMV
www.hmv.com

Jungle.com
www.jungle.com

Kilberry Bagpipes
www.kilberry.com

Music & Games
www.musicandgames.com

Music in Scotland
www.musicinscotland.com

Nice Price
www.niceprice.net

Odeon Filmstore
www.filmstore.com

Odeon Videostore
www.filmstore.co.uk

Our Price
www.ourprice.co.uk

Ross Records
www.rossrecords.com

Scots Market
www.scotsmarket.com

Scotweb Music
www.scotwebshops.com/shopping/music

Temple Records, Scotland
www.templerecords.co.uk

Tower Records
www.towerrecords.co.uk

Virgin Megastore
www.virginmega.com

WH Smith
www.whsmithonline.co.uk

Yalplay
www.yalplay.com

photography

Charles Tait
www.charles-tait.co.uk

Denver Gallery Online
www.photoworkshops.co.uk

Dixons
www.dixons.co.uk

Internet Cameras Direct
www.internetcamerasdirect.co.uk

Jessops
www.jessops.co.uk

Mega Pixels
www.megapixels.co.uk

Olan Mills
www.olanmills.com

Photo Gold
www.photogold.co.uk

Photo Me
www.photo-me.co.uk

Scottish Photography
www.scottishphotography.com

shoes & accessories

Church & Co
www.buckinghamgate.com/bgate

Timberland
www.timberland.com

Wolford
www.wolfordboutique-kenmode-kensington.co.uk

Accessories

Accessorize
www.accessorize.co.uk

Claire's Accessories
www.claires.com

James Lock
www.lockhatters.co.uk

Lulu Guinness
www.luluguinness.com

Marsden's leather
www.marsdens-leather.co.uk

Mulberry
www.mulberry-england.co.uk

Sak
www.thesak.com

Whitehouse & Cox
www.whitehouse-cox.co.uk

Glasses

Arnette
www.arnette.com

The Eye Shop
www.the-eye-shop.com

Oakley
www.oakley.com

Ray-Ban
www.rayban.com

Sunglass Shop
www.sunglassshop.co.uk

Shoes

Barratts
www.barratts.co.uk

Birkenstock
www.birkenstock.co.uk

Cheaney
www.cheaney.co.uk

Clarks
www.clarks.co.uk

DASCO
www.shoeworld.co.uk/dasco

Dolcis
www.dolcis.co.uk

Dr Martens
www.drmartens.com

Ecco
www.ecco-shoes.co.uk

Faith
www.faith.co.uk

Gordon Scott
www.gordonscott.co.uk

Gucci
www.gucci.com

Hush Puppies
www.hushpuppiesshoes.com

Jones Bootmaker
www.jonesbootmaker.com

Office
www.office.co.uk

Rockport Shoes
www.walking-shoes.com

Skechers
www.skechers.com

Timpson
www.timpson.com

specialist

Ann Summers
www.annsummers.co.uk

Anything Left Handed
www.anythingleft-handed.co.uk

Innovations
www.innovations.co.uk

The Left Hand
www.thelefthand.com

sports & outdoor

Allsports
www.allsportsretail.co.uk

Altberg Boots
www.altberg.co.uk

Barbour
www.barbour.com

Berghaus
www.berghaus.com

Blacks
www.blacks.co.uk

Brasher Boot Company
www.brasher.co.uk

Edge2Edge
www.edge2edge.co.uk

Ellis Brigham
www.ellis-brigham.com

Farlows
www.farlows.co.uk

Field & Trek
www.field-trek.co.uk

Fila
www.fila.com

Golf Classics
www.golf-classics.com

Gore-Tex
www.gorefabrics.com

Hawkshead
www.hawkshead.com

Intersport
www.intersport.co.uk

James Lock
www.lockhatters.co.uk

JD Sports
www.jdsports.co.uk

JJB Sports
www.jjb.co.uk

Kitbag.com
www.kitbag.com

Musto
www.musto.co.uk

Nikwax Waterproofing
www.nikwax.co.uk

ProLine
www.proline-sports.co.uk

Rohan
www.rohan.co.uk

Snow & Rock
www.snowandrock.co.uk

Sports Connection
www.sportsconnection.co.uk

Sports Division
www.sports-division.com

Sweatshop
www.sweatshop.co.uk

Timberland
www.timberland.com

TSI Exercise Equipment
www.tstleisure.co.uk

Online Shops

Cotswold
www.cotswold-outdoor.co.uk

Extreme Pie
www.extremepie.com

M & M Sports
www.mandmsports.com

Newitts 4 Sports
www.newitts.com

Worldwide Sports
www.worldwidesports.com

Scottish Based

Baw Faces Golf Balls
www.bawfaces.co.uk

Freeze Scotland Site
www.freeze-scotland.com

International Outdoor Clothing
www.outdoor-wear.com

Scotland's Golf Shop
www.scotlandsgolfshop.com

Service Sports
www.servicesports.co.uk

toys

Action Man
www.actionman.com

Barbie
www.barbie.com

Beanie Babies
www.eurobeenie.co.uk

Brio
www.brio.co.uk

Caledonian Bears
www.banavie4.freeserve.co.uk

Corgi
www.corgi.co.uk

Crayola
www.crayola.com

Dawson & Son
www.dawson-and-son.com

E-Toys
www.etoys.co.uk

Early Learning Centre
www.earlylearningcentre.co.uk

English Teddy Bear Company
www.teddy.co.uk

FAO Schwartz
www.faoschwarz.com

Fisher Price
www.fisher-price.com

Fun & Games Toyshop
www.funandgamestoyshop.co.uk

Game Store
www.tgs.co.uk/games

Hamleys
www.hamleys.co.uk

Hasbro
www.hasbro.com

Hobbycraft
www.hobbycraft.co.uk

Hornby
www.hornby.co.uk

Kikaflik
www.kikaflik.com

Knex
www.knex.co.uk

Lego
www.lego.com

Little Tikes
www.rubbermaid.com/littletikes

Matchbox
www.matchboxtoys.com

Mattel
www.mattel.com

Meccano
www.dircon.co.uk-meccano

Paddington Bear
www.paddingtonbear.co.uk

Playmobil
www.playmobil.com

Pokemon
www.pokemon.com

Polly Pocket
www.pollypocket.co.uk

Quadro
www.quadro-toys.co.uk

Scalextric
www.scalextric.co.uk

Tiger Toys
www.tigertoys.co.uk

Tomy
www.tomy.co.uk

Toy City
www.toycity.com

Toys R Us
www.toysrus.co.uk

TP Activity Toys
www.tptoys.com

Wicksteed
www.wicksteed.co.uk

Woolworths
www.woolies.co.uk

trade associations

Alliance of Independent Retailers
www.indretailer.co.uk

Booksellers Association of Great Britain & Northern Ireland
www.booksellers.org.uk

British Antique Dealers Association
www.bada.org

British Association of Toy Retailers
www.batr.co.uk

British Footwear Association
www.shoeworld.co.uk

British Toy & Hobby Association
www.btha.co.uk

Central Scotland Chamber of Commerce
www.central-chamber.co.uk

Company of Master Jewellers
www.company-of-master-jewellers.co.uk

Independent Footwear Retailers Association
www.shoeshop.org.uk

LAPADA: Association of Art & Antique Dealers
www.lapada.co.uk

Toymaster
www.toymaster.co.uk

wallcovering

Armourcoat
www.armourcoat.co.uk

Coleman Brothers
www.colemanbros.co.uk

Coloroll
www.adroit.co.uk/the.pattern.of.life

Farrow & Ball
www.farrow-ball.co.uk

Graham & Brown Wallcoverings
www.grahambrown.com

Monkwell
www.monkwell.com

watches

Baume & Mercier
www.baume-et-mercier.com

Breitling
www.breitling.com

Casio
www.casio.co.uk

Citizen
www.citizenwatch.com

Direct Watch Company
www.directwatch.com

Jaeger le coultre
www.jaeger-lecoultre.com

Longines
www.longines.com

Omega
www.omega.ch

Panerai
www.panerai.com

Patek Philippe
www.patek.com

Rado
www.rado.ch

Rolex
www.rolex.com

Rotary
www.rotarywatches.com

Seiko
www.seiko.co.uk

Sekonda
www.sekonda.com

Swatch
www.swatch.com

TAG Heuer
www.tagheuer.com

Timex
www.timex.com

Tissot
www.bme.es/tissot

Watch Heaven
www.watch-heaven.com

Wrist Watch Depot
www.wristwatchdepot.com

- american football
- athletics
- badminton
- baseball
- basketball
- bowls
- boxing
- canoeing
- combat
- cricket
- croquet
- curling
- cycling
- darts
- fencing
- field sports
- football
- golf
- gymnastics
- handball
- highland games
- hockey
- horseracing
- inline & roller skating
- international games
- korfball
- lacrosse
- magazines & websites
- motor racing
- netball
- orienteering
- personalities
- polo
- promotion & education
- rounders
- rowing
- rugby
- sailing & boating
- shinty
- show jumping
- snooker & billiards
- softball
- sportswear & equipment
- squash
- sub-aqua
- surfing
- swimming
- table tennis
- target sports
- tennis
- tenpin bowling
- volleyball
- water skiing
- weightlifting & strength
- winter sports
- wrestling

american football

British Collegiate American Football League
www.bcafl.org

National Football League
www.nfl.com

Scottish Claymores
www.claymores.co.uk

Scottish Claymore's fan Site
www.touchdownclaymores.com

Sky Sports American Football
www.sky.co.uk/sports/nfl

Super Bowl
www.superbowl.com

Under Centre Scotland
www.undercenter.f9.co.uk

athletics

Amateur Athletics Association
www.englandathletics.demon.co.uk

Athletic News
www.athleticsnews.com

British Athletics Federation
www.british-athletics.co.uk

British Triathlon Association
www.britishtriathlon.org

British Wheelchair Sports Foundation
www.britishwheelchairsports.org

European Athletic Federation
www.eaa-athletics.ch

Health Development Agency
www.hea.org.uk

International Amateur Athletics Federation
www.iaaf.org

International Paralympic Committee
www.paralympic.org

International Pentathlon Union
www.pentathlon.org

International Triathlon Union
www.triathlon.org

London Marathon
www.london-marathon.co.uk

National Coaching Foundation
www.ncf.org.uk

Runner's World
www.runnersworld.co.uk

Scottish Athletics Federation
www.saf.org.uk

Scottish Disability sport
www.scottishdisabilitysport.com

Sports Aid
www.sportsaid.org.uk

Sydney 2000 Olympics
www.sydney.olympic.org

Youth Sport Trust
www.youthsport.net

badminton

Badminton UK
www.badmintonuk.ndo.co.uk

International Badminton Federation
www.intbadfed.org

Scottish Badminton Union
www.scotbadminton.demon.co.uk

baseball

British Baseball & Softball
www.baseballsoftballuk.com

International Baseball Federation
www.baseball.ch

Scottish National team
www.leaguelineup.com/welcome.asp?url=teamscotland

basketball

Basketball Players Association
www.woods.demon.co.uk/bpa

Britball-Scotland
www.britball.com/scotland.html

Budweiser Basketball League UK
www.basketball-league.co.uk

Global Basketball News
www.eurobasket.com

International Basketball Federation
www.fiba.com

National Basketball Association
www.nba.com

Scotball News
www.size10.com/scotball

Scottish Basketball League
www.basketball-scotland.com

XXL Basketball
www.xxl.co.uk

bowls

Bowls Club
www.bowlsclub.co.uk

International Bowling Federation
www.fiq.org

Official Lawn Bowls
www.lawnbowls.co.uk

Scottish Bowling Clubs
www.scottishsport.co.uk/bowling

Scottish Indoor Bowls
www.scottishindoorbowls.org.uk

boxing

Boxing Monthly Magazine
www.boxing-monthly.co.uk

British Boxing Board of Control
www.dspace.dial.pipex.com/bbbc

International Amateur Boxing Association
www.aiba.net

International Boxing Organisation
www.iboboxing.com

World Boxing Association
www.wbaonline.com

canoeing

British Canoe Union
www.bcu.org.uk

European Canoe Association
www.canoe-europe.org

International Canoe Federation
www.canoeicf.com

Scottish Canoe Association
www.scot-canoe.org

combat

British Aikido Association
www.aikido-baa.org.uk

British Council for Chinese Martial Arts
www.bccma.demon.co.uk

British United Taekwon-do Federation
www.butf.com

Eastwinds Tai Chi
www.eastwinds.co.uk

International Judo Federation
www.ijf.org

Judo Scotland
www.scotjudo.org

Muay Thai Scotland
www.muaythai-scotland.co.uk

Scottish Karate Club
www.scottishkarate.com

Scottish Kempo Academy
www.kempo.co.uk

Scottish Wingchun
www.scottishwingchun.homestead.com

Temple Martial Arts, Scotland
www.templekickbox.freeserve.co.uk

UK Taekwon-do Association
www.ukta.com

World Judo Organisation
www.worldjudo.org

World Karate Federation
www.wkf.net

World Kickboxing Association
www.worldkickboxing.com

Wossobama Martial Arts Gym
www.wossobama.co.uk

cricket

Cricket Index Directory
www.cricketindex.com

Cricket World
www.cricketworld.com

Cricketer International Magazine
www.cricketer.com

Edinburgh Accies
www.eacc.co.uk

Glasgow High Kelvinside
www.ghk-cricket.co.uk

Highland Cricket Club
www.highlandcc.co.uk

Rampant Lion
www.scotlandcricket.rivals.net

Scottish Cricket Clubs
www.scotlandinter.net/cricket.htm

Scottish Cricket Union
www.cricketeurope.org/SCOTLAND/home.shtml

Scottish National Cricket League
www.sncl.btinternet.co.uk

West of Scotland Cricket Club
www.westofscotlandcricketclub.co.uk

Grounds

Lord's
www.lords.org

Sydney
www.scgt.oz.au

Organisations

Federation of International Cricketers
www.ficahof.com

International Cricket Council
www.cricket.org/link_to_database/national/icc

Minor Cricket Counties Association
www.mcca.cricket.org

Trophies

NatWest Trophy
www.natwest.co.uk/cricket

World Cup
www.ecb.co.uk/worldcup

Websites & Magazines

BBC Cricket
http://news.bbc.co.uk/hi/english/sport/cricket

CNN Cricket
www.cnnsi.com/cricket

Cricket Info
www.cricket.org

Cricketer International Magazine
www.cricketer.com

Live from Lord's Webcam
www.lords.org/mcc/camview

Sky Sports Cricket
www.sky.co.uk/sports/cricket

Wisden
www.wisden.com

croquet

Scottish Croquet Association
www.grue.demon.co.uk/sca/intro.htm

curling

Curling Shoes
www.curlingshoes.com

Royal Caledonian Curling Club
www.rccc.org.uk

cycling

Association of Cycle Traders
www.cyclesource.co.uk

Batavus
www.batavus.com

Beastway MTB
www.beastway.com

BMX
www.ebmx.com

British Cycling Federation
www.bcf.uk.com

British Cyclo-Cross Association
www.cyclo-cross.co.uk

British Mountain Biking
www.bmb.org

British Pedal Car Championship
www.pedalcars.info

Cycling in Scotland
www.scottishcycling.co.uk

Cycling UK Directory
www.cycling.uk.com

Cyclists Touring Club
www.ctc.org.uk

E-cycles
www.ecycles.uk.com

Falcon
www.falconcycles.co.uk

London Cycling Campaign
www.lcc.org.uk

Mountain Biking UK
www.bikinguk.net

National Cycle Network
www.nationalcyclenetwork.org.uk

On Your Bike
www.onyourbike.com

Orbit
www.orbit-cycles.co.uk

Prutour
www.prutour.co.uk

Raleigh
www.raleighbikes.com

Road Time Trials Council
www.rttc.org.uk

Scottish Cyclists' Union
www.scuweb.com

Sturmey Archer
www.sturmey-archer.com

Tour de France
www.letour.fr

Trail Cyclists Association
www.trailquest.co.uk

Union Cycliste Internationale
www.uci.ch

Wheelie Serious
www.wheelie-serious.com

darts

Bulls Eye Magazine
www.bullsinet.com

Embassy World Darts
www.embassydarts.com

Planet Darts
www.planetdarts.co.uk

Scottish Darts Association
www.geocities.com/scotland_darts

fencing

British Academy of Fencing
www.baf-fencing.org

British Fencing Association
www.britishfencing.com

Scot-Fencing
www.scottishfencing.8m.com

Scottish Fencing
www.scottish-fencing.com

field sports

British Shooting & Fishing
www.premier-pages.co.uk/sports/british.htm

Galloway Country Sports
www.country-sports.co.uk

Gateside
www.gatesidefieldsports.com

Glen Osprey
www.glenosprey.co.uk

Harris
www.sol.co.uk/h/Harrisfieldsports

football

Clubs

AC Fiorentina
www.acfiorentina.it

AC Milan
www.acmilan.com

Arsenal
www.arsenal.co.uk

AS Roma
www.asromacalcio.it

Aston Villa
www.astonvilla-fc.co.uk

Barcelona
www.fcbarcelona.com/select_language.sps

Barnsley
www.barnsleyfc.co.uk

Berwick Rangers
www.brfc.mcmail.com

Birmingham City
www.bcfc.com

Blackburn Rovers
www.rovers.co.uk

Blackpool
www.blackpoolfc.co.uk

Bolton Wanderers
www.boltonwfc.co.uk

Bournemouth
www.afcb.demon.co.uk

Bradford City
www.bradfordcityfc.co.uk

Bristol City
www.bcfc.co.uk

Burnley
www.clarets.co.uk

Cambridge United
www.cambridge-united.co.uk

Carlisle
www.cufconline.org.uk

Charlton Athletic
www.charlton-athletic.co.uk

Chelsea
www.chelseafc.co.uk

Cheltenham Town
www.cheltenhamtown.co.uk

Chester City
www.chester-city.co.uk

Colchester United
www.cufc.co.uk

Coventry City
www.ccfc.co.uk

Crewe Alexandra
www.s-cheshire.ac.uk/cafc

Crystal Palace
www.palace-eagles.com

Darlington
www.darlingtonfc.co.uk

Derby County
www.dcfc.co.uk

England
www.englandfc.com

Everton
www.evertonfc.com

Fulham
www.fulhamfc.co.uk

Huddersfield Town
www.huddersfield-town.co.uk

Hull City
www.hullcity.demon.co.uk

Ipswich Town
www.itfc.co.uk

Leeds United
www.lufc.co.uk

Leicester City
www.lcfc.com

Lincoln City
www.redimps.com

Liverpool
www.liverpoolfc.org

Macclesfield Town
www.mtfc.co.uk

Manchester City
www.mcfc.co.uk

Manchester United
www.manutd.co.uk

Middlesbrough
www.mfc.co.uk

Millwall
www.millwallonline.co.uk

Newcastle United
www.nufc.co.uk

Northampton Town
http://web.ukonline.co.uk/ntfc

Norwich City
www.canaries.co.uk

Nottingham Forest
www.nottingham-forest.co.uk

Notts County
www.nottscounty.net

Parma AC
www.acparma.it

Peterborough United
www.theposh.com

Plymouth Argyll
www.argyll.org.uk

Queens Park Rangers
www.qpr.co.uk

Reading
www.readingfc.co.uk

Scunthorpe United
www.scunthorpe-united.co.uk

Sheffield United
www.sufc.co.uk

Sheffield Wednesday
www.swfc.co.uk

Shrewsbury Town
www.shrewsburytown.co.uk

Southampton
www.saintsfc.co.uk

Sunderland
www.sunderland-afc.com

Tottenham Hotspur
www.spurs.co.uk

Watford
www.watfordfc.com

West Bromwich Albion
www.wba.co.uk

West Ham United
www.westhamunited.co.uk

Wimbledon
www.wimbledon-fc.co.uk

Wolverhampton Wanderers
www.wolves.co.uk

York City
www.yorkcityfc.co.uk

Clubs – Scottish

Aberdeen
www.afc.co.uk

Airdrie
www.airdrie-football.co.uk/club.htm

Alloa Athletic
www.nevis.cwc.net

Arbroath
www.arbroathfc.co.uk

Ayr United
www.ayr-united.org.uk

Brechin City
www.brechincity.co.uk

Celtic
www.celticfc.co.uk

Clyde
www.irw.co.uk/clydefc/

Dundee
www.dundeefc.co.uk

Dundee United
www.dundeeunited.net

Dunfermline
www.dunfermline-athletic.com

Falkirk
www.falkirkfc.co.uk

Forfar Athletic
www.forfarathletic.co.uk

Hearts
www.heartsfc.co.uk

Hibernian
www.hibernianfc.co.uk

Inverness CT
www.caley-thistle.co.uk

Kilmarnock
www.kilmarnockfc.co.uk

Livingston
www.livingstonfc.co.uk

Motherwell
www.motherwellfc.co.uk

Partick Thistle
www.ptfc.co.uk

Queen of the South
www.qosfc.co.uk

Raith Rovers
www.rrfc.co.uk

Rangers
www.rangers.co.uk

Ross County
www.rosscountyfootballclub.co.uk

St Johnstone
www.stjohnstonefc.co.uk

St Mirren
www.stmirren.net

Magazines & Websites

Fanzine
www.soccer-fanzine.co.uk

Football 365
www.football365.com

Football Scotland
www.football-scotland.co.uk

Nationwide League
www.football.nationwide.co.uk

Planet Football
www.planetfootball.com

Roy of the Rovers
www.royoftherovers.com

Scottish Football
www.scottishfootball.com

Scottish Football Museum
www.scottishfootballmuseum.org.uk

Scottish Premier League Online
www.thespl.cjb.net

Soccernet
www.soccernet.com

Organisations

FIFA
www.fifa.com

Football Association
www.the-fa.org

Football Supporters' Association
www.fsa.org.uk

League Managers Association
www.leaguemanagers.com

Scottish Football Association
www.scottishfa.co.uk

UEFA
www.uefa.com

Tournaments

England 2006
www.fa2006.org

FA Carling Premiership
www.fa-carling.com

Scotland & Ireland Euro 2008
www.euro2008bid.com

Scottish First Division
www.firstdivision.co.uk

Scottish Premier League
www.scotprem.com

golf

Associations

Golf Foundation of Britain
www.golf-foundation.org

Ladies' Professional Golf Association
www.lpga.com

Professional Golf Association of America
www.pga.com

Scottish Golf
www.scottishgolf.com

Scottish Golf Schools
www.golfscotland.co.uk

Scottish Golf Society
www.scottishgolfsociety.com

Scottish Ladies' Golfing Association
www.slga.scottishgolf.com

World Amateur Golf Council
www.wagc.org

Courses

All Scottish Golf Clubs
www.golfeurope.com/clubs/scotland.htm

Carnoustie Golf Course Hotel & Resort
www.carnoustie-hotel.com

Gleneagles
www.gleneagles.com

Muirfield
www.waimea.demon.co.uk/muirfield.html

Prestwick
www.prestwickgc.co.uk

Royal Birkdale
www.royalbirkdale.com

Royal Troon
www.royaltroon.co.uk

St Andrews
www.standrews.org.uk

UK Golf Guide
www.uk-golfguide.com

Magazines, Websites & TV

Fore Magazine
www.scga.org/fore

Golf
www.golfonline.com

Golf Channel
www.thegolfchannel.com

Golf Digest
www.golfdigest.com

Golf Europe
www.golfeurope.com

Golf Link Scotland
www.golf-link-scotland.com

Golf Monthly
www.nexusinternet.co.uk/gm

Golf Today
www.golftoday.co.uk

Golf.com
www.golf.com

Scotland-Home of golf
www.scotland-for-golf.com

Thistle Golf Holidays
www.thistlegolf.co.uk

UK Golf
www.uk-golf.com

Tournaments

British Open
www.opengolf.com

European Masters
www.golf.european-masters.com

LPGA Classic
www.lpgaclassic.com

Open Championship
www.opengolf.com

PGA European Tour
www.europeantour.com

Times MeesPierson Corporate Golf Challenge
www.timescorpgolf.com

US Masters
www.masters.org

US Open
www.usopen.org

gymnastics

British Amateur Gymnastics Association
www.baga.co.uk

International Gymnastics Federation
www.fig-gymnastics.com

Scottish Gymnastics
www.scottishgymnastics.com

handball

International Handball Federation
www.ihf.ch

highland games

Dufftown Highland Games
www.dufftownhighlandgames.org

Scottish Games Association
www.st-andrews.ac.uk/%7Eig2/SGA/SGAhomepage.html

hockey

Field Hockey
www.fieldhockey.com

Field Hockey Foundation
www.fieldhockeytournament.com

Hockey Network
www.hockey-net.co.uk

International Hockey Federation
www.fihockey.org

Scottish Hockey Union
www.scottish-hockey.org.uk

horseracing

Betting

Barry Dennis
www.barrydennis.co.uk

Blue Sq
www.bluesq.com

IG Index
www.igindex.co.uk

InterBet
www.inter-bet.com

Ladbrokes
www.bet.co.uk

Sean Graham
www.seangraham.com

Sporting Index
www.sportingindex.com

Sportingbet.com
www.sportingbet.com

Sunderlands
www.sunderlands.co.uk

Surrey Racing
www.surreyracing.co.uk

Totalbet.com
www.totalbet.com

Victor Chandler
www.victorchandler.com

William Hill
www.willhill.com

Magazines & Websites

Channel 4 Racing
www.channel4.com/sport/racing

Direct Racing Information
www.directracing.com

Discover Racing
www.discover-racing.com

Race Horses.com
www.race-horses.com

Racenews
www.racenews.co.uk

Scottish Racing
www.scottishracing.co.uk

Sporting Life
www.sportinglife.co.uk

Organisations

British Betting Office Association
www.bboa.co.uk

British Bloodstock Agency
www.bba.co.uk

British Horseracing Board
www.bhb.co.uk

Horserace Betting Levy Board
www.hblb.org.uk

Jockey Club
www.jockeyclub.com

National Trainers Federation
www.martex.co.uk/racehorsetrainers

Racecourse Association
www.comeracing.co.uk

Tattersalls
www.tattersalls.com

Weatherbys
www.weatherbys-group.com

Racecourses

Aintree
www.aintree.co.uk

Ascot
www.ascot.co.uk

Catterick
www.catterick.com

Cheltenham
www.cheltenham.co.uk

Chepstow
www.chepstow-racecourse.co.uk

Chester
www.chester-races.co.uk

Cork
www.aardvark.ie/cork-racecourse

Curragh
www.curragh.ie

Doncaster
www.britishracing.com

Down Royal
www.downroyal.com

Epsom
www.epsomderby.co.uk

Galway
www.iol.ie/galway-races

Goodwood
www.goodwood.co.uk

Haydock Park
www.haydock-park.com

Huntingdon
www.huntingdonracing.co.uk

Kempton Park
www.kempton.co.uk

Market Rasen
www.demon.co.uk/racenews/marketrasen

Newbury
www.raceweb.com/newbury

Newmarket
www.newmarketracecourses.co.uk

Newton Abbot
www.eclipse.co.uk/naracecourse

Nottingham
www.nottinghamracecourse.co.uk

Punchestown
www.punchestown.com

Sandown Park
www.sandown.co.uk

Stratford on Avon
www.stratfordracecourse.net

Towcester
www.demon.co.uk/racenews/towcester

Tramore
www.tramore-racecourse.com

Uttoxeter
www.uttoxeterracecourse.co.uk

Warwick
www.warwickracecourse.co.uk

Wetherby
www.wetherby.co.uk

Wincanton
www.wincantonracecourse.co.uk

Windsor
www.windsorracing.co.uk

Wolverhampton
www.parkuk.freeserve.co.uk

Racecourses – Scottish

Ayr
www.ayr-racecourse.co.uk

Hamilton Park
www.hamilton-park.co.uk

Kelso
www.kelso-races.co.uk

Musselburgh
www.musselburgh-racecourse.co.uk

Perth
www.perth-races.co.uk

inline & roller skating

Federation of Roller Skating
www.bfrs.org.uk

Inliners
www.inliners.co.uk

International Roller Skating Federation
www.rollersports.org

international games

Athens 2004 Olympics
www.athens.olympic.org/gr

British Olympic Association
www.olympics.org.uk

International Olympic Committee
www.olympic.org

International Paralympic Committee
www.paralympic.org

Olympic Games
www.olympics.com

World Anti-Doping Association
www.wada-ama.org

korfball

International Korfball Federation
www.ikf.org

lacrosse

International Lacrosse Federation
www.intlaxfed.org

Scottish Lacrosse Association
www.scottish-lacrosse.org.uk

magazines & websites

BAA Millennium Youth Games
www.baamyg.org.uk

BBC Sports academy
www.bbc.co.uk.sportsacademy

SportLive
www.sportlive.co.uk

Sports.com
www.sports.com

motor racing

Circuits

Anglesey
www.anglesey-race-circuit.co.uk

Brands Hatch
www.brands-hatch.co.uk

Castle Combe
www.castlecombecircuit.co.uk

Donington Park
www.donington-park.co.uk

Knockhill
www.knockhill.co.uk

Le Mans
www.24h-le-mans.com

Mallory Park
www.mallorypark.co.uk

Monaco
www.monaco.mc/monaco/gprix

Monza
www.monzanet.it

Nürburgring
www.nuerburgring.de

Oulton Park
www.oultonpark.co.uk

Pembrey
www.barc.net/pembrey.htm

Silverstone
www.silverstone-circuit.co.uk

Events

Automobile Club de l'Ouest
www.lemans.org

British Rallycross Drivers Association
www.rallycrossuk.com

British Touring Car Championship
www.btcc.co.uk

Formula One
www.formula1.com

New Pig Scottish Rally Championship
www.newpigsrc.co.uk

Scottish Formula Ford Zetec Championship
www.scottishzetec.co.uk

World Rally Championship
www.wrc.com

F1 Teams

Arrows
www.arrows.com

BAR-Honda
www.britishamericanracing.com

Ferrari
www.shell-ferrari.com

Jaguar
www.jaguar-racing.com

Jordan
www.jordangp.com

McLaren
www.mclaren.co.uk

Minardi
www.minardi.it

Prost
www.prostgp.com

Renault
www.renaultf1.com

Sauber
www.sauber.ch

Toyota
www.toyota-f1.com

Williams
www.williamsf1.co.uk

Grand Prix

America
www.usgpindy.com

Austria
www.a1ring.at

Belgium
www.spa-francorchamps.be

Canada
www.grandprix.ca

France
www.magnyf1.com

Germany
www.hockenheimring.de

Italy
www.monzanet.it

Japan
www.suzukacircuit.co.jp

Malaysia
www.malaysiangp.com.my

Monaco
www.f1-monaco.com

San Marino
www.formula1.sm

Magazines & Websites

Autosport
www.autosport.com

British Motor Racing Circuits
www.bmrc.co.uk

F1 Today
www.f1today.com

F1-Live
www.f1-live.com

ITV
www.itv-f1.com

Motor Sport
www.motorsport.com

Motorsports UK
www.motorsportsuk.co.uk

Scottish Motor Sport
www.scottishmotorsport.com

Manufacturers

Lola Cars International
www.lolacars.com

Organisations

British Racing & Sports Car Club
www.brscc.co.uk

British Trials & Rally Drivers Association
http://freespace.virgin.net/liz.cox/BTRDA2/Entry/indexSS.htm

Federation Internationale de l'Automobile (FIA)
www.fia.com

Royal Scottish Automobile Club (motor sport)
www.rsacmotorsport.co.uk

Scottish Motor Racing Club
www.smrc-uk.com

netball

All England Netball Association
www.england-netball.co.uk

International Federation of Netball Association
www.netball.org

Scottish Netball Association
www.netballscotland.freeserve.co.uk

orienteering

British Orienteering Federation
www.cix.co.uk/~bof

Scottish Orienteering Association
www.scottish-orienteering.org

personalities

Alan Shearer
www.fly.to/shearer

Ally McCoist MBE
www.aquestionofally.co.uk

Andre Agassi
www.andresite.com

Anna Kournikova (Fan Club)
www.annak.org

Ayrton Senna
www.ayrton-senna.com

Babe Ruth
www.baberuth.com

Chris Bonington
www.bonington.com

Damon Hill
www.damonhill.co.uk

David Coulthard
www.davidcoulthard.com

David Ginola
www.ginola.net

David Leadbetter
www.leadbetter.com

Diego Maradona
www.diegomaradona.com

Don Bradman
www.bradman.sa.com.au

Eddie Irvine (Fan Club)
www.exclusively-irvine.com

Evander Holyfield
www.evanderholyfield.com

Evel Knieval
www.evel.com

Gary Player
www.garyplayer.com

Geoff Billington
www.geoff-billington.com

Heinz-Harald Frentzen
www.frentzen.de

Jack Nicklaus
www.nicklaus.com

Jacques Villeneuve
www.jacques.villeneuve.com

John Whitaker
www.john-whitaker.com

Johnny Herbert
www.johnnyherbert.co.uk

Lee Westwood
www.westy.com

Lennox Lewis
www.lennox-lewis.com

Lionel Dunning
www.lionel-dunning.com

Mark Spitz
www.cmgww.com/sports/spitz

Michael Jordan
www.jordan.sportsline.com

Michael Schumacher
www.michael-schumacher.com

Mika Hakkinen
www.mikahakkinen.net

Mika Salo
www.micasalo.net

Mohammed Ali
www.ali.com

Nadia Comaneci (Fan Club)
www.nadiacomaneci.com

Pedro De La Rosa
www.pedrodelarosa.com

Pele
www.pele.net

Pete Sampras
www.sampras.com

Phil Mickelson
www.phil-mickelson.com

Prince Naseem Hamed
www.princenaseem.com

Ralf Schumacher
www.ralf-schumacher.de

Ronaldo
www.r9ronaldo.com

Steffi Graf
www.steffi-graf.com

Steve Waugh
www.stevewaugh.com.au

Tiger Woods
www.tigerwoods.com

Tim Henman
www.henmagic.freeserve.co.uk

polo

Federation of International Polo
www.fippolo.com

Hurlingham Polo Association
www.hpa-polo.co.uk

International Women's Polo Association
www.polo.co.uk

Polo World Cup on Snow
www.polostmoritz.com

promotion & education

UK

British Association of Sport & Exercise Sciences
www.bases.co.uk

British Wheelchair Sports Foundation
www.britishwheelchairsports.org

Central Council of Physical Recreation
www.ccpr.org.uk

National Coaching Foundation
www.ncf.org.uk

National Playing Field Association
www.npfa.co.uk

Sports Council (United Kingdom)
www.uksport.gov.uk

Sports Industries Federation
www.sportslife.org.uk

SPRITO
www.sprito.org.uk

Women's Sports Foundation
www.wsf.org.uk

Youth Sport Trust
www.youthsport.net

Scottish

Scottish Disability Sport
www.scottishdisabilitysport.com

Scottish Sports Association
www.scottishsportsassociation.org.uk

Scottish Sports Council
www.ssc.org.uk

Sport Scotland
www.sportscotland.org.uk

SPRITO Scotland
www.spritoscotland.org.uk

rounders

National Rounders Association
http://rounders.punters.co.uk

rowing

Amateur Rowing Association
www.ara-rowing.org

Boat Race
www.boatrace.co.uk

Coxless Fours
www.coxless4.com

FISA (international body)
www.fisa.org

Henley Royal Regatta
www.hrr.co.uk

International Rowing Federation
www.worldrowing.com

Ocean Rowing Society
www.oceanrowing.com

Regatta Magazine
www.regatta.rowing.org.uk

Scottish Amateur Rowing Association
www.scottish-rowing.org.uk

rugby

Clubs

Aberdeen
http://members.tripod.co.uk/aberdeenshirerfc

Avondale
www.avonvalerfc.freeserve.co.uk

Bath
www.bathrugby.co.uk

Bedford
www.bedfordrugby.co.uk

Belfast Harlequins
www.belfastharlequins.com

Bristol Rugby
www.bristolrugby.co.uk

Canterbury Crusaders
www.crusadersrugby.com

Cardiff
www.cardiffrfc.com

Coventry
www.coventryrugby.co.uk

Dungannon
www.dungannon-rugby.co.uk

Gloucester
www.kingsholm-chronicle.org.uk

Harlequins
www.quins.co.uk

Henley
www.henleyrugbyclub.org.uk

Leeds
www.leedsrugby.co.uk

Leicester
www.tigers.co.uk

Llanelli
www.scarlets.co.uk

London Irish
www.london-irish-rugby.com

London Welsh
www.london-welsh.co.uk

Manchester
www.manchester-rugby.co.uk

Moseley
www.moseleyrugby.co.uk

Neath
www.k-c.co.uk/neathrfc

Newcastle Falcons
www.newcastle-falcons.co.uk

Nothampton Saints
www.northamptonsaints.co.uk

Pontypridd
www.pontypriddrfc.co.uk

Richmond
www.richmondrugby.com

Sale
www.salerugby.com

Saracens
www.saracens.com

Shannon
www.shannonrfc.com

Swansea
www.swansearfc.co.uk

Vulcan
www.vulcanrufc.co.uk

Wakefield
www.wakefieldrugby.com

Wasps
www.wasps.co.uk

West Hartlepool
www.west-rugby.org.uk

Worcester
www.wrfc.co.uk

Clubs – Scottish

Ayr
www.sellitontheweb.com/ayrrfc

Boroughmuir
www.boroughmuirrfc.co.uk

Currie
www.currierfc.co.uk

Gala
www.galashiels.bordernet.co.uk/rugby

Glasgow Hawks
www.glasgowhawks.com

Hawick
www.hawickrfc.co.uk

Kircaldy
www.kirkcaldyrfc.co.uk

London Scottish
www.londonscottish.com

Melrose
www.melroserugby.bordernet.co.uk

Stirling County
www.stirlingcountyrfc.co.uk

Magazines & Websites

Rugby League
www.rleague.com

Rugby World
www.rugbyworld.com

Scottish Rugby directory
www.scotlandinter.net/Rugby.htm

Scrum.com
www.scrum.com

This is Rugby
www.thisis-rugby.com

Organisations

British Amateur Rugby League Association
www.barla.org.uk

Caledonia District Rugby Union
www.caledoniarugby.org.uk

International Rugby Board
www.irb.org

Rugby Football League
www.rfl.uk.com

Rugby World
www.rugbyworld.com

Scottish Rugby League
www.scotlandrugbyleague.org.uk

Scottish Rugby Union
www.sru.org.uk

Tournaments

Allied Dunbar Premiership
www.rugbyclub.co.uk

Melrose Sevens
www.melrose7s.com

Rugby League
www.rleague.com

Rugby World Cup
www.rwc99.com

Rugby World Cup 2003
www.rwc2003.com.au

Six Nations Rugby
www.sixnationsrugby.com

Super 12
www.super12rugby.com

World Sevens Series
www.irbsevens.org

sailing & boating

Boats & Equipment

Banks Sails
www.banks.co.uk

Corsair Marine
www.corsairuk.com

Garmin
www.garmin.com

International Coatings
www.yachtpaint.com

Laser
www.lasersailing.com

Moody
www.moody.co.uk

Nauquip
www.nauquip.com

Online Marine
www.on-line-marine.com

Raytheon Marine
www.raymarine.com

Saturn Sails
www.saturn-sails.co.uk

Sobstad Sailmakers
www.sobstad.co.uk

Suzuki Marine
www.suzukimarine.co.uk

Tenrag
www.tenrag.com

Yamaha Motor
www.yamaha-motor.co.uk

Clubs & Organisations

Association of Sea Training Organisations
www.asto.org.uk

British Universities Sailing Association
www.busa.co.uk

Coastguard Agency
www.coastguard.gov.uk

International Sailing Federation
www.sailing.org

Jubilee Sailing Trust
www.jst.org.uk

National Federation of Sea Schools
www.nfss.co.uk

Ocean Youth Club
www.oyc.org.uk

Royal & Sun Alliance Challenge
www.rsachallenge.com

Royal Institute of Navigation
www.rin.org.uk

Royal Yachting Association
www.rya.org.uk

RYA – Scotland
www.ryascotland.org.uk

Sail Scotland
www.sailscotland.co.uk

Scottish Sailing Institute
www.scottishsailinginstitute.com

Team Philips
www.teamphilips.com

Trinity House
www.trinityhouse.co.uk

UK Team Racing Association
www.teamracing.org

Yacht Charter Association
www.yca.co.uk

Holidays

Alba Sailing
www.alba-sailing.co.uk

Intersail
www.intersail.co.uk

Moorings
www.moorings.co.uk

Nautilus
www.nautilus-yachting.co.uk

Neilson Holidays
www.neilson.co.uk

Portway Yacht Charters
www.portwayyachtcharters.com

Sunsail Holidays
www.sunsail.com

Sunvil Activity Holidays
www.activity-holidays.co.uk

Clubs & Organisations

British Disabled Water Ski Association
www.bdwsa.org.uk

British Water Ski Federation
www.bwsf.co.uk

International Surfing Association
www.surfing.worldsport.com

International Water Ski Federation
www.iwsf.com

World Underwater Federation
www.cmas.org

Events, Regattas & Trophies

America's Cup
www.americascup.org

America's Cup Jubilee
www.amcup2001.com

BT Global Challenge
www.btchallenge.com

Champagne Mumm Admiral's Cup
www.admiralscup.org

Cowes Week
www.cowesweek.co.uk

Fastnet Race
www.fastnet.org

Hamble Week
www.hamble-week.org.uk

Millennium Round the World Yacht Race
www.millennium-rtw.co.uk

Royal & Sun Alliance Challenge
www.rsachallenge.com

Sail for Gold 2000
www.sailforgold.co.uk

Magazines & Websites

Boat Exchange
www.btx.co.uk

British Waterskiing
www.waterski-uk.com

Classic Boat Magazine
www.classicboat.co.uk

Cruising Association
www.cruising.org.uk

Dinghy Trader
www.dinghytrader.co.uk

Motor Boat & Yachting
www.ybw.co.uk

Sailing Now
www.sailingnow.com

Sailing Today
www.sailingnet.co.uk

UK Harbours Guide
www.harbours.co.uk

UK Sailing Index
www.uksail.com

Yachting & Boating World
www.ybw.co.uk

Yachting World
www.yachting-world.com

shinty

Shinty Governing Body
www.shinty.com

show jumping

Scottish Branch of the British Show Jumping Association
www.bsjascotland.co.uk

Events

Badminton Horse Trials
www.badminton-horse.co.uk

Hickstead
www.hickstead.co.uk

Horse of the Year Show
www.hoys.co.uk

Windsor Horse Trials
www.windsor-horse-trials.co.uk

Magazines & Websites

British Dressage
www.britishdressage.co.uk

Jump Magazine
www.jumpmagazine.com

Scottish Equestrian
www.thescottishequestrian.co.uk

Organisations

British Endurance Riding Association
www.british-endurance.org.uk

British Equestrian Federation
www.bef.co.uk

British Horse Driving Trials Association
www.horsedrivingtrials.co.uk

British Horse Society
www.bhs.org.uk

British Horse Trials Association
www.bhta.co.uk

British Show Jumping Association
www.bsja.co.uk

International Equestrian Federation
www.horsesport.org

Pony Club
www.pony-club.org.uk

snooker & billiards

Andy Gibbs, snooker cue maker
www.smartsnooker.com

Billiards Congress of America
www.bca-pool.com

Crucible Theatre
www.embassysnooker.com/crucible.htm

EJ Riley
www.ejriley.com

Embassy World Snooker
www.embassysnooker.com

English Pool Association
www.epa.org.uk

International Billiards & Snooker Federation
www.ibsf.org.uk

Peradon
www.peradon.co.uk

Pot Black Magazine
www.potblack.co.uk

Scottish Pool Association
www.scottishpool.com

Snooker Market
www.snookermarket.co.uk

Snooker Nations Cup
www.snooker.forceg.co.uk

Snooker Net
www.snookernet.com

Snooker Scene
www.rileyleisure.com/sscene.htm

World Snooker
www.worldsnooker.com

World Snooker Association
www.wpbsa.com

softball

International Softball Federation
www.internationalsoftball.com

sportswear & equipment

Adidas
www.adidas.com

American Golf Discount
www.americangolf.co.uk

Armour
www.armourgolf.com

Belfe
www.belfe.com

Berghaus
www.berghaus.com

Bogner
www.bogner.com

Chase Sport
www.chase-sport.co.uk

Columbia
www.columbia.com

Couloir
www.couloir.com

Crag Hoppers
www.craghoppers.com

Fat Shaft
www.wilsonsports.com/golf

Footjoy
www.footjoy.com

Golf Pride Grips
www.golfpride.com

Gryphon
www.gryphonhockey.com

Head
www.head.com

Helly Hansen
www.hellyhansen.com

Hi-Tec
www.hi-tecsports.com

Hill Billy Powered Golf Trolleys
www.hillbilly.co.uk

JJB Sports
www.jjb.co.uk

Luhta
www.luhta.com

Maxfli
www.maxfli.com

Mitre
www.mitre.com

Mizuno
www.mizunoeurope.com

Monarch
www.monarch-hockey.com

National Golf Show
www.golflive.co.uk

Nevada Bob Golf Superstores
www.nevadabob.co.uk

Nike
www.nike.com

North Face
www.thenorthface.com

O'Neill
www.oneilleurope.com

Oakley
www.oakley.com

Ping
www.pingeurope.com

Pinnacle
www.pinnaclegolf.com

Powakaddy
www.powakaddy.com

Proline
www.proline-sports.co.uk

Puma
www.puma.com

Reebok
www.europe.reebok.com

Riley Leisure
www.rileyleisure.com

Salomon
www.salomonsport.com

Schoffel
www.schoffel.com

Slazenger
www.slazenger.co.uk

Speedo
www.speedo.com

Taylor Made
www.taylormadegolf.com

TearDrop
www.teardropgolf.com

Tenson
www.tenson.com

Titleist
www.titleist.com

Topflight
www.topflight.com

Umbro
www.umbro.com

Wilson
www.wilsonsports.com

Zevo
www.zevoeurope.com

Zoppo Hockey Sticks
www.hippo-zoppo.demon.co.uk

squash

British Squash Open Championship
www.britishopensquash.com

International Racquetball Federation
www.racquetball.org

Internet Squash Federation
www.squash.org

Scottish Squash
www.scottishsquash.org

Squash Player
www.squashplayer.co.uk

Squash Rackets Association
www.sportuk.com/sra

Squash UK
www.squash.uk.com

World Squash Federation
www.squash.org/wsf

sub-aqua

Aberdeen Dive Centre
www.aberdeenwatersports.com

British Sub-Aqua Club
www.bsac.com

British Underwater Sports Association
www.busa1.freeserve.co.uk

Diver Magazine
www.divernet.com

Historical Diving Society
www.thehds.com

PADI (Professional Association of Dive Instructors)
www.padi.com

Puffin Dive Centre, Oban
www.puffin.org.uk

Scot Dive Magazine
www.mounthigh.co.uk/scotdive

Scottish Sub-Aqua Club
www.scotsac.com

Sub-Aqua Association
www.saa.org.uk

surfing

Clubs & Organisations

International Surfing Association
www.isa-wsg.org

Surfers Against Sewage
www.sas.org.uk

UK Surf Index
www.britsurf.org

Magazines & Websites

Surf Scotland
www.surf-scotland.co.uk

Surf System Forecast
www.surfsystem.co.uk

swimming

Federation Internationale de Natation Amateur (FINA)
www.fina.org

International Life Saving Federation
www.ilsf.org

Scottish Swimming Association
www.scottishswimming.com

Speedo
www.speedo.com

Swimming Teachers' Association
www.sta.co.uk

table tennis

European Table Tennis Union
www.ettu.org

International Table Tennis Federation
www.ittf.com

Scottish Table Tennis Association
www.tabletennisscotland.com

target sports

Airgun UK
www.airgun.org

Clay Shooting Magazine
www.clubclayshooting.com

Firearms News
http://firearms-news.webjump.com

Gun Trade News
www.brucepub.com

International Archery Federation
www.archery.org

Archery

European & Mediterranean Archery Union
www.emau.com

Grand National Archery Society
www.gnas.org

International Archery Federation
www.archery.org

Scottish Archery
www.scottisharchery.org.uk

Magazines & Websites

Airgun UK
www.airgun.org

Clay Shooting Magazine
www.clay-shooting.com/mainpage_.htm

Firearms News
www.firearmnews.com

Gun Trade News
www.brucepub.com/gtn

Organisations

British Shooting Sports Council
www.bssc.org.uk

Clay Pigeon Shooting Association
www.cpsa.co.uk

International Practical Shooting Confederation
www.ipsc.org

International Shooting Sport Federation
www.issf-shooting.org

Muzzle Loaders' Association of Great Britain
http://user.itl.net/~dale

National Rifle Association
www.nra.org.uk

National Smallbore Rifle Association
www.nsra.co.uk

Practical Shooting Association
www.ukpsa.co.uk

Scottish Rifle Association
www.hugon.demon.co.uk/sra

Scottish Smallbore Rifle Association
www.ssra.co.uk

Shooters' Rights Association
www.tsra.demon.co.uk

tennis

ATP Tour
www.atptour.com

AXA Cup
www.axatenniscup.com

Champions Tennis
www.championstennis.com

International Tennis Federation
www.itftennis.com

Lawn Tennis Association
www.lta.org.uk

Real Tennis
www.real-tennis.com

Royal Tennis Court, Hampton Court Palace
www.realtennis.gbrit.com

Tennis Organisation UK
www.tennis.org.uk

Tennis Scotland
www.tennisscotland.org

US Open
www.usopen.org

Wimbledon
www.wimbledon.org

WTA Tour
www.wtatour.com

tenpin bowling

Bowlers Web
www.bowlersweb.com

Bowling Tips
http://eteamz.com/bowling/instruction/tips

Bowling.org.uk
www.bowling.org.uk

British Tenpin Bowling Association
www.btba.org.uk

East Cork Superbowl
www.perksfunfair.com

Go-TenPin
www.gotenpin.co.uk

Megabowl
www.megabowl.com

Scottish Tenpin Bowling Association
www.stba.org.uk

SuperBowl
www.superbowl.co.uk

Universal Bowling Services
www.universalbowlingservices.com

Universities & Colleges Tenpin Bowling Association
www.dataweb.co.uk/uctba

volleyball

Association of Volleyball Professionals
www.volleyball.org

International Volleyball Federation
www.fivb.ch

Scottish Open Volleyball Tournament
www.sovt.info

Scottish Volleyball Association
www.scottishvolleyball.org

water skiing

Clubs & Organisations

British Disabled Water Ski Association
www.bdwsa.org.uk

British Water Ski Federation
www.bwsf.co.uk

International Water Ski Federation
www.iwsf.com

Magazines & Websites

British Waterskiing
www.waterski-uk.com

weightlifting & strength

British Amateur Weightlifters' Association
www.bawla.com

British Tug of War Association
www.tugofwar.co.uk

International Weightlifting Federation
www.iwf.net

World's Strongest Man Competition
www.strongestman.com

winter sports

Ice Hockey

English Ice Hockey Association
www.eiha.co.uk

Hockey Player Magazine
www.hockeyplayer.com

Ice Hockey UK
www.icehockeyuk.co.uk

International Ice Hockey Federation
www.iihf.com

National Hockey League
www.nhl.com

Scottish Ice Hockey Association
www.siha.net

Sekonda Ice Hockey Superleague
www.iceweb.co.uk

Ice Skating

International Skating Union
www.isu.org

Scottish Ice Skating Association
www.sisa.org.uk

Torvill & Dean (Fan Club)
http://members.aol.com/sandsonik/tanddfans.html

US Figure Skating Association
www.usfsa.org

Other

British Association for Snowsport Instructors
www.basi.org.uk

British Bobsleigh Association
www.british-bobsleigh.com

Great Britain Luge Association
www.gbla.org.uk

International Biathlon Union
www.ibu.at

International Bobsleigh & Tobogganing Federation
www.bobsleigh.com

International Luge Federation
www.fil-luge.org

Salt Lake City Winter Olympics 2002
www.saltlake2002.com

Torino Winter Olympics 2006
www.torino2006.it

Skiing & Snowboarding

Alpine World Cup Skiing news
www.irisco.net/ski

Aviemore & Cairngorms Experience
www.aviemore.co.uk

British Association of Ski Instructors
www.basi.org.uk

British Ski & Snowboard Federation
www.bssf.co.uk

Cross Country Skier Magazine
www.crosscountryskier.com

Freeze-Scotland
www.freeze-scotland.com

International Ski Federation
www.fis-ski.com

Scottish National Ski Council
www.snsc.demon.co.uk

Ski Club of Great Britain
www.skiclub.co.uk

Ski Injury
www.ski-injury.com

Ski Magazine
www.skimag.com

Ski Scotland
www.ski-scotland.com

Ski World Cup
www.skiworldcup.org

Skier & Snowboarder Magazine
www.ski.co.uk/skimag

Skinet Scotland
www.skinet.uk.com/scotland

Snowboarding Scotland
www.snowboardingscotland.net

Snowboarding UK
www.snowboardinguk.co.uk

Snowsport Highland Holidays
www.snowsport-highland.com

Snowsport Scotland
www.snsc.demon.co.uk

Tamworth Snowdome
www.snowdome.co.uk

wrestling

International Federation of Associated Wrestling Styles
www.fila-wrestling.org

International Sumo Federation
www.amateursumo.com

NWO Wrestling
www.nwowrestling.com

Scottish Wrestling Bond
www.scotwrestle.co.uk

Scottish WWF Page
www.angelfire.com/tx/andertl

WCW Wrestling
www.wcwwrestling.com

World Wrestling Entertainment
www.wwe.com

World Wrestling Federation
www.wwf.com

technology

- cable
- computers
- internet companies
- internet service providers
- magazines & websites
- search engines
- telecommunications
- web censors

cable

Blueyonder
www.blueyonder.co.uk

Cable & Wireless
www.cableandwireless.com

Cable Communications Association
www.cable.co.uk

Cable Net
www.cablenet.net

Cable Tel
www.cabletel.co.uk

Channel One TV
www.channel-onetv.co.uk

Crimptech National
www.crimptech.co.uk

Diamond Cable
www.diamond.co.uk

Inside Cable
www.inside-cable.co.uk

NTL
www.ntl.com

Power Check
www.powercheck.demon.co.uk

Telewest
www.telewest.co.uk

computers

ACER
www.acer.com

Acorn
www.acorn.co.uk

ACT
www.act.org.uk

Adobe
www.adobe.com

AMEC
www.amec.co.uk

Amiga
www.amiga.com

Amstrad
www.amstrad.com

Apple
www.apple.com

AST
www.astcomputer.com

Audiogalaxy
www.audiogalaxy.com

Broderbund Europe
www.broderbund.com

Bull
www.bull.co.uk

Canon
www.canon.com

Claris
www.claris.com

Commodore
www.commodore.net

Compaq
www.compaq.co.uk

DEC
www.dec.com

Dell
www.dell.com/uk

Demon
www.demon.net

Digital
www.digital.co.uk

Eidos
www.eidos.co.uk

Elonex
www.elonex.co.uk

Epson
www.epson.com

Ericsson
www.ericsson.com

Eudora
www.eudora.com

Fujitsu
www.fujitsu-pc.com

Gateway
www.gw2k.co.uk

Gnutella
www.gnutella.com

Hewlett Packard
www.hp.com

Hitachi
www.hds.co.uk

Honeywell
www.honeywell.com

IBM
www.ibm.com

Imesh
www.imesh.com

Intel
www.intel.co.uk

Iomega
www.iomega-europe.com

Kazaa
www.kazaa.com

Lexmark
www.lexmark.co.uk

Lotus
www.lotus.com

Mesh
www.meshplc.co.uk

Microlease
www.microlease.com

Microsoft
www.microsoft.com

MISys
www.misysinc.com

Mitel
www.mitel.com

Morpheus
www.morpheus.com

MP3 Café
www.mp3cafe.net

MP3 Yes
www.mp3yes.com

NEC
www.nec-global.com

Netcom
www.netcom.net.uk

Nintendo
www.nintendodirect.com

Nokia
www.nokia.com

Novell
www.novell.com

Olivetti
www.olivetti.com

Open Universal Software
www.universal.com

Oracle
www.oracle.co.uk

Packard Bell
www.packardbell.com

Palm
www.palm.com

Peoplesound
www.peoplesound.com

Playstation
www.playstation-europe.com

Psion
www.psion.com

Racal
www.racalworld.com

Real
www.real.com

Sibelius (Music Software)
www.sibelius.com

Siemens
www.siemens.com

Silicon Graphics
www.sgi.com

Sony
www.sony.com

Sunsoft
www.sunsoft.com

Texas Instruments
www.ti.com

Tiny
www.tiny.com/uk

Toshiba
www.toshiba.com

Tulip
www.tulip.com

Unisys
www.unisys.com

Universal
www.universal.com

Viglen
www.viglen.co.uk

Vitech
www.vitech.net

Wang
www.wang.com

Widget Software
www.widgetsoftware.com

Winamp
www.winamp.com

internet companies

Cisco
www.cisco.com

Freeserve
www.freeserve.net

Jellyworks
www.jellyworks.com

Morse
www.morse.com

Netbenefit
www.netbenefit.com

NicNames
www.nicnames.co.uk

internet service providers

Aardvaak
www.aardvaak.co.uk

Abel
www.abel.co.uk

Abel Gratis
www.abelgratis.com

Activeware
www.activeware.co.uk

ADSL Internet Access
www.adslinternetaccess.co.uk

AOL
www.aol.co.uk

Barclays
www.is.barclays.co.uk

Beeb Net (from the BBC)
www.beeb.net

Beebware
www.beebware.com/internet

Bigwig
www.bigwig.net

Blueyonder
www.blueyonder.co.uk

Breathe
www.breathe.com

BT Click
www.btclick.com

BT Internet
www.btinternet.com

BT Openworld
www.btopenworld.com

Cable & Wireless
www.cwcom.net

Channel One
www.channel-one.co.uk

Claranet
www.uk.clara.net

Colloquium
www.colloquium.co.uk

Demon
www.demon.net

Direct Connection
www.dircon.net

EasyNet
www.easynetdial.co.uk

Eclipse
www.eclipse.net.uk

Ecosse
www.ecossetel.co.uk

Egg
www.egg.com

Enterprise
www.enterprise.net

Fish
www.fish.co.uk

Free UK
www.freeuk.com

Free4All
www.free4all.co.uk

Freebie List (Internet access directory)
www.freebielist.com/isp.htm

FreeNet
www.freenet.co.uk

Freenetname
www.freenetname.co.uk

Freeserve
www.freeserve.co.uk

Freewire
www.freewire.net

FreeZone
www.freezone.co.uk

Gael
www.gael-net.co.uk

Global
www.global.net.uk

IberPass (International Internet access)
www.iberpass.com

Internet for Business
www.ifb.net

LineOne
www.lineone.net

Lycos
www.lycos.com

Madasafish
www.madasafish.com

Net4Nowt (Internet access directory)
www.net4nowt.com

NetDirect
www.netdirect.net.uk

Netscape
www.netscape.com

Netscape
www.netscape.co.uk

Nildram
www.nildram.net

NTL
www.ntl.com

One Tel
www.onetel.co.uk

Pipemedia
www.pipemedia.co.uk

Prestel
www.prestel.co.uk

Scotland Online
www.scotlandonline.com

The Scottish Webring
www.albee.org/scotland

Supanet
www.supanet.com

Talk 21
www.talk21.com

TescoNet
www.tesco.net

Tiny
www.tinyonline.net

Tiscali
www.tiscali.co.uk

Tiscali
www.tiscali.co.uk

UK ISP Directory
www.uk-isp-directory.co.uk

UK Online
www.ukonline.co.uk

Virgin
www.virgin.net

Virtual Glasgow
www.virtualglasgow.com

WH Smith
www.whsmith.co.uk

X-Stream
www.x-stream.com

Yahoo!
www.yahoo.co.uk

magazines & websites

Computer Games

Acorn Gaming
www.acorn-gaming.org.uk

Computer & Video Games
www.game-online.com

Future Gamer
www.futureview.co.th

GameSpot UK
www.gamespot.co.uk/pcgw

Lara Croft
www.laracroft.com

Total Games
www.totalgames.net

Computers

Bluetooth
www.bluetooth.com

British Computer Society
www.bcs.org.uk

Computer Shopper
www.compshopper.co.uk

Computer Weekly
www.computerweekly.co.uk

Computeractive
www.computeractive.co.uk

Computing
www.vnunet.com

IT Weekly
www.itweek.co.uk

MacUser
www.macuser.co.uk

Macworld
www.macworld.com

Net
www.thenetmag.co.uk

PC Advisor
www.pcadvisor.co.uk

PC Plus
www.pcplus.co.uk

PC Zone OnLine
www.pczone.co.uk

search engines

About
www.about.com

Alta Vista
www.altavista.co.uk

Ask Jeeves
www.askjeeves.co.uk

DejaNews
www.dejanews.com

Direct Hit
www.directhit.com

Dogpile
www.dogpile.com

Electric Library
www.elibrary.com

Excite
www.excite.co.uk

Fish4
www.fish4.co.uk

Galaxy
http://galaxy.einet.net

Go To
www.go2.com

Google
www.google.com

HotBot
www.hotbot.com

Infoseek
www.infoseek.co.uk

LookSmart
www.looksmart.com

Lycos
www.lycos.co.uk

Maxisearch
www.maxisearch.com

Metacrawler
www.metacrawler.com

Mirago
www.mirago.co.uk

MSN
www.msn.co.uk

Northern Light
www.nlsearch.com

Open Text Index
www.opentext.com

Scottish Borders
www.scottishborders.com

Search UK
www.searchuk.co.uk

UK Directory
www.ukdirectory.co.uk

UK Max
www.ukmax.co.uk

UK Online
www.ukonline.co.uk

UK Plus
www.ukplus.co.uk

WebCrawler
www.webcrawler.com

Yahoo!
www.yahoo.co.uk

telecommunications

Alcatel
www.alcatel.com

Alpha Telecom
www.alphatelecom.com

Breathe
www.breathe.com

BT
www.bt.com

BT Pagers
www.btmobility.com

Cable & Wireless
www.cwcom.co.uk

Com One
www.com1.fr/uk

Dolphin
www.dolphin-telecom.co.uk

Energis
www.energis.co.uk

Ericsson
www.ericsson.co.uk

Esprit
www.esprittelecom.com

Eurobell
www.eurobell.com

First Telecom
www.first-telecom.com

Hagenuk
www.hagenuk.de

Maxon
www.maxon.co.uk

MCI Worldcom
www.wcom.co.uk

Mercury
www.mercury.co.uk

Mondial
www.mondial-gsm.com

Motorola
www.mot.com

NEC
www.euronec.com

Nokia
www.nokia.co.uk

Nortel
www.nortel.com

Norweb
www.norwebcomms.com

Nynex
www.nynex.co.uk

O2
www.o2.co.uk

Odyssey
www.odysseycorp.co.uk

OFTEL
www.oftel.gov.uk

One.Tel UK
www.onetel.co.uk

Orange
www.orange.co.uk

Panasonic
www.mcuk.panasonic.co.uk

Philips
www.pcc.philips.com

Planet Talk
www.planet-talk.co.uk

Sagem
www.sagem.com

Samsung
www.samsungelectronics.com

Siemens
www.siemens.co.uk

Sony
www.sony-europe.com/cons/pce

T-Mobile
www.t-mobile.co.uk

Telecom UK
www.telecom.co.uk

TeleWest
www.telewest.co.uk

Torch
www.torch.co.uk

Virgin
www.virgin.com/mobile

Vizzavi
www.vizzavi.co.uk

Vodafone
www.vodafone.co.uk

World Online
www.worldonline.com

web censors

Cyber Patrol
www.cyberpatrol.com

Cybersnoop
www.cyber-snoop.com

Net Nanny
www.netnanny.com

Surf on the Safe Side
www.surfonthesafeside.com

X-Stop
www.xstop.com

Xcheck
www.xcheck.net

travel

- accommodation
- airlines
- airports
- bus & coach companies
- camping/caravan sites
- car hire
- ferries
- hotels
- magazines & websites
- parking
- professional bodies & trade associations
- resorts
- tourist boards
- trains
- travel agents, tour operators & cruises

accommodation

Bed & Breakfast

Accomodate Scotland
www.scotland2000.com/accom

B&B Directory
www.bedandbreakfast-directory.co.uk

B&B Nationwide
www.bedandbreakfastnationwide.com

B&B Scotland
www.b-and-b-scotland.co.uk

B&B UK
www.bedandbreakfasts-uk.co.uk

Scotland Accomodation
www.scotlandaccom.co.uk

Visit Us
www.visitus.co.uk

Guest Houses & Hotels

Accommodation in Scotland
www.accommodation-in-scotland.co.uk

Directory of UK Hotels
www.directoryofukhotels.co.uk/scotland-map.html

Scotlands Website
www.scotlandswebsite.co.uk/hotel

Scottish Accommodations Index
www.scottishaccommodationindex.com

Scottish Hotel Guide
www.scottishguide.co.uk

Vacations Scotland
www.vacations-scotland.co.uk

Webreaks
www.webreaks.co.uk/scotland

Hostels

Celtic Budget Accommodation Ireland
www.celtic-accommodation.com

International Youth Hostels Association
www.iyha.org

Irish Youth Hostel Association
www.irelandyha.org

Scottish Youth Hostels Association
www.syha.org.uk

SCS International – Budget travel in Scotland
www.scsinternational.co.uk

Youth Hostels Association (England & Wales)
www.yha.org.uk

Hotel Booking Services

Bookhotels (UK only)
www.bookhotels.co.uk

Bookings
www.bookings.org

Eurohotels (mainly Germany & Italy)
www.eurohotels.com

Hotel Book
www.hotelbook.com

Hotels Chains Online
http://hotel-chains-online.com

Hotelworld
www.hotelworld.com

Quikbook (US only)
www.quikbook.com

Sinohotel (China only)
www.sinohotel.com

Hotels – Scottish

Airds Hotel (Argyll)
www.airds-hotel.com

Ardsheal House (Highland)
www.ardsheal.co.uk

Auchendean Lodge (Speyside)
www.auchendean.com

Balbirnie House Hotel (Fife)
www.balbirnie.co.uk

Ballathie House Hotel (Perthshire)
www.ballathiehousehotel.com

Boath House (Morayshire)
www.boath-house.demon.co.uk

The Ceilidh Place (Highland)
www.theceilidhplace.com

Clifton House (Morayshire)
www.cliftonhousehotel.co.uk

Craigellachie Hotel (Speyside)
www.craigellachie.com

Craigsanquhar (Fife)
www.craigsanquhar.com

Creggans Inn (Argyll)
www.creggans-inn.co.uk

Crieff Hydro
www.crieffhydro.com

Cringletie House Hotel (Borders)
www.cringletie.com

Cromlix House (Stirling)
www.cromlixhouse.com

The Cross (Highland)
www.thecross.co.uk

Culloden House (Inverness)
www.cullodenhouse.co.uk

Gleneagles Hotel (Perthshire)
www.gleneagles.com

Greywalls (East Lothian)
www.greywalls.co.uk

Hilton Dunkeld House (Perthshire)
www.hiltondunkeldhouse.co.uk

Inverlochy Castle (Highland)
www.inverlochy.co.uk

Isle of Eriska Hotel (Argyll)
www.eriska-hotel.co.uk

Kinfauns Castle (Perthshire)
www.kinfaunscastle.co.uk

Kinloch House (Perthshire)
www.kinlochhouse.com

Kinnaird Estate (Perthshire)
www.kinnairdestate.com

Loch Melfort Hotel (Argyll)
www.lochmelfort.co.uk

Marcliffe at Pitfodels Hotel (Aberdeenshire)
www.marcliffe.com

Maryculter House Hotel (Aberdeenshire)
www.maryculterhousehotel.co.uk

Muckrach Lodge (Speyside)
www.muckrach.co.uk

Old Course Hotel (Fife)
www.oldcoursehotel.co.uk

The Peat Inn (Fife)
www.thepeatinn.co.uk

Peebles Hydro
www.peebleshotelhydro.co.uk

Roman Camp Hotel (Trossachs)
www.roman-camp-hotel.co.uk

Rufflets Hotel (Fife)
www.rufflets.co.uk

Rusacks Hotel (Fife)
www.macdonald-hotels.co.uk

Scarista House (Harris)
www.scaristahouse.com

Skibo Castle (Ross-shire)
www.carnegieclub.co.uk

Taychreggan Hotel (Argyll)
www.taychregganhotel.co.uk

The Three Chimneys (Skye)
www.threechimneys.co.uk

Turnberry Hotel (Ayrshire)
www.turnberry.co.uk

Hotels – Edinburgh

The Balmoral
www.thebalmoralhotel.com

The Bonham
www.thebonham.com

The Caledonian Hilton
www.hilton.co.uk

Channings Hotel
www.channings.co.uk

The George Intercontinental
www.edinburgh.interconti.com

Malmaison
www.malmaison.com

The Point Hotel
www.point-hotel.co.uk

Prestonfield House Hotel
www.prestonfieldhouse.com

Rick's Hotel
www.ricksedinburgh.co.uk

The Roxburghe
www.macdonald-hotels.co.uk

The Scotsman Hotel
www.thescotsmanhotel.co.uk

Hotels – Glasgow

Arthouse Hotel
www.arthousehotel.com

The Brunswick
www.brunswickhotel.info

Carlton George
www.carlton.nl

Groucho St Judes
www.saintjudes.com

Inn on the Green
www.theinnonthegreen.co.uk

Langs
www.langshotels.co.uk

Malmaison
www.malmaison.com

Millennium Hotel
www.millenniumhotels.com

One Devonshire Gardens
www.onedevonshiregardens.com

Piper's Tryst
www.thepipingcentre.co.uk/hotel.html

Quality Central Hotel
www.choicehotels.com

International Hotel Chains

Choice Hotels
www.choicehotels.com

Flynn Hotels
http://flynnhotels.com

Four Seasons
www.fourseasons.com

Grand Heritage Hotels
www.grandheritage.com

Great Southern Hotels
www.gsh.ie

Hilton
www.hilton.com

Holiday Inn
www.holidayinn-ireland.com

Ibis Hotels
www.ibishotel.com

Intercontinental Hotels & Resorts
www.intercontinental.com

Jury's Hotels
www.jurys.com

Le Meridien
www.lemeridien-hotels.com

Mandarin Oriental
www.mandarin-oriental.com

Marriott Hotels
www.marriott.com

Novotel
www.novotel.com

Oberoi
www.oberoihotels.com

Posthouse Hotels
www.posthouse-hotels.com

Queens Moat Houses
www.queensmoat.com

Radisson
www.radisson.com

Raffles Singapore
www.raffles.com

Red Carnation
www.redcarnationhotels.com

Regal
www.regal-hotels.com

Regency Hotels
www.regencyhotels.com

Ritz
www.theritzhotel.co.uk

Savoy
www.savoy-group.co.uk

Sol Melia
www.solmelia.com

Self-Catering Europe

Escape Overseas
www.escapeoverseas.com

French Connections
www.frenchconnections.co.uk

Holiday Leaders
www.holidayleaders.com

Individual Traveller
www.indiv-travellers.com

International Chapters Villa Rental
www.villa-rentals.com

Simply Travel
www.simplytravel.co.uk

Spanish Web
www.spanish-web.com

Villa Holiday
www.villa-holiday.co.uk

Villa Vacation
www.villa-vacation.com

Self-Catering Scottish

Aberfeldy Cottages
www.aberfeldycottages.co.uk

Achan Drilleach
www.selfcateringhighland.co.uk

Ardnacross
www.ardnacross.com

Ardoch Cottage
www.holiday-cottage-scotland.co.uk/index.htm

Cottage & Castles
www.cottages-and-castles.co.uk

Cottage Guide
www.cottageguide.co.uk

Discover Scotland
www.discoverscotland.net

Drum Croy Lodges
www.highland-lodges.com

Glenaros Farm Cottages
www.glenaros.co.uk

Good Cottage Guide
www.goodcottageguide.com/scotland/
map.html

Large Holiday Houses
www.lhhscotland.com

Loch Lomond Holiday Park
www.lochlomond-lodges.co.uk

Mackays Agency
www.mackays-scotland.co.uk

Preferred Places
www.preferredplaces.co.uk

Scottish Holiday Cottages
www.scottish-holiday-cottages.co.uk

Seaside Cottages
www.seasidecottages.co.uk/scotland.htm

Stronvar House
www.stronvar.co.uk

Self-Catering UK

Beautiful Devon
www.beautiful-devon.co.uk/
accommodation.htm

Come Stay with Us
www.comestaywithus.com

Cumbrian Cottages
www.cumbrian-cottages.co.uk

Heart of the Lakes
www.heartofthelakes.co.uk

Hideaways
www.hideaways.co.uk

Holidaybank
www.holidaybank.co.uk

Lake Lovers
www.lakelovers.co.uk

Preferred Places
www.preferredplaces.co.uk

Rural Index
www.ruralindex.net/selfcatering.html

Somerset Cottages
www.somersetcottages.com

Walking Britain
www.walkingbritain.co.uk/accommodation/l_selfcater.shtml

airlines

AB Airlines
www.abairlines.com

AccessAir
www.accessair.com

Aer Arann
www.aerarann.ie

Aer Lingus
www.aerlingus.ie

Aeroflot
www.aeroflot.org

Aerolineas Argentinas
www.aerolineas.com.ar

Aeromexico
www.aeromexico.com/ingles

Aeroperu Airlines
www.rcp.net.pe/AEROPERU/ingles/indice.htm

Air 2000
www.air2000.co.uk

Air Afrique
www.airafrique.com

Air ALM
www.airalm.com

Air Aruba
www.interknowledge.com/air-aruba

Air Asia
www.airasia.com

Air Atlanta Icelandic
www.atlanta.is

Air Baltic
www.airbaltic.lv

Air Berlin
www.airberlin.com

Air Canada
www.aircanada.ca

Air Caribbean
www.aircaribbean.com

Air China
www.airchina.u-net.com

Air Fiji
www.airfiji.net

Air France
www.airfrance.co.uk

Air Georgia
www.air-georgia.com

Air India
www.airindia.com

Air Jamaica
www.airjamaica.com

Air Kazakhstan
www.airkaz.com

Air Lithuania
www.airlithuania.lt

Air Madagascar
www.africaonline.co.ke/airmalawi

Air Malawi
www.airmalawi.net

Air Malta
www.airmalta.com

Air Mauritius
www.airmauritius.com

Air Moldova
www.ami.md

Air Namibia
www.airnamibia.com.na

Air New Zealand
www.airnz.com

Air Philippines
www.airphilippines.com

Air Portugal
www.tap-airportugal.pt

Air Seychelles
www.airseychelles.it

Air Tahiti
www.airtahiti-nui.com

Air UK
www.airuk.co.uk

Air Zimbabwe
www.airzimbabwe.com

Airlanka
www.airlanka.com

Alaska Airlines
www.alaska-air.com

Alitalia
www.alitalia.it

Alitalia
www.alitalia.co.uk

All Nippon Airways
www.ana.co.uk

American Airlines
www.americanair.com

Ana Europe
www.ana-europe.com

Ansett
www.ansett.com

Ariana Afghan Airlines
www.tzetze.simplenet.com/sam/srfgafg.htm

Asiana Airlines
www.asiana.co.kr/english

Atlas Air
www.atlasair.com

Austrian Airlines
www.aua.com

Avro
www.avro.co.uk

Azzurra Airlines
www.azzurraair.it

Bahamasair
www.bahamasair.com

Balkan Airlines
www.balkan.com

Bhoja Air
www.bhojaair.com.pk

BMI Baby
www.bmibaby.com

BMI British Midland
www.flybmi.com

Bouraq Indonesia Airlines
www.bouraq.com

Braathens
www.maviation.se

Britannia
www.britanniaairways.com

British Airways
www.british-airways.com

British European
www.british-european.com

British Midland
www.britishmidland.co.uk

British World Airlines
www.british-world.co.uk

Brussels Airlines
www.brussels-airlines.com

Buzz
www.buzzaway.com

BWIA
www.bwiacaribbean.com

BWIA
www.bwee.com

Cameroon Airlines
www.airnautic.fr/camair.htm

Cape Air
www.flycapeair.com

Cathay Pacific
www.cathaypacific.com

Cayman Airways
www.caymanairways.com

China Airlines
www.china-airlines.com

Continental
www.flycontinental.com

Corsair
www.corsair-int.com

Croatia Airlines
www.ctn.tel.hr/ctn

Crossair
www.crossair.ch

Cubana Airlines
www.cubana.cu

Cyprus Airways
www.cyprusair.com

Cyprus Turkish Airlines
www.kthy.net

Czech Airlines
www.csa.cz/en

Delta
www.delta-air.com

Dragon Air
www.dragonair.com

Eastern Airways
www.easternairways.com

EasyJet
www.easyjet.com

El Al
www.elal.co.il/worldwide/uk

Emirates (UAE)
www.ekgroup.com

EVA Air
www.evaair.com/html/global/english/
gb_en_home

EVA Air
www.evaair.com.tw/english

Finnair
www.finnair.co.uk

Garuda Indonesia
www.garudausa.com

Ghana Airways
www.ghana-airways.com

Go
www.go-fly.com

Greek Airlines
www.cronus.gr

Greenlandair
www.greenland-guide.dk/gla

Gujarat Airways
www.gujaratairways.com

Gulf Air
www.gulfairco.com

Guyana Airways
www.turq.com/guyana/guyanair.html

Hapag-Lloyd Airlines
www.hapag-lloyd.com

Hawaiian Airlines
www.hawaiianair.com

Iberia
www.iberia.com

Icelandair
www.icelandair.co.uk

Indian Airlines
http://indian-airlines.nic.in

Japan Airlines
www.jal.co.jp

JAS Japan Air System
www.jas.co.jp

Jersey European Airways
www.jea.co.uk

Kenya Airways
www.kenyaairways.co.uk

Kiss Air
www.kissair.com

KLM
www.klm.uk.com

Kuwait Airways
www.travelfirst.com/sub/kuwaitair

Lauda Air
www.laudaair.com

Loganair
www.loganair.co.uk

LOT Polish Airlines
www.lot.com

Lufthansa
www.lufthansa.co.uk

Lynx Air International
www.lynxair.com

Malaysia Air
www.malaysiaair.com

Malaysia Airlines
www.malaysiaairlines.com.my

Malev
www.malev.hu

Mandarin Airlines
www.mandarinair.com/english

Manx Airlines
www.manx-airlines.com

Martin Air
www.martinairusa.com

Middle Eastern Airlines
www.mea.com.lb

Monarch
www.monarch-airlines.com

North West Airlines
www.nwa.com

Pakistan International
www.piac.com

Pan Am
www.panam.org

Philippine Airlines
www.philippineair.com

Polynesian Airlines
www.polynesianairlines.co.nz

Portugália Airlines
www.pga.pt/uk

Qantas
www.qantas.com.au

Qatar Airways
www.qatarairways.com

Royal Air Maroc
www.royalairmaroc.com/ver_en

Royal Brunei
www.bruneiair.com

Royal Jordanian Airlines
www.rja.com.jo

Royal Nepal Airlines
www.royalnepal.com

Ryanair
www.ryanair.com

Sabena
www.sabena.com

SAS Scandanavian Airlines
www.flysas.co.uk

Saudi Arabian Airlines
www.saudiarabian-airlines.com

Scandanavian Airlines
www.flysas.co.uk

ScotAirways
www.scotairways.co.uk

Singapore Airlines
www.singaporeair.com

SkyKing Airlines
www.skykingairlines.com

Solomon Airlines
www.pacificislands.com/airlines/solomon.html

South African Airways
www.saa.co.za

SriLankan Airlines
www.lanka.net/airlanka

Star Alliance
www.star-alliance.com

Surinam Airways
www.cqlink.sr/slm

Swiftair
www.swiftair.com

Swissair
www.swissair.ch

Tahiti Airlines
www.airtahitinui-usa.com

Tasmania Airlines
www.tasair.com.au

Thai Airways
www.thaiair.com

Turkish Airlines
www.turkishairlines.com

TWA
www.twa.com

Tyrolean Airways
www.tyrolean.at

Ukraine International Airlines
www.uia.ukrpack.net

United Airlines
www.ual.com

United Airlines Belgium
www.ual.be

Uzbekistan Airways
www.uzbekistanairways.nl

VARIG Brazil
www.varig.com.br/english

Vietnam Airlines
www.vietnamair.com.vn

Virgin Airways
www.fly.virgin.com

Virgin Atlantic
www.fly.virgin.com/atlantic

World Airways
www.worldair.com

Yemen Airways
http://home.earthlink.net/~yemenair

Yugoslav Airlines JAT
www.jat.com

Zimbabwe Express Airlines
www.zimsurf.co.zw/zex

airports

UK

Aberdeen Airport
www.baa.co.uk/main/airports/aberdeen

Belfast City Airport
www.belfastcityairport.com

Belfast International
www.bial.co.uk

Birmingham
www.bhx.co.uk

Bristol International Airport
www.bristolairport.co.uk

British Airports Authority
www.baa.co.uk

British International Airports
www.bia.co.uk

Dundee
www.dundeecity.gov.uk/a-z/a005.htm

Edinburgh
www.baa.co.uk/main/airports/edinburgh

Exeter
www.eclipse.co.uk/exeterair

Gatwick
www.gatwickairport.co.uk

Glasgow
www.baa.co.uk/main/airports/glasgow

Glasgow Prestwick International
www.glasgow.pwk.com

Heathrow
www.heathrow.co.uk

Highland & Islands Airports
www.hial.co.uk

Inverness
www.hial.co.uk/inverness-airport.html

Isle of Man
www.iom-airport.com

Knock International Airport
www.knockinternationalairport.ie

Leeds Bradford International Airport
www.lbia.co.uk

Liverpool
www.livairport.com

London City
www.londoncityairport.com

London Luton Airport
www.london-luton.com

Manchester
www.manairport.co.uk

Newcastle International Airport
www.newcastle-airport.co.uk

Southampton Airport
www.baa.co.uk/main/airports/southampton

Stansted
www.baa.co.uk/stansted

Foreign

Aer Rianta
www.aer-rianta.ie

Albuquerque
www.cabq.gov/airport/index.html

Alicante
www.aena.es

Amsterdam
www.schiphol.nl

Atlanta
www.atlanta-airport.com

Auckland
www.auckland-airport.co.nz

Baltimore Washington
http://bwiairport.com

Bangkok
www.airportthai.or.th

Barcelona
www.aena.es/ae/bcn/homepage.htm

Beijing
www.bcia.com.cn

Berlin
www.berlin-airport.de

Boston
www.massport.com

Brisbane
www.brisbaneairport.com.au

Brussels
www.brusselsairport.be

Calgary
www.calgaryairport.com

Cape Town
www.airports.co.za

Charlotte/Douglas
www.charlotteairport.com

Chicago
www.ohare.com

Cincinnati
www.cvgairport.com

Cologne
www.airport-cgn.de

Copenhagen
www.cph.dk

Dallas Fort Worth
www.dfwairport.com

Dehli
www.delhiairport.com

Denver
www.flydenver.com

Detroit
www.metroairport.com

Donegal International Airport
www.donegalairport.ie

Dubai
www.dubaiairport.com

Dublin International Airport
www.dublin-airport.com

Dusseldorf
www.duesseldorf-international.de

Faro
www.ana-aeroportos.pt

Frankfurt
www.frankfurt-airport.de

Geneva
www.gva.ch/en

Gothenburg
www.lfv.se/scaa/airport/landvetter

Hannover
www.flughafen.hannover.de

Helsinki
www.ilmailulaitos.com/english/lentoase/helvan

Hong Kong
www.hkairport.com

Honolulu
www.hawaii.gov/dot/airports/visitor_info.htm

Ibiza
www.aena.es

Istanbul
www.dhmiata.gov.tr

Johannesburg
www.airports.co.za

Kansas
www.kcairports.com

Kuala Lumpur
www.klia.com.my/klia

Madrid
www.aena.es/ae/mad/homepage.htm

Marseille
www.marseille.aeroport.fr

Melbourne
www.melbourne-airport.com.au

Memphis
www.mscaa.com

Mexico City
www.asa.gob.mx/grupo_aicm/aicm_set.html

Milan
www.sea-aeroportimilano.it

Montreal
www.admtl.com

Moscow
www.sheremetyevo-airport.ru

Munich
www.munich-airport.de

Nashville
www.nashintl.com

New York
www.panynj.gov

Newark
www.newarkairport.com

Nice
www.nice.aeroport.fr

Orlando
http://fcn.state.fl.us/goaa

Osaka
www.kiac.co.jp

Paris
www.adp.fr

Perth
www.perthairport.com

Pusan
www.kimhae-airport.co.kr

Rome
www.adr.it

San Diego
www.portofsandiego.org/sandiego_airport/index.html

San Francisco
www.sfoairport.com

Seattle
www.portseattle.org

Seoul
www.kimpo-airport.co.kr

Shannon Airport
www.shannonairport.com

Singapore
www.changi.airport.com.sg

Stockholm
www.arlanda.com

Stuttgart
www.stuttgart-airport.de

Sydney
www.sydneyairport.com.au

Taipei
www.cksairport.gov.tw

Tampa
www.tampaairport.com

Tokyo
www.narita-airport.or.jp/airport

Toronto
www.gtaa.com

Vancouver
www.yvr.ca

Venice
www.veniceairport.it

Vienna
www.viennaairport.com

Washington (Dulles)
www.mwaa.com

Zurich
www.zurich-airport.com

bus & coach companies

Airbus
www.airbus.co.uk

Airlinks
www.airlinks.co.uk

Arriva
www.arriva.co.uk

Big Bus Tours
www.bigbus.co.uk

Blue Line
www.blueline.demon.co.uk

Bus Web
www.busweb.co.uk

Citylink
www.citylink.co.uk

Citylink
www.citylink.co.uk

Clarkes of London
www.clarkes.co.uk

Coach Hire directory
www.coach-hire.uk.com

Eurolines
www.eurolines.co.uk

First Group
www.firstgroup.com

First Group
www.firstgroup.com

GB Bus Timetable
www.xephos.com/GBBTT

Go Ahead
www.go-ahead.com

Go By Coach
www.gobycoach.com

Green Line
www.greenline.co.uk

London Transport
www.londontransport.co.uk

Lothian Buses
www.lothianbuses.co.uk

National Express
www.nationalexpress.co.uk

Nicolsons (Isle of Skye)
www.gael-net.co.uk/nicolsons/index.html

Oxford Bus
www.oxfordbus.co.uk

Skye-Ways
www.gael-net.co.uk/skyeways/index.html

Speedlink
www.speedlink.co.uk

Stagecoach
www.stagecoachholdings.com

Stagecoach
www.stagecoachbus.com

Yellow Buses
www.yellowbuses.co.uk

camping/caravan sites

British Holiday & Home Parks Association
www.ukparks.co.uk

Camping & Caravanning Club
www.campingandcaravanningclub.co.uk

Camping Club Europe
www.campingclubeurope.com

Caravan & Camping Ireland
www.camping-ireland.ie

Caravan Club
www.caravanclub.co.uk

Caravan Sitefinder
www.caravan-sitefinder.co.uk

The Caravanning Site
www.thecaravanningsite.co.uk

car hire

1car1
www.1car1.com

A G Lees (Galashiels)
www.aglees-cars.com

Alamo
www.alamo.com

Alamo
www.goalamo.com

Alldrive 4x4
www.scottish-towns.co.uk/perthshire/auchterarder/alldrive/index.html

AMK Self Drive
www.amkselfdrive.co.uk

Avis
www.avis.co.uk

BCR British Car Rental
www.bcvr.co.uk

British Vehicle Rental Association
www.bbi.co.uk/bvrla

Budget
www.budget-rent-a-car.co.uk

Clarkson Glasgow
www.carhirescotland.com

Direct Car Hire
www.direct-car-hire.co.uk

Disabled Car Hire Companies
www.mobility-unit.dft.gov.uk/mavis/fact19.htm

Easy Car
www.easycar.com

Easy-autos
www.easyautos.co.uk

Enterprise
www.erac.com

Eurodrive Car Rentals
www.eurodrive.com

Europcar
www.europcar.com

Guy Salmon
www.guysalmon.co.uk

Hertz
www.hertz.co.uk

Holiday Autos
www.holidayautos.com

Kenning
www.kenning.co.uk

Motorhome Rentals
http://freespace.virgin.net/montana.motorhomes

National
www.nationalcar-europe.com

Portree Coachworks
www.portreecoachworks.co.uk

Practical Car & Van Rental
www.practical.co.uk

Scotland Car Hire
www.scotland-carhire.co.uk

Thrifty
www.thrifty.co.uk

U-Drive
www.udrive.co.uk

Woods Car Rental
www.woods.co.uk

ferries

A Ferry To
www.aferry.to

Brittany
www.brittany-ferries.com

Calais
www.calais-port.com

Calmac
www.calmac.co.uk

Channel Hoppers
www.channelhoppers.com

Clyde SPT Ferries
www.spt.co.uk/Travel/ferries.html

Color Line
www.colorline.com

Condor
www.condorferries.co.uk

DFDS Seaways
www.dfdsseaways.co.uk

Emeraude Lines
www.emeraudelines.com

Glenelg – Kylrhea
www.skyeferry.co.uk

Hover Travel
www.hovertravel.co.uk

Hoverspeed
www.hoverspeed.co.uk

Irish Ferries
www.irishferries.ie

Island Ferries Teo
www.aranislandferries.com

Northlink Ferries
www.northlinkferries.co.uk

P & O European
www.poef.com

P & O Scottish
www.poscottishferries.co.uk

P & O Stena Line
www.posl.com

P & O North Sea
www.ponsf.com

Red Funnel
www.redfunnel.co.uk

Scandinavian Seaways
www.scansea.com

Sea France
www.seafrance.co.uk

Seacat
www.steam-packet.com

Seaview
www.seaview.co.uk/ferries

Stena
www.stenaline.co.uk

Swansea Cork Ferries
www.commerce.ie/cs/scf

Wightlink
www.wightlink.co.uk

hotels

Accor
www.accor.com/accor/english

British Hotel Reservation Centre
www.bhrs.co.uk

Choice
www.hotelchoice.com

Crowne Plaza
www.crowneplaza.com

Dan
www.danhotels.co.il

De Vere
www.devereonline.co.uk

Elounda Beach
www.eloundabeach.gr

Forte & Le Meridien
www.forte-hotels.com

Four Seasons
www.fourseasons.com

Gleneagles
www.gleneagles.com

Goodnight Inn
www.thegoodnightinn.com

Grand Heritage
www.grandheritage.com

Hilton
www.hilton.com

Holiday Inn
www.holiday-inn.com

Intercontinental
www.interconti.com

Lanesborough
www.lanesborough.co.uk

Late Rooms.com
www.laterooms.com

Le Meridien
www.lemeridien-hotels.com

Mandarin Oriental
www.mandarin-oriental.com

Marriott Hotels
www.marriott.com

McDonald
www.mcdonaldhotels.co.uk

MKI Hotels
www.mki.ltd.uk

Novotel
www.novotel.com

Oberoi
www.oberoihotels.com

Orient Express
www.orient-expresshotels.com

Posthouse
www.posthousehotels.com

Queens Moat
www.queensmoat.com

Radisson
www.radisson.com

Raffles Singapore
www.raffles.com

Red Carnation
www.redcarnationhotels.com

Regal
www.regal-hotels.com

Relais & Chateaux
www.relaischateaux.fr

Ritz
www.theritzhotel.co.uk

Savoy
www.savoy-group.co.uk

Shangri-la
www.shangri-la.com

Sheraton
www.sheraton.com

Stakis
www.stakis.co.uk

Swallow
www.swallowhotels.com

Thistle
www.thistle.co.uk

Travel Inns
www.travelinn.co.uk

Travelodge
www.travelodge.co.uk

Virgin
www.virginhotels.com

Wyndham
www.mki.ltd.uk/wyndham.htm

magazines & websites

Condé Nast Traveller
www.cntraveller.co.uk

Fodor's Guide
www.fodors.com

Go By Coach
www.gobycoach.com

Good Holiday Guide
www.goodholidayguide.com

Good Ski Guide
www.goodskiguide.com

Holiday Which?
www.which.net/holiday

Lonely Planet
www.lonelyplanet.com

National Geographic
www.nationalgeographic.com

Public Transport Information
www.pti.org.uk

Rough Guides
www.roughguides.com

UK Street Map
www.streetmap.co.uk

Virgin Net Travel
www.virgin.net/travel

International

Backpackers Australia
www.backpackers.com.au/bpaus.htm

Condé Nast Traveller
www.cntraveller.co.uk

Discover Northern Ireland
www.discovernorthernireland.com

Europe Links
www.europelinks.ndo.co.uk/tourist.html

Fodor's Guide
www.fodors.com

Footprint Guides
www.footprintbooks.com

Good Holiday Guide
www.goodholidayguide.com

Good Ski Guide
www.goodskiguide.com

Holiday Ireland
www.nci.ie/holiday

Holiday Which?
www.which.net/holiday

Lonely Planet
www.lonelyplanet.com

National Geographic
www.nationalgeographic.com

Public Transport Information
www.pti.org.uk

Rough Guide
www.roughguides.com

Virgin Net Travel
www.virgin.net/travel

Scotland

Destination Scotland
www.destination-scotland.com

Guide to Scotland
www.scotland-info.co.uk

Scotland Calling
www.scotland-calling.com

Scottish Travel Services
www.scottishtravelservices.com

Travel Scotland
www.holiday.scotland.net

parking

BAA Parking
www.baa.co.uk

Britannia Parking
www.britannia-parking.co.uk

Flypark
www.flypark.co.uk

National Car Parks
www.ncp.co.uk

Parking Express, APCOA Parking
www.parkingexpress.co.uk

professional bodies & trade associations

ABTA
www.abtanet.com

Association of Independent Tour Operators
www.aito.co.uk

Railway Industry Association
www.riagb.co.uk

resorts

Butlins
www.butlins.co.uk

Center Parcs
www.centerparcs.co.uk

Club Mark Warner
www.markwarner.co.uk

Club Med
www.clubmed.com

Disneyland (California)
www.disney.co.uk/usa-resorts/disneyland

Disneyland (Paris)
www.disneylandparis.com

Disneyworld (Florida)
www.disney.co.uk/usa-resorts/wdw

Pontins
www.pontins.com

Sandals
www.sandals.com

tourist boards

National

Austria National Tourist Information
www.austria-tourism.at/index_e.html

Belgium Tourist Office
www.visitbelgium.com

British Tourist Authority
www.visitbritain.com

Canadian Tourism Commission
www.travelcanada.ca

Croatia Tourist Board
www.croatia.hr

Czech Republic Tourist Board
www.czechtourservice.cz

Danish Tourist Board
www.denmark.dt.dk

Estonian Tourist Board
http://visitestonia.com

Finnish Tourist Board
www.finland-tourism.com

France Tourism
www.tourisme.fr

Germany Tourism
www.germany-tourism.de

Greek National Tourism Organisation
www.gnto.gr

Hungary Tourist Board
www.hungarytourism.hu

Irish Tourist Board
www.ireland.travel.ie/home

Italian State Tourist Board
www.enit.it/default.asp?Lang=UK

Luxembourg National Tourist Office
www.ont.lu

Netherlands Tourist Board
www2.holland.com/uk

Northern Ireland Tourist Board
www.discovernorthernireland.com

Norwegian Tourist Board
www.visitnorway.com

Polish National Tourist Office
www.polandtour.org

Portugal's Official Tourism Site
www.portugal.org/travelAndTourism/index.html

Russian National Tourist Office
www.russia-travel.com

Spain
www.tourspain.co.uk

Swedish National Tourist Office
www.visit-sweden.com

Switzerland Tourism
http://uk.myswitzerland.com

Tourist Office listings
www.tourist-office.org

Travel England
www.travelengland.org.uk

United States Official Portal
www.tourstates.com

Welsh Tourist Board
www.visitwales.com

Scottish

Aberdeen & Grampian Tourist Board
www.agtb.org

Angus & Dundee Tourist Board
www.angusanddundee.co.uk

Ayrshire & Arran Tourist Board
www.ayrshire-arran.com

Dumfries & Galloway Tourist Board
www.galloway.co.uk

Edinburgh & Lothians Tourist Board
www.edinburgh.org

Greater Glasgow & Clyde Valley Tourist Board
http://seeglasgow.com

Highlands of Scotland Tourism Board
www.host.co.uk

Kingdom of Fife Tourist Board
www.standrews.co.uk/fife/index.html

Orkney Tourist Board
www.visitorkney.com

Perthshire Tourist Board
www.perthshire.co.uk

Scottish Borders Tourist Board
www.scot-borders.co.uk

Scottish Heartlands Tourist Board
www.scottish.heartlands.org

The Scottish Tourist Board
www.visitscotland.com

Shetland Islands Tourism
www.visitshetland.com

Western Isles Tourist Board
www.witb.co.uk

trains

Alphaline Regional Railways
www.alphaline.co.uk

Amtrak
www.amtrak.com

Anglia Railways Train Services
www.angliarailways.co.uk

Association of Train Operating Companies
www.rail.co.uk/atoc

C2C
www.c2c-online.co.uk

Central Trains
www.centraltrains.co.uk

Chiltern Railways
www.chilternrailways.co.uk

Connex
www.connex.co.uk

Docklands Light Rail
www.dlr.co.uk

English Welsh & Scottish Railways
www.ews-railway.co.uk

Eurostar
www.eurostar.com

First Great Western
www.great-western-trains.co.uk

First North Western
www.firstnorthwestern.co.uk

Gatwick Express
www.gatwickexpress.co.uk

Great Eastern Railway
www.ger.co.uk

Great North Eastern Railway
www.gner.co.uk

Heathrow Express
www.heathrowexpress.co.uk

Jubilee Line Extension
www.jle.lul.co.uk

London Transport
www.londontransport.co.uk

London Transport Season Tickets
www.tickets-on-line.co.uk

London Underground
www.thetube.com

Midland Mainline
www.midlandmainline.com

National Rail Info
www.nationalrail.co.uk

NI Railways
www.nirailways.co.uk

North Western Trains
www.nwt.rail.co.uk

Northern Spirit
www.northern-spirit.co.uk

Railtrack
www.railtrack.co.uk

Scotrail
www.scotrail.co.uk

Silverlink Train Services
www.silverlink-trains.com

South West Trains
www.swtrains.co.uk

Stansted Express
www.stanstedexpress.com

Thames Trains
www.thamestrains.co.uk

Thameslink Rail
www.thameslink.co.uk

The Trainline (UK ticket service)
www.thetrainline.com

Virgin Trains
www.virgintrains.co.uk

Wales & West
www.walesandwest.co.uk

International

Amtrak
www.amtrak.com

Deutsche Bahn
www.bahn.de

European Rail Guide
www.europeanrailguide.com

Eurostar
www.eurostar.com

Irish Rail
www.irishrail.ie

RENFE
www.renfe.es/ingles/index.html

SNCF (in French)
www.sncf.com

Tren Italia
www.fs-on-line.com

travel agents, tour operators & cruises

Abercrombie & Kent
www.abercrombiekent.co.uk

Air Miles
www.airmiles.co.uk

Airtours
www.airtours.com

American Holidays
www.american-holidays.com

Arctic Experience & Discover the World
www.arctic-discover.co.uk

Austravel
www.austravel.com

British Airways Holidays
www.britishairwaysholidays.co.uk

Budget Travel
www.budgettravel.com

Cadogan Holidays
www.cadoganholidays.com

Carnival
www.carnival.com

Carribbean Connection
www.carribbean-connection.com

Citalia
www.citalia.co.uk

Club 18-30
www.18-30.co.uk

Club 25
www.club25.ie

Co-op Travel
www.extratravel.co.uk

Cosmos
www.cosmos.co.uk

Cresta Holidays
www.crestaholidays.co.uk

Crystal Holidays
www.crystalholidays.co.uk

Cunard
www.cunardline.com

Deck Chair Com
www.deckchair.com

Destination Group
www.destination-group.com

Direct Holidays
www.directholidays.co.uk

Disney Cruise Line
www.disney.co.uk/usa-resorts/waltdisneyworld/IV/index.html

Dream Travel Africa
www.dreamtravelafrica.co.uk

E-Bookers
www.ebookers.com

Eclipse
www.eclipsedirect.com

Elegant Resorts International
www.elegantresorts.com

Erna Low
www.ernalow.co.uk

Expedia
www.expedia.co.uk

First Choice
www.first-choice.com

Fred Olsen
www.gbnet.co.uk/fred.olsen

Going Places
www.going-places.co.uk

Hayes Travel
www.hayes-travel.co.uk

Headwater
www.headwater.com

Hoseasons
www.hoseasons.co.uk

Inghams
www.inghams.com

Internet Travel Services
www.its.net

JMC
www.jmc-holidays.co.uk

Kuoni
www.kuoni.co.uk

Lastminute.com
www.lastminute.com

Lunn Poly
www.lunn-poly.co.uk

Magic Travel Group
www.magictravelgroup.co.uk

Moorings
www.moorings.co.uk

Nautilus
www.nautilus-yachting.co.uk

Neilson Holidays
www.neilson.co.uk

Norwegian Cruise Line
www.ncl.com

Orient Express Trains & Cruises
www.orient-expresstrains.com

P & O Stena Line
www.posl.com

Page & Moy
www.pagemoy.com

Portland
www.portland-holidays.co.uk

Portman Travel
www.portmantravel.co.uk

Powder Byrne
www.powderbyrne.com

Princess
www.princess.com

Royal Carribean Cruise Line
www.royalcaribbean.com

Saga Holidays
www.saga.co.uk

Scantours
www.scantoursuk.com

Silversea
www.silversea.com

Simply Travel
www.simply-travel.com

Skidream
www.skidream.com

Sovereign
www.sovereign.com

STA Travel
www.statravel.co.uk

Sunsail Holidays
www.sunsail.com

Sunvil Activity Holidays
www.activity-holidays.co.uk

Sunworld
www.sunworld.co.uk

Swan Hellenic
www.swan-hellenic.co.uk

Tenrag
www.tenrag.com

Thomas Cook
www.thomascook.com

Thomson Cruising
www.thomson-holidays.com/cruises

Thomson Holidays
www.thomson-holidays.com

Tradewings
www.tradewings.co.uk

Trailfinders
www.trailfinders.co.uk

Travel for the Arts
www.travelforthearts.co.uk

Union Castle Line
www.union-castle-line.com

Virgin Holidays
www.virginholidays.co.uk

Voyages Jules Verne
www.vjv.co.uk

Wallace Arnold
www.wallacearnold.com

Windjammer
www.windjammer.com